India's Economic Reforms and Development

Prof. A. Vaidyanathan is currently *Emeritus* Professor at the Madras Institute of Development Studies and is a member of the Prime Minister's Economic Advisory Council.

Born in 1931, he was educated in Madras, and did his post graduation in the USA. After obtaining a Ph.D from Cornell University, he worked for six years (1956-62) as economist in the National Council of Applied Economic Research (NCAER), New Delhi. Thereafter he joined the Perspective Planning Division of the Planning Commission, Government of India.

After 10 years in the Planning Commission, and 4 years in the World Bank, he shifted to the Centre for Development Studies, Trivandrum, in 1976 and worked there as Professor for 8 years and has been in the Madras Institute of Development Studies since 1984.

He has been president of the Indian Society of Agricultural Economics since 1993. Currently he is also Chairperson of the Board of Trustees of the Institute of Social Studies Trust, New Delhi.

Prof. Vaidyanathan has served on a number of Government Committees : as Member of the Planning Commission in New Delhi and Tamilnadu State Planning Commission; and Chairperson of a Committee on Irrigation Pricing set up by the Planning Commission.

India's Economic Reforms and Development

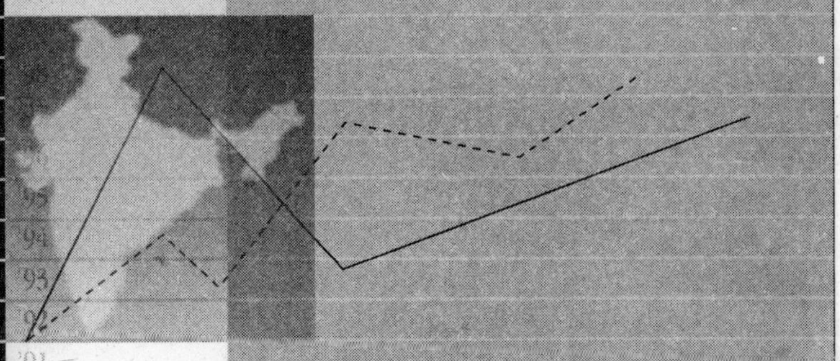

A Vaidyanathan

Academic Foundation
NEW DELHI

Reprint 2005

Published in 2003 by
ACADEMIC FOUNDATION
4772-73 / 23 Bharat Ram Road,
(23 Ansari Road), Darya Ganj,
New Delhi - 110 002.

Phones : 23245001, 02, 03, 04.

Fax : 011-23245005

e-mail : academic@vsnl.com

www : academicfoundation.com

INDIA'S ECONOMIC REFORMS AND DEVELOPMENT
by A. Vaidyanathan
ISBN 81-7188-305-2

Laser-Typeset at AF's DTP Division.
Printed at Print Perfect, Mayapuri, New Delhi.

To
my wife Shanta,
and daughters
Rama and Radhika

Contents...

Section – II

Poverty, Inequality and Development Policy

Preface

THE body of work presented in this collection owes much to several institutions where I have worked and to colleagues and friends too numerous to be listed. I take this opportunity to acknowledge my thanks and gratitude to all of them. My understanding of developmental issues and approaches to dealing with them were influenced and shaped during the sixties. It was a period marked by intense and stimulating debates on development both intellectually and at the practical policy making level. The Perspective Planning Division of the Planning Commission, where I worked at that time, was an excellent vantage point to observe and participate in this process. Pitambar Pant, who headed the division, played a major role in articulating a long-term developmental vision. Besides building a multi-disciplinary team to work out its implications for policy, he was instrumental in bringing together an exceptionally talented group of economists and statisticians in the Planning Unit of the Indian Statistical Institute. The close collaboration between these teams, and with a wide circle of scholars, both Indian and foreign, was very productive and enriching to everyone who participated. Personally, my work, then and since, owes a great deal to continuing friendships and intellectual interaction with several members of these groups. Perhaps my greatest debt is to Pitambar Pant who inculcated the habit of looking at development from a long-term viewpoint and in a broader social perspective. He made me appreciate the importance of careful empirical analysis without being overwhelmed by quantitative techniques of analysis, and the need to go beyond economic analysis to recognise the key role of technology, institutions and, yes, politics and the interactions among them.

Issues relating to development strategy, planning and poverty continued to be important foci of my work in academia — first at the Centre for Development Studies and later at the Madras Institute for Development Studies. Moving out of Delhi to the periphery changed my perspectives in significant ways. It made me realise how excessive preoccupation with policy issues and suggesting policy prescriptions tends to distract attention and effort from trying to unravel actual happenings in the real world and better understand the forces that shape them. My growing interest in institutional and political economy aspects of development, and the historical context, is also related to this change of perspective. At the Centre for Development Studies, then in its infancy, I was specially lucky to have colleagues with similar perceptions. They, together with an unusually motivated, questioning and able student body, provided the ambience and the stimulus to pursue work in this perspective. I cannot adequately thank them for what has been an enriching, rewarding experience.

I have continued this effort in the Madras Institute of Development Studies for nearly two decades. I am grateful to the institute for providing me generously the space, opportunity and facilities to pursue my fancies even after retirement in 1991. A special word of thanks and appreciation are also due to colleagues in the Institute who spared time to discuss half baked ideas and analytical issues and react to draft papers.

All this would not have been possible without patience, understanding support at home. My wife Shanta, and daughters

Rama and Radhika have left me free to pursue my professional interests, suffered my workaholic habits and borne the brunt of dislocations caused by my several changes of jobs and locations. To them I dedicate this volume in love and gratitude.

— **A. Vaidyanathan**

Chennai
February, 2003

Introduction

RAPID economic growth and eradication of abject poverty have been core concerns of India's polity and government throughout the last five decades. Coordinated planning with the state playing the leading role in initiating and regulating the process of development in pursuit of these objectives has been a distinctive feature. Specific targets, perceptions of the problems involved and their solutions have been changing over time. The essays in this collection provide an overview of evolution of this process culminating in the far-reaching reorientation of strategy and policies during the nineties and a critical assessment of their rationale, implementation and impact from the political economy perspective.

The essays are divided into two sections: Those in the first part, mostly written in the nineties, focus on key elements of overall development strategy being pursued from the early nineties. Selection 2, dating back to 1992, voiced some concerns over the rationale and the thrust of the structural adjustment package soon after it was unveiled by Dr. Manmohan Singh. Issues relating to subsidies and foreign direct investment, two important concerns of the new policy, are examined in selections 3 and 4. Broader issues of the role of the state generally and of planning in particular in the changed context are discussed in selections 5, 6 and 7. The nature and sources of demand for manufactures and the basis for the hype of the eighties and early nineties about the huge domestic market as the potential driving force of rapid industrial growth are discussed in selection 8. The last piece in this section (No.9) reviews trends in the cottage and small-scale industry sector and highlights the ineffectiveness of policies meant to protect and promote them. The lead piece in this section pulls together the assessment of different aspects and attempts an overall assessment of the antecedents of the reforms of the nineties, their halting and meandering course and the reasons for their less-than-expected achievements. It also reflects on the prospects for the future.

Selections in the second section span a much longer period. The earliest (selection 11) dating back to 1972, reviews various attempts at measuring poverty incidence, mapping its morphology and assessing trends. Others focus on problems relating to concepts, data and measurement of poverty (selections 13, and 14); regional variations (No.15 and 16); the evolution of poverty alleviation programmes (No.17); critical commentary on their design, implementation and measures to improve their efficacy (Nos 12,and 18). Though written over a span of nearly three decades, it will be apparent from the most recent and comprehensive review of the subject (in the Kale Memorial lecture of 2001, (selection no.10 in this volume) that most of them remain relevant in the current context.

The general thrust of the essays is critical of the design and implementation of the reform package and skeptical of its impact on growth and socio economic inequality. By way of a general introduction it may be useful to recapitulate the main grounds for my skepticism about the reasoning underlying the reforms as well as their implementation.

It is a fact that attitudes to planning, as it had been practiced since Independence, began to show perceptible changes even during the seventies for several valid reasons: (a) the consistent failure of successive five year plans to accelerate the overall growth rate and the rather tardy pace of improvement in income and employment opportunities for the poor and socially disadvantaged; (b) the fact that the system of elaborate and complex direct controls over the private sector did not achieve its objectives and was proving to be counter productive; (c) waste, inefficiency and corruption in the functioning of government and public institutions were becoming more widespread and massive; and (d) the fiscal position of the public sector, and hence its capacity to sustain investments in essential infrastructure was eroding rapidly.

The sharp contrast between the economic performance, in terms of growth and poverty reduction, of India and that of east Asian countries further contributed to this trend. The explanation that the latter's performance was the result of a policy regime based on an "open economy" and a market friendly state gained increasing credence among political leaders, bureaucracy, the media and the private sector. The collapse of the Soviet Union and the impressive increase in China's growth rate following its shift towards a market economy, profit incentives and large-scale foreign private investment further intensified this trend. By the time the crisis of 1991 occurred, there was considerable support among key figures in and out of government for the view that a thorough going reform was necessary to pull the economy out of the morass it had gotten into.

The reform package outlined by Manmohan Singh in 1991 had three distinct components: (1) fiscal stabilization to check the growing fiscal deficit and contain it at a much lower level in such a manner that public investments in basic social and economic infrastructure could be substantially stepped up without generating inflationary pressures; (2) internal liberalization to increase competitive pressures, leaving enterprises free to make their production and investment decisions in the light of market conditions and enlarging the scope and freedom for private enterprise; (3) integration with the global economy by removing controls on foreign trade and exchange rates, lowering tariffs and rationalizing their structure and substantially relaxing regulations regarding external capital flows and a proactive policy for attracting foreign direct investment. This package, it was claimed, would release powerful growth impulses and lift the economy to a high growth trajectory comparable to that of east Asia. This view prevailed and has come to be accepted by successive governments since.

This expectation was, and remains, altogether unrealistic for several reasons: For one, the reform package did not address the problems of agriculture. Besides being an important source of output and employment, accelerated overall growth required a substantial step up in the rate of growth in this sector. Except for reduction of input subsidies, the proposals for fiscal reforms and internal and external liberalization would not have had much of an impact on agriculture. Liberalisation of foreign trade in agricultural products came much later. The process is however incomplete. The nature and extent of consequent changes in the relative price structure of various crops. and how sustained they will be, cannot be predicted with confidence.

Expectations of large increases in agricultural productivity through more efficient allocation of resources and stimulus to investment in technology from changes in output prices were, and still are, exaggerated. There is ample basis in experience to suggest that inadequate supply and poor management of water, land degradation, relatively slow pace of improvement in varieties and practices for several crops and for rain-fed agriculture, and excessively subsidized inputs are far more important in constraining the pace of agricultural growth. Measures to tackle these constraints – by way of more and better public investment and more importantly, improvements in the institutional arrangements to handle these tasks û have simply not been addressed seriously and purposefully so far.

Internal and external liberalization measures have no doubt significantly increased both the opportunities and the incentives for greater efficiency and dynamism in non-agricultural sectors. But the presumption that they would propel production and investment to a much higher and faster trajectory was far too facile. Attitudes and mindset of indigenous entrepreneurs had been shaped by a regime when survival and growth depended, not on innovation and efficiency, but on influencing government decisions on licences, taxes and controlled prices. It was unrealistic to expect that liberalisation by itself would transform them into dynamic and proactively innovative entrepreneurs of the kind seen in East Asia. The policy of wooing foreign direct investment, besides being overoptimistic about the scale of inflow, added to a sense of vulnerability among indigenous firms and made them more defensive.

Expectations of the scale of foreign direct investment, based on the experience of China and south East Asian countries, were also far too optimistic. Most of the FDI into China came from overseas Chinese entrepreneurs with skills and experience in producing and exporting a wide range of modern manufactures. In south East Asia much of the investment came from Japanese multinationals. The Indian Diaspora by contrast consists mostly of professionals, traders and semiskilled workers. Their investments in India, though sizeable and growing, are mostly in financial assets. Except for software, they are unlikely to invest directly in productive sectors on any significant scale. Therefore FDI in India is largely dependent on multinationals that did not, and still do not, show much enthusiasm for investing in India.

The implementation of the reform package has also been fitful and patchy. All its elements have been opposed, and several strongly resisted, by different groups, in varying degrees and for diverse reasons. Nevertheless some major changes in the policy regime – especially dismantling of licensing and controls on domestic industry, financial institutions, foreign trade and exchange markets as well as creating regulatory institutions – have had relatively smooth passage. Some others, like privatization of public enterprises, foreign direct investment, and changes in labour laws to give greater freedom in hiring and firing and flexibility in deployment of workers, have been pushed to a considerable degree in the face of strong resistance.

The biggest, and in many ways the most critical, failure is the inability to reduce the fiscal deficit, and stepping up public investment in infrastructure. The combined fiscal deficit of the Centre and the states remains as high as it was in 1991. And the public sector has been unable to step up investments in basic infrastructure or restructure its management. Shortages and poor quality of infrastructure continue to be serious. This is clearly an important factor impeding and constraining private investment in productive sectors.

That the reform proposals did not command widespread, not to speak of general, acceptance was all too obvious from the beginning. In part the opposition was on ideological grounds. These include concerns over strident suggestions from some proponents of reform for drastic reduction in State participation and regulation of economic activity; winding down poverty alleviation and safety net programmes; apprehensions about the vulnerability of the country's political and economic institutions to external pressures by allowing large scale entry of multinationals and foreign finance capital; and agreeing to be bound by unequal international arrangements like WTO.

All the objections were not purely ideological. There are several well founded concerns on important substantive issues such as the nature, extent and modalities of divestment, utilisation of its proceeds, restructuring of public enterprises to ensure greater accountability, and the distributional impact of privatization, desirability or even the necessity for relying on FDI and multinationals. It has been pointed out that Japan and S.Korea achieved rapid growth without relying on FDI. Nevertheless, it should be recognized that particular interests all too often use ideological arguments to cloak opposition to specific measures.

A case in point is the argument that the World Bank and the International monetary Fund are dictating fiscal adjustment as conditions of their assistance to tide over the payments crisis. While it was certainly part of the agreement with these institutions, the rapid deterioration in the fiscal position was obvious long before 1991. The dangers of allowing the trend to continue, and the necessity to arrest it have been emphasized by economists in and out of government, and recognized in official pronouncements The measures to arrest the trend figuring in agreements with donor agencies had been widely discussed within the country for a long time.

The truth is that the needed measures would adversely affect several influential groups and the political classes, across the entire spectrum, were unwilling to confront them. Thus the strong opposition from public sector employees to both divestment and labour reforms stem from apprehensions of loss of secure jobs and the not-inconsiderable benefits and privileges, which they now enjoy. The strong farm lobby is bitterly opposed to increase in electricity and water charges and fertiliser prices. The urban population is opposed to increase in real estate taxes, utility charges; and the better off in both rural and urban areas agitate against charging their children for higher education. Measures (such as decentralization, right to information, computerization) to achieve greater transparency, and accountability of functionaries in public agencies are opposed by unions.

There are also instances where a broad based consensus cannot be implemented because of opposition and subversion by vested interests. Restructuring poverty alleviation programmes is a striking case in point. That they are poorly designed, inefficiently implemented and open to huge leakages and corruption is common knowledge. Politicians recognize it and accept the need for corrective action. The passage of the 73rd and 74th Constitutional amendments mandating transfer of resources and power for local development to elected panchayats was a major step meant to ensure better targeting, and improving the relevance, quality and economy, and accountability for the programmes. But having found the programmes a convenient means for appropriation of public resources for patronage and private gain, the bureaucracy and the political class have so far successfully resisted attempts to implement these reforms.

All this points to a colossal failure of political management. The Centre decided the scope and content of the reforms without any attempt to build a broad based political consensus. A particularly serious lapse was the failure to recognize the crucial role of the states and their cooperation for the success of fiscal adjustment and liberalization. Suggestions to convene a meeting of the NDC or the Inter State Council to explain the rationale of the reforms, discuss their implications for the states, their role in the reform process and accommodate their interests were not heeded. And until recently there has been no serious discussion of these issues between the center and the states. The centre's unilateral approach to reforms was compounded by the appointment of a pay commission for the central staff in the face of states' explicit concern over its fallout on their precarious finances. The disastrous consequences of this for both central and state finances are now manifesting. Though there is more of an effort to interact with states on these issues and the states themselves are beginning to show signs of willingness to confront them, the process is still far too ad hoc and anemic.

There has also been no serious effort at forging a broad based consensus on the reforms and devising a political strategy to steer them through the welter of interests opposing them. This requires (a) clear sorting out of the ideological posturing from substantive issues and opposition of different interest groups; (b) promoting informed public debate on the policy options and their implications as part of a concerted effort to secure broad based understanding and support for the reform agenda across a wide political spectrum both at the centre and the states; and (c) working out the priorities and sequencing of different reform measures and formulating a political strategy to steer through the opposition from a welter of vested interests.

The growing severity of the fiscal crunch has forced more and more chief ministers and the Prime Minister to speak publicly about the problem and emphasise the necessity and urgency for corrective action. Several states have tried to reduce subsidies by raising user charges and to withhold, or postpone, allowances and perquisites of their staff in the face of strong and even violent agitations. These are welcome and hopeful signs. The nature and content of needed reforms are now better understood (though not always clearly worked out). But it is still a story of one step forward and three quarters of a step backward.

The unwillingness or inability of governments to walk the talk in fiscal matters and public sector reform stands in contrast to the enthusiasm with which privatization, eagerness to get World Bank loans and foreign direct investment are being pursued at all levels and by all parties in power. One cannot help wondering if they see these as a way of avoiding politically difficult and contentious reforms of taxes, public expenditure, public institutions and governance in the hope that multinationals and private enterprise in a free market will be a sure and painless way to faster growth and poverty eradication. This is dangerous illusion based on simplistic understanding of the factors underlying the East Asian "miracles".

The notion that unprecedented, rapid growth of east and south East Asia was achieved under a minimalist, non-interventionist state and a free market system is a gross misreading of their experience. Maintaining an open economy and strategic intervention in the exchange rates, interest rate and fiscal policy to maintain an appropriate incentive environment were no doubt important contributory factors. But there was much more to it.

East and south east Asian countries have several other distinguishing features: (a) control of state power by a 'modernising' elite led by the military and comprising professionals and capitalists; (b) the existence /emergence of a dynamic entrepreneurial class; (c) the ability to encourage and support entrepreneurs, enable them to acquire the technical and organizational capacity and devise effective inducements (through a mixture of incentives and penalties) to encourage performance; (d) a determined pursuit of modernization and growth without being concerned by considerations of equity and environmental sustainability; (e) electoral system designed to exclude significant sections (especially workers and agriculturists) from centres of state power; and (f) active discouragement of dissent and agitations and no hesitation in putting them down with an iron hand, when deemed necessary.

These features are the result of a historical process, in many ways unique to them. In Japan, Korea, Taiwan and China, the political clout of the agriculturists was contained by radical land reforms. These reforms, invariably the product of violent and revolutionary upheavals, eliminated the lords and large land owners. Together with egalitarian redistribution of land, it also weakened the ability of the rural classes for political mobilisation. But this alone could not have been sufficient. Given that the bulk of the population of all these countries in the initial stages was agricultural and rural, additional devices were necessary to make sure that their numerical strength did not give them significant influence or voice in the shaping of state policy. One such mechanism is to so frame the constitution as to restrict representation of rural/agricultural interests and their effective participation in legislative and executive bodies of the state. At some stage (as happened in China) the farm sector's interest was assuaged by allowing agricultural prices to rise by relaxing/removing restrictions on production/marketing or (as in Japan and Korea?) by higher state guaranteed prices for farm products.

The Indian scene is very different in crucial respects. The conditions prevailing in India are very different by virtue of its size and diversity, and its commitment to democracy based on universal adult franchise. A complex intermeshing of land ownership and caste, together with constitutional guarantees against expropriation of private property without adequate compensation, has frustrated even attempts at modest land reform. This certainly precludes radical reforms of the kind accomplished in East Asia. Parliamentary democracy based on adult franchise has given agricultural interests a strong, and growing presence in legislatures and in the executive. Their voice has been influential enough to claim and extract significant concessions from state resources. Trade unions, sanctioned and protected by law, are an important means for mobilising workers in organized sectors for protecting their interests. Though limited to a small fraction of the work force, they are a factor to be reckoned with in the political process.

The state has also to address the claims of a vast underclass handicapped by their current poverty and accumulated disadvantages arising from the caste system. The Constitution and the way it has worked has significantly enlarged the space and opportunity for underprivileged castes and poor groups to press their claims openly, actively, and forcefully in the councils of governance. The sheer size of this class makes their support often crucial in determining electoral outcomes. With time, they have become increasingly assertive in voicing their claims that no elected governments can ignore.

On the other hand, the phenomenal increase in overseas employment and income opportunities for the highly educated class has made the elite much more outward oriented. They are more interested in pressing for programmes and policies that would help more of their class to access external opportunities than in addressing domestic economic and social issues that concern the large mass of the population.

In all these respects India is in a very different situation from that of east and south East Asia. Politics in India is far more fluid; governments are less stable and single-minded pursuit of growth and strong governance inherently more difficult than in east or Southeast Asia. Numerous distortions in the way politics, government and institutions function have added to the difficulties. Excessive centralization of resources and power, lack of transparency in the way public institutions operate, shortsighted populism and weak regulatory institutions are part of the problem. Relations between the elected representatives, legislative bodies and the executive agencies of the government and the oversight institutions have become far too fuzzy and blurred. This fuzziness – at once deliberate and increasing – is responsible for the enormous waste, inefficiency and corruption characteristic of the way public sector carries out economic activity and the lack of both information and effective institutions needed to ensure public accountability.

These internal weaknesses are far more important factors constraining development than the slow pace of privatisation, export growth and inflow of foreign investment on which state policy and influential segments of elite opinion set so much store. Indeed, quite apart from their desirability, these policies are unlikely to make much headway unless internal systemic constraints are addressed and remedied. The focus should therefore be much more, and primarily, on reforms on the domestic front. Fortunately the nature of needed changes are widely discussed in civil society, academia, judiciary and to some extent even in the political sphere. Several promising initiatives (such as the constitutional amendments for decentralization, creation of autonomous regulatory institutions, and stricter norms for elections and functioning of public officials) have been set in motion. The focus should be on efforts for mobilization of far more broad based and much stronger pressure for carrying this process much further. Widening and deepening of the democratic process will help the process.

Major changes of institutions and policy in a plural, open and democratic society are difficult: The process is bound to be jerkier, slower and trajectories more erratic. We may not achieve east Asian GDP growth rates. But there is no reason to be defensive on that account. Even a 5 – 6 percent growth rate for a country of India's size is no mean achievement. What would lend distinction and uniqueness to Indian development is its ability to achieve a different quality of development: one which mitigates and eventually eliminates accumulated disadvantages arising from social and economic exclusion of underprivileged groups; effective public action to ensure a decent, and progressively higher, minimum standard of living in terms of personal consumption, living environment and access to basic social amenities; and effectively addresses issues of sustainable and eco-sensitive development.

Section – I

Planning, State and Development

1

A Decade of Reforms

Antecedents

THE nineties have been a decade of momentous changes in the country's development strategy and policies. Ever since Independence these have been premised on the belief that comprehensive planning combined with direct participation and control of economic activity by the state are both necessary and desirable to achieve rapid economic growth, poverty eradication and a just and equitable society. This belief, its concrete expression in successive five year plans and their implementation has long attracted criticism. Some of it — for example that of the Swatantra Party — was ideological. Several economists also criticised excessive state involvement and interference, obsession with heavy industry and highly autarkic policies on grounds that they made the system rigid, reduced their capacity for flexible adaptation to changing conditions and inhibited innovation.

Despite the Plans, Gross Domestic Product (GDP) growth rate remained more or less stuck at 3-4 per cent per annum and the pace of improvement in the conditions of the poor and the underprivileged remained excruciatingly slow. No doubt, democracy gave greater political voice for the poor and compulsions of electoral politics made governments of all hues to launch 'direct attack' on poverty, initiate a variety of poverty alleviation programmes and commit substantial resources for them. But experience showed that they did not benefit the weak and the vulnerable in full measure. On the other hand, they have led to massive corruption and abuse of power by the functionaries and institutions of the state to further their own interests and the interests of the rich and the powerful.

Meanwhile, by the seventies, the sharp contrast between India's performance and that of east Asian and south-east Asian countries began to attract increasing attention. The latter were achieving very high and historically unprecedented rates of growth in output and employment, and improvement in living standards. Their expansion was widely attributed to reliance on the market mechanism, rather than state sponsored central planning, openness of their economies, a dynamic export trade, and import of foreign capital and modern technology.

The sharp contrast between the performance of these countries and that of India was influential in persuading the emerging generation of political and bureaucratic elite as well as the middle class that India needed to change track. The collapse of the erstwhile Soviet Union and east European communist regimes further reinforced this trend. All this, taken together with the comparatively lack lustre achievements of India's own efforts at planned development, gave credence to the notion that 'free market — free enterprise — free trade system' would produce better results in terms of efficiency, growth of income and employment and reduction of poverty. This perception became ascendant and gained greater acceptance, internationally and in India, among influential segments of academia, opinion makers, media, the bureaucracy and politicians and became quite pronounced during the 1980's. It is also reflected in the reports of some government committees and in the limited and half hearted attempts at 'liberalisation' during the 1980's. The intellectual ground for reforms of the 1990's had thus been prepared much earlier.

Limited as 'liberalisation' during the eighties was, the expansionist fiscal policy and larger investments in infrastructure pursued during the decade resulted in a significant improvement in the growth rate. But it was accompanied by a growing strain on government finances, balance of payments and prices. Warnings about the implications of continuing the policy of larger public investments financed out of borrowings — especially high cost short-term external borrowings — went unheeded. The economy moved predictably, and inexorably, to the crisis of 1991. With foreign reserves practically exhausted the government was forced to seek external assistance.

This was a period when the philosophy of 'free markets, free trade and globalisation' was being pushed aggressively on several crisis – ridden Third World countries in the name of 'structural adjustment programmes'. In our case too the donors exerted strong pressure for far reaching changes. The necessity to reduce the fiscal and balance of payments deficits and drastically reducing, if not total dismantling of controls on the private sector was widely recognised and several, though not all, measures suggested by the donors had been advocated by Indian economists spanning a wide range of ideological persuasions. But external donor agencies and governments went considerably further in asking for restricting and cutting back public sector involvement in productive activity, a strong push towards privatisation of the economy, and allowing free flow of private foreign capital. That external pressure was an important factor in getting the government to accept the entire package cannot be denied. But we should not forget that the launching of reforms was facilitated by the fact that a sizeable and influential segment of the ruling elite in the country was already persuaded of its necessity and were actively lobbying for it.

The key elements of the reform original package unveiled by Dr. Manmohan Singh included the following:

- Dismantling the import and export licensing system, reducing tariffs, and moving towards a more or less free trade regime to increase the pressure of competition and thereby induce domestic industry to increase efficiency.
- Simultaneously, opportunities and space for greater efficiency were sought to be enhanced by dismantling all controls over industrial investment, choice of technology, scale and location of plants, production and pricing; relaxing restrictions on foreign direct investment and adopting a proactive policy of wooing such investment;
- Liberalisation of the financial sector by drastically reducing direct state intervention in mobilisation of resources, lending policies as well as in the interest rates and opening it to the private sector including foreign institutions;
- Reducing the central government's fiscal deficit from 8 per cent of GDP in 1990-91 to 3 per cent by 1996-97 by tax reform to raise revenue, cutting implicit and explicit subsidies on food, fertilisers and exports and compressing and re-orienting public sector plan expenditure.

Measures for trade liberalisation went through fairly smoothly. Import and export trade are now more or less free; tariff rates have been lowered and rationalised substantially; exchange rates are left to be determined by the market subject to strategic intervention by the Reserve Bank; and a limited degree of convertibility on capital account is now permitted. The dismantling of the control system, widely welcomed by large-scale private sector industries, was also completed in a relatively short time. The financial sector and markets have also been opened up and permitted to operate more freely But fiscal consolidation and privatisation (especially of public enterprises) have floundered in the face of severe opposition.

Expectations and Achievements

The impact of the reforms on the performance of the economy has not been as large or as sustained as predicted by its protagonists. Prima facie, the most striking achievement of the decade of 'reforms' is the turn around in the balance of payments. Despite considerable year-to-year variation, total commodity export earnings have doubled during the 1990's. The increase during the 1980's being of more or less the same magnitude, trade and exchange rate policy reforms cannot be considered a great success. But they have undoubtedly contributed to the phenomenal and sustained expansion of software exports.

Imports have grown faster after liberalisation. But total export earnings (including software) rose fast enough to prevent any significant deterioration in the trade balance. On the other hand, the current account has been in surplus for much of the decade. External reserves have risen from a little over 9 billion dollars in March 1992 to 38 billion dollars in March 2000 and over 50 billion dollars currently. Policy changes have no doubt contributed significantly to this increase and strengthened the capacity to withstand unexpected shocks to the country's balance of payments. But it must also be noted that very little of it is contributed by surpluses from our own exchange earnings. Practically the entire increase of 29 billion dollars over this period is accounted by the huge influx of funds from foreign institutional investors and accretions to foreign currency deposits. That, despite this, the nation's financial system was insulated from the contagion effects of crises and 'melt-down' experienced by east and south-east Asia during the mid nineties is, nevertheless, an unquestionably major achievement of policy.

The domestic financial system has also been progressively liberalised. Private sector banks, including foreign banks have grown rapidly. Control over interest rates has been greatly relaxed leaving market forces to play a larger role. Regulatory mechanisms are being put in place and gradually extended and strengthened. That they are yet incomplete and have not been as effective as it should be is reflected in the high incidence of non-performing assets of banks and the two major, and several minor, financial scams during the decade. Much remains to be done to insulate the financial system from manipulation and political interference.

The most striking failure of the reforms is in the sphere of fiscal consolidation. There have been major changes in taxation regime at the Centre: Direct tax rates have been substantially reduced. But the system continues to be complicated by numerous exemptions/concessions to benefit one or the other interest group. Tariff rates have been substantially reduced and the structure simplified. Rationalisation of excise taxes has also made some progress. Introduction of a nationwide value-added-tax is in process. The expectation that lower rates of direct tax rates would reduce incentives for evasion and increase compliance has however been belied. While the number of income tax payers has increased, measures to tighten tax administration have not been as conspicuous or successful. There has been hardly any tax reform of significance in the states. In the event, tax revenues of the centre and the states as a proportion of GDP has in fact declined.

Compounding it is the failure to check expenditures. On the contrary: the largesse handed out by the Central Pay Commission has meant a huge increase in outlays on salaries and benefits both at the centre and in the states. Efforts to reduce subsidies have been stalled by strong and widespread opposition across the political spectrum. As a result, the revenue deficit has increased and public savings have dwindled. Despite slowing down of public investment (which has fallen as a proportion of GDP), government borrowing and therefore interest payments have sky rocketed. Consequently, while there was some reduction in gross fiscal deficit of the centre initially, the gain was short-lived. The trend was soon reversed. While the centre's deficit is now below pre-reform levels, the combined deficit of the centre and the states is currently around 10 per cent of GDP, roughly the same level as before the launching of the reforms.

The reforms, it was claimed, would unleash the latent, but repressed, forces for growth by exposing enterprises to international competition and leaving them free to exploit the opportunities. The country, it was said, would be propelled to a much higher growth path: Some euphoric protagonists of the reforms spoke breezily about achieving growth rates of 8 to 10 per cent a year. According to official estimates, actual GDP growth during the 1990's (excluding the 2 crisis years) averaged around 6.5 per cent per annum. This is higher than the estimated 5.6 per cent annual growth during the 1980's, but considerably short of expectations.

Closer examination of sector-wise growth reveals some puzzling features: The average annual growth rate (average of year to year changes) of commodity producing sectors during the nineties has not been very different from that during the eighties, especially the latter half of the eighties. Tertiary sector output has grown much faster than that of commodity sectors. The conceptual and measurement problems in estimating real output in this sector are well-known. They are the same for the 1980's and for the 1990's. But this cannot account for the differences in growth between the two periods: According to the revised national income estimates at 1993-94 prices, growth of trade, transport and communications is higher than the earlier estimates (at 1980-81 prices) and the elasticity of this sector's output relative to that of commodity sectors is considerably higher and increasing during the 1990's compared to the eighties. It also seems odd that the rate of growth of finance, insurance and business services (which includes software) during the nineties (when the real boom in software industry occurred) is more or less the same as in the eighties. To what extent does the steep increase in the growth rates of public administration, defense and other services during the latter half of the nineties reflect the increase in salaries and benefits following the implementation of Pay Commission recommendations?

Another puzzling feature is that the rates of output growth relative to that of employment during the 1980's and the 1990's show striking differences. During 1980's, output growth (estimated from National Accounts Statistics) was higher than employment growth (estimated from National Sample Survey Organisation employment surveys) in primary, secondary and tertiary sectors; the implied improvement in value added per worker in all of them being modest. However, during the post-reform period (1993-94 to 1999-2000) the implicit growth in value added per worker in industry and services is much higher than in the 1980's.

There is no evidence that changes in underlying factors (e.g. capital per worker, technological change or managerial improvements) have been of an order which can explain such a sharp and abrupt rise in productivity. One is forced to be somewhat circumspect in assessing the extent of quickening in the pace of growth during the post-reform period. That the last 2 years have witnessed a marked slow down in overall growth, and in industrial growth, only underlines the need for caution in assessing the growth impact of reforms.

Factors Affecting Reforms and Their Impact

In assessing the impact of the reforms, it needs noting, that they were launched in the midst of a crisis, without a coherent overall design, without a clear idea of the strategy to be adopted and without any attempt to forge a broad based political support. Elements of the package unraveled over time in a piece meal fashion and implementation was halting, often partial. The necessity for a regulatory system for proper functioning of markets, including financial markets did not figure prominently, if at all, in the original proposal. They came to the fore much later, in the mid-nineties, after the second report of the Narasimham Committee and in the context of privatisation of electricity. The idea of first and second-generation reforms was not there to begin with; it came much later.

The original package was also incomplete in key respects: For one thing, it did not cover the states though it was obvious that states' finances were also in bad shape, in fact worse than that of the centre. Subsidies for power, surface irrigation, public transport, higher education and food incurred by states were much larger than the central subsidies. They were facing increasingly severe constraints in finding resources to expand and improve infrastructure essential to support and sustain overall economic growth.

The omission of the states in the initial stage was justified on the ground that it would create wider controversies and make it politically more difficult to push through the reforms. Arguments that the fiscal problem of the states, especially in relation to subsidies, was as important as that of the centre, that centre's actions had major direct and indirect impact on state finances, and that therefore states must be taken into confidence did not cut much ice. Suggestions that a special meeting of the National Development Council (NDC) be called were not heeded. It is only much later that the necessity for fiscal reform in the states came to the centre stage.

There was hardly any attempt to explain the compulsions for and the rationale of the contemplated measures even to leaders of key political parties; anticipate criticisms that reforms would hurt the poor and show why the fear was misplaced and how that possibility would be avoided. By failing to highlight the fact that the impending crisis and the need for many (though not all) of the measures had long been stressed by economists within the country (including the Planning Commission during the V.P. Singh regime), the impression that the reforms were wholly at the dictate of the Bank and the Fund was allowed to gain credence.

While a wider debate on these aspects may have delayed the reforms and made it more difficult to steer it through Parliament, it would have served the interests of openness and transparency so essential in a democracy; helped counter criticism of acting under external pressure; and to explain the issues involved to the public, try to assuage misgivings, and persuade a wide cross section of politicians about the necessity for the proposed changes. There was thus hardly any attempt to prepare the ground for a broad political consensus for such far-reaching reforms.

Not only did the centre shy away from doing so, but compounded the difficulties by appointing another Pay Commission for its staff with wide terms of reference without informing, not to speak of consulting, the states even as the latter were urging restraint on expenditure (including a Dearness Allowance freeze). Subsequently, the centre decided to grant more than the generous package recommended by the

Pay Commission again without consulting the states. These rank amongst the most disastrous and short-sighted decisions which may prove near fatal to the prospect of fiscal stabilisation and also impede other reforms. They have not only compromised the centre's ability to reduce its own fiscal deficit, but aggravated the problem of the states. Once the centre accepted the Pay Commission recommendations for its staff, the states, having earlier accepted the principle of parity, could not resist demands of their staff. The increase in salary bill (and arrears) payment has imposed a crushing burden on state finances.

The second noteworthy feature of the reform is that it did not address the problems of agriculture seriously. Changes in foreign trade regime did not have much of an impact on prices of agricultural inputs and outputs. Only a miniscule proportion of agricultural output entered foreign trade; and it continued to be subject to regulation. Attempts to reduce input subsidies were frustrated, though support and procurement for major crops were raised often against market signals.

People who played a key role in shaping the reform tended to underestimate the importance of raising agricultural growth rate to sustain faster overall growth and the difficulty of achieving it. They assumed, rather facilely, that judicious use of allocations in agricultural and rural infrastructure — augmented if need be — will accelerate agricultural growth. There was breezy talk of accelerating agricultural growth to 4 per cent per annum and more. The fact is that the rate of agricultural growth remains well under 3 per cent a year. If anything the signs of a slow down in yield growth and resource degradation in the Punjab and Haryana give cause for concern about sustaining past high growth rates in these regions.

Over the years, the emphasis gradually shifted to trade liberalisation and integration with the World markets for agricultural products. This, it was argued, would raise domestic farm prices and correct the asymmetry in the implicit protection given to agriculture and industry under the earlier regime. The profitability of agriculture would increase and provide a powerful impetus to increased investment, technical progress and growth in this sector. That there is little evidence to indicate a high aggregate supply response to changes in terms of trade and that non-price factors were far more crucial was either ignored or played down. The deeper and more difficult tasks — namely improving the quality of land and water management, creating the conditions necessary for raising productivity of rainfed agriculture, and correcting the uneven pace of technological improvement between crops, between irrigated and rainfed areas and across regions – which have to be tackled in order to step up agricultural growth, have not been addressed.

The expectation that the reforms would lead to a big increase in production of manufactures has also been belied. There was a brief spurt in investment and output growth in the organised manufacturing sector for 3-4 years after the launching of the reform, much of it in the so-called fast moving consumer goods sector. Traditionally important sectors, especially textiles, machinery and metal manufacturers and small-scale industry, have found it difficult to withstand import competition. The worst affected being the engineering industry. Foreign Direct Investment (FDI) inflows are no doubt much higher compared to the negligible levels of the past, but they are far less than expected and miniscule compared to south-east Asian countries.

The initial buoyancy in organised industry, however, petered out and growth rates have since declined to near stagnation levels. To some extent this may be due to over-optimistic hype regarding the potential of the 'huge' middle class market and the domestic demand for FCMG. Even so, that demand growth in this segment should have slackened so sharply despite a huge increase in incomes of the organised sector employees, and the middle class, is somewhat of a puzzle. Deceleration of investment, especially public investment together with the free import of equipment at lower tariff rates, was also a contributory factor.

The disappointing impact on industry is sought to be rationalised on the grounds that the process of expanding and improving energy and transport infrastructure have been far too slow and that the government has been unable to implement needed restructuring and legal reforms (especially labour reform). There is force in these arguments. Shortages and poor quality of infrastructure has undoubtedly impeded industrial growth. Rigidity of labour laws is, however, a less convincing alibi.

These laws do not apply to the unorganised sector which still accounts for the bulk of industrial employment and a substantial proportion of the sector's output. The organised private sector, on the other hand, has long found effective ways to circumvent the law: This is evident from the fact that output has grown at a fairly rapid rate during the eighties with practically no increase in number of workers: Output growth in the nineties is also much faster than employment.

Ironically, it is the public sector enterprises which, not being in a position to adopt strategies to get around the law, have borne the brunt of the rigidities of the labour laws and trade union pressure against retrenchment and restructuring of work force. And yet public enterprises are damned for their inefficiency and private enterprise held out as models of efficiency!

More important, entrepreneurs in the private sector have not shown a sufficiently vigorous, confident and far-sighted response to the opportunities opened by liberalisation. No doubt, competitive pressures are forcing industries to upgrade technology, improve quality and cut costs. But their initial enthusiasm for globalisation and free flow of FDI has distinctly weakened and even turned into opposition for several reasons. In some cases — especially metal/engineering and small industries — the pace of trade liberalisation and tariff reduction seem to have compounded difficulties of domestic industry. A deeper problem — and one reflected in the attitudes and perceptions of industrialists and the revealed placement patterns of management graduates — is that finance and marketing are seen as for more interesting and challenging functions than production. It is difficult to see what financial management and indigenous marketing can do unless the products offered are of good quality and competitive.

Moreover, unlike their east Asian counterparts, Indian enterprise (and official policy) has chosen to depend on foreign collaborations rather than develop their own knowledge, skills and competence necessary to meet competition. Their initial enthusiasm of indigenous firms to liberalisation and globalisation has distinctly waned. They now emphasise the unevenness of the field of competition because of the multiple advantages which Multi-National Corporations (MNCs) have in access to and cost of capital, superior technology and innovative capacity and established brand names. That several MNC collaborators seem more interested in setting up their own plants rather than transferring latest technology and designs to their current collaborators may also have been a contributory factor. Pressures for greater protection and further fiscal concessions to domestic industry have therefore grown. These arguments have evidently been persuasive enough to induce government to shift gradually towards a general lowering of interest rates and slowing down the pace of reduction in tariffs.

Political Resistance to Reform

Political resistance to the reform measures was to be expected from diverse sources, for diverse reasons and with varying force. Industrialists and exporters had most reason to welcome the new economic policy. But we have noted that their enthusiasm has waned over time and given place to demand for a variety of protective measures.

The 'middle class' with access to higher professional education constitute perhaps the most enthusiastic supporters of the new dispensation. Most of the large and growing number of Non-Resident Indians (NRIs) and those employed in the burgeoning software industry belong to this group. Globalisation has vastly improved the opportunities and earning potential of this class both within and outside the country. One has only to see the veritable explosion in salaries of executives and professional personal in recent years. Some of the most ardent and passionate advocates of free markets, globalisation and capital account convertibility belong to this class.

The strongest opposition comes from farmers and from workers in the organised sector including, especially those employed in the public sector. Farmers have fiercely, and so far successfully, resisted any increase in the price of inputs in the name of reducing subsidies. Their argument is that farmers are unable to recover costs at current level of input and output prices and that farm prices are too low to enable them to have a 'decent' income. Subsidising inputs and pegging output prices higher than warranted by the balance between supply and demand is neither fiscally feasible nor a viable way of raising farmers' incomes to a higher level and even less so for ensuring their progressive improvement. Moreover, since there is much scope for increasing the productivity of water and fertilisers, higher prices do not necessarily mean an increase in unit costs. On the other hand, by encouraging profligate use of scarce resources, low input prices damage the environment and endanger long-term sustainability of agriculture.

All these arguments cut little ice with the farm lobby and politicians. Nor does the fact that the support price and public procurement mechanisms work effectively only for some crops, regions and some classes of farmers. High procurement prices for rice and wheat benefit mostly Punjab, Haryana and west Uttar Pradesh, and paddy surplus areas in states like Andhra Pradesh and Tamil Nadu. Much of the benefits of price support and subsidised provision of inputs also accrue to be relatively larger, better-off farmers. Small farmers, farmers in rain-fed areas, and those growing 'coarse cereals; and pulses benefit hardly, if at all.

Nevertheless, the use of purchased inputs and sale of produce in the market is sufficiently, even if unevenly, widespread across the country and farmers of all size groups to facilitate political mobilisation against raising input prices and for higher support/procurement prices. In the case of rice and wheat, during the past few years, the farm lobby has successfully pressured the government not only to raise prices but also to dilute specifications of quality standards for procurement. The huge and growing accumulation of foodgrain stocks is the direct consequence of this perverse policy.

Labour in the organised sector is the other locus of strong and organised resistance to the reform: Organised sector (registered factories, financial institutions, government agencies, public sector undertakings) constitute barely 10 per cent of the country's for work force (and 20 per cent of the non-agricultural work force). Trade unions, though largely confined to this segment of the economy, have played, and continue to play a key role in protecting the interests of their members and in influencing state policy. They comprise an important section of the better-off segments of the population (most of them belong in the top quartile of the population in terms of per capita income) and get the lion's share of the benefits of subsidised or free facilities and services (higher education, healthcare, public transport, electricity, water) provided by the state.

Unions in the organised sector have had considerable success in securing better wages, working conditions and other benefits for workers in this sector and also legislative protection against lay-off and retrenchment. Several of the activities, especially in the public sector, being crucial to the orderly governance and smooth functioning of economy and society, those employed in them are strategically positioned to resist lay-offs, redeployment, restraint on salaries and benefits.

All this is threatened by proposals to permit flexibility in hiring and firing, retrenchment and redeployment of excess work force, privatisation of public undertakings, allowing market forces a greater role in determining wages; and measures to check leakages and corruption. As consumers, they also stand to lose by increased user charges for public services and possibly having to pay more taxes. The fierce resistance of trade unions to reforms — especially in the public sector — is hardly surprising.

Self employed and wage paid workers in agriculture and unorganised non-agricultural activities far outnumber the above mentioned interest groups. For the most part they are economically weak, socially underprivileged and ill-equipped to articulate their interests on employers or the state in concerted manner. The sheer weight of their numbers, however, has given them a crucial place in electoral politics. Over the year, parties of all hues have been compelled to woo their support by promising to address their problems. While initially these may have been limited to the rhetoric of election manifestoes, over the years, these promises have come to be backed by concrete programmes and commitment of resources.

The rapid growth in the variety and scale of poverty alleviation programmes reflect this trend. Reinforcing it is the growing assertiveness and active participation of Backward Castes and Dalits in the political process and increasing presence in centres of power. The misuse and large leakages in funds allocated for these programmes and their limited effectiveness in improving the conditions of the poor are increasingly the subjects of public discussion.

The 73rd and 74th Constitutional Amendments have opened a space for local leaders and their pressure for a larger, more meaningful role in matters relating to local development is increasing. There is an ongoing contest over sharing of power between Panchayat Raj Institutions (PRIs) and state and central level politicians. There are also indications that local communities, being frustrated with the apathy and inefficiency of government agencies and programmes, are beginning to take the initiative to solve local problems on their own. These are all positive developments to be welcomed.

Among the less wholesome features of this welcome churning in the polity are indications of a resurgence and reinforcement of caste as the basis of political mobilisation even among the 'backward' castes and Dalits; accentuation of differences and conflicts among the underprivileged; and focus on demands for subventions and concessions rather than on pressing for using the resources being spent ostensibly for their benefit to enable and equip their constituents to better access the opportunities opened by economic growth and achieve a durable and sustained improvement in living standard and social dignity. The accentuation of caste divisions and intrusion of party politics in village communities are impeding collective action in several important areas.

Overarching the resistance from particular interest groups are wider concerns about the larger social and political implications of the reform. These include several apprehensions:

- that trade liberalisation and domestic regulation and disbanding protection for small industry would have huge and widespread adverse effects on employment and incomes;
- that in the name of fiscal consolidation, expenditures are being squeezed and the compression is at the expense of pro-poor programmes (like basic social services, social welfare, security and poverty alleviation);
- that in the name of providing incentive for enterprise and professional skills, inequalities are allowed to increase;
- that the policy of open door for foreign capital and agreeing to the jurisdiction of international organisations (like World Trade Organisation) created under unequal treaties in an unequal world dominated by the developed countries reduces the country's autonomy and makes, it vulnerable to external pressure and interference.
- an added dimension is the increasing concern about the consequences of pursuing current patterns of development for the environment and sustainability.

To dismiss, as protagonists of the reform often tend to, criticism based on these concerns as paranoia or ideologically motivated, would be serious mistake.

Some influential protagonists of the free market ideology have argued that far too much is spent on poverty alleviation programmes, that they are prone to large leakages, and that they do not bring about a sustained improvement in the condition of the poor. In their view, faster growth is a better and surer instrument for this purpose. On this questionable premise, and citing the necessity to reduce the fiscal deficit, they advocate scaling down poverty alleviation programmes and diverting the resources to augment growth-promoting investment.

The more sophisticated version of the argument stresses the necessity and scope for better targeting, more effective implementation and shifting emphasis from subsidies and relief to augmenting of productive asset base. This is certainly valid and must be pursued. But the suggestion that poverty alleviation programmes are the main or even an important cause for the mounting fiscal deficit is specious and untenable. The fact is that, compared to the loss of revenue due to rampant tax evasion by the well-to-do and the magnitude of implicit subsidies accruing to the better-off, the resources expended on poverty alleviation pales into insignificance.

Another source of larger concern relates to the importance attached to wooing foreign direct investment and multinationals to speed up development. The examples of China and south-east Asia are often cited in support of this policy. The volume of FDI flowing into China in the post-Maoist era is indeed phenomenal. From practically nothing in 1980, total foreign direct investment in 2000 is estimated to be over 400 billion dollars. That it has been a major factor in the impressive growth of manufacturing output (and exports) during the last 2 decades is undisputed. But what is not recognised, certainly not emphasised, is that much of this investment was made by overseas Chinese enterprises (from Taiwan, Hong Kong,

Singapore etc.) who had acquired considerable experience in a wide variety of manufacturing and built a world-wide trading network. In 1993, the latest year for which I could get the data, of the 57 billion dollars inward FDI stock in China only 5-6 per cent originated from United States of America and European Union, and 5 per cent from Japan. Even in 1997, 80 per cent was from countries with large overseas Chinese presence.

In sharp contrast, the volume of foreign capital inflow into India during the nineties is but a fraction of that into China. The cumulative total of direct and financial investments up to 2000 was barely 50 billion dollars. Most of it has been in the form of bank deposits and financial investments by institutional investors. Neither has a significant direct impact on production or technology improvement. Direct investments, mostly from multi-nationals, are very small : around 2 billion dollars a year currently and total stock around 20 billion dollars. This is not surprising. The number of Indian emigres abroad is large. But those with industrial experience are nowhere comparable in range or depth with that of Chinese. The great bulk of the new generation emigres from India are professionals. Remarkably, successful but hardly interested and, with the significant exception of software, not equipped to make a large direct contribution to industry on the scale recorded in China. Much of FDI comes from multi-nationals.

Developed countries are exerting intense pressure on the developing world through the WTO negotiations to permit MNCs to invest freely. The vastly superior financial resources, and technological capacity of MNCs taken together with the new IPR regime (to which India is a signatory) does place indigenous business at a disadvantage. At another level, the political clout that MNCs can command — legitimately or otherwise — is also a source of concern. India may not be a banana republic. But our decision makers are by no means immune to the influence of MNCs (as is evident from the Enron experience). And as the Bhopal Gas tragedy case showed, nor can MNCs be effectively brought to book even for serious and criminal negligence. Concerns about the impact of FDI cannot therefore be dismissed as fanciful or paranoiac.

A single-minded pursuit of FDI is fraught with serious risks. It is only through a purposive, long-term strategy that these risks can be met. From this view point, the east Asian strategy of acquiring know-how through purchase or licensing, and simultaneously investing in Research and Development capacity to master, adapt and improve technology is worthy of emulation. Collaborations with MNCs and foreign universities/research institutions are far better, far more advantageous in the long-run than FDI in manufacturing/ infrastructure. That would however require Indian Government and domestic enterprises to muster the courage and grit to pursue a conscious, proactive long-range strategy to upgrade their technological competence. Government policy can facilitate this but cannot implement it except with through industry. Some industries — software; pharmaceuticals, biotechnology — have shown the inclination and capacity to follow this route. Perhaps, that defines the starting point for implementing a national strategy.

There are also much deeper reasons to be concerned about the impact of globalisation. Whether one likes it or not, the communications revolution and the growing exposure to mass media have opened an ever widening window to the outside world. Through this the mass of Indian people are made aware of happenings the world over in practically every sphere of human activity. We have to accept that little can be done to stop this exposure and that, whether we like it or not, it has, and will have, a powerful influence in shaping tastes preferences and aspirations of all classes. Across the board, aspirations and expectations are rising faster than what most can afford or can expect in a reasonable period to afford, even as a small minority is visibly able to afford it. That this could be a source of aggravating social tension is one source of concern.

Whether the adoption of life styles and consumption patterns of 'developed' countries, even for a relatively small but growing minority, is at all sustainable is cause for deep concern. Our resource base is already much smaller relative its population than 'developed' countries. Signs of ecological stress in the country are manifest in continued deforestation, depletion of groundwater and increasingly widespread pollution of land, water and atmosphere. Optimism that international trade and free inflow of foreign capital and technology can take care of the problems is misplaced. Also under question is the belief that science and technology is capable of taking care of all these problems.

Resources everywhere are under severe stress and there is growing concern over unabated resource depletion and deterioration of the earth's biosphere. The unwillingness of developed countries to accept responsibility for checking these trends by restraining their consumption, and checking the relocation of polluting industries to the developing countries are likely to aggravate the problems of pollution and resource depletion in the Third World. While continuing to press the developed world hard to accept that they are the major cause of environmental degradation and should accept the major responsibility for corrective action, it is also imperative that we address the task of reducing pollution and preventing its spread as well as that of reshaping domestic consumption pattern seriously.

The solution is not to hard back to Gandhiji's concept of

simple living but to explore low available modern technology can be used, or can be made through imaginative research, to improve capabilities and functioning of the mass of ordinary people in an environment friendly way. This is a challenge, which we have hardly begun to address. Some promising work along these lines is being done: Amulya Reddy's work on energy being a notable example. But they are only a beginning, a hint of the lines along which this task needs to be addressed.

Prospects

What are the prospects for the future and how should strategy and policy be reoriented to address these tasks? These are too large and too complex issues to be dealt with in a lecture of this kind. In any case, I am not equipped to deal with them. I will only touch on three key issues to which I have given some thought: strengthening Panchayati Raj Institutions; fiscal consolidation, and agriculture. Effective tackling of these will help, and is indeed essential, to facilitate addressing others. There is also a need for reorienting the scope and techniques of planning.

Decentralisation

By mandating creation and empowerment of elected representative Panchayat Raj bodies with authority and responsibility for local development, the 73rd and 74th Constitutional Amendments have opened the possibilities of major changes in the configurations of political power and in the way local development programmes area planned and implemented. Underlying these amendments is the premise that effective decentralisation of the authority and responsibility, along with resources, for local development to elected, representative local bodies will help ensure that programmes are better adapted to local needs, that stronger pressures will be generated to ensure that the works are completed, maintained and managed properly, and that the have-nots and underprivileged can exert effective democratic pressure on the local government to address their needs. The process is still in an incipient stage and has to overcome several obstacles and strong resistance.

They have also the potential to bring about substantial shift in the configurations of political power from the state and central political leaders to local leaders. The implementation of the provisions of the amendments has been halting because of resistance from the former. But already one can see signs of growing pressure from the emerging class of leaders in the PRIs for a greater and more effective power in local development matters. The central and state level political leaders will not yield their power easily. But the contest is poised to intensify and it is important to stoke this process so that the balance of power shifts significantly in favour of the PRIs. It will deepen democracy and at the same time create conditions for better (that is, more meaningful and efficient) management of public resources for local development. In doing so, it is essential to ensure that resources allocated to local development and poverty alleviation programmes are not diminished in the name of fiscal stabilisation.

The focus should, however, not be limited to the quantum of resources alone, but equally on ways to ensure that they are utilised effectively and that the benefits in fact reach the disadvantaged. There is much scope for improving local development programmes in both respects by, among other things: (a) ensuring that the spirit of the 73rd and 74th amendments are implemented by holding free and fair elections regularly and full devolution of authority and resources to the PRIs; (b) reducing duplication and fragmentation by consolidating poverty alleviation programmes into two broad groups: namely those relating to provision of basic amenities and those meant to provide immediate employment and simultaneously augment the productive base to sustain growing employment and incomes; (c) eliminating subsidies, doles and handouts; (d) rationalising the criteria for distribution of resources across regions and within regions, so that, allocations are proportional to the deficiencies; and (e) strengthening mechanisms to increase accountability of elected executives.

Improvement on the Fiscal Front

Improvements in the efficiency of local development and poverty alleviation programmes can contribute significantly to easing the fiscal constraint, but would not solve it. Improvement in the fiscal situation at all levels of government will remain a major challenge. The required measures are well-known; (a) increase tax-revenues to absolute taxes and as a proposition of GDP by rationalising tax system and more importantly by tight or enforcement of tax laws and collection of tax dues; (b) enable rationalisation and flexible redeployment of staff in the light of changing requirements; (c) restructure public enterprises/undertakings to make their management autonomous of government in all respects subject only to broad guidelines to be monitored by regulatory bodies independent of and outside government.

Issues concerning salary levels and structure of government employees, difficult as it is, have also to be faced. There is abundant evidence of over-staffing which is compounded by acceptance of more or less uniform pay and benefits to employees at all levels of government without regard to affordability, and with little flexibility to try alternative ways of performing the tasks. Governments at the center and in the states simply do not have the resources to compensate for cost of living increases much less to grant periodic increases in salaries and benefits. PRIs simply cannot afford salaries and benefits paid by higher levels of government. It is therefore necessary to evolve a national policy for determining level and structure of salaries and benefits to government employees at different levels consistent with their resources, the capacity of the economy and remuneration in non-government sectors.

All these measures are essential ingredients of any credible programme of fiscal stabilisation. Governments at every level have long viewed them as political hot potatoes and, therefore, been unwilling to even consider such reforms seriously. However, the picture is changing. The fiscal position of the governments everywhere has deteriorated to such an extent that several of them do not have cash even to pay salaries on time; many have accumulated huge arrears for supplies of power and face cut-off in supplies, if they don't clear dues.

All possible stratagems (such as overdrafts and ways and means advances from the Reserve Bank, drawing on various funds, allowing public undertakings to borrow on the strength of government guarantees, loans from international donors) for increasing expenditure without worrying about mobilising matching resources have been tried and pretty much exhausted. This experience is by now familiar to every major political party as they are, or have been, in power in one or other state. They are increasingly, if painfully, conscious that they cannot avoid confronting the difficult task of fiscal reform.

Already several state Chief Ministers and even the Prime Minister are speaking publicly about the problem and explaining the necessity for unpopular corrective measures such as raising utility user charges; stricter collection of tax revenue; suspending or reducing benefits to employers and even retrenchment through voluntary retirement and similar schemes. Some have also implemented some of these measures in the face of strong opposition. More can be expected to follow. Their task will be easier, if strategies can be devised by which opposition can be reduced and corrective measures made more palatable.

A first, and essential, step to this end is to make the public aware that the benefits of subsidies implicit in under-pricing of goods and services provided by the public sector as well as revenue leakages and corruption accrue largely to the relatively better-off segments. Corrective measures may seem harsh but it can be shown that they will fall mainly on the better-off. The resulting improvement in public resources will help government to devote more resources and attention to the needs of the poor, the needy and the underprivileged. The existence of huge 'fat' in the system by way of leakages could also be used as the bargaining counter to persuade key groups opposed the reforms.

For instance, in agriculture subsidies can be shown to be inimical to the long-term interests of the farmers' because it encourages wasteful use of inputs, causes degradation of soil, dwindling of groundwater supply and deterioration of water quality. There is much scope for increasing output per unit of water and fertilisers. If exploited, higher input prices need not result in any reduction in output or net returns. To make this credible, a substantial part of the resources generated by reduced subsidies could be earmarked for a programme of research and extension, improvement in the quality of services, and providing better amenities and infrastructure in rural areas.

Similarly, in the case of electricity, irrigation and amenities, if only leakages of revenue were plugged by eliminating theft and proper billing and collection of charges, finances of these undertakings would improve dramatically. For this purpose, it is essential to make these undertakings autonomous of government, and insist that they cover their costs from their own earnings giving them freedom, subject to approval by independent regulatory authority, to fix the prices for their products. It further means banning subsidies from the budget except for clearly specified purposes and showing them explicitly as such in the budgets. The ongoing reforms are ostensibly meant to bring about these changes. But progress is very slow, because of none of interests involved in running these undertakings — political executive, bureaucracy and the workers — wants them.

Workers' opposition to such reforms is understandable. But current blanket opposition to labour reforms seems short-sighted and inimical to their long-term interests. The brutal truth is that the fiscal situation simply does not permit indefinite continuation of the current dispensation. The long-term interests of the undertakings and their employees would be better served, if they cooperate in measures to increase operating efficiency, reduce leakages and improving the financial position of the enterprises. In exchange for their cooperation, an arrangement could be negotiated whereby restructuring and redeployment of the work force is so phased as to mesh with programmes for future expansion; and a portion of improved revenue collections and cost reductions shared with the employees. Given the widespread disenchantment among users with the poor quality of service and corruption at the interface between functionaries and users, such a reform would also be welcomed by the public. Failure to do realise this can only make the situation worse for workers and make outright privatisation unavoidable.

Agriculture

The importance of agriculture to achieving and sustaining development of the rest of the economy is not sufficiently appreciated. The sense of satisfaction of having solved the food problems on the ground that we no longer depend on imports and that there is a huge stock of foodgrains reflects a dangerously complacent attitude. We need to remind ourselves that foodgrain self-sufficiency has been achieved largely because of an unexpectedly large and rapid diversification in the pattern of food demand. Foodgrain consumption per capita has in fact remained nearly stagnant though per capita incomes have been growing by more than 3 per cent a year. And at current levels of food consumption, the calorie intake of the majority of the Indian population falls short of the norms considered by nutritionists to be necessary for active and healthy life. The huge foodgrain stocks are the result of a perverse pricing and procurement policy. Acceleration in overall growth in the measure contemplated by Planning Commission would call for faster growth of agricultural production (nearly double the levels achieved so far) and for rapid diversification in the pattern of production. What kinds and degrees of diversification, where and by what means — are 'questions' which are not being addressed seriously.

Quickening of overall growth requires much faster rates of yield improvement. There is much hype about bio-technological revolution as holding the key. But the fact is that much of it is as of now more promise than reality. The progress of varietal and agronomic improvements in rainfed crops and non-cereal crops is remains very uneven. On the other hand, there are legitimate concerns that the green revolution technology is running out of steam and that it has created serious problems of land degradation, groundwater depletion and deterioration of water quality which threaten sustainability. Vast improvements in the quality of land, soil and water management are an essential precondition to effectively exploit the potential of advance in biophysical technology. The potential for augmenting water availability for irrigation being increasingly constrained by several factors (technical, financial and social); therefore improving the quality of soil and water management for more effective use of available water has become imperative. Of course, this will call for more investments. Bur far more important and far more difficult are institutional reforms, which are urgently needed but are being addressed fitfully and in a halting manner.

Role of Planning

What should be the role of planning in the changed context? To begin with, it is necessary to recognise that the role of the state will be different from that envisaged in the fifties and sixties. The state's direct involvement in production, marketing and finance will be reduced. These activities will be increasingly and largely with the private sector or with undertakings in which government may directly or indirectly have a stake but without supervision and direction by the political executive.

Reducing the sphere of the state's direct involvement or interference in economic activity does not imply a shrinking in its activities. Only its spheres of activity will change.

The responsibility of the state to provide a legal framework and regulatory mechanisms and ensure that they function effectively and in a fair manner will be much greater. It will need to play a much more effective role in checking pollution and issues concerning sustainable development. It has the responsibility to deliver constitutionally mandated social goals of ensuring universal elementary education, healthcare and basic amenities, adequate employment and a reasonable minimum living to all citizens; reduce entrenched social and economic inequalities generally. Besides ensuring that adequate public resources are allocated to these ends, the state has to strengthen, and where needed create institutional framework to ensure that these programmes are effectively implemented.

The role of the government in deciding inter-sectoral allocations of resources will be reduced. But this does not mean dismantling of planning only its reorientation. In the past, at the national level, the Planning Commission played an important role in providing governments at the center and, through the NDC, in the states, an overall national perspective on development. Such agreed perspective is indispensable to enable all concerned to appreciate the interconnections between its constituent elements and formulate sectoral programmes and policies consistent with it. The Planning Commission has also served as a bridge between the centre and the states in evolving a national development strategy, ensuring central assistance for the states' programmes and evolving a consensus on the criteria for allocation of this assistance between the states. These functions will continue to be important, in fact more so in the future.

The focus and style of the commission's work will however change. The practice of detailed reviews of schemes under central and state plans to decide overall plan size and sectoral allocations has outlived its utility. The states should be encouraged to devise and try out innovative approaches to tackle problems in their spheres and equip their institutions for this purpose.

The Planning Commission must concentrate on providing an independent overview of the trends in key aspects of the economy; the trends in the conditions of the poor and the disadvantaged social groups; strategic long-term planning for key sectors; and serving as a bridge to promote interaction and exchange of experiences between states and between government and Non-Governmental Organisations (NGOs). This will require the Commission to be far more selective in the kinds of issues on which it will concentrate.

Instead of spreading its attention on details of all sectors and schemes, it needs to concentrate on key aspects, and key sectors, which are likely to pose major problems (for example agriculture, energy, and transportation) or present significant new opportunities in the long-term (as in the case of software, communications, bio-technology and pharmaceuticals).

In particular, there is need for identifying technologies and products which can enhance the quality of life of the mass of people even while minimising adverse environmental consequences; and exploring strategies and instruments by which the selected technologies can be adapted and engineered for that purpose by appropriate selection and R&D. In this perspective, the technological and organisational aspects of land and water, energy, transportation and construction are some of the most important and challenging areas for such an effort.

With problems of resource depletion and degradation getting more intense and widespread, measures to ensure long-term sustainability of development. Therefore, apart from strategic sector planning, the Commission needs to keep a close watch on emerging trends in the environment, and examine consumption patterns and the technology used to meet them from the view point of long-term sustainability and impact on the environment. Technological innovations and production systems need to be scanned from such a broad and long-term perspective.

The approach will however have to be very different from the past. It will require Planning Commission to become leaner, more professional and at higher level of quality. They cannot expect to do a satisfactory job of strategic planning without considering the vastness and diversity of the country. They cannot do this on their own. It is essential to encourage and stimulate states to set up professionally competent organisations to develop plans for the development of activities falling in their spheres. Such bodies, whether at the center or the states, cannot, and should not, rely solely (or even mainly, on their own staff or that of government). It is essential to explore innovative ways to bring together entrepreneurs, technologists, NGOs, universities, and research establishments for a continuing, but focused, interaction and collaboration to address these important and challenging tasks.

D.P. Dhar Memorial Lecture delivered at the Giri Institute of Development Studies, Lucknow, April 19, 2002.

2

Structural Adjustment in the Indian Economy

THE famous Bombay Plan, published in 1945, outlined a vision of India's transformation from a poor and stagnant economy into a prosperous and dynamic industrial power on the basis of modern technology. Dr. John Mathai, who had a career spanning academia, business and government, was one of the group of economists and businessmen who prepared this plan which saw a strong positive role for the state in initiating and sustaining the process. Soon after Independence, Dr. Mathai became the Finance Minister in the Union Cabinet but quit the Government when it decided to set up the Planning Commission. He did so perhaps not so much out of opposition to planning as such, as the implications of creating a body with wide ranging functions which was not envisaged in the Constitution and whose formal position in relation to other organs of Government was left vague. His fears have proved to be unfounded. The Planning Commission did not turn out to be a supercabinet and yet played a useful role in providing a framework in which public investment decision could be coordinated and in mediating between the Centre and the States in matters relating to development. If anything, there is reason to lament the steady erosion in the importance and the role of the Planning Commission since the Seventies.

Approach to Planning

Nowadays 'planning' itself has become something of a dirty word. Critics of Indian planning have been blaming the modest performance of the Indian economy, its inefficiency and corruption on excessive state involvement and interference in the functioning of the economy in the name of equity and self-reliance. The dramatic collapse of the socialist regimes in east Europe and the USSR has added much grist to the proponents of "market driven" development against planning. One must note, however, that the choice is no longer posed in terms of market Vs state intervention. State intervention and guidance is now conceded as being desirable, even essential. The plea is that the state should play a "market friendly" role. Our own policies have been gradually veering, over the past decade or more, towards "liberalisation" in respect of trade and industry. The larger questions — such as the role of the state and public sector enterprises, the balance between the growth and equity, and the appropriateness of the pattern of development pursued — which have been debated in a rather desultory, fitful fashion so far have suddenly acquired a compelling immediacy in the context of our present economic crisis. A basic restructuring of the approach to planning and the role of the state now occupies centre stage.

It is worth recalling that during the first three decades of planning India experienced and weathered numerous "crises" — military conflicts, food and foreign exchange shortages, and inflation — without giving up the basic approach. During this period, the economy recorded steady, though moderate, rate of growth in output. The widening and deepening of the industrial base were noticeable, but employment problems persisted; and the pace of improvement in terms of average living standards and of reducing the incidence of unemployment and poverty has been slow. On the other hand, the macro economic management was guided by prudence — some might even say conservatism — and succeeded in containing the domestic rate of inflation and the recourse to foreign borrowings within reasonable limits. In these two respects, India's record compares very favourably with most other countries of the developing world.

India entered the Eighties with a fairly comfortable position in terms of food and foreign exchange reserves — with food stocks around 20 million tonnes and foreign exchange reserves equivalent to five months imports. The rate of domestic savings was at a record level of 21 per cent of GDP, savings performance of the public sector had visibly improved in the late Seventies with total public savings averaging an all time high of 4.5 per cent of GDP during 1975-79; and the inflation rate during the latter half of the Seventies (hardly 4-5 per cent a year) was the lowest in three decades.

The Eighties witnessed a paradoxical situation: For reasons which are far from clear, the overall rate of growth was significantly higher than the average of the previous three decades even as both the balance of payments and the public sector finances deteriorated rapidly. On the external front, the deficit on the current account of balance of payments rose progressively from around $ 3 billions equivalent at the beginning of the decade to over $ 9 billion at the end. During the first half of the decade both exports and import grew rather slowly, the latter in large measure due to the rise in domestic crude oil output from Bombay High and a consequent reduction in POL imports. But a decline in remittances and a big increase in interest payments, consequent on a deliberate policy of encouraging NRI deposits and taking recourse to commercial borrowing, led to a widening of the current account deficit.

Payment for Imports

During the second half of the decade, partly due to the switch in exchange rate policy (reflected in the crawling devaluation of the rupee), there was an unprecedented increase in exports. But this was more than neutralised by the increase in payments for imports. The latter was contributed by two factors; an increase in normal imports and an even larger increase in the payments on account of credit purchases of defence, aircraft and other items which do not figure in the recorded trade statistics. Continued increase in NRI deposits and commercial bank borrowings — outstandings under these heads nearly quadrupled between 1984-85 and 1989-90 — meant a further large rise in interest payments. There was no improvement in remittances. The current account deficit more than doubled in the course of the Seventh Plan. This was met partly by higher borrowings and partly by a drawing on reserves, which fell by $ 2.7 billions in just three years. But the end of 1989-90, foreign exchange reserves were equivalent to two months imports.

On the domestic front, the comfortable food, foreign exchange and savings position along with the low rate of inflation encouraged the government to step up public investments rapidly, despite a progressive deterioration in the savings performance of the public sector. As a percentage of GDP, public investment which stood at around 8.5 per cent in 1980-81 averaged 10.5 per cent through the Eighties, while public sector savings declined from around 4.5 per cent in 1981-82 and 1982-83 to 1.2 per cent by the end of the decade. The government was not deterred by the steep rise in the fiscal deficit at a time when private savings rate was also lower and the interest rate on government securities had been increased in accordance with the Chakravarthy Committee recommendations. In the event the government's recourse to borrowing from the Reserve Bank also rose substantially from an average of 2.1 per cent in GDP in 1980-1981 to 2.4 per cent in subsequent quinquennium. Warnings about the dangers of allowing this situation to continue were countered by pointing to the relatively high growth rate in GDP and the fact that the policy did not generate extra inflationary pressures.

The dangers implicit in allowing the fiscal and BOP trends to continue unchecked were however obvious enough. This consideration weighed heavily with the Planning Commission in formulating the approach to the Eighth Plan early in 1990: While the document argued for many basic changes to make planning more sensitive to the needs of the poor and the unemployed, to encourage decentralisation of power and responsibility for local development and pay more attention to the content of development in terms of environmental impact and sustainability, it also pointed out "with the fiscal system and the BOP being under such severe stress, the margin for manoeuvre in the coming few years is limited. This makes it all the more necessary to undertake a close scrutiny of existing expenditures to accommodate new commitments. Accordingly the emphasis has to be more on restructuring both economic priorities and the pattern of spending as well as getting much more out of what is spent than on large financial outlay".

POLICY PACKAGE AND GROWTH RATE

The Commission resisted pressures to set a high growth target. Even the maintenance of growth rate achieved in the Eighties did not seem feasible without determined action to tackle the fiscal and the BOP deficits. And the elements of the medium term policy package suggested in the Approach document were consciously designed to address these problems. This package included: decentralisation and integrated local planning were not only inherently desirable, but would also improve efficiency of public spending; vigorous conservation efforts to reduce the rate of growth in demand for capital/foreign exchange intensive inputs notably energy and fertilizers; a thorough review of the rationale and incidence of explicit and implicit subsidies to help decide on how to trim them without affecting the poor; and measures to maintain and improve upon the export growth achieved in the latter half of the Eighties. Following the Gulf War the elements of a medium term programme to cope with the situation were spelt out in some further detail.

But the debate on this document was never really joined. There was a great deal of shadow boxing on the question of quantification and on what the target growth rate should be. To some degree this may reflect a concern among influential segments in government and the media that the formulations of the approach document may threaten the efforts at liberalisation. The idea of opening the economy to external competition and dismantling the control system had gradually gained support in the government. Rajiv Gandhi was openly committed to it and V.P. Singh was quite persuaded that liberalisation was inevitable and necessary. The kind of agenda proposed in the Approach document — emphasising internal structural changes, the problems of the poor, the unemployed and traditional craftsmen, and sustainable development — was perhaps seen as retrograde; at any rate it might divert attention and blunt the momentum of liberalisation. Perhaps the opinion makers did not have much faith in the longevity of the JD government much less its capacity to implement any reform, not to speak of radical reform. Whatever the reason, the proposals of the Planning Commission did not get serious attention.

The Gulf war precipitated the BOP crisis earlier than might have happened in the normal course. In 1990-91 the import bill on account of POL is estimated to have increased by as much as $ 1.7 billions — largely on account of the steep rise in oil prices during the conflict and to some extent higher volume of imports necessitated by shortfall in indigenous production. Remittances fell in the wake of the conflict and there were substantial withdrawals in the NRI deposits. The weak policy response to these developments, reflecting the fluid political situation at the Centre, had an adverse effect on our international credit rating and further intensified the withdrawal of NRI deposits. Meanwhile reserves kept falling and by early 1991 dipped to barely one month's imports. The foreign exchange liquidity crisis became so acute as to raise the spectre of default. Even roll over of short term commercial credit was difficult. The new government was forced by these circumstances into a series of measures such as pawning gold to stave off the crisis. But eventually it had to apply for assistance from the IMF and the Bank. Under the circumstances there was hardly any other option.

It was well known that assistance from the Fund as well as the prospects of additional aid from other donors would be contingent on our taking effective steps to reduce the fiscal and the BOP deficits. It was also known that the Fund and the Bank expected the adjustment package to go well beyond the conventional prescriptions, namely controlling growth of government expenditure generally, trimming of subsidies, restricting the government dependence on borrowing and improvement in public enterprise operations on the fiscal side and exchange rate adjustments on the foreign trade side. These, in their view, would need to be accompanied by a substantial lowering of tariffs and permitting free import of goods, capital and knowhow; dismantling controls on investment, production and prices of domestic industry; creating conditions, including freedom to lay off workers and close down non-viable units, in which enterprises could rationalise their operations;

reorganising the financial institutions by giving them autonomy and permitting them to function in a competitive environment; and generally restricting the area of public sector operations in the economy.

This package has provoked a great deal of concern and criticism partly on the ground that acceptance of the package as part of the conditionalities of assistance from IMF and other foreign donors implies surrender of national sovereignty but also, and more importantly, on the ground that these changes were being rushed without thinking through its implications, without paying sufficient attention to content and sequencing of various measures, and without sufficient political preparation.

To reject the reforms merely on the ground that they are conditions for getting foreign assistance would be inappropriate. The deterioration in the BoP and the fiscal situations has been going on for some time and nothing prevented us from working out a package of corrective measures to prevent them assuming crisis proportions. Many of the measures needed to reduce the fiscal and the BoP deficits are as unexceptionable as they are obvious.

Thus, there can be hardly any disagreement that the tendency of government to depend increasingly on borrowings not only for investments but also for meeting current expenditures is fraught with grave danger; that a great deal is wrong in the way public enterprises work and that they must be made more efficient and generate substantially more surpluses for reinvestment if they are to serve the purposes they were meant to; and that the system of detailed, direct and discretionary controls on the private sector is ineffective if not counterproductive. All these are by now widely accepted across practically the entire political spectrum. They have also been repeatedly emphasised in discussions within the government, in the NDC and in public debates on the economy. And, as mentioned earlier, the May 1990 document on the Eighth Plan had drawn pointed attention to these and outlined a programme to deal with them in a medium term framework.

If nevertheless no action was taken to prevent the crisis and attempt to correct the situation no outside agency can be blamed. It is lamentable that the government launched on such wide ranging policy changes only after the crisis occurred and IMF and other donors had to be convinced not only about our willingness to address the problem but to negotiate a package acceptable to them. One cannot expect to have much room for manoeuvre when negotiating emergency assistance with barely four to six weeks of reserves. It must be noted however that a significant segment of domestic opinion, in and out of government, had also been working for quite some time to push through more or less a similar package.

Problem of Liberalisation

Given the magnitude of the fiscal and the balance of payments problems, there can be no question about the need for structural adjustment; but there are questions about its content as well as viewing it primarily as a problem of liberalisation and opening of the economy. Much faster export growth, freer access to imports and allowing enterprises, private and public, greater freedom are all necessary. But questions concerning the wisdom of an open-door policy to multinationals, the action necessary to stimulate greater technological dynamism and innovation within the country, and the kinds of strategic intervention which the state should attempt in the long term interests of society cannot be brushed aside lightly. These are not adjudicable in the market place.

Further the way the problem is posed reflects an excessive preoccupation with large industry. What about the impact of liberalisation on small industry (traditional and modern) which have been so assiduously fostered in the last four decades? And what relevance does liberalisation have for agriculture? Agricultural growth is not being impeded by excessive state intervention. It requires more effective intervention in strengthening institutions and by way of public investment. Improvements of infrastructure are again not mediated by markets but need restructuring of the way they are organised and managed. And if adjustment involves adverse effects (even temporarily) on employment and incomes, both considerations of humanity and political compulsions of democracy make it necessary to ensure that costs are shared equitably. All these issues are germane to formulating an adjustment programme but we do not yet have an articulation of how precisely they will be handled. The Planning Commission's latest paper on the Eighth Plan, which provided an opportunity for addressing these issues, has chosen to confine itself to generalities. Moreover, its quantitative projections seem quite out of line with the realities of adjustment. It is not possible to deal with all these issues in this lecture. My subsequent comments are limited to the problem of reducing the BoP and the fiscal deficits to manageable proportions in a reasonable period of time.

Devaluation and After

The central case for devaluation and changes in foreign trade policies is that they will help promote a faster export growth and generate pressures for improvement in efficiency of domestic industry which will eventually be reflected in faster growth of income and employment. The crucial question is how long will these effects take to manifest?

On the export front, the immediate impact of devaluation has not been at all striking; while the reported six per cent decline in dollar earnings during the first six months is almost entirely due to the steep fall (over 50 per cent) in exports to east Europe and USSR, the earnings from exports to other hard currency countries rose by only six per cent. By comparison it is estimated that total exports should grow by about 15 per cent a year if the current account deficit is to be brought down to manageable levels in the course of the next five years.

This is more than double the rate achieved during the latter half of the 1980s when the domestic inflation rate was lower and periodic adjustments in the exchange rate compensated for inflation. The current inflation rate being much higher, there is reason for apprehension that unless it is brought down quickly or we resume the policy of crawling adjustments in the exchange rate, the impact of devaluation on export growth would soon be blunted. In any case accelerated export growth is contingent not only on competitive prices but on a sustained effort to cultivate foreign markets, build a reputation for reliability in delivery schedules and quality and domestic producers showing the resilience to adapt speedily in the light of changing conditions in overseas markets.

The past record of Indian business — especially the large corporations — in these respects is not particularly good. While a change of attitude is reported to be occurring as a result of the new policy initiatives, a doubling of the growth rate of overall export earnings beginning next year can hardly be taken for granted. Hopes of diverting, to any substantial extent, earnings flowing through illegal channels are unlikely to be realised so long as the sources of demand for foreign exchange for smuggling (mainly gold) or for building foreign balances remain untouched.

Altogether it would be realistic to go on the assumption that the response is likely to be gradual. Meanwhile, government should take up, in collaboration with industry and trade, a concerted drive in selected products/markets to lay the basis for a sustained 15 per cent growth in exports at least by mid 1990s. A 15 per cent export growth must become a target of very high priority.

Imports have been substantially reduced during the current year despite considerable liberalisation of licensing and quota restrictions because of the substantial premium which the eximscrips command, the stringent conditions for opening letters of credit and high interest rates. But as these are relaxed and the proposed tariff reduction is implemented — the government is apparently committed to both — there is bound to be a significant increase in the demand for imports and the rate of import growth relatives to national income will also be much higher than in the past. No one quite knows by how much import demand will go up as a result of liberalisation. In the past imports have grown roughly at 5 per cent a year; some projections assume — they are no more than assumptions — a 10 per cent annual growth under the new regime.

Supposing, for argument sake, one accepts the latter figure and assumes that it takes three to four years (rather than one or two) to attain the 15 per cent annual export growth. Under reasonable assumptions concerning the growth of factor services (largely determined by the level and structure of debt already committed) and with no significant change in remittances, one should expect a substantial increase — on a rough estimate by an average of five billion dollars a year) — in the current account deficit in the next 3-4 years. Reserves at the end of 1990, being still barely two months imports, do not permit drawing down. Any further increase in commercial borrowing and NRI deposits is undesirable — the levels are already too high, costly, and have shown themselves to be volatile at times of difficulty. This means that the volume of multilateral and bilateral assistance needed to tide over the transitional phase of BOP adjustment will also be substantially more than appears to be visualised by external donor agencies.

If this extra assistance is not available and the inflow of foreign resources is limited to the magnitude of current account deficit projected on the basis of export growth rate reaching 15 per cent in 1992-93, the import capacity of the economy will be severely constrained in the coming three-four years. While this can be managed without reimposing import controls by allowing the eximscrips premium to increase, there is bound to be a severe recession in aggregate output with no means to regulate its incidence across sectors or regions.

Precisely because the BOP outcomes of the recent policy changes are uncertain and highly sensitive to the assumptions one makes about the economy's response to the regime change, and foreign exchange is a critical resource, it would be prudent to phase trade liberalisation and tariff reduction over a longer period, negotiate for larger assistance for the transition and also accept the possibility that the transition will involve a recession in the overall rate of growth. Acting on misplaced optimism is risky and almost certainly a recipe for a repetition of the crisis.

Risks of recession are likely to be aggravated by the measures to reduce the fiscal deficit. The 1991-92 budget promised that deficit financing will be contained at Rs. 7,500 crores without imposing any additional levies largely by controlling non-plan expenditures and effecting substantial cuts in food and fertilizer subsidies. If needed non-development expenditures are contained at budgeted levels by these measures, it would be an unprecedented achievement deserving the utmost commendation. Even so, the fact that revenue collections are running substantially below projections and reports that the centre is holding back on payments (eg. of amounts due to the financial institutions on account of the farm loan waivers of last year), give room for apprehension that deficits may not be really contained at projected levels. The latest available information suggests that Reserve Bank lending to government is running at a higher level than projected.

1992-93 BUDGET PROSPECTS

The prospects for the coming budget are more daunting; Even ignoring the unease on account of revenue collections, if the present trends continue, several difficulties would remain. Reducing tariffs to fulfil commitments about trade liberalisation would mean substantial revenue reduction; and a cut in the statutory liquidity ratio (i.e. the proportion of the commercial banks' resources which they are required by statute to invest in government securities) will substantially reduce the magnitude of borrowings from the market and/or raise their cost. The government has in any case agreed to bring down the fiscal deficit to 5 per cent of GDP by 1991-92. Substantial cuts in non development expenditure are not feasible in the immediate future; Nothing can be done about interest payments. It would be surprising if defence and expenditure on civilian staff can be brought down significantly in a year or two; and the scope for further cuts in central subsidies is limited.

Given all this there is every likelihood that the resources available for the plan will be squeezed. A slow down in public sector plan outlays would affect growth via aggregate demand and depressing growth of industries dependent directly on public investments. It also raises difficult questions of where the cuts should fall; should it be in the central plan or in reduced assistance to States? How should cuts be distributed as between energy, transport and other infrastructure, agriculture and rural development, industry and anti-poverty/ employment programmes? Cuts in infrastructure investment will adversely affect growth, while cuts in antipoverty programmes restrict the scope of the "safety net" for the poor at a time when they need it most. On the other hand to insist on a certain magnitude of financial outlays for the plan, irrespective of what happens to non-plan expenditures and the impact of various fiscal measures on resources available to the government, can only exacerbate the dangers of stagflation.

It is thus necessary to be realistic about the economic and political problems involved in reducing the fiscal deficit and the time it will take to accomplish it without causing serious dislocations. To try and 'sell' the adjustment package on the promise of a speedy and dramatic turn around in the economy's performance in respect of output growth, employment, inflation and balance of payment, is tempting but shortsighted. Not all the elements of the package have been worked out; none of them is easy to implement and the economy's response is uncertain. The risk of one or more promises regarding improved performance not being redeemed is very high. Therefore, it is better to administer the bitter medicine without sugar coating it with false hopes. Adjustment will be a slow and painful process and should be projected as such.

Major Changes

Reducing fiscal deficits calls for measures both on the revenue and on the expenditure sides. Major changes in the structure of taxation — especially as between excise and customs — are in the offing. The nature of these changes and the net revenue impact is as yet unclear; the apprehension is that there may be a loss of revenue. Partly for this reason and on grounds of equity, a substantial increase in the share of direct taxes relative to total revenue and to GDP is desirable and feasible. Wider coverage of direct taxes, simplification of the system by eliminating exemptions are as necessary as effective enforcement of tax laws. There is clearly much room for improvement in the latter respect.

However, much more important concern should be on economising expenditure both by cutting non-development items to the bare bone and improving the efficiency of development spending. Among the non-development expenditures, defence, staff salaries and subsidies are the principal areas where potential for economies is large.

The need for a close look at manning and equipment programmes with a view to cutting down defence spending without compromising security has long been emphasised but to no avail. The upheavals in USSR so far the major source of our hardware, may have significant consequences for the cost of maintenance of existing equipment and for replacements both of which may call for large expenditures. Changes in the world geopolitical situation on the other hand argue for a reassessment of our "threat perceptions". and long term defence strategy. What the overall impact would be can only be a matter of speculation at this stage. But there can be no question that any reassessment should keep in mind the severe fiscal crisis and the need to contain the growth of defence expenditure to the minimum, and, if possible even reduce them so that resources for development are not jeopardised.

In order to contain the growth of staff salaries it is essential to (a) check any increase in the number of government staff and eventually reduce it; (b) redeploy personnel along with rationalisation of activities to raise their effectiveness and (c) observe a great deal of restraint in the matter of revision of pay scales, allowances and benefits. Government employees are among the more privileged segments of Indian society in terms of level of emoluments and security of jobs and can reasonably be expected to share in the cost of structural adjustment.

The third area is subsidies. Apart from explicit subsidies

given by the Centre on account of food, fertilizers and exports, the quantum of implicit subsidies largely on account of the difference between the cost of providing various goods and services and the recoveries from their users is much larger. The National Institute of Public Finance Policy and Research estimates the total value of unrecovered costs on account of social and economic services at Rs. 42,000 crores in 1987-88 — nearly as large as the total public sector plan outlay in that year. About 40 per cent of the unrecovered costs is on account of social services and 60 per cent for economic services (including irrigation, power and transport). A substantial reduction in the magnitude of these subsidies would release sizeable resources for the plan and should therefore be very high on the agenda of reform.

These unrecovered costs however, do not at all represent subsidies to the consumers of these services. A good part of it is attributable to inefficiencies in production and inappropriate pricing for different categories of users. Therefore, any attempt at reducing the magnitude of unrecovered costs must address both aspects of the problem: Increases in user charges are inevitable — notably for irrigation, power and road transport. However, it is essential to be discriminating while deciding which category of uses and users should be made to pay more and by how much. At the same time, the task of raising the efficiency in the production and distribution of the goods and services should receive far greater emphasis and attention than so far.

Price Increases

One way to generate the necessary pressures would be to subject increases in administered prices to review by independent tribunals and make them contingent on explicitly commitments on the part of the department/enterprise concerned to achieve a reasonable level of operational efficiency and reduce unit costs. The present system of unilateral announcement of price increases without any question as to whether the costs and cost increases are kept to the minimum is indefensible. Clearly too the discipline must cover both the Centre and the states inasmuch as the latter account for nearly 60 per cent of the total unrecovered costs on social economic services and nearly half that on economic services.

That there is considerable scope for improvement in efficiency in practically every sphere is all too obvious. Efforts in this respect must focus specially on energy and transport — which are largely in the public sector and are used throughout the economy. Greater efficiency through better use of existing capacity of such universal intermediates reduces unit costs of producing them, and therefore the potential for cost push inflation through administered price rises. It also reduces the quantum of additional capacity, and hence, investment needed to meet a given growth in demand for these inputs. If these were combined with effective measures to conserve and economise these capital intensive inputs in the activities using them, the additional capacity needed to meet a given growth of demand will be further reduced, thereby releasing investment resources for other uses. A strong and purposive policy of conservation of energy generally and of petroleum products in particular, as well as in fertilizer use is essential. These are all highly capital intensive and import intensive; domestic resources of oil are limited and measures to contain the growth of demand for oil and oil-based products is essential for long term viability in balance of payments.

Improvements in enterprise efficiency however require concerted efforts in which the Centre, the state governments and the workers of the enterprises concerned all need to cooperate. This cannot be achieved by exhortation, pressure or confrontation but only by assiduous fostering of a sense of the serious stakes involved and collaboration in evolving a restructuring programme which seeks to minimise the costs of adjustment — in terms of redeployment and even retrenchment of workers. To imagine that the problem can be solved through privatisation is altogether unrealistic; in the case of infrastructure, one cannot duck the problem of improving efficiency of investments already made by the public sector; the scope, manner and implications of privatisation in sectors like power, coal and transport have in any case to be thought of far more carefully and in detail before taking that route.

Another area where potential efficiency gains are significant is in the plan itself. These include a stricter scrutiny of all new public investment proposals in terms of the social and economic justification and a review of ongoing projects (especially larger projects) with a view to speedy completion of ongoing schemes and eschewing non-viable projects. By far the most important is reducing duplication and waste in implementation of agriculture, rural development and antipoverty programmes which now account for nearly one fifth of public sector plan outlay. The efficacy of these programmes can be greatly increased by integrating and pooling the resources being spent on those elements of the programmes which consist of works to be done locally and making them available to elected representative local bodies for deployment in accordance with specific needs and potentials of each district block and panchayat.

Duplication and leakages can be substantially reduced in the framework of such decentralisation even as it creates political space in which local leaders can meaningfully participate in developmental activity. The creation of such a political space at the local level is also a much needed antidote and corrective to the present excessive centralisation of power and patronage. Democratic decentralisation is therefore important both for more effective use of resources for local development and for more healthy politics.

All these reforms — and the list is far from exhaustive — calls for a high order of political management. In the first place, the sense of the crisis, the imperative need for systemic reform and the rationale for the main element of the reforms need to be effectively communicated to all levels of government and to the people at large. Second, the task of structural reform should not be viewed as the responsibility of the Centre alone. States spend nearly as much as the Centre. They are responsible for key segments of infrastructure (namely electricity, roads and water supply) as well as the social welfare and antipoverty programmes; the implicit subsidies (unrecovered costs) passing through the State budgets are some 60 per cent more than in the Central budget; and the State governments taken as a whole also show a substantial and growing revenue deficit. Unless the States also show a high degree of fiscal discipline — which must necessarily consist of a mixture of measures designed to raise revenues, contain expenditure growth and improve the effectiveness of expenditure — it would be hardly possible to bring down the overall fiscal deficit without impinging adversely on the expansion and improvement of essential infrastructure (so crucial for the success of trade and industrial liberalisation) and on the employment and anti poverty programmes (which provide a safety net of sorts for the vulnerable segments).

On the other hand, the condition of the States' finances is affected in myriad ways by the Centre. The manner in which the Centre mobilises additional resources, the Centre's policies regarding salaries, allowances and benefits for employees, the operational efficiency and pricing policies of public enterprises, the decisions regarding the overall size of the plan, the magnitude of Central assistance and the nature and scale of centrally sponsored schemes — all these have a large impact on the State resources. Given this, and the vast ramifications of structural adjustment, one would expect a serious and sustained effort by the Centre to take the States fully into confidence about the nature and magnitude of the crisis facing the economy and the rationale for and implications of the "structural adjustment" programme, even while impressing on them the contribution they have to make and the responsibilities they have to share in order to make the programme a success. What we need is a national structural adjustment programme based on the maximum possible understanding and consent among the States and the Centre. Apart from informal meets, the NDC and the inter-State Council provide formal mechanisms for informing, counselling and discussing these issues with the States. That these have not been used to any significant extent in shaping the adjustment reforms is to be regretted.

In the final analysis no structural adjustment programme can be effectively implemented without broadbased political support. This support will not be easy to muster merely on the basis of promises of faster growth of income and employment and of lower rate of inflation at the end of the adjustment process. It requires not only a great deal of public education about the need for and rationale of policy changes but also to generate a feeling that the costs of adjustment — by way of lower subsidies, higher price of utilities and services, higher taxes, insistence on productivity norms, the redeployment and even some retrenchment of workers, restraints on increase in wages and salaries, restricting the scope for using public institutions for political patronage at every level — are being shared equitably. As it is farmers are being asked to pay more for water, electricity and fertilizers; workers to accept wage restraints, retrenchment and closures; and the users of PDS to pay higher prices for foodgrains, sugar, kerosene and transport services. Necessary as all these are, they also provoke — and understandably so — a great deal of resistance. And the farm lobby and trade unions are forces to reckon with. Their opposition can, however, be to some extent mitigated by measures to contain the adverse effects on employment and incomes specially for the vulnerable segments of the population.

Safety Net

A "safety net" for workers in the organised sector who may lose their jobs in the process of adjustment is on the agenda. But there is hardly any talk of the far more numerous rural wage labour and workers in urban unorganised activities who are relatively worse off, whose jobs and incomes are also at risk and who have neither legislative nor union protection. It is extremely important, at a minimum, to ensure that the employment and antipoverty programmes and access of the poor to the PDS do not get whittled down in the name of fiscal crisis.

Above all it is essential to demonstrate that the better off segments, especially in urban areas, bear their due share of the costs of adjustment. The Government must show greater willingness and ability to deal with this class, make them pay the taxes due from them, pay for the full cost of public services they use, and take measures to enforce greater austerity among them than is currently in evidence. Regrettably, the tendency is to assume that nothing much can be done to make tax administration effectively enforce existing tax laws relating to income, wealth and property. Amnesties and incentives to flush out black money reflect this presumption and tantamount to sanctifying a culture of noncompliance with the law among the well-to-do. So is the plea for lowering of the tax rates on the ground that it will reduce incentives for evasion. There is also a vocal lobby for raising the exemption limit for income tax, removing restrictions on the level of executive compensation, and reducing excise duty on durables and other goods largely catering to the better-off segments in the face of recession. Should the government yield to these pressures, the effective tax burden on the well-to-do will be reduced — even as all other classes are being asked to bear hardships for the sake of the "larger good". Can we really expect a democratic polity to support, or is it even proper to expect it to support, such an inequitous sharing of the cost of adjustment?

3

Attitude Towards Multinationals

THE current euphoria and hype about wooing multinationals to invest in India rests on the belief that such investment will significantly augment capital available for investment, bring in up-to-date technology and improve access to foreign markets. These arguments, which seem to be widely and unquestioningly accepted, need to be examined critically in the light of experience of other countries, especially those of east and southern east Asia.

The Magnitude

It is well known that east and south Asian countries have received huge and rapidly growing amounts of direct investment in recent years: the annual inflow of such investment in this region has grown from 8 billion US dollars in the early 1980's to 59 billion US dollars in 1994. This region has also become an increasingly important destination of such investments. Thus 80 per cent of the total increase in the stock of foreign direct investment between 1980 and 1990 (122.8 billion dollars) was within the developed countries; Asia accounted for a mere 10 per cent of the total. During the first half of the 1990's nearly 30 per cent of the increase ($610 billion) in this stock went to east and south east Asia, the biggest beneficiary being China.

Huge as these magnitudes are in absolute terms, they

constitute but a small fraction of the total investments taking place in these economies. In 1994, direct investment by multinational accounted for about 9 per cent of total gross fixed capital formation in Asia as a whole; in most south east Asian countries (except Malaysia) the rate was less than 5 per cent; in China however this proportion has been rising very rapidly to touch about 20 per cent in 1994. But in none of these countries has increased inflow of more capital been accompanied by an increase in the overall rate of capital formation. The belief that FDI will bring about a sizable rise in capital formation is thus ill founded. The great bulk (upward of 90 per cent in most cases and 80 per cent even in China) continues to be funded by domestic savings. Whether or not export performance and overall growth rates have a positive relation to FDI as a proportion of GDB or gross domestic capital growth remains to be established.

TNC's and MNC's

The term "transnational" and "multinational" corporations is associated in our minds with giant corporations of the developed countries like General Motors, IBM, Shell, Toyota, and Coca Cola. While these are no doubt important, they are far from being the sole and, in many cases, even the dominant players in the arena. Innumerable firms (which are "small and medium" relative to these giants) collaborate (or set up on their own) industrial enterprises outside their countries. According to the World Investment Report there are some 38,000 firms which are multinational in character. The 100 largest MNCs in 1993 accounted for only about a third of the total MNC owned capital stock in the world – an average of nearly $ 7.5 billion per firm. But the stock held by the remaining firms averages only $ 40 million per firm.

Nor is it correct to assume that MNCs from developed countries are everywhere the main source of foreign direct investment. Much of the FDI in south Asian countries no doubt is coming from developed countries — Japan, Europe and US. But in China there are as many as 45,000 foreign affiliates of MNCs. The average cumulative investment per firm being only $ 2.7 million. As much as 80 per cent of the FDI Stock in China is owned by overseas Chinese mainly from the developing countries of Hongkong and Taiwan. FDI in this case is the vehicle through which modern manufacturing and trading skills and experience gained by overseas Chinese in these countries — which is truly remarkable in terms of the range, depth and speed — is being put to use in the development of mainland China.

The Experience of South Asian Countries

The experience of Japan, South Korea and Taiwan provide strong grounds for contesting the belief that large FDI is necessary for technological progress or rapid growth. Before and during the second world war Japan built a wide industrial base — comprising both light and heavy industry — largely through indigenous effort. Its efforts to upgrade technology and restructure industries in the post war period continued the policy of making national companies the principal agents of development and restricting foreign equity investment. Technology transfer was effected not through FDI but mainly through non equity means such as licensing agreements and subcontracting to acquire advanced technologies, designs and, in some cases, marketing tie-ups with foreign companies for exports.

Immediately after the war, when Japan sought to enter export markets for light manufacturers (garments, footwear, sports goods), it did not have an overseas network for commercial information on foreign firms (not all of which were MNCs) for product and packaging design, style, sizes etc. Often sheer copying was a source of learning. Gradually

Japanese firms built their own capability through R&D and setting up trading houses to compete in world markets on their own. In the case of automobiles, government encouraged learning from MNCs through ".... joint ventures and foreign exchange allocation for knockdown assembly of foreign models". This helped Japanese auto makers to learn basic techniques of mass production. But simultaneously there was a vigorous and organised effort to adapt and improve technology and organisation of manufacturing to such an extent that they eventually — and within a surprisingly short time — became world leaders in the industry.

Much the same pattern was followed by Taiwan and Korea. Both relied on non-equity arrangements rather than FDI to access technology initially, but eventually built up their own capability to innovate, and to set up and manage complex manufacturing processes. For instance Korea's electronics industry started with assembly (including assembly of imported components for TNCs). This formed the basis for building up local skills and absorptive capacity to make use of imported technology. Once this capacity matured, the local firms resorted to licensing arrangements more frequently as means to acquire and digest advanced technique. This, together with an aggressive domestic R&D effort actively encouraged and supported by government, enabled them to rapidly eliminate the technology gap vis-a-vis developed countries in such a sophisticated product as micro chips. The establishment of the electronics industry in both countries owed much to the entrepreneurial knowledge and skills of their people (including expatriates educated and trained in developed countries). Essentially similar strategies were successfully pursued in a large range of industries leading to the building of industrial capability of extraordinary range and depth within a short span of 3-4 decades.

Both in Korea and Taiwan the point of entry into modern

manufacturing was export of labour intensive products often starting with simple assembly — type operations. And exports remained an important driving force even after the scale and complexity of industrial activity increased. The progress of industry in these countries has been characterised as a "step-by-step" capitalising on learning opportunities made available through its external relations with more advanced world and the tendency for TNCs to relocate production in low wage countries. TNCs decisions on which processes, products or technology are to be located in a developing country are determined by TNC's interest in maximising its profits or securing other advantages and not by the interests of the host country.

It has been suggested that as labour costs increase in developed countries their firms shift production to low wage developing countries, starting with assembly, progressing through the manufacture of components and intermediate products for particular industries and then across industries. Whether this progression (referred to as the flying geese pattern) would have taken place in Korea and Taiwan if they had relied heavily on technology through FDI is open to serious doubt. The motivation and ability of the indigenous firms, most of which do not have foreign collaborations and which account for much the larger part of total manufacturing activity has been crucial factor.

Government policy can facilitate and encourage but ultimately it is the entrepreneurs' motivation and ability which will determine how much and how fast the available opportunities can be exploited. Economic incentives alone cannot explain why the Koreans, who were complete novices in automobile making, chose to take up the challenge of becoming automobile manufacturers of world class; much less can they explain how they made a such huge success of it. The development of indigenous capability for design, manufacture and marketing of automobiles and building purposefully on such knowledge and technology as were available in the market was crucial.

The south east Asian countries seem unlikely to replicate the path of Korea and Taiwan if they continue to depend largely on TNCs for setting up and operating modern manufacturing. It is possible that their indigenous entrepreneurs, being predominantly ethnic Chinese, may be able to accomplish, in due course, what their counterparts did in Taiwan and Hongkong. They may also be able to draw on the latters' accumulated technological and organisational expertise. But that will mean development of capabilities through essentially non equity routes. The future course of development in south east Asia merits careful watching.

Lessons for India

The experiences of east and south east Asia have important lessons for India. After decades of a policy strongly opposed to foreign investment, the pendulum has swung to the other extreme of wooing it at any cost. The organised sector of industry gave an unqualified welcome to this policy initially. But they now seem apprehensive of their position if multinationals were allowed free entry. The emphasis has shifted in favour of encouraging foreign direct investment in areas (power, road, oil) where presence of indigenous private enterprise is small, and on ensuring "level playing field" to counter advantages (such as easier access to finance at lower cost, capacity to carry aggressive sale campaigns taking advantage of their brand names etc.) enjoyed by MNCs. The apprehension flows from the realisation that the interest of TNCs — especially the larger ones — is in the large, and growing domestic market for a variety of mass consumer goods which is currently almost entirely controlled by indigenous firms. The likely effect of staffing and remuneration policies of TNCs on labour costs (via higher wages and salaries), faster turn over of skilled workers and executives is also a source of concern.

Even after seven years of liberalisation, Indian industry has not overcome its mindset under the earlier regime where a highly protected domestic market with little internal competition made them indifferent to production. Though pressures for improving product quality and reducing costs are increasing, they have not mustered the will to address these problems seriously and purposefully. They seem more inclined to seek to escape their predicament through better management of finance and marketing and manipulation of state policy (on tax rates, special concessions, and subsidies).

The international playing field has meanwhile changed in the wake of the recent agreement on intellectual property rights, pressures for widening their scope and stiffening their terms, as well as for according home country firms and MNCs equal treatment. The IPR regime makes it much more difficult to follow the older route (followed by east Asian countries) of learning through copying and imitation followed by adaptation and then innovation. The TNCs, being keen on accessing the domestic market for mass consumer goods, may be less willing to part with technology through arrangements other than equity participation. Nor do we have as large and diverse a pool of expatriate experience and skills (as the Chinese do) to draw upon in setting up and operating modern industry under conditions of rapid technological progress and competition.

Under these circumstances the strategy and policy in regard to foreign capital and know how need careful review. In the first place we need to recognise that free entry of MNCs into mass consumption market on the basis of majority control is not in the national interest. Apart from political considerations, the difficulty of enforcing MNC compliance with national laws (eg. in the case of Bhopal) and their ability to interfere in domestic politics to protect their interests, the branded products of MNCs do not necessarily and always make the users better off. Competition from MNCs as a spur to efficiency is neither necessary, nor is it the best way to protect the Indian consumer. Active policy to promote greater competition among indigenous firms deserves much greater emphasis. On the other hand, the products of MNCs and life styles associated with them are in many cases unattainable for the large mass of the people, and give rise to serious environmental problems threatening long term sustainability. It is essential to give ourselves as much autonomy as possible to shape products and life styles in the long term interests of our people.

All this would suggest that we should disallow MNC investment in mass consumption goods. Policy focus should shift from FDI per se to active encouragement of non-equity routes to access available technology by creating differential incentives favouring arrangements such as purchase or licensing of technology and against FDI. This should be complemented by a strong and active policy of pressure and persuasion of indigenous firms to spend on R&D, and for absorption, adaptation and upgradation of imported technology. We must look at the east Asian experience for pointers on the elements of this strategy and what it takes to make it work.

Efforts to attract FDI should be focussed on areas where technology is changing rapidly; in sectors producing intermediate and capital goods. In this connection, a concerted effort must be made to identify areas in which Indians overseas have established a presence in manufacturing and/or technology development (or have an interest in doing so), compile and maintain and up-to-date inventory of such individuals/firms and make the information freely available to interested Indian firms; and afford them reasonable incentives to set up and/or manage facilities in India with Indian collaborators.

Finally policy must create an environment in which indigenous firms in the domestic market for mass consumer goods are under strong pressure to upgrade the products and for lower costs. This means freedom for firms to set up and expand plants; and where domestic competitive pressures are weak, to allow import of consumer goods with some tariff. At the same time firms should have flexibility to retool, and redeploy their resources and men in the light of changing needs.

Above all, indigenous firms and business houses must shed the mind set of looking to foreign collaborations for their development and growth, and adopt a more proactive and purposeful approach to developing their own technological competence. They certainly need government support. Indeed greater interactive cooperation between government and industry is essential. But this will not go far without the business capacity to self reliance and willingness to confront the challenges it poses. Sonys and Hyundais do not come about simply because of a friendly government or because there are large and potentially profitable markets at home or abroad.

Distribution of FDI Stock by Host Countries in Different Regions

Billion US $

	1980	*1993*
World	481.0	2319.0
S.SE and E.Asia	32.2	305.0
Newly industrialising Economics	11.4	72.7
ASEAN	19.0	120.0
China	5.7 (1984)	54.2

There are 38,000 parent MN firms in the world. They have 2,50,000 affiliates operating in different countries.

Source: World Investment Report 1995

FDI Stocks and Flows in Select Host Countries/ Regions by Origin

billion US $

	Stock		*Flows/annum*	
	1980	*1993*	*1985-87*	*1990-93*
NIE	10.8	72.7	13.5	2.9
EUSUS	4.9	30.1	7.5	1.3
Japan	2.2	14.0	2.2	0.8
Other	3.7	28.6	3.8	0.8
ASEAN	19	120	2.25	16.9
EU/US	4.7	29.6	0.71	6.5
Japan	4.4	26.8	0.72	3.2
Other	9.9*	63.6**	0.82	6.2
China	5.7	57.2	2.0	11.6
EU/US	1.8	6.3	0.4	2.7
Japan	0.3	5.2	0.2	0.8
Other	3.6	45.7@	1.4	8.1

* 6.4 from Asia ** 46 from Asia @ 45 from Asia

Source: World Investment Report 1995

Stock of FDI in Select Asian countries by Origin 1993

$ billion

Origin	*Host country*			
	Indonesia	*Malaysia*	*Thailand*	*Singapore*
NIE (incl Singapore)	17.2	11.5	4.5	2.7
Asean	0.3	1.4	—	2.6
China	—	.2	—	—
Japan	13.9	7.4	4.6	2..6
EU US	13.7	9.4	3.9	16.0
Other	22.1	4.2	0.9	14.7
TW	67.6	34.1	13.9	38.6

4

Subsidies in India

THE discussion paper on "Government Subsidies in India", (1998) published by the Finance Ministry of the Central government, gives a comprehensive and up-to-date estimate of all "subsidies", visible and hidden, given by the central and state governments in 1994-95. The word "subsidies" is however, somewhat loaded and misleading: To be precise, the estimate measures the difference between costs incurred in producing and distributing various social and economic services provided by government and the charges recovered from those who use these services. "Unrecovered costs" would therefore be a more appropriate description than "subsidies".

The document, which is based on a detailed study done by the National Institute of Public Finance and Policy, brings out the magnitude of the problem and the challenge it poses for fiscal management. It has attracted some amount of comment and criticism. But the expectation that the publication could stimulate a serious public discussion of the rationale for various "subsidies", the necessity to contain them and the ways in which they can be reduced has unfortunately been belied. Hence this attempt at raising some of these issues.

Magnitudes

The most obvious and striking finding of the study is the staggering magnitude of "subsidies". In 1994-95 the Centre and the states taken together gave Rs. 137,000 crores on this account. This amounts to a little under 14 per cent the countrys' GDP; about 1.4 times the gross fiscal deficit of the Centre and states; and 1.3 times their combined plan outlays.

- Two thirds of the total unrecovered costs are on account of states whose total amounts to about three times of their combined gross fiscal deficit and 2.4 times their total plan outlays.
- Economic services account for most of the unrecovered costs at the Centre, while at the state level the major portion is on account of social services, their share ranging from about 40 per cent (Haryana) to 61 per cent (Kerala). Education is the single largest element of unrecovered costs on account of social services. Irrigation, power, agriculture and transport, generally in that order, account for the bulk of unrecovered costs of economic services. (Table 1).

TABLE — 1

Magnitude of Unrecovered Costs of Social and Economic Services, India 1994-95*

Rs. in crores

	Social services	*Economic services*	*Total*	*Total as % of GDP*
Central	5102	48983	43048	4.0
State**	37945	45307	94290	9.9
Total	43047	94290	137338	14.4

* gross of surpluses

** covers 15 major states

- Unrecovered costs of social and economic services provided by states relative to their respective state domestic product ranges from a minimum of 9 per cent in Punjab to as much as 15 per cent in Orissa and Rajasthan. They add up to twice the state plan outlay at a minimum (AP) to over five and a half times (in Bihar). Their magnitude every where exceeds the gross fiscal deficit, ranging between 70 per cent (Punjab) and 240 per cent (for Tamilnadu and West Bengal)!

- The burden of uncovered costs has been rising at a rapid rate: Based on earlier NIPFP study (which used broadly similar concepts and assumptions), unrecovered costs of the centre have risen 2.4 times over a 7 year period: from Rs. 16,000 crores in 1987-88 to Rs. 38,500 crores in 1994-95. The increase at the state level is considerably larger: 2.6 times over a 6 year period (ie. 1987-88 to 1993-94). Unrecovered costs of economic services have risen faster than that of social services, the difference being more pronounced in the states (Table 2).

TABLE — 2

Changes in Uncovered Costs between 1987-88 and 1993-94

	1987-88	*1993-94*	*1993-94/1987-88*
Social Services			
Centre	2300	5702	2.22
States	14460	43954	2.42
Economic Services			
Centre	13765	33344*	2.42
States	11799	34380	2.91
Total			
Centre	16065	38446*	2.39
States	26259	69334	2.64

* relates to 1994-95.

- Both at the Centre and the states the uncovered costs have risen much faster than plan outlays. In 1987-88 central plan outlays were 50 per cent higher than the unrecovered costs; by 1994-95 this difference had fallen to around 43 per cent. At the state level unrecovered costs have consistently exceeded plan outlays during the last 2 decades. But the ratio has widened dramatically from 1.28 in 1977-78 and to 1.75 in 1987-88 and 2.65 in 1993-94 (Table 3).

Implications

These figures should dispel any doubt that large and growing magnitude of unrecovered costs of goods and services provided by the government are a major factor contributing to the deteriorating fiscal health of government at both levels. Moreover, uncovered costs — which are in effect a recurrent subsidy to producers and/or users of these goods and services — do not contribute to expanding and improving the infrastructure facilities or add to the economy's productive capacity. Uncovered costs are increasingly outstripping plan outlay. This means that an increasing diversion of resources away from activities while promote faster economic growth and larger, more widely diffused employment. A determined and bold effort to reduce "unrecovered costs" is necessary-both in the interests of restoring governments' fiscal health and to release much needed resources for development.

Uncovered costs consist of several different elements. At one extreme are interest subsidies, loan waivers, subsidies under various plan schemes and poverty alleviation programmes. Here the main issue is whether the subsidies accrue fully and exclusively to the targetted population. That there are large "leakages" and that mistargetting is widespread in such hand-outs is common knowledge. The task therefore is to device ways to check these tendencies and also to explore alternative ways of accomplishing their underlying objectives more effectively.

TABLE — 3

Unrecovered Costs and Plan Outlay in Major States 1977-78, 1987-88 and 1996-97

Rs. in Million

Major States	*1977-78*			*1987-88*			*1993-94*			
	Unrecover Cost	*Plan Outlay*	*Ratio 1/2*	*Unrecover Cost*	*Plan Outlay*	*Ratio 1/2*	*Unrecover Cost*	*Plan Outlay*	*Ratio 1/2*	*Gross Fiscal Deficit*
Gujarat	3411	3270	1.04	20071	11020	1.82	55540	19310	2.88	14068
Haryana	1314	1470	0.89	7757	4640	1.67	19840	8070	2.46	6744
Maharashtra	5067	6480	0.78	27967	21910	1.28	94630	37780	2.5	33877
Punjab	2796	2220	1.26	11430	7900	1.45	26680	10950	2.44	15662
Andhra Pradesh	4385	3610	1.21	22893	11230	2.04	57750	28670	2.01	21226
Karnataka	3088	2460	1.26	17047	7020	2.43	48010	20000	2.4	15162
Kerala	2740	1590	1.72	11611	3900	2.98	29540	10130	2.92	13387
Tamilnadu	3968	2420	1.64	23300	12770	1.82	62830	22340	2.81	18503
West Bengal	4923	2250	2.19	19880	7830	2.54	45960	12170	3.78	23662
Bihar	4212	2660	1.58	19160	11950	1.6	45800	8120	5.64	13421
Madhya Pradesh	3524	3470	1.02	20576	14130	1.46	51450	22360	2.3	14852
Orissa	2118	1360	1.56	10427	7010	1.49	26450	10950	2.42	12017
Rajasthan	2790	1730	1.61	16674	6450	2.59	42460	17430	2.44	18307
Uttar Pradesh	8045	5850	1.38	33795	22150	1.53	83390	32500	2.57	46023
Total of above	52381	40840	1.28	262588	149910	1.75	690330	260780	2.65	266911

The case for a drastic reduction of uncovered costs is unassailable but it does not mean that the only means of achieving it is to raise user charges. In the first place, basic education and health facilities, water supply, sanitation, roads and other such services give rise to significant beneficial effects not only for individual users but for the economy. Better educated and healthy people are likely to be more productive. It is also in the larger social interest to make sure that all segments (and particularly the poor and the disadvantaged) have access to these minimum basic facilities. On all these grounds, it is now widely accepted that the government should provide such facilities free or at highly subsidised rates.

The precise boundaries of these so called "merit goods" has been the subject of some debate. While in principle a society is free to decide this, its freedom is constrained by the availability of resources. A government with large revenue surplus can afford to be liberal in offering subsidies; though even in such a situation there is a choice between using the surplus for investments as against subsidizing current consumption. The present state of public finances clearly does not permit widening the scope of subsidies much beyond the above mentioned basic social amenities.

The social argument against levying user charges on these amenities is strong. The brunt of the effort at reducing uncovered cost in this segment has to be an improving efficiency which in effect would yield more and better quality services from resources devoted to them. That there is much scope for efficiency improvement is again undeniable: There is a general complaint that teachers are irregular in attending schools and indifferent about conducting classes. A similar situation prevails in the primary health care system. Departmental supervision is not effective in ensuring proper functioning of these and most other public services. Additional resources for teaching and medicines and other necessary supplies are needed and will help increase quality of service. But unless local communities are interested and have the authority to supervise and monitor the working of these institutions, and, ideally, the necessary disciplinary powers, the pressure for public accountability will remain weak. Giving greater freedom and flexibility to panchayats to appoint additional teachers and improve facilities from local resources would also help. There is ample of evidence of growing community concern about getting good education, health care etc. but reforms have to overcome strong and unreasoning opposition from the unions.

The third, and by far the most important, category comprises goods and services produced and/or distributed by the public sector. This includes irrigation, electricity, transport, telephones and several other elements of economic infrastructure provided mostly by the public sector. It also includes a variety of manufactures (like fertilisers, steel, machinery to name but a few) in the production of which the government, as a matter of policy, has invested large amounts. Perceptions regarding the role of the public sector in both categories of activity has changed a great deal in the last two decades. This is reflected in the growing shift of emphasis in policy in favour of deregulation and dismantling of controls, giving private sector greater scope and freedom, privatising existing public enterprises and strengthening the public regulatory framework.

Irrespective of the outcome of these changes, the massive resources already invested in public enterprises and the large and growing losses in their operation are a major problem demanding urgent attention. Moreover, the public sector will continue to play the major role in the infrastructure sector. Therefore, measures to check and reduce the current level of losses and also avoid recurrence of such losses are essential.

In all the above mentioned cases, underpricing of output is responsible for a part, but only a part, of low cost recovery. The supply of free electricity for agriculture in several states is the most dramatic example; but by no means confined to it. For nearly twenty years all governments at the centre and states, and all parties, have revised prices charged to users marginally, if at all, despite all around rise in costs. Indeed in some cases, like water and electricity for pumping, user charges have infact been reduced! The country's public finances are paying a high price for the unbridled populism of the last two decades!

While substantial price increases of most publicly provided goods and services are necessary, the adjustment has to be gradual. Since the prices charged have not changed even as costs rise, the order of increase needed to breakeven is often very high. For example, in the case of surface irrigation, it is estimated that a five fold increase in rate is needed even to recover the current operation and maintenance costs and a small part of capital charges! It is also imperative to recognise that a good part of the low cost recovery is due to high costs of producing and supplying these goods and services. It would be palpably unfair to make users pay for the inefficiencies in their production and distribution.

A policy of increasing users charges would have greater chances of being accepted by the users provided (a) The adjustments are spread over a specified number of years: (b) credible steps are taken to raise efficiency of enterprises and reduce their costs: (c) the price increases are accompanied by an improvement in the quality of service and future increases are subject to review by regulatory authorities independent of government; and (d) the impact of the increase in user charges is socially equitable in the sense that their incidence falls more heavily on better off segments of the population.

That there is gross inefficiency in the way public agencies providing goods and services can hardly be contested. They arise in part from poor design of projects; inordinate delays in their completion; widespread corruption in construction and other elements in process of investment. At the operational level employing far more workers than are strictly needed for operating the facilities efficiently and the rapid rise in wages and salary costs is a common feature of public enterprises. Under-utilisation of capacity is also quite common. For example, the ratio of the utilisation of power generating capacity (measured by the number of KWA generated per annum per KW of capacity) is known to be well below the technically feasible levels. There is compelling evidence that a large part of the recorded transmission and distribution losses, and reported agricultural consumption in fact represents theft of electricity. By allowing this to go unchecked, the electricity board loses a large amount of revenue due to under-billing. If effective steps were taken to plug this leakage, and agricultural users were charged a nominal 50 paise per unit, the SEB can practically wipe out its current deficit. Similar problems exist in irrigation, public transport and other services.

Tackling these problems is as important for reducing the burden of unrecovered costs, as raising user charges. It is in this context that issues like autonomy of enterprises, credible social monitoring and audit systems, rationalisation of work force, increasing productivity and ensuring that dues from customers are properly collected become directly relevant to fiscal stabilisation. None of these can be done without general consensus among all political parties to curb the tendency to use public funds and jobs as instruments of patronage or as means of mobilising political funds. The cooperation of employees manning these facilities is also essential.

It would be unrealistic to expect those who are already employed to accept significant retrenchment in order to cut costs; or for politicians to accept it as the central focus of policy. However, it is not un-reasonable to seek the cooperation of public sector employees in achieving better capacity use, plugging leakages in purchase and use of materials and ensuring proper billing and collection of dues from customers. The potential gains from these sources are substantial. And workers in public services are beginning to be aware that the government cannot bale them out indefinitely if they continue to make looses and that efficiency improvements are essential for their survival. Under these circumstance we can think of, and work towards, a collective agreement under which gains from efficiency improvement are shared between employees, the enterprise/departments, and for a long term programme of bringing down redundant work force.

Cooperation of workers in the concerned enterprises is critical to the success of needed reforms. Threats of privatisation or closure are unlikely to work. A two pronged approach of generating pressure for better performance along with incentives is the only practical course. The former can be done in several ways: (1) making enterprises autonomous and withdrawing all budgetary support within a specified period. (2) Bringing the enterprises under to the jurisdiction of consumer protection law and making all price rises of public utilities subject to review of their efficiency and cost of operations by independent regulatory agencies. (3) Devolve more powers to elected panchayatraj institutions for planning and implementation of local development works and for management of basic school and health related services in the community. (4) In many cases (e.g. irrigation) active cooperation of users is essential for efficient operation and reducing costs. User participation in management at all levels, and transfer of more of the responsibility or maintenance and cost recovery to users will help in the process.

While it is obvious that the subsidies mostly benefit the better off segments, no one political party on its own dares to tackle the problem in an atmosphere of unbridled competitive politics. The magnitude of subsidies as well as the number of beneficiaries of each subsidy being large, each group which benefits is capable of exerting organised pressure on the State. No government or, for that matter no political party, is willing to confront the problem. The significant recent exception in Andhra Pradesh under the Chief Ministership of Sri. Chandrababu Naidu. He speaks publicly about the untonability of the current subsidies and the need to cut food subsidies, raise prices of water and electricity and restructure the electricity board. That he has not succeeded yet in denting opposition is another matter. Otherwise most leaders behave like ostriches with their heads buried in sand, pretending that the problem does not exist or will go away. Worse still, populist policies continue to flourish in the face of manifest and worsening fiscal crisis.

About a year back a report of the NDC committee on austerity (consisting of chief ministers of periodically all shades of political opinion) recognised the need for determined measures both at the centre and in the states to tackle the fiscal problem and rightly called for a common approach. It could have been used to evolve a measure of consensus for the needed measures. Instead of using this to create a political climate conducive for wide ranging fiscal and public sector reform, the central government leadership in effect sabotaged the initiative for the sake of its immediate interest to avoid confrontation with its employees.

It is imperative that efforts be revived to forge a common approach encompassing the centre and the states, and the major political parties, on this issue. Failure to do so can only worsen the fiscal problem and the capacity of the government to invest in development. If the trend of the last five years is allowed to continue, the magnitude of unrecovered costs will reach Rs 350,000 crores a year by the end of the 9th plan! On top of it the central and states exchequers have to find an extra Rs. 35,000-40,000 crores per annum by way of increased salaries.

We need a serious national debate on the magnitude and implications of subsidies; classes and regions which benefit from different categories of subsidies; whether they are equitable and serve any social purpose; and whether the avowed aims can be better achieved in other, less expensive, ways. It should also focus on designing a balanced package of increased user charges, greater efficiency in the functioning of the services which would be acceptable to the concerned interests. The political leadership at all levels, the media and academics have an important role to play in raising these issues sharply, make people aware of the stakes and churn public discussion of ways in which policies should be reshaped so that subsidies can be kept to a minimum and that too limited to only clearly identified group of poor and disadvantaged.

5

Planning, State and Development

While the Indian planning structure and mechanisms are indeed due for an overhaul, it is altogether simplistic to view the problem solely in terms of greater freedom for the private sector and switching over to a market-based economy.

WHILE national planning and particularly the role of the state in guiding and shaping economic development in our country has always been a contentious subject, there was a rather wide consensus around the time of independence about the necessity for the state to play a leading role in the development process. The reasoning of course varied:

The Bombay Plan prepared by leading Indian businessmen saw massive public investments in infrastructure and basic industries as being necessary to facilitate growth of the private sector and set the country on the road to rapid development. The socialists emphasised the importance of public ownership and state control over the private sector to correct the existing inequities and injustices, as well as inequities and injustices associated with unfettered capitalist development. In the event a compromise evolved in which the basic concept of overall national planning with a major role for the public sector was accepted but the bulk of production and a large part of fresh investment was still left with the private sector.

Over the years, while significant progress has been made in many directions, criticisms of its shortcomings and failures have also grown: One cannot but take note of the fact that actual achievements — be it in growth, employment, standard of nutrition, health and education among the mass of the people, greater regional balance or reduction of inequality — have been rather less than expected and promised. In some respects, especially in respect of disparities across regions and between different classes (e.g, agriculture and non-agriculture; organized vs unorganised sectors; wage labourers vs property owners), the situation has deteriorated or, at any rate, is perceived to have deteriorated. The social and political unrest, and the increasingly violent expression thereof, is palpable. The public sector has not lived up to the expectation of its becoming an increasingly important source of surpluses for investment or as an instrument for achieving a more egalitarian income distribution and a more just social order. Instead the vast expansion in the developmental and regulatory roles assumed by the state has led to the creation of a huge centralised bureaucracy which is at once rigid, costly and insufficiently responsive to its social responsibilities. The consequences of widespread corruption, both administrative and political, generated by the vast discretionary powers vested in the state functionaries over the access to and use of facilities and resources in the system is also a cause for serious concern.

Criticism of Planning

All this has naturally spurred criticism of the planning process and of the government's role to the point where the very rationale of planning and of state intervention have come under increasing question. Recent developments in the socialist countries would seem to reinforce this trend. There is a massive retreat throughout the socialist world from the tenets of near-complete state ownership of the means of production and a system of planning in which the details of investment, production, pricing and distribution decisions of individual enterprises are sought to be determined by a central authority. Few would deny that these countries succeeded in eliminating abject poverty and ensured everyone a reasonable minimum of food, shelter, educational and health services and social security; and also in building up the productive forces of their economies at a reasonably rapid rate. But disenchantment set in partly because the system was unable to sustain high overall growth, ensure efficiency, and adapt to changing technological and market conditions. This has led almost all socialist countries to experiment with various ways of loosening the centralised bureaucratic control and move to more decentralised forms of decision-making in economic matters mediated through market as an institutional device, and evolving a system of incentives to encourage more efficient and responsive behaviour on the part of various economic agents. Some have gone considerably beyond this to experiment with privatisation of economic activity.

These developments have undoubtedly encouraged those who feel that India's development strategy needs a basic change in favour of the private sector, free markets and liberal trade policies, and away from public enterprise and state intervention. Even as this viewpoint is finding more and more forceful expression, the traditional votaries of the public sector and planning display a certain amount of puzzlement, if not confusion, about the significance of the changes in Soviet Union, China and east Europe for our planning.

While both our experience and that of the socialist countries does underscore the limits to central planning and control, one should not overdraw the parallel between our economy and the socialist economies. For one thing, with nearly 75 per cent of India's GDP being produced by the private sector, the government's influence in the Indian economy is more restricted than in socialist countries. Also market-type institutions are better developed and play a far more extensive role in the Indian economy while they are non-existent or exist in a rather rudimentary form in the socialist countries.

Second, the argument is about restructuring and reorienting government's role, *not* of eliminating it. The fact remains that the government appropriates a substantial part of the national product by way of taxes, and accounts for an even larger part of national expenditure. The way government spends its resources and the efficiency of this spending will therefore continue to exercise a very important influence on the rest of the economy. Furthermore, unlike the socialist countries, poverty, malnutrition, ill health and illiteracy remain widespread. Given political democracy, adult franchise and expectations roused by mass media and mass politics, no government can afford to take the position that inequality is not its concern or that poverty and unemployment can be left to be taken care of by growth in due course. Governments have perforce to address these problems here and now and that necessarily means state intervention.

Third, it is not particularly meaningful to pose the problem, in either context, as a simple choice between planning and the market mechanism. Even in free market economies practically all intra-firm allocation decisions — and these cover small enterprises as well as the giant corporations like General Motors and US Steel — surely are made outside the market. The scale, variety and complexity of the operations of some of the large corporations being comparable to the whole economy of some of the east European countries, one cannot maintain that non-market, hierarchical forms of organisation are inherently incapable of ensuring efficient allocation and use of resources. Moreover, even in the domain where markets and planning can be viewed as alternatives, it is rarely an either-or choice: it is more a question of finding effective combinations and mixes of the two instruments.

The problem of reform of the planning system is therefore much wider and more complex than is implied in the 'planning' vs 'market' formulation. In the Indian context we must distinguish between at least three levels of reform: one has to do with the reforming of the interrelations between and internal functioning of the organs of government at different levels; second, there is the problem of restructuring public sector enterprises to make them more efficient instruments for achieving their objectives; and the third relates to the demarcation of the sphere of private activity and the extent and modalities of state intervention to regulate such activity.

With nearly half the new investments in India being done by the government and public enterprises, the manner in which projects, programmes and policies are conceived, evaluated and implemented within the governmental machinery has a direct bearing on the success or failure of the plans. That there are a great many weaknesses in the way these functions are handled hardly needs to be stressed. The mismatch between the distribution of functions and the command over resources between the centre and the state, excessive concentration of power in the hands of the central government, the erosion of various check-and-balance mechanisms envisaged in the Constitution, problem of federal finance, the balance between state autonomy and national priorities — all these have been widely discussed. Here I want to focus on one aspect which has lately come to the fore, namely, the mechanisms for planning development at the sub-state level, i e, at the level of districts and below.

Planning Development at Sub-State Level

A great many development projects — specifically schools, PHCs, district hospitals, water supply, local roads, small or even medium irrigation projects, soil and moisture conservation, development of degraded lands — are by their nature local in character and are amenable to planning, co-ordination and management on a decentralised basis. However, for historical reasons even these local developmental activities have been undertaken in a centralised fashion through schemes largely formulated and financed by the state governments and implemented through the state bureaucracy. Increasingly the centre has sought to play a significant role in determining the scale and content of such programmes and priorities. It has become clear over the years that in this system there is very little scope for effective participation of the local population in determining what investments are undertaken in their respective localities, much less to make sure that what is done bears a reasonable relationship, in terms of both scale and content, to the needs of and possibilities in each locality.

A situation has been created in which the local communities tend to look to the state and central governments to take up projects which in principle can and should be conceived and implemented locally on the basis of locally available resources. This has in turn led to a climate of dependence, of developmental schemes becoming the bone of contention in local politics and a medium through which state or central level political power-centres can seek to dispense patronage of one kind or the other.

Furthermore local development works have tended to get fragmented into innumerable departmental schemes with little concern for the problems of overlap and lack of co-ordination between related activities and between the programmes and the needs of each region. This together with the 'softness' of many of the programmes and the opportunities they provide for leakages at almost every step have greatly reduced the effectiveness of the large and growing resources devoted to these activities.

The emphasis on area planning *and* democratic

decentralisation by the reconstituted Planning Commission is really aimed at correcting these deficiencies. The idea, simply put, is to pool the resources currently being spent on various departmental schemes at the district level and below and to give the appropriate local developmental agency the power to decide on the disposition of these resources on the basis of the conditions specific to each district and mandal or panchayat as the case may be. By cutting down fragmentation and duplication of programmes and facilitating a better fit between the scale and content of the programmes on the one hand and the local needs and possibilities on the other, the effectiveness of public spending on these activities can be increased substantially.

The other strand of reform in the planning of local development is to set up and empower representative and accountable local government institutions. Such institutions would give the opportunity for the local citizenry, with the support and assistance of the voluntary organisations, local education/research institutions as well as expertise available in the government bureaucracy, to play a more active and informed role (a) in deciding the relative priorities of local development works and (b) to exercise a closer supervision on the implementation of these projects as well as their subsequent maintenance. The provision for mandatory periodic elections to the panchayats and other local institutions with safeguards for reasonable representation to the more vulnerable segments of the population (and in particular the scheduled castes, scheduled tribes and women) is seen as a necessary condition to ensure that the local institutions are responsive and accountable.

These two elements of the proposed reform — namely, local area planning and democratic decentralisation — are thus mutually reinforcing and must be viewed as an integrated package. That this calls for drastic change in the approach to and procedures of local planning is all too obvious. Fortunately, there is a near general consensus in the country among all shades of political opinion about the necessity for democratic decentralisation and there is a good prospect that a general legislation to give effect to this concept will be passed in the near future.

But this is only a beginning and one must anticipate many problems and difficulties in putting these arrangements actually on the ground. There is bound to be resistance from those — and in particular political and bureaucratic functionaries of the state and the central governments — who wield considerable influence and power under the existing arrangements. It is particularly important to make sure that the creation of an additional tier of the government at the local level does not lead to further growth in the state or central level bureaucracies. As far as possible the existing staff at the district level and below must be redeployed to serve these panchayati raj institutions. They must be encouraged to secure such personnel and expertise as they may need without adding to the permanent bureaucracy. The new arrangement must allow ample scope for experimentation with diverse approaches.

It is no one's case that all this will happen merely by legal formalities. Local despotisms are a fact of life and one may readily grant that they may not be dislodged and indeed may, in some places, even get strengthened under a system of elected panchayats. But despotisms are not universal and certainly not uniformly strong everywhere. Nor are they immortal or immutable. The electoral process, with the above safeguards, would give an opportunity for a fuller articulation of interests and concerns of different groups and pave the way for a more democratic, collective endeavour for local development. The expectation is that as the credibility of this type of participatory local planning gets established it will serve as an effective instrument to keep local despotisms in check, hopefully even to dislodge them. The people can also be then induced to mobilise more of local resources to augment what is received from the state governments.

Doubts have been raised that the local level agencies may end up merely by making claims for devolution of more resources from the states or the centre without any concern about husbanding the resources available to them efficiently and consistent with overall social concerns. This can be contained to some extent through a budget constraint on the overall amount which will be made available for such local development works from the state. Generalised criteria need to be evolved for determining the amounts which will be allocated to particular districts or parts thereof. Some, albeit limited, attempts in this direction have been made in states like Maharashtra and Andhra Pradesh. In the case of Karnataka, a special state level Finance Commission has gone into the basis on which to determine amounts to be allocated to each zilla parishad and from then on to the mandal panchayats. It is possible to work out these arrangements on a more systematic basis.

In doing so, one could also include provisions by which a certain portion of devolution is made conditional on the magnitude of the resources mobilised by the local agencies on their own. Whether or not there should be additional conditionalities to make sure that the local bodies spend their moneys on activities of high social priority is more debatable. There is persuasive logic in the position that the elected local bodies should be given the freedom to determine appropriate priorities. If this process results in serious neglect of elementary education, public health and other social amenities or of the welfare of vulnerable segments, then the necessary correctives have to be sought through the electoral process. Efforts to generate greater consciousness of the importance of these programmes and the relative position and performance of different districts/local units to create a sense of healthy competition will also help.

All this suggests the outline of possible rearrangement of local development planning which could bring about a less wasteful and a socially more responsive development at the local level. But clearly it is far from being a blueprint. To attempt such a blueprint which seeks to tie up all the loose ends is neither possible nor desirable. There are simply too many things we do not know; there are far too many diversities; and it is desirable to leave ample room for different kinds of approaches to be tried out. We should also recognise that the changes of this kind, even if initiated more or less simultaneously in all parts of the country, are likely to take on different trajectories and occur at different paces. One cannot and should not attempt to pre-empt this process and cast it in a rigid mould. We must encourage plurality of approaches within the broad guidelines that have been outlined above and leave ample room for learning from experience.

Management of Public Enterprises

The second major area of institutional reform within the public sector relates to the management of public enterprises of all kinds. These enterprises are largely concentrated in infrastructure, public utilities and the production of certain basic intermediates and capital goods. They are of course not confined to these activities having been extended over the years into a variety of other spheres not all of which serve an essential social purpose. While there are arguable grounds for checking the indiscriminate proliferation of public enterprises, few would question that the state has to continue to play a key role in infrastructure and public utilities. Efficient functioning of these sectors is also essential for the sustained and efficient growth of the private sector.

The investments involved in these activities are already very large and they will continue to absorb a substantial proportion of fresh investments which will be made in the future. They are also relatively capital intensive and, in some cases, lay large claims on scarce foreign exchange and non-renewable domestic resources. The operational efficiency in many of these enterprises is much below what is desirable and feasible. And with a few significant exceptions, their earnings are generally insufficient to cover costs and leave a reasonable surplus as return on the investment. Improvement in the operational efficiency of these enterprises is essential both for increasing their contribution to the resources available for fresh investment and also to bring down the costs of a number of important intermediate goods which find widespread use in all segments of the economy. The state of public finances being what it is, efficiency improvements in public enterprises is imperative if even moderate expansion of public investment is to be sustained without aggravating dependence on market borrowings deficit financing or progressive increase in the prices of energy, transport and other basic intermediates.

This will require a major reorganisation and restructuring of public enterprises. The relationship between parliament, the political executive and enterprise managements has to be redefined in such a way as to drastically reduce the scope for political or administrative intervention — formal or informal — in day-to-day functioning of enterprises. Subject to certain broadly agreed guidelines on objectives and operational performance, professional managers must have the necessary freedom to take operational decisions. They should be held accountable only for the overall performance with respect to clearly specified goals and not for the rightness or wrongness of individual decisions. Non-commercial objectives expected to be served by each enterprise must be explicitly stated and the costs involved should be at least quantified. Ideally the burden should be shifted progressively and within a reasonable period of time to the general budget. Pending that due allowance must be made for this element while assessing financial results. Workers and the management alike need to be persuaded to accept the importance of efficiency and of earning a reasonable return on investment as well as the impracticability of the government subsidising losses indefinitely.

A hardening of the overall 'budget constraint' on the public enterprises by putting them on notice that the state will not indefinitely absorb the losses or less-than-reasonable returns on investments is a minimum necessary condition. But it is also necessary to give a great deal more thought to the nature of incentive system operating in the interface of the enterprises with the rest of the economy as well as between and within these enterprises in order to create inbuilt pressures for more efficient performance. A much closer and critical evaluation of the economic viability of major investment decisions in all of these enterprises and some way of subjecting these decisions to public scrutiny is needed. It will serve as a check on any temptation to approve major investments without proper scrutiny and on political considerations. The relations between different public enterprises must be governed by efficient contractual agreements. And the experience of large corporations may have useful and practical lessons to offer on incentive and control systems within each enterprise.

State-Private Sector Relationship

The third major area of reform concerns the state-private sector relationships. One aspect of it relates to the domain in which the private sector should operate. A major argument for public enterprise is that it is supposed to play a pioneering role in setting up a variety of industries and activities involving large investments due to the shortage of industrial entrepreneurship capable of investing in such activities. It is arguable that the situation has changed materially in the last 40 years. India now has a very much larger and more broad-based corpus of industrial entrepreneurs both willing and able to set up and manage large projects.

Whatever may be one's ideological predilection on public enterprises — and there are strong arguments in their favour — the persistent failure of several public enterprises to earn a reasonable surplus is proving to be a persuasive argument in the hands of those who would like to see the role of public enterprise to be substantially reduced. The *ad hoc* but recurrent entry of the public sector into areas which do not really serve any social purpose has added to the difficulties of discharging its assigned role in the more important areas.

The other aspect concerns the nature and extent of regulations on the private sector. It is by now generally accepted that the elaborate system of direct and detailed controls over investment, location, imports, etc, have not succeeded in achieving their objectives. Instead they have created opportunities for extensive corruption; promoted strategic behaviour on the part of private enterprise *vis-a-vis* the state rather than create pressures for efficient production; and has shackled private enterprise from exploiting available opportunities efficiently. This has led to the growing advocacy for doing away with *all* controls on private enterprise and letting the market decide what is to be produced where, by whom and how in a competitive environment with equal freedom for entry as well as exit.

Leaving the market free for individual entrepreneurial production decisions would still leave the problem of macro-economic management and of the pattern of industrial development. The uncompromising liberalisers would argue that appropriate macro-economic management policies can ensure the necessary overall price stability and viability in balance of payments by appropriate fiscal, monetary and exchange rate policies. However, there is much more to it than this.

The east Asian countries — which are usually held out as the outstanding examples of success of market-oriented policies of this type — in fact were marked by a strong direct role for the state in setting long-term task for the private sector (both overall and for specific enterprises) and backing it up with both incentives (in the form of preferential allocation of resources, particularly credit) and also sanctions to make sure that the enterprises did in fact fulfil the tasks assigned to them. This was possible because the state and the private sector were in a collaborative rather than adversorial relationship. At the same time — and this is of crucial importance — the public sector was in a position to enforce the necessary discipline on private enterprise. This aspect of the role of the state in the east Asian economies needs much more attention and emphasis than has been given in the Indian debates on liberalisation.

It goes without saying that unless the state brings to bear a strong and well focused long-term strategy and is in a position to induce the private sector to conform, the model will not quite work. We need to reflect whether such conditions exist and whether and how far they can be created in the Indian context. The nature of the relationships between the Indian state and that of private sector tend to be much more an adversorial and in any case the state machinery has not built sufficient expertise and clout to effectively orient private sector to long-term development goals.

There is also the question about the social consequences of the pattern of development which may occur in a free market environment. This is important for several reasons. Given the pattern of income distribution and the powerful impact of modern communications, there is a strong demand for a variety of consumer goods which are intensive in the use of scarce resources including imports. The institutionalisation of such consumption patterns can have far-reaching social consequences: only a small minority of the population can afford them. Those who cannot are understandbly aggrieved, the more so when the vast majority of them cannot afford the bare essentials for existence. This is a source of frustration and social tension. The other problem is that the resources needed for upper class consumption are scarce and the present rate of expansion may not be sustainable for long without giving rise to large additional demands for imports, unacceptably rapid depletion of renewable domestic resources, creating serious problems of congestion, pollution and other forms of environmental degradation, or a combination of all these.

On the other hand, given the abject poverty of the vast masses of people and the need for increasing the rate of savings and capital formation to build up the productive base rapidly, there is a strong case for restraining the growth of consumption of the better-off segments — specially conspicuous consumption — and to devote much more resources for guaranteeing a tolerable minimum standard for the bulk of the population. The state has the primary and overriding responsibility to guarantee everyone adequate work at a minimum wage, access to food, education, health services, water supply and other services which have a bearing on the quality of life and on the capacity of individuals to augment their skills and enlarge opportunities in life.

Ideally this calls for a direct attack on the sources of inequality in income distribution including the highly unequal distribution of wealth, inequitable access to education and highly differentiated structures of wages and salaries particularly as between organised and unorganised sectors. But if this cannot be effectively tackled directly, there is a strong case for at least containing the consumption of the well-to-do through progressive direct taxation and/or through measures to make the goods and services consumed by the well-to-do much more expensive.

The implication of all this is that while Indian planning structure and mechanisms are indeed due for an overhaul, it would be altogether simplistic and wrong to view the problem solely in terms of greater freedom for the private sector and switching over to a market-based economy. The state is, and will continue to be, a significant actor in the economy both as a provider of infrastructure essential for agriculture and industry, and by politically and morally necessary interventions to take care of the poor and neglected. In what manner and how effectively these functions are performed have as important a bearing on the opportunities and resources available to the private sector as the dismantling of the control system and allowing 'free' market price mechanisms to guide resource allocation. Discussions of the nature and content of structural reform in the management of the Indian economy should therefore view the problem in a wider perspective comprehending government, public enterprises and private sector, and the interrelations among them.

Economic and Political Weekly, June 30, 1990.

6

Planning in India

Retrospect and Prospects

Introduction

PLANNED development of the kind that India has been pursuing since independence is now under severe attack. The attack centres not so much on the objectives as on the way planning has worked and on the role that the State has sought to play in the process. There has never been much disagreement on the necessity for sustained rapid expansion and diversification of economic activity or about the State's responsibility to ensure that everyone has access to means of satisfying basic minimum needs. Planning is criticised for not accomplishing these aims in the last four decades; for consistently failing to fulfill its targets; and for not checking the deterioration of the fiscal position and the balance of payments position during the 1980s.

These failures are attributed variously to (a) the wrong strategies (specifically preoccupation with heavy industry to the neglect of agriculture, over-protection of domestic industry, and insufficient concern for increasing exports); (b) the way these strategies were sought to be implemented, particularly the excessive reliance on the public sector and the stifling effects of the control system on the private sector; and (c) weaknesses in the process of formulating and implementing the plans. Much has been written on the first two aspects.[1] This paper is largely concerned with the third aspect.

Indian planning is characterised by a strong interventionist role for the State within the framework of a mixed economy and a federal system of government. Initially the government was seen, even by the leading private industrialists, as essential to undertake direct investments, to develop infrastructure and basic industry which were beyond the competence and resources of the nascent private sector and thereby stimulate and support the growth of private sector.[2] State intervention in the form of direct public ownership of key sectors, regulation of the private sector and controls over allocation of scarce resources came to be considered as essential for achieving growth with social justice. Apart from the ideal of socialism, which appealed to a sizable segment of political opinion, the Directive Principles of State Policy in the Constitution spelled out some of the major social concerns which should guide policy.

Indian Planning: Distinctive Features[3]

The nature and effectiveness of interventions are conditioned by several factors of which two are fundamental: (1) the federal structure of government; (2) the fact that government, both central government and state governments, are democratically elected and have to renew their mandate periodically.

Planning in a Federal Setup

The domains over which the centre and the states may exert authority are clearly defined in the Constitution. Some (such as heavy industry, railways, atomic power) are exclusively in the centre's jurisdiction, while others (including agriculture, land reform, irrigation, electricity, education, health and roads) are in the domain of the states.

Securing a consensus on the national plan, and ensuring the consistency of programmes and policies pursued by different constituents of the federation with the objectives and priorities of the overall plan, are major problems. The political consensus on plan-related matters is sought to be achieved formally through the National Development Council (where the central and the state governments are represented) and informally through the party conclaves. The Planning Commission plays a crucial role in articulating the overall plan and working out the size and content of programmes at the centre and in the states through an extended consultative process. Various instruments have been used to get the states and departments to comply with the plan. These include the central government's power to make policy on subjects in which the centre and the states have concurrent jurisdiction; earmarking parts of central assistance to state plans for specified programmes; and special central funding for programmes conceived by the centre in areas that formally fall under the exclusive jurisdiction of the states. These worked reasonably well, though not always and not uniformly successfully, for nearly two decades after independence when the Congress Party held sway at the centre and in most states. Once this pattern was broken, achieving and enforcing consensus on development plans has become increasingly difficult.

The Political Environment

Vision and farsightedness are essential to planning. Both were very much in evidence for some time after independence thanks to the undisputed leadership of Nehru and the supremacy of the Congress Party. Even so, in a democratic system, politicians in power tend to be preoccupied with immediate survival, or at the best with the next elections. They are therefore not particularly interested in the long-term consequences of their actions. This tendency has become progressively more acute with the passing of Nehru, the end of Congress supremacy and the growing fluidity of politics.[4] Altogether, the working of the political and the administrative system has become strongly biased in favour of promises and actions which have electoral appeal in the short run, even when it is known that they will turn out to be unsustainable or harmful over the long run. The Planning Commission has been unable to check this tendency.

Thus even though actual growth has fallen consistently short of targets, suggestions that it would be prudent to lower targets and trim the size of the plan to a realistic assessment of the capacity to mobilise resources were seldom accepted.[5] It is considered a cardinal political sin to set targets lower than in earlier plans or those proposed by the party that held power earlier. That promises of land reform and other means of reducing inequality have proved to be empty rhetoric has not prevented them from being repeated ritually in every plan. The shift of emphasis from reduction of relative inequality to removal of absolute poverty — reflected in the emergence and spread of various poverty alleviation programmes — no doubt reflects the compulsion of democratic politics and is not wholly based on its inherent merits. Being convenient instruments for distributing patronage on a wider scale, such programmes also serve the interests of politicians in power. This adds to their political appeal.

By the same token there is unwillingness to take action which is necessary for the stability of the economy but which may hurt the interests of one or other powerful or numerically strong groups in the society. This fear is heightened by the compulsions of electoral politics and the precariousness of power and largely explains the reluctance to implement measures acknowledged to be necessary to restore fiscal stability — be it strict enforcement of tax laws, raising prices of publicly provided goods and services to meet costs, reducing subsidies which benefit the well-to-do, or improving efficiency of public agencies and enterprises.

Attitudes of the politicians and the bureaucracy are also strongly coloured by the fact that control over decisions on the scale and location of projects (be it a road, school, hospital, irrigation work or factory), the award of contracts, the appointment of personnel or determination of which individuals or groups will benefit from a poverty alleviation or welfare scheme are all instruments for securing the political support base and simultaneously a convenient source of much-needed funds for party and personal purposes. Gradually offices in public institutions (public corporations, cooperatives and the like) have come to be seen and used as part of what has become virtually a 'spoils system'.

Independent professional advice, public scrutiny of major investment decisions, enforcement of rules and regulations (intended to ensure that projects are designed and executed to achieve the end result at the lowest cost) and the functioning of Public Accounts Committees and Estimate Committees of the Parliament and State legislatures, the Comptroller and Auditor General, the judiciary and other watchdog institutions (which are meant to ensure that public funds are handled with probity and in the public interest) have all been compromised, softened and made increasingly ineffective in various ways. The cumulative effect of all this has been to give planning a bad time.

Changes in Political Environment

Political configurations and processes have also been changing rapidly and this naturally affects the planning as well. On the one hand there is a significant trend towards centralisation reflected in the progressive expansion of the 'concurrent list' to include areas which were originally in the exclusive jurisdiction of the states; the worsening financial status of the states making them more dependent on the centre and also more amenable to taking up central and centrally sponsored programmes; and the growing tendency for the centre to influence the scope and content of state-level programmes through various types of special programmes funded by it.

This centralising tendency is manifest at the state level too. Local government institutions have been weakened by supercession, postponement of elections and meagre resources and powers. The staff under the control of local governments have in most cases agitated successfully to have themselves incorporated as part of the State government bureaucracy. Politicians in power at the state level have tightened their control over the funds available for development and also over the public institutions (like co-operatives and public corporations) for use as instruments of patronage.

Even as these centralising tendencies have gained ground at the governmental level, there has been a progressive loosening of centralised political control. This control, which was characteristic of the heyday of Congress Party hegemony, began to change with the death of Nehru. Since then, the Congress Party has split; new political parties like the BJP and Janata Dal have emerged at the national level, even as purely regional parties gained ascendency in some states (notably Tamil Nadu and AP, Punjab). The tension between the centre and the states has intensified with the states becoming increasingly resentful of attempts by the centre to unseat duly constituted state governments in arbitrary ways and to use its superior access to financial resources to secure its political interests. Competitive electoral politics has sponsored competitive populism, making it more difficult to achieve the minimal consensus necessary to ensure effective collection of taxes, efficient running of public services and keeping subsidies in check.

The balance of political forces has also been changing. Being a vast and diverse polity, regional, linguistic and caste differences have always been important factors weighing on the side of pluralism. Unlike in many other developing countries, neither the capitalist, nor a modernising managerial elite, has been able to establish undisputed hegemony over State power. On the contrary, electoral politics gave an opportunity for the relatively large landed classes from rural areas and the urban professional and middle classes to enter the legislatures and the government. Some observers characterise these groups as part of a distributive coalition running the State. Workers in the organised sector, including the government and the public sector, have also been influential because of their strategic positioning in the economy and the emergence of powerful trade unions.

However this is arguably an oversimplification. One of the most striking developments of the past two decades is the rapid growth in scale and variety of poverty alleviation programmes designed to woo the electoral support of the poor. The poor, though not organised to press their interests directly in the political arena, are numerous. In an electoral system based on universal adult franchise, almost every party finds it necessary (following the dramatic demonstration that 'Garibi Hatao' is a very effective vote-catching platform) to demonstrate their interest in and concern for the welfare of the poor. While this has, at one level, led to unrestrained populism, it can also been seen as an indication that the democratic process is an effective means of forcing the powers-that-be to pay attention to the interests of the poor. Moreover, these programmes have increased the awareness of the poor of their importance in the political process and the potential for more active pressing of their claims. The emergence of OBC-minorities-SC alliances, and the sharp increase in political tensions in several parts of the country on this account, could be read as a reflection of this.

This loosening of central power is accompanied by the emergence of religion as a more primary and contentious issue in politics, and the erosion of the consensus of the Nehruvian era on the planning and the role of the State in fostering economic development and social justice. The cumulative effect of all this is hardly conducive to planning which is dependent on forging a wide enough political consensus to make policy informed by a coherent long-term vision and to ensure that the policies needed to realise the vision are made and implemented consistently.[6] The recent economic reforms, which are as much the result of ideological shifts as of the compulsions created by the failures of the past, and the resources crisis have called into question the original concept of planned development, the role of the State and the functions of the Planning Commission.

The Functioning of the Planning Commission

The Planning Commission, appointed by the central government in 1950, has a wide mandate including the determination of the overall strategies of development, the quantum of resources to be devoted for that purpose and their allocation between different programmes. It is supposed to review all major projects before clearance, advise on important policy matters and monitor the performance of the plan as a whole and of individual programmes. Its composition was designed to give it sufficient political weight in the councils of government. the National Development Council, comprising key central ministers and all state chief ministers, provided the forum for discussing important issues concerning the national plans and development policy.

So long as there was political commitment to planning and the government was stable — as was the case during the 1950s and early 1960s — the Commission did play an important role in all the above respects. The first two plans presented a long term vision and a coherent strategy to realise it. The Commission emerged as a bridge between the centre and the states. It mediated the competing claims of the centre and the states, of different states for central assistance and of various central ministries. But after Nehru's death, the weakening of the Congress and the emergence of governments ruled by parties other than Congress in several states, led to the gradual erosion of the role of the Commission as an independent professional body focusing on the medium and long-term problems in a wide, national perspective.[7]

The Planning Commission has successfully persuaded the states to set up their own overall planning organisation. Although most states now have planning boards or commissions of their own, few are equipped to play an effective role in devising overall plans appropriate to the needs of each state. In most cases they are no more than ornaments; they are not accorded the status and power to play anything like an important role in determining development priorities and allocations in the state plans within a coherent long-term perspective of their growth.

The Commission however has not taken the same degree of sustained interest in strengthening sectoral planning. Occasionally sectoral studies have been commissioned either from individual experts or expert committees. Some useful detailed studies on transport, energy, fertilisers, and steel – to mention a few examples – have come out of this process.[8,9] These serve rather as *ad hoc* exercises without any arrangement for monitoring actual developments in relation to projections and the changing conditions or resources, technology and market conditions. It is also difficult to see evidence of their findings shaping, in any systematic or sustained way, investment priorities, technology choices, price policy and technology development and the policy framework to realise them. Neither the Commission, nor the ministries and the concerned public enterprises, have done much to build design organisations and promote forward-looking research and technology development on their own or in collaboration with research laboratories. The situation in the states – which are responsible for electricity, water resource development, and roads – is, if anything, worse.

As for its role in decision-making, the executive ministries, and to some extent the states, had from the beginning looked again at the Commission's role and its power to influence decisions which were in their domain.[10] The ministries have been zealously guarding their prerogative in policy making. While the Commission was usually consulted on major policy and investment decisions, its views were not always decisive. The technical sophistication of the five-year plans in articulating implications of overall goals for investment allocation, production targets and resource mobilisation is indeed remarkable.[11] But the Commission has been less than successful in working out, and getting the government to accept, a coherent set of policies needed to implement the programme.[12]

The Commission's effectiveness in respect of specific investment decisions was also compromised by the reluctance of departments to provide the information needed to evaluate the viability of particular projects or programmes and track their actual progress fully, accurately and promptly. The Commission had no independent channel for such information.

The creation of the Project Appraisal Division within the Commission, and making it the secretariat to the Public Investment Board, gave it some power but not enough.

Soon after its constitution, the Planning Commission created a Programme Evaluation Organisation to obtain an independent assessment of the working and impact of various programmes. This organisation has shown remarkable candour and objectivity in its reports, which are also published. However, the evidence of their impact in terms of improving the design of interventions is much less striking. Most states also have their own evaluation organisations. Their reports not being in the public domain, it is difficult to assess their impact. A notable and serious gap in post-evaluation exercises is the conspicuous absence of systematic critical reviews of the performance of large investment projects in terms of the deviation of actual time schedules, costs, utilisation of facilities, and impact on production from the original assumptions.

Until recently Indian planning was based on the understanding that direct and detailed firm and product specific controls over allocation of foreign exchange, capital and other scarce inputs, as well as controls over production, creation of new capacities and pricing are necessary in the larger social interest. The control system however has grown in a piecemeal fashion, rather than as a well-thought-out, coherent set of instruments to achieve clearly stated goals. The elements constituting the control system were introduced and altered to meet particular exigencies. The resulting incoherence and inconsistency is at least part of the reason why rationing and price controls did not achieve their ostensible aims.[13]

India's experience, and the experience of the centrally planned economies, has also shown that the central authority simply cannot get the relevant information in necessary detail, promptly and without any distortion, from individual enterprises and agencies. And attempts to digest this information and reach decisions on who is to get what material in what quantities, what is to be produced, by whom, and how, have simply failed. Such decisions as have been made could not be enforced. The shroud of secrecy surrounding project approvals and policy decisions, and the fact that the public does not have access to the relevant information or the opportunity to raise objections and seek reviews has also compromised the accountability of public authorities for their decisions.

Reorientation of Planning

It is for these reasons that we see a strong swing of opinion against central planning and in favour of dismantling the control regime, freer access to imports, foreign capital and technology; and other liberalisation measures. The search for fewer, simpler impersonal and indirect mechanisms — operating via fiscal policy — as a way of creating an incentive environment conducive to efficient but decentralised decisions by both public and private enterprise is understandable and justified. The need for planning is not, however, eliminated in the process.

Planning in its widest connotation calls for anticipation of longer term significance and consequences of emerging social, economic and technological trends; and taking action soon enough in advance to ensure that agreed basic social objectives (particularly meeting basic needs for everyone and equality of opportunity) are realised and that bottlenecks do not impede the progress of the economy.

Some problems are obvious enough. The country's endowment of several key natural resources (like land, forests, water and oil) is not only limited in absolute terms but is also rather modest in relation to the population. Some of these resources (like oil) are rapidly depleting in the rest of the world too. More effective use of these resources (by increasing their productivity, conservation and by the use of cheaper/ more abundant substitutes preferably based on renewable resources) is therefore imperative. Major technological developments need to be constantly monitored, developments which are of significance in the Indian context need to be identified, and their acquisition and/or future development need to be encouraged. There is also the wider, long-term problem of 'sustainable' development. Action on all these fronts must be informed by a clear understanding of the interconnected implications of broadly defined social goals in terms of mutual consistency, potential conflicts, trade-offs, etc.

Both past experience and the reforms currently in process call for major changes in the organisation and processes of planning. The Planning Commission has to adapt its organisation and functioning in the light of the inevitable changes in the nature and scope of the State's role both directly and in regulating the private sector. It needs to build up a wider, stronger information base, acquiring, if need be, the power and the capacity to establish its own channels for collecting data on key aspects of the economy. Instead of devoting so much of its staff and time to discussing details of innumerable individual schemes of the central government and the states, the Commission should focus more on evolving long-term strategy and policy for key sectors, evaluating major investment decisions and their actual implementation records, expert evaluation of selected important sectoral and regional programmes consisting of a large number of small schemes and questions concerning long-term technology and resource management for sustainable development. It should hand over detailed planning at the state level to state planning agencies, and confine itself to providing an independent critical review of the overall performance of states and of key sectors of the economy. The Commission cannot and should not attempt to perform all these activities with its own staff but should rely more and more on outside experts either by commissioning them to carry out studies on selected, well-defined problems or by inducting them for such tasks within the Commission.

Second, the Commission should pay special attention to widening and deepening the competence for sectoral and regional planning. This is particularly important in energy, transport, water and some major industries, as well as in activities (like urban planning) which involve (a) large long-gestating investments; (b) a high degree of inter-sectoral linkage; (c) rapid technological change; and (d) depletion of non-renewable resources and/or high pollution risks. Institutions need to be strengthened at the sectoral level to periodically assess future needs and alternative ways of meeting the needs in the long term as a basis for guiding pricing, investment and technology policies in respect of key sectors (like energy, land and water, transport, environment and important raw materials). Such assessments are best organised under the auspices of the Planning Commission whose function is to view sectors and projects in a comprehensive economy-wide perspective. The Commission should also take an active interest in assessing the nature and scale of specialised design-engineering organisations needed at the centre, in the states and outside the government and to recommend policies to encourage the formation of such organisations.

Both link up with building long-term technological capabilities through programmes for making up current gaps. for the adaptation and improvement of available technology, and for developing new technologies. Here again the Planning Commission is, in principle, best placed to provide the wide and long-term perspective and get the sectoral specialists from the public and private sector, research institutions, design-engineering organisations and technology experts into a creative interaction on a continuing basis. This does not mean that the Planning Commission should become a mammoth organisation. Rather, it should play the kind of role that MITI plays in Japan — it should be a forum of strategic thinking, a medium for getting the relevant expertise from concerned enterprises, universities, and laboratories together to examine the problems and come up with solutions, and an interlocutor with the government to establish appropriate policies and institutional arrangements.

The third major task is to improve the performance of public sector institutions and agencies both in setting up new facilities and in operating them. This calls for fundamental changes in the way government and its enterprises work. We need credible and effective mechanisms to ensure that investment decisions are made after objective techno-economic appraisal by professionals and that the political considerations in such decisions are made explicit and kept to a minimum. Greater autonomy and flexibility for the enterprises to plan their operations in the light of market conditions must be an essential part of reforms to improve efficiency. But efficiency is not only a function of allowing enterprises to adapt flexibly to market signals; it depends equally on how the non-market institutions function. One crucial aspect of this concerns the relation between the enterprises, the political executive, the Parliament and the watchdog institutions. The other relates to the internal structure and functioning of enterprises.

Not all decisions on resource allocations are made with reference to the market. Within each firm — irrespective of whether it is publicly or privately owned and whether its ownership is concentrated or diffused — such decisions are invariably made in the framework of a hierarchical organisation, each with its own rules, procedures and control systems to ensure efficient operation. This would suggest that the central issue is not ownership but internal structures, procedures and incentive systems within the firms. Transferring a part — even a substantial part — of the equity in PSUs to the private sector will not automatically solve the problem unless these questions are addressed. Devising a programme for such institutional reform is therefore one of the major tasks of planning and planners.

The fourth area of reform in planning has to do with setting up and managing facilities to develop common production resources used by a large number of users. The most important examples of this are land development, irrigation, research, and credit. The present system whereby such programmes are conceived, set up and operated by the State without much, if any, interaction with the beneficiaries leaves a great deal to be desired. In the case of land, water and credit the success of the programmes depends crucially on the beneficiaries agreeing to certain discipline in terms of the allocation of the resources between uses and users, and an effective mechanism for ensuring compliance.[14]

The State alone cannot accomplish this; nor can such facilities be left wholly to user organisations (especially in relatively large projects). What we need is an arrangement whereby the users are made to acquire a stake in the facility and are actively involved along with State officials and professional managers of the facilities in evolving a set of generally acceptable rules and enforcement mechanisms. In the case of research and extension, again, the problem is to evolve incentive systems to promote active interaction between the research workers, extension agents and the farmers; to ensure that the research system is responsive to the needs of users; and to make the researchers accountable for their performance.

Finally, the institutional arrangements for planning and implementation in the states need a thoroughgoing reorganisation. Apart from strengthening the state-level planning agencies and getting them to play a more active role in providing an overall perspective, there is much scope for improving the content and efficacy of programmes. Apart from power, major irrigation, major roads and road transport, the bulk of state-level development outlays happen to be on local development activities which are widely dispersed in space. Their efficacy is seriously impaired by three features: (a) a great deal of overlapping and duplication between different schemes; (b) the top-down approach designing programme content and deciding how the resources are to be allocated in space; and (c) ensuring that programmes targeted at particular groups do in fact reach them in full measure.[15]

The solution, as has been widely recognised, involves rationalisation of programmes to minimise duplication. More importantly, in respect of all local development activity, state-level schemes of standardised design should give place to integrated local-level plans whose content reflects the specific needs, opportunities and priorities of each district, block and village. The funds allotted to such local development projects should be pooled and allocated across districts (possibly blocks) on the basis of the magnitude of unemployment and poverty and the deficiency in basic amenities with due allowance for the potential for further resource development. And democratically elected local government institutions should be given the opportunity and the necessary support to plan the content of these local development programmes and to implement them.

The passage of the 74th constitutional amendment on Panchayati Raj sets the stage for such reforms. But it would take much patient and sustained effort before those who exercise power under the existing, highly centralised political system and bureaucracy can be persuaded, perhaps even forced, to accept a different role in a more decentralised arrangement. This institutional reform is crucial to the success of investment and other interventions by the public sector for promoting rural development and protecting the vulnerable.

Some of these reforms are now on the agenda. Significant progress has been made in dismantling central government controls over industry and in rationalising foreign trade and exchange rate policies; some subsidies have been cut; forcing public undertakings to mobilise their own resources has increased pressure on them to improve efficiency; and the 74th constitutional amendment creates space for better regional planning with meaningful local participation in development. But all these initiatives are limited to the centre; the states have been largely left out of the process and no serious effort has been made to enlist their active involvement and co-operation. Without the latter, the reforms under way, which are already facing resistance, cannot go far. The Planning Commission has a key role to play in promoting, through the NDC, a minimal political consensus on the necessary reforms in the above areas and also on the way planning has to be reoriented in the changed context. That this has not happened, and that the Planning Commission has chosen to play a passive role, is therefore regrettable.

Notes

1. For recent critiques of Indian planning see Ahluwalia 1985, Lucas and Papanek (eds) 1988, Adiseshaiah (ed.).
2. The need for a strong government role in India's development was emphasised by Visveswarayya and by the Bombay Plan prepared by industrialists (Thakurdas, 1944).
3. An excellent historical review of the evolution of Indian Planning – both at the level of concept and implementation – up to the mid 1960s is available

in Hanson, 1966. For a critical assessment of the functioning of the planning process see Paranjape, 1975.

4. For a political economy interpretation of Indian Planning see Frankel, 1978; Rudolph and Rudolph, 1987; and Bardhan, 1982.

5. The controversy between 'bold planning' and 'realistic planning' has of course been characteristic of all plans. But while, in the first three plans, the debate centred around the relative merits of alternative strategies and their feasibility, the political pressure for over-pitching targets and for approving large plans came into prominence from the late 1960s and early 1970s. There was a public controversy over the wisdom of the Planning Commission yielding to such pressures in the early 1970s, leading to the resignation of one of the members of the Commission (see Minhas, 1974, for one view of this controversy). Although this issue has kept surfacing since, successive governments and the Planning Commission have been most reluctant to reduce the overall growth targets below 5-5.5 per cent a year even though actual growth (until the 1980s) averaged 3.5 per cent per year.

6. This is part of the wider debate on centre-state relations which intensified in the 1970s and led to the appointment of the Sarkaria Commission (GOI, 1987-88).

7. For a brief overview of this process see Krishnaswamy et. al, 1992.

8. The Perspective Planning Division in the early 1960s prepared a series of papers spelling out the main tasks involved in translating long-term targets for sectors like transport, electricity, steel, fertilisers and machinery into concrete projects and the nature and scale of specialist organisation needed. These papers are unpublished. Pant, who headed PPD, repeatedly drew attention to this aspect in the Commission, the working groups, and the ministries. Attempts to develop indigenous design organisations in steel and fertilisers ran into difficulties. One can obtain some idea of the kind of problems involved, and the reason for the slow progress in this field, from Desai's study of Bokaro Steel Plant (Desai, 1979).

9. During the early 1960s, some pioneering studies were done to determine the optimum location, scale and time phasing of capacity in key industry (such as fertilisers and cement) within the framework of an overall perspective plan (Manne (ed.) 1967). The reports of the Energy Survey Committee (GOI, 1965); the working group on Energy Policy (GOI, 1979); the National Transport Planning Committee (GOI, 1980) and recent (unpublished) studies on long-term plans for energy and steel commissioned by the Planning Commission are examples of such work. The lack of continuity, the weak institutional memory, and the failure systematically to review actual experience in relation to earlier analyses and recommendations as a basis for subsequent sector studies are conscious weaknesses.

10. It needs recalling that John Mathai resigned as Finance Minister soon after the Planning Commission was set up in 1950 on the ground that the commission was an extra constitutional body which would become a 'parallel Cabinet'.

11. A variety of planning models ranging from the simple harrod-Domar type

macro models, to multisector, multiperiod optimisation models have been constructed and estimated in India. For an excellent review see Rudra, 1975.

12. Gadgil (1967) appropriately called it as 'planning without a policy frame'.
13. For a critique of the control system see GOI, 1967, 1979 and Jha, 1980.
14. The rationale of this approach in the case of large surface irrigation works has been discussed at length in the report of a committee on Irrigation Pricing set up by the Planning Commission (GOI, 1992).
15. For a powerful statement of the case for decentralisation see Jain, 1985.

References

Ahluwalia, I.J. 1985. *Industrial Growth in India; Stagnation since the Mid-Sixties* (OUP, New Delhi).

Bardhan, P.K. 1984. *The Political Economy of Development in India* (OUP, New Delhi).

Desai, Padma. 1979. *Bokaro Steel Plant: A Study of Soviet Economic Assistance.*

Frankel, Francine R. 1978. *India's Political Economy 1947-1977: The Gradual Revolution*, (Princeton University Press, Princeton).

Gadgil, D.R. 1967. 'Planning without a Policy Frame', *Economic and Political Weekly*, Annual Number, February 1967.

GOI, 1987. Report of Commission on Centre-State Relations, parts I and II (GDI Press, New Delhi).

GOI, 1988. Centre-State Relations, Parts I and II (GOI, Press, New Delhi).

GOI, Planning Commission. 1965. *Energy Survey of India.*

GOI. Planning Commission. 1967. *Report of the Industrial Planning and Licensing Policy Inquiry Committee*, Main Report.

GOI. Planning Commission 1979. *Report of Working Group on Energy Policy.*

GOI. Planning Commission 1980. *Report of the National Transport Planning Committee.*

GOI. Planning Commission (Undated). *Perspective Planning for Transport Development: Report of Steering Committee.*

-GOI. Ministry of Finance. 1979. *Report of the Committee on Controls and Subsidies.*

GOI. Ministry of Energy and Coal. 1980. *Report of the Committee on Power.*

Hanson, A.N. 1966. The Planning Process (OUP, London).

Jain, L.C. 1985. *Gross without Roots* (Sage, New Delhi).

Jha, L.K. 1980. *Economic Strategy for the 80s* (Allied, New Delhi).

Krishnaswamy, K.S., I.S. Gulati and A. Vaidyanathan. 1992. 'Economic Aspects of Federalism in India', in Mukherjee Nirmal and B. Arora (eds), *Federalism in India. Origins and Development* (Vikas, New Delhi).

Lucas, Robert and Gustav, Papanek (eds). 1988, *Indian Economy, Recent Development and Future Progress* (West View, London).

Manne, A.S. (ed.). 1967. *Investment for Capacity Expansion Size Location and Land Time Phasing* (George Allen & Unwin, London).

Mukherjee, Nirmal and Balveer Arora, 1992. *Federalism in India: Origins and Development,* (Vikas, New Delhi).

Paranjape, H.K. 1964. *The Planning Commission: A Discriptive Account* (Indian Institute of Public Administration, New Delhi).

Rudra Ashok, 1975. *Indian Planning Models*, Allied Publishers, New Delhi.

Rudolph Lloyd and Suzanne Rudolph, 1987. *In Pursuit of Lakshmi: The Political Economy of the Indian State* (Orient Longman, Bombay).

Thakurdas, Purushothamdas and others. 1964. *Plan for Economic Development of India.*

7

Development Planning Models

The Indian Experience

THE scope and manner of state involvement in the economy is undergoing major changes. The idea of coordinated mobilisation of resources and their allocation under the auspices of government to achieve rapid development with social justice is losing its appeal in recent years. There is a shift in favour of reducing the role of the state and allowing private sector to operate freely subject only to the discipline of the market place. However few would advocate a return to laissez faire.

It is now generally accepted that the state has the responsibility to provide public goods, a minimum standard of basic amenities like elementary education, primary health care and water supply and to ensure a reasonable minimum living standard to all its citizens. It also accepted that the state will need to play a major role, either as provider or as regulator, of certain types of infrastructure. A sizeable segment of opinion goes further to recognise that the phenomenally rapid growth of several developing countries was facilitated by strong purposeful and resilient state intervention.

All this implies that government will continue to play an important role — both directly and through its policies affecting the non government sector — in development.

Therefore the need for compctent, informed and objective analyses based on good data as essential input into policy making remains. The focus and techniques of such analyses will of course be different from these obtaining in the past. Presumably the purpose of this conference is to take stock of past experience in this respect and to see how modelling in the broader sense of empirical analysis of development related issues in a rigorous and technically sound analytical framework can make a more effective and useful contribution to policy in the changed context.

Technical aspects of modelling, and their application for policy formulation, will no doubt be discussed in detail by experts specialising in the field. But perhaps it is appropriate given the accent on "relevance and approaches" in the conference theme, to make a few general observations on the role which modelling has played in the formulation of Indian plans and the areas in which they could play a more useful role in the changed context. I offer these observations not as an expert practitioner of the art but on the basis of knowledge and impressions gained from being closely associated with modelling work in the Planning Commission during the 1960s and subsequently by keeping touch of major development in this sphere from outside.

The use of formal models in Indian planning dates back to the first plan which projected the long term trajectory of growth using a simple Harrod-Domar type growth the model. This was subsequently refined to incorporate foreign trade and aid in the so called two gap models (Tendulkar 1971). The first moves towards multisectoral models came from Prof. Mahalanobis (in his famous two and four sector models which formed the basis of the second plan) and from Professors Raj and Sen (1961). During the mid fifties the Indian Statistical Institute started work on construction of multisector models and the collection of the empirical data (including the construction of an input — output table) necessary for estimating them. These early exercises (Frisch 1960 and Sandee 1960) were pursued further in the ISI and provided the basis for estimation of input-output models (Manne and Rudra 1965, Srinivasan etal 1965) which were used in the Planning Commission for preparing the first detailed outline of a long term plan (PPD 1964). These models were designed to project the levels of sectoral outputs consistent with specified overall targets of GDP, consumption and capital formation in the terminal year of the plan as well as the total investment needed and its sectoral allocation. By varying the relevant parameters, the model could also track the impact of different combinations of export growth and import substitution and inequality in consumption.

Then followed a period of close and active interaction between Planning Commission and academia through the Planning unit of the ISI both in preparing more detailed and up-to-date input-output tables and in extending the scope of the models. One exercise (Bergman and Manne 1966) sought to work out-under specified assumptions about the time required to construct and commission projects in various sectors and on rates of export growth and import substitution — the appropriate phasing of investment to ensure that the trajectory of supplies and requirements match. Besides dynamising the models, (Manne and Weisskopf 1970, and Weisskopf 1967) there have also been attempts to construct and estimate models to determine optimum allocations of investment (Chakravarthy and Eckhaus and Parikh 1966).

But this phase did not last long. For various reasons, the interaction between the Planning Commission and the ISI diminished in the late sixties. Much of the subsequent work on plan models was internalised in the Planning commission. More detailed and refined I/O tables were constructed. Special Sub models for projecting consumer demand, exploring interaction between income distribution and output patterns, the volume and pattern of employment likely to be generated by the projected growth of output, and assessing the prospects for agriculture were developed as an adjunct to the main model. Attempts at constructing and estimating dynamic or optimisation models were however more or less abandoned. The models in operational use have focussed on projecting internally consistent terminal year configurations for the national plan. Interest in extending and refining these models for state level planning has been conspicuously weak. And academic interest in this area has also been limited even when planned development was not in dis-repute! There are several reasons for this:

In the first place, even the most disaggregated models used by the Planning Commission provide only an approximate indication of the overall output targets for some important sectors. But typically, this is not enough in as much as the products of particular sectors is varigated (as is clearly the case in energy, textiles and steel). Moreover questions like the desirable mix of different energy sources or transportation modes cannot be answered by the models used. This limitation arises partly because of the level of aggregation but more importantly because the models assume fixed input coefficients and therefore do not permit exploration of the implications of different (extant and prospective) technologies as well as of changing relative prices for the composition of final and intermediate demands. They are even less suited to assess the merits of alternative output and technology mixes from the economic view point.

In principle these limitations can be mitigated by the dovetailing economy-wide input-output models with detailed sectoral models. That overall economy-wide planning models need to be supplemented by sectoral level analysis for deciding sector specific investment strategies and policies was recognised early. In fact the PPD, in the 1960s, prepared a series of papers detailing the steps needed (in terms of resource surveys, advance planning of projects, the creation of design and engineering organisation and coordination of investment in related activities in time and space) to realise the long term targets for some key sectors. However the preparation of detailed sector programmes were largely remitted to the various working groups consisting of representatives of concerned ministries/enterprises, the planning commission and some non-official experts. These usually turned out to be lobbies for larger allocations for particular sectors/projects. They were neither designed, nor equipped to produce sectoral programmes or policies based on objective indepth studies. Special expert committees set up by the Planning commission to work out long term programmes for energy transport and steel came closer to accomplishing this.

In the case of transport there have been 2 or 3 such studies over the past 4 decades. Formal modelling to work out optimum location, phasing and scale of investment in a few sectors (cement, fertiliser, and paper) was tried in the 1960's (Manne, 1967). Subsequently detailed sector studies have been done in respect of, energy and steel. Some of these have used quite elaborate models to assess optimum long term strategies in respect of produce mix, technology, location and scale (Sengupta, 1990, 1993).

But these have been sporadic exercises; nor have they become as widespread and sustained as they need to be. Neither the Planning Commission nor the concerned departments have institutionalised arrangements necessary for updating data, revising and refining the models in the light of experience and new information; and provide a constant feed back into the process of decision making in respect of specific projects or plans. The extent to which the findings of the few systematic sectoral studies shaped the targets, strategy and policies of the government is also in some doubt.

Undoubtedly, data deficiencies have impeded the process. While considerable improvements have no doubt taken place in terms of coverage, reliability and level of disaggregation of data, problems remain. Input-output data for unorganised industry, trade transport and services continue to be inadequate in terms of the level of detail and reliability even at the national level. The problem gets compounded because technology and product mix is changing at different rates in different industries. Data on unorganised industries leaves much to be desired. A particularly serious problem is the lack of data needed for constructing capital coefficient matrices, differentiating between various construction materials machinery and equipment. Pioneering work on this aspect was done in the 1960's. But it has not been pursued further even though Planning Commission, the Ministries and the Financial Institutions (such as ICICI & IDBI) have been accumulating a massive amount of data on these aspects.

The more serious impediment is institutional : A high level of interaction between modellers and the policy makers is essential to make the technique an effective instrument for decision making. But policy makers typically have neither the time, the patience or even the interest for such interaction. Informed and rigorous analysis as a basis for policy choices has not been encouraged and cultivated by politicians or for that matter bureaucrats in the concerned departments. With some significant exceptions, those responsible for policy decisions have shown little interest in such analysis. The prospects of debate and controversy in public forums (including Parliament) on the factual basis and rationality of decisions seems to make executives take at best a cautions, and invariably secretive, attitude to commissioning expert analysis. The general secretiveness about making data accessible to outsiders severely restricts the possibility of such work being done by interested academics and non-governmental agencies.

That there is considerable interest among academics in systematic empirical analysis of policy relevant issues is evident in the work on behavior of consumer demand, modelling of water allocation in large irrigation systems like Bhakra Nangal, estimation of fertiliser response functions and of optimum allocation between crops and regions, and evaluation of alternative poverty alleviation policies in a general equilibrium framework. But these remain sporadic. While they do help more informed discussion of the issues among experts, they do not feed systematically and effectively in public discussions of such issues or in policy making.

As the government's direct involvement in productive activity and its role in regulating resource allocation in the non-government sector diminish the role of elaborate economy-wide models for determining output targets and investment allocations will naturally decline. Macro economic modelling for relatively short term predictions and for assessing macro policy alternatives is likely to be more prominent. In recent years interest in this aspect has grown especially outside the government. There is also growing interest in using general equilibrium models to analyse the ramifications of major changes in domestic and international spheres and of alternative policies in pursuit of particular goals such as poverty alleviation. Efforts at improving both the analytical framework underlying such models and the quality of empirical data entering their estimation, as well as widespread discussion of their findings among professionals in and out of government, should of course be encouraged.

While the use of input-output models for target setting will decline, rigorous sectoral modelling deserves much greater emphasis even under a regime of indicative planning or for that matter market-driven private sector development. In the context of fast changing technology, which has far reaching effects on both the demand for, and the supply of, various key materials (e.g. energy and metals) and services, in-depth studies of key sectors from a long term perspective are particularly important. The choice of strategic sectors which the government should support and encourage, as well as the kind of policies appropriate for key sector will require such analysis. These considerations are also relevant for planning long term corporate strategies of individual enterprises both public and private.

Such studies — of which modelling is an important component — are however very demanding in terms of both data and technical expertise. Therefore work on these sector specific studies should be organised as a collaborative effort involving concerned government agencies, technical experts from within and outside government, the industry associations and academics. Wider and freer sharing of data and open discussion of techniques, assumptions and inferences could greatly enhance the value of such studies for developing an informed consensus on policy.

In the Indian context, given its size and diversity, both macro and sectoral studies and associated modelling need to be extended to the states. There has been little work in this area, largely because state level planners and policy makers have shown even less interest in data based analysis as an input into decision making than their central counterparts. This would however call for a significant improvement in the coverage and quality of macro economic and sectoral data relating to states and regions. Most states produce annual economic reviews. But these tend to be descriptive with no attempt at integrating the data into an overall macro economic framework, much less analysing and interpreting the trends. There is also much room for rigorous modelling at the state/

regional level of a number of policy relevant issues such as pricing of goods and services provided by the public sector; the impact of programmes and policies in areas (such as agriculture, animal husbandry, electricity and road transport) which are largely in the states' domain; the design of appropriate strategies in respect of energy supply, transport and other infrastructure to stimulate industrial development in specific regions; and the like.

To sum up, the shift from centralised planning of production and investment may diminish the role and relevance of particular type of models (especially economy wide, input-output models); but it does not reduce the need for rigorous and objective analysis as a basis for informed deliberation of important matters of policy. In the changed context, models for analysing trends and assessing policy issues at the macro-economic level, general equilibrium type analysis to understand the ramifications of alternative policies relating to particular issues and, above all detailed studies of development prospects of key sectors in a long term perspective will have a much more important role in policy making and in facilitating more informed public debate on policy. However the realisation of this potential will require greater interest on the part of government agencies in using expert analysis as an input in policy making; a willingness to involve non governmental experts in such work; to follow a more open policy in giving access to the relevant data and placing the findings of analyses in the public domain. It is also essential to devote for more resources and attention to institutionalised arrangements for improving the coverage and quality of data, making them more easily accessible and for continuity in policy-relevant modelling.

Presented at the International Seminar on '*Development Planning Models: Relevance and Approaches*'. Institute of Economic Growth, New Delhi, March 19-21, 1996.

8

Growth of Indian Industry

Role of Demand Factors

1. BACKGROUND

THE role of demand factors in shaping the growth of Indian industry has been the subject of some discussion in the context of the debate on the slowing down of manufacturing output growth since the mid-sixties. On the domestic side, these discussions have focussed on the role of three elements: viz., agricultural growth, shift in sectoral term-of-trade and public investment.

Agricultural growth affects the demand for manufactures both directly and indirectly. The direct effects operate through the farm sector's demand for manufactured farm equipment, intermediates and consumer goods. The indirect effects are felt via marketed surplus of food and the availability of raw material for the agro-processing industries. Since foreign exchange shortages put a severe limit on the import option, expansion in non-agricultural incomes which generates a faster growth in demand for foodgrains relative to its supply triggers off inflation and a shift in relative prices against manufactures. The impact of these factors on the level of public investment, together with the squeeze on manufacturers profits on account

I am grateful to K. Nagaraj and S.D. Tendulkar for their comments on an earlier draft. The usual disclaimer applies.

of the increase in relative price of wage goods, also adversely affects private investment and output growth[1].

There was also a widespread view that the new agricultural technology (embodied in the HYV's) and the liberal price support policies were biassed in favour of the larger farmers. The resulting increase in rural income inequalities was seen to be reinforced by the shift in the terms-of-trade in favour of agriculture. It was argued that under these conditions, growth of demand for luxury goods accelerated at the expense of manufactures for mass consumption. This shift in the demand pattern for manufactures impeded full utilisation of installed capacity for intermediate and capital goods production. As Nayyar (1978) argued, only a broad based demand for mass consumption goods can lead to a full utilisation of capacity and generates sustainable increase in output[2].

More recently, Chakravarty (1986) went further to suggest that demand factors may have contributed in some ways to increasing the realised ICORs and hence cause a persistent slow overall growth of incomes and aggregate demand. The deceleration of real investment growth (since the mid sixties) meant slowing down in the growth of demand leading to unutilised capacity in capital goods industries; the worsening distribution of income meant a shift in the pattern of demand from mass consumer goods to capital intensive production of luxuries. The steep rise in energy prices at a time when energy intensity of production was increasing raised costs and dampened demand. Indian industry could not take advantage of foreign markets because of several structural difficulties characterising the domestic and the international economy.

The sharp reduction in public sector's plan outlays in the latter half of the sixties directly affected the demand for a variety of equipment, especially railway rolling stock, electrical equipment and machinery for steel, coal and other heavy industry, for which substantial indigenous capacities had been built during the second and the third plan periods. The indirect effect on growth-via its influence on aggregate demand, the climate for private investment and on the expansion in the availability of infrastructure, skills and basic intermediate goods — was no less important.

There is a fairly widespread consensus that the slow pace of agricultural growth and the serious set back to public investment growth from the mid sixties have dampened the growth of demand for manufactures. But the role of the agricultural sector's terms of trade, and income distribution in general, has been contested mainly on factual grounds. It has been pointed out that agricultural output has not decelerated after the mid sixties; that the growth of marketed surplus of foodgrains has expanded more rapidly after the mid sixties despite near constant trend growth of crop output: that percapita availability of foodgrains admittedly a major element of the wage goods basket, had not declined and may even have increased marginally; that the available evidence did not show any persistent trend either way in the terms-of-trade for agriculture or in the distribution of income either in rural or urban areas; and in any case consumer goods industries did not show any sign of deceleration since the mid sixties (Ahluwalia, 1985)[3].

Indeed it is being questioned whether inadequate consumer demand for manufacture is at all the major constraint on industrial growth. Results of some recent market surveys for 1980s are cited to support an argument that the market for manufactures including durables, with rural India accounting for a sizeable portion of their sales is not limited to the urban rich, but is much wider and deeper than it is supposed to be. Production would grow faster if only the government did not discourage investment in industries for whose products there is considerable unsatisfied demand. Slow growth of industry according to this view, is due fundamentally to wrong policies affecting the supply side. Excessive emphasis on import substitution. Over-protection of domestic industry, elaborate controls on the private sector and inadequacies of infrastructure reflecting an inefficient public sector are seen as the more basic causes (Bhagwati and Srinivasan, 1975 and Ahluwalia, 1985).

The purpose of this paper is not to join the larger debate on the performance of Indian industry. It is concerned only with the behaviour of the level and pattern of demand for manufactured consumer goods and evaluating, in the light of the available evidence, the validity of various hypotheses concerning this aspect. Specifically, we consider the relation between income distribution and the demand for manufactures; and the extent to which "structural changes" in tastes and preferences of consumers may have affected the aggregate demand for manufactures and its composition.

2. OVERALL TRENDS

To begin with, there is a problem of defining "manufactures". In principle, the term should cover the processing and transformation of all raw materials — agricultural, mineral or manufactured materials. There are, however, practical problems when it comes to precisely delineating the boundaries of "manufacturing industry" from that of services, determining whether output is to be measured in gross terms or as value added and of course getting the actual data.

For the economist, "production" is production for exchange. The process of "development" typically involves a shift in the way production is organised: from processing for own use to making processed products for exchange. The volume of manufacturing activity as defined by the economists can, therefore, increase without any increase in the total volume of processing or transformation activity. This has probably been happening in India even during the post-Independence period, especially in processing of agricultural and food products; But its extent and incidence cannot be quantified.

The definitional difficulty is compounded by data inadequacies. We do have estimates of the level and composition of consumption derived from statistics of production and disposition by end use as in the National Accounts Statistics (NAS) and from direct enquiry from households through sample surveys of which the National Sample Survey (NSS) is the most important. The NAS provides a continuous time series of private consumption expenditure at current and constant prices for 38 commodity groups since 1950-1. (GOI, 1989, 1989a) NSS estimates of commodity composition of household consumption are available for most years from 1960 to 1972 and thereafter at five year intervals.[4] The published NSS estimates, however, mostly give a break-up for only 10-12 commodity groups and that too at current prices. It is of course possible to estimate the level of real household consumption overall and by different commodity groups and the total in real terms at different points of time. Such exercise have been undertaken but the time profile of change reconstructed from NSS is very different from NAS even in respect of the aggregate. Difference in respect of individual commodities, as we shall see later, are even more divergent.[5]

According to NAS the aggregate value of private consumption of selected major manufactures at constant (1980-81) prices nearly quadrupled between 1950-51 and 1986-87, the trend rate of growth being around 3.7 per cent a year, nearly the same as GDP growth rate. The trend growth rate of both real NDP and of manufacture consumption per capita during the seventies and eighties is substantially higher the implied elasticity of the latter with respect to per capita NDP being somewhat above unity.

Estimates based on NSS data suggest that upto 1966-67 per capita expenditure on industrial products fell progressively and by a substantial amount (40 to 50 per cent) in both rural and urban areas (Table 1). While it steadily rose thereafter, the average during the second half of the sixties was substantially below the averages for 1960-64. The level in 1973-74 was still below that in the early sixties. This is quite out of line with the NAS estimates for this period even in terms of direction of change not to speak of its magnitude.

TABLE — 1

Per Capita Consumption Expenditure on Industrial Products 1960-61 to 1973-74

Rs. at. 1964-65 prices

Period	*Bottom 40%*		*Middle 40%*		*Top 20%*		*All*	
	Rural	*Urban*	*Rural*	*Urban*	*Rural*	*Urban*	*Rural*	*Urban*
1960-61 to 1964-65	35	51	78	125	257	427	97	156
1965-66 to 1969-70	29	37	63	88	192	290	75	108
1970-71	30	42	67	110	195	385	78	138
1973-74	32	43	69	92	228	313	86	117

Source : Roy's estimate cited in Sundrum (1987). Estimates have been rounded to the nearest rupee.

A rough estimate for years subsequent to 1972-73 based on published NSS tabulations and the NAS estimates both show increase in real per capita consumption of manufactures (Table 2). But the time profile of increase from 1972-73 to 1986-87 obtained from the two sources is quite different. Between the end points of this period, the NSS shows a larger percentage increase in per capita manufactures consumption and in the share of manufactures in total private consumption compared to NAS. The respective time profiles of change within the period differ markedly.

TABLE — 2

Estimated Growth of Per Capita Real Consumption of Manufactures

	Index at constant prices			
	1972-73	*1977-78*	*1983*	*1987-88*
NAS[1]				
Value (Index)	100	105	131	132
Share of manufactures in total consumption	32.3	31.4	34.5	33.0
NSS[2]				
Value (Index)	100	126	128	150
Share of manufactures in total consumption	23.5	27.9	26.4	27.7

Notes : Estimated from CSO's latest revised series of private consumption at 1980-81 prices. (GOI, 1989, 1989a)

1. "Manufactures" included the following commodity groups: Sugar and gur; oils and oilseeds; coffee, tea spices and other food; beverages, pan and intoxicants; tobacco and product; hotels and restaurants; clothing and footwear, furniture, furnishings, household equipment etc; and personal transport equipment.
2. The estimates of percapita expenditure manufacturers at current prices are available separately for rural and urban areas (GOI, NSS, 1990). Manufacturers are taken to include the following categories in the NSS. Sugar, edible oils, salt and spices; beverages and refreshments; pan, tobacco and intoxicants; clothing and footwear, and durable goods. The weighted average is obtained using the share of the two sectors in total population in the respective years.

   The average percapita total consumption corresponding to NSS is estimated as the sum of the deflated expenditure on food and non food items on rural and urban areas the deflators being the respective price indexes as estimated by Minhas et al 1991.

There are also significant differences in the pattern of change in the consumption of manufactures since the early seventies shown by the two sources. According to the NAS, judging by its share in total manufactures consumed, the consumption of textiles grew relatively faster than that of other manufactures. No such tendency is revealed by the NSS data. Indeed, except for 1983-84, the share of textiles and that of other manufactures in total manufactures has been more or less constant (Table 3).

It is difficult to reconcile the two estimates or even to say which one is more reliable. They differ in terms of scope, sources of data and basis of valuation between the two sets of estimates. The commodity classifications of the two sources are also not comparable. The NSS estimate relates only to household consumption while NAS covers all private consumption. The NAS relies on incomplete and often unreliable production data and various ad-hoc assumptions about allocation between end uses. In principle the NSS is expected to be better in that it seeks to obtain commodity-wise details directly from the households. But it is not free of problems either.

The concept of "consumption" in the case of clothing and durables is not always clearly and consistently defined. Both estimates are subject to errors and biases of unknown magnitude; further, changes in the scope and coverage of data, source and estimation methods in the case of NAS and changes in commodity categories, reference' period and sample design in the case of NSS affect the comparability of the estimates overtimes[6]. For these reasons, it is difficult to be sure which of the two series are more reliable as the basis for assessing the behaviour of total consumption of manufactures over time[7].

Only in the case of textiles — which is by far the biggest single item of manufactured consumer goods — estimates from a survey conducted by the Market Research Wing (MRW) of the Textile Directorate permit an independent cross check of the NSS and the NAS (Table 4). According to official estimate, the per capita consumption of all textiles stagnated at 14-15 meters in the early 1970s to less than 14 meters in the mid

TABLE — 3

Estimated Composition of Consumption Expenditure on Manufactures as Per National Accounts and National Sample Survey 1972-73 to 1987-88

Item	1972-73			1977-78			1983-84			1986-87		
	NAS[1]		NSS[2]	NAS		NSS	NAS		NSS	NAS		NSS
	Constant prices	Current prices	Current prices	Constant prices	Current prices	Current prices	Constant prices	Current prices	Current prices	Constant prices	Current prices	Current prices
Sugar[2], edible oils	32.6	31.1	32.0	31.9	25.9	21.8	32.9	30.7	27.8	30.0	28.2	28.3
Beverages[3], Tobacco, etc.	29.1	29.9	29.7	22.2	28.3	22.0	22.5	25.9	25.5	20.8	24.5	28.7
Clothing and footwear	29.8	30.6	29.1	36.1	37.2	29.7	34.5	35.0	37.6	38.1	38.0	29.1
Durables[4]	9.2	8.2	9.1	9.8	8.5	26.5	10.1	8.3	9.7	11.1	9.9	13.9
All manufactures	100	100	100	100	100	100	100	100	100	100	100	100

Notes: 1. The NSS estimates for the total population is estimated as the weighted average of rural and urban figures of per capita consumption, the weights being the population of the total population in these 2 sectors.

2. Includes 'sugar' and 'edible oils' in the NSS tabulations and 'sugar and gur' and 'oils and oilseeds' in the NAS

3. Includes 'salt and spices' 'beverage and refreshments' 'pan, tobacco and intoxicants' in the NSS categorisation and 'coffee tea, spices and other food', beverages, pan and intoxicants, tobacco and restaurants in the case of NAS.

4. Includes the item 'durable goods' in NSS and 'Furniture, furnishing the household equipment' and 'personal transport equipment' on NAS.

The NSS estimate relates only to household consumption and the NAS to total private consumption. The NAS estimates relate to the fiscal year; the NSS year is from July to June (except 1972-73 when it is Oct-Sept.). NSS estimates for durable in 1977-78 is believed to be defective (Tendulkar 1989) and this would affect comparisons of level and composition of manufactures between the sources.

eighties and that of cotton textiles from 13-14 metres to 10 metres. This is often cited as evidence of deceleration in the demand for mass-consumption goods. But the MRW survey data, while corroborating the declining trend in cotton cloth consumption measured by length, suggests a moderate rise in total cloth consumption and much larger rise in non-cotton fabrics than the official estimate (Table 5). Quantity estimates are not published by the NSS.

TABLE — 4

Estimate of Household Purchases of Textiles Derived from Market Research Wing Survey[1]

Year	Per capita purchase (meters)			Per capita purchase value at 1972 prices (Rs)	Per capita[1] availability official estimates[2] (metres)		
	Cotton	non[3] cotton	Total		Cotton	non[3] cotton	Total
1972	12.48	1.29	13.77	52.36	13.2	2.0	15.2
1973	11.23	1.37	12.60	49.31	12.0	1.9	13.9
1974	11.85	1.77	13.62	55.61	12.9	1.7	14.6
1975	11.72	1.59	13.31	53.48	12.6	2.0	14.6
1976	10.79	1.18	11.97	46.32	11.4	2.4	13.8
1977	11.60	1.65	13.25	53.58	9.5	4.0	13.5
1978	11.60	1.99	13.59	57.21	10.2	4.8	15.0
1979	11.46	2.19	13.65	58.89	10.1	4.6	14.7
1980	10.56	2.87	13.43	63.16	11.0	3.7	14.7
1981	9.57	2.74	12.31	59.15	10.2	4.2	14.4
1982	10.04	3.48	13.52	68.58	9.9	3.7	13.6
1983	10.12	3.59	13.69	69.55	10.8	4.0	14.8
1984	9.94	3.89	13.83	71.72	10.6	3.9	14.5
1985	10.79	4.66	15.45	82.25	10.8	4.0	14.8
1986	10.71	5.08	15.79	86.53	10.6	4.4	15.0
1987	10.75	5.60	16.75	92.58	10.5	4.2	14.7

1. *Source* : Divatia (1990)
2. *Source* : GOI, Economic Survey, 1989
3. Cotton + mixed/blended.

A better index for cloth consumption one which takes into account changes in quality composition — would be the value of consumption at current prices deflated by a price index for cloth than merely the length of cloth. The NAS estimates of per capíta cloth consumption at constant prices, which better approximates to this concept[8], show rise at an average rate of over 3 per cent a year since 1950-51. During the 70's and 80's the constant price value of consumption rose by 3.4 per cent a year even as in terms of meters it was stagnant or falling. Over the same period, according to the MRW survey data, cloth consumption per capita at constant prices grew by nearly 4 per cent per annum (Table 5).

TABLE — 5

Trend rates of Growth of Percapita Textiles Consumption as per NAS and MRW 1972-1987

(per cent per annum)

	Official[1]	*MRW*[2]
All textiles (meters)	0	+1.18
Cotton (meters)	-1.5	-1.05
non-cotton (meters)	+6	+10-11
Value of consumption at constant prices	+3.4	+3.98

1. 'meters' as published in the Economic Survey. Value from NAS series on private consumption at constant prices. NAS, GOI, (1989, 1989a)
2. *Source*: Divata (1990).

The NSS data which are available for a few points of time do not permit estimation of the trend growth rate. But the overall increase between 1972 and 1986 is substantially below that shown by the other two sources (Table 6). It therefore seems reasonable to infer that at least in textiles, the growth in quality adjusted real consumption of clothing obtained from NAS is a better approximation of the trends than the NSS.

There is clearly no deceleration in the demand growth after the mid sixties.

TABLE — 6

Value of Per capita Consumption of Textile According to Different Sources

Year	Current prices[1] (Rs/annum)			Constant prices Index 1972-73=100		
	NAS[1]	MRW[2]	NSS[3]	NAS[1]	MRW[2]	NSS[4]
1972-73	59.9	52.4	38.2	100	100	100
1977-78	135.9	101.1	75.4	129	102	112
1983-84	202.2	217.8	127.3	160	133	158
1986-87	275.1	315.9	142.4	169	165	137

Sources :
1. GOI, (1989, 1989a)
2. Divatia (1990)
3. GOI, (1990) (weighted average of estimated per capita expenditure in rural and urban areas)
4. Estimated current prices values deflated By

3. IMPACT ON INCOME DISTRIBUTION CHANGES

Among the contentious issues in the earlier debate is the impact of changes in income distribution on the demand for manufactures. There are two distinct aspects to this. First, how is the level of aggregate demand for manufactures affected by changes in inter-sectoral and inter-class income distribution? Second, What has happened to intersectoral and inter class distribution of income?

Terms of Trade for Agriculture: The average urban consumer spends more, both in absolute and relative terms, on manufactured products than his rural counterpart[9] (Table 7). Consequently, any shift in distribution of real incomes between the two sectors may be expected — other things being given — to have a significant affect on the aggregate demand for manufactures.

TABLE — 7

Changes in Consumption of Manufactures and Associated Variable According to NSS, 1972-73 to 1987-88.

	1972-73	*1977-78*	*1983*	*1987-88*
Per capita real consumption[1]:				
Total	100	126.8	110.3	127.7
Manufactures	100	126	128	150
Proportion of manufactures[2] in total consumption:				
Rural	22.4	28.0	25.0	26.1
Urban	26.7	32.6	28.1	28.3
Gini coeff. of consumption[3] at constant prices:				
Rural	.308	.330	.293	NA
Urban	.350	.347	.335	NA
Ratio of rural[3] pce to urban pce at constant prices	68.2	70.6	68.0	NA
Share of rural areas[4] in total consumption of manufactures	69.8	68.2	64.7	61.9

1. See note (2) to table 1. These are expressed as indices with 1972-73 = 100
2. at current prices
3. estimated by Jain and Tendulkar (1989)
4. estimated

TABLE — 8

Indices of Inequality in Consumption Distribution
Rural and Urban India

Year	1961-62	63-64	64-65	66-67	67-68	68-69	69-70	70-71	71-72	72-73	73-74	77-78
Rural												
Nominal	.313	.297	.294	.297	.293	.291	.305	.293	.283	.299	.276	.336
Real	.316	.302	.309	.312	.314	.320	.329	.318	.304	.324	.345	.352
Urban[1] Real	.363	.369	.371	.362	.371	.380	.366	.395	.373	.378	.344	.360
CV of real per capita consumption[2]												
Rural	16.0	10.8	16.4	15.2	18.1	16.5	19.0	18.2	16.3	23.2	16.9	24.1
Urban	15.3	16.7	12.9	15.5	16.0	14.0	11.9	13.9	12.9	11.3	9.1	10.4

Sources: Suryanarayana (1986) pce = per capita consumption expenditure

1. not available
2. CV across states (in percentage terms) of mean per capita consumption at 1961-62 prices.

However terms-of-trade changes do not affect all segments of the rural and urban population uniformly. When food and agricultural products become relatively more expensive, consumers with fixed incomes or incomes not fully indexed with reference to the cost of living are likely to cut back their consumption of manufactures more than others. In the agricultural sector, the medium and large farmers (who account for most of the marketed surplus) are likely to benefit (lose) much more from an increase (decrease) in the relative price of farm products than small farmer and agricultural labourers.

It so happens (see Table 1) that, though the average rural consumer spends substantially less (some 30-40 per cent less according to NSS) on industrial products than his urban counterpart, the top 20 per cent of the rural population (which would be among the principal beneficiaries of a terms-of-trade shift) spend more than twice on industrial products compared to the middle 40 per cent of the urban population, which is likely to include the organised working class. Because of this, an improvement in the terms of trade of agriculture, other things given, should result in a net increase, even as a deterioration will tend to depress, the aggregate demand for manufactures.

The thesis concerning the role of agriculture's terms of trade as a factor explaining industrial growth has, however lost much of its relevance because there is no secular or sustained increase in the prices of food and agricultural products relative to manufactures especially since the mid 1970s. The latest available evidence suggests that the income terms of trade moved in favour of agriculture through the sixties till the early 1970s. But then followed a phase of progressive fall till around 1980. While there has been a mild reversal of this trend, the terms of trade in the late 1980's are considerably less favourable to agriculture than they were in the early 1970's. The relative rates of population and income growth in rural and urban areas and changes in income distribution within each sector are far more important determinants of the growth in consumer demand for manufactures.

Urbanisation: Urban population has been increasing nearly twice as fast as rural population. The share of population dependent on agriculture has fallen much less than the share of income derived from this sector and rural non-farm activities are for the most part in the unorganised sector. Urban incomes (total and percapita) must therefore be growing considerably faster than rural areas. Given the relatively higher manufacturing intensity of urban consumption, one would expect the share of urban areas in total consumption of manufactures to become progressively more important. The NSS, the only source of data on these aspect, does not suggest any sustained change in rural-urban disparities in real per capita's consumption but the share of urban areas in total consumption of manufactures in 1983 and 1987-88 was higher than in 1972-73 and 1977-78.

Inter class inequality: Those who assert that there has been no increase in inequality rely primarily on the estimates of the Gini coefficient of concentration (GCC) of assets and consumption expenditure obtained from the National Sample Survey and the rural income surveys done by the NCAER. The NSS data show a general decline in the inequality index for nominal consumption in rural India through the sixties, with wide fluctuations at a relatively higher level thereafter; (Table 8) that of land holdings and assets also do not show a marked change between 1960-61 and 1980-81. However, estimates of consumption inequality at constant prices (Suryanarayana, 1986) suggest that for the rural areas of the country as a whole inequalities in real consumption were rising through the sixties, fell to somewhat lower level in the early seventies only to rise again in 1977-78 (Table 8). A more recent estimate (Tendulkar and Jain 1989) also suggests that real consumption in rural areas during 1977-78 and 1983 was more unequally distributed than in the early 1970s. Both studies do not show any sustained trend in the distribution of real consumption in urban areas (Table 7).

The NSS consumption surveys are designed to provide estimate for the population as a whole at each point of time. But there have been significant changes in the methodology and sample design[10] whose effects on comparability over time remains a debatable issue. (See Vaidyanathan 1986). Estimates of the inequalities in distribution of assets suffer from a twin limitation. They are available only at current prices:

(correction) for changes in relative prices of different assets are not feasible at present. Moreover, asset holdings relate to the distribution of households arranged by size of household assets and not of households arranged by size of per capita assets. The latter is arguably the more appropriate criterion for ordering households.

An independent survey of the level and distribution of incomes in rural India conducted by the National Council of Applied Economic Research (NCAER) at two points of time, namely, 1970-71 and 1981-82, provided estimated for a common panel of sample households covered in both years, as well as for the rural population as a whole. More than one fourth of the 1970-71 sample households could not be matched in the resurvey of 1981-82, and the non-response rate in the latter year was high (5 per cent). Consequently the comparisons of levels and distribution of income based on the panel sample are not reliable. Estimate for the entire population are more appropriate for assessing distributional changes. Even here there are questions about the comparability of sample designs and therefore of the estimates from the two surveys and about the plausibility of the pattern of income growth suggested by the data[11]. Subject to these caveats, it is noteworthy that the NCAER survey reports no significant change in inequality of rural income distribution between the two years.

Other evidence points to a worsening income distribution across regions, between wage labourers and cultivators in rural areas, and between workers in organised and in unorganised sectors. More specifically it is important into the following:

(a) Inter state disparities in per capita SDP has risen progressively. Broadly speaking, the more prosperous areas (namely Punjab, Haryana and West UP) have recorded relatively high per capita growth while large parts of eastern and central India, where poverty is concentrated, recorded little or no growth in per capita output.

(b) In rural areas, inter-state disparities in foodgrains and total crop output per head — which is a major source of rural incomes have also increased progressively.[12] The coefficient of variation (across states) in per capital real consumption in rural areas also seems to have risen steeply through the sixties and seventies (see Table 8). Even as the proportion of wage labour has risen, the total demand for labour from agriculture has grown, if at all, rather slowly. While non-agricultural employment opportunities have grown, the total availability of work in terms of number of days, per usually employed worker, has fallen.[13] Real Wage rates too have been stagnant in several states, and declined in some, till the early 1980s.[14] This would suggest a worsening in the relative position of wage labourers in terms of real income compared to cultivators.

(c) Taking the non-agricultural sector as a whole, there is a strong tendency for the relative importance of unorganised sector employment to grow. Between 1971 and 1991, according to census data, the proportion of non-agricultural workers engaged in the unorganised sector is estimated to have risen from 68 per cent to over 69 per cent, provisional results of the 1991 census suggest that this proportion has gone up further to nearly 74 per cent.[15] Many of the unorganised sector activities are not covered by minimum wage regulations or, where applicable, are not enforced. They, of course, do not get any of the other protections and privileges (like health insurance, leave, and workers compensation) or the bargaining power which organised sector employees have.

(d) Real wage rates in the public sector have risen by nearly 80 per cent between the early seventies and the mid eighties and by some 40 per cent in organised industry.[16] The disparities between workers in organised and unorganised sectors are therefore likely to have widened. This tendency will, if anything, be aggravated by the tendency for the proportion of unorganised sector employment in rural areas to rise.

The apparent puzzle of a sustained rapid increase in marketed surplus and the absence of any sustained rise in the price of food (and agricultural products generally) relative to manufactures in the face of a slow-down in per capita crop output growth may also be "explained in terms of (or at any rate seen to be consistent with) a worsening income distribution across regions and classes because the growth of agricultural output and marketed surplus largely occurred in the relatively prosperous regions the poorer states slow overall growth meant that the effective demand for food also grew slowly. This together with the relatively high support prices helped the public agencies to procure large and growing quantities of food.

If income distribution across regions and classes has worsened, one expects the increase in consumer demand for manufactures relative to income to increase over time. Since the manufacturing intensity of urban consumption is higher, progressive urbanisation will also have the same effect. Changes in consumer's tastes and preference due to commercialisation, spread of education, growing inter-action between rural and urban population and the enormous expansion in the reach of mass media are all likely to further induce greater demand for manufactures.

The available evidence does not quite corroborate the above expectation. The time series income elasticity of clothing consumption during 1971-86 was indeed substantially higher than doing the previous 2 decades (Table 9).

TABLE — 9

Estimates of Demand Elasticity for Manufactures

	All manufacturers	*Clothing*
1977-88 Cross section data[1]		
Rural	1.3	2.1
Urban	1.46	1.9
Changes between 1972-3[2] and 1987-88	1.79	1.34
NAS Time Series[3]		
1950-70	1.16	1.11
1971-86	1.15	1.87

1. Estimated from a double log function relating expenditure on clothing to percapita consumer expenditures in different size classes of expenditure.
2. The ratio of the percentage change in per capita expenditure on manufacture, clothing and total pce in real items, estimated using the corresponding implicit NAS deflators.
3. estimated by fitting double log function to the time series of consumption of selected items w.r.t that of pce, both at constant prices as per revised NAS series.

But the elasticity for total manufactures is not very different in the two periods. By implication, the elasticity for manufactures other than clothing, which was higher than that for clothing in 1950-70, has not only declined since but has fallen substantially below that of clothing. A point-to-point comparison based on NSS data, however, suggests the opposite, i.e., the increase in per capita consumption of all manufactures relative to per capital total consumption has been much higher in the case of clothing and also higher than the elasticity estimated from cross section data for 1977-78. The NSS data suggest a steady rise in the share of non-food expenditures (in real terms) in total real consumption of urban India, but no such tendency is noticed in rural areas where the share has in fact progressively declined after 1977-78. One cannot on the above evidence, infer with confidence, a structural change in consumer preferences in favour of manufactures.

Two other surveys — one a survey in 1985-86 of sample households in rural Bengal covered by NSS consumption enquiry in 1973-74 and another the NCAER's panel survey of household income in 1971-72 and 1981-82 seem, at first sight, to provide stronger evidence of structural changes in consumer demand patterns. The former shows that in real terms per capita expenditure on cereals and food as a whole had remained more of less constant between the two points of time while that on manufactures rose by nearly 40 per cent[17]. (Bhattacharya et.al., 1987)

A similar picture emerges from the NCAER surveys, which show that mean per capita total consumption of the panel households surveyed in 1980-81 was about 15 per cent higher in real terms than the mean for the same set of households 10 years earlier. Cereal consumption fell marginally, even as non cereal food expenditure rose by 10-11 per cent; and outlays on clothing, footwear and durables rose by 40 per cent (NCAER, 1986). However, one has to be cautious in drawing any inferences on structural changes in consumption patterns from these survey data. They deal only with rural areas and the survey of the NSS sample is confined to West Bengal. The NCAER panel survey could not locate more than a fourth of the 1971-72 sample and even if they had been, the sample would not be representative of the population in 1981-82.

4. PATTERN OF CONSUMER DEMAND FOR MANUFACTURES

We have so far considered only the effect of urbanisation, income distribution and consumer preferences on the aggregate demand for manufactures. All these also have a major bearing on the pattern of demand for manufactures. NSS data show that, compared to his urban counterpart, the average rural consumer spends a relatively higher proportion of total outlay on manufactured good on sugar, pan and tobacco, and clothing and relatively less on beverages and refreshments and durables. As one moves up the income scale, the share of manufactures in total consumption rises and the pattern change. The relative importance of edible oil, sugar and pan tobacco and beverages and refreshments declines sharply while that of clothing and footwear and, especially durable increases. This pattern of behaviour is observable both in rural and urban areas; only the extent of the shift seems far more marked in the latter (Table 10).

TABLE — 10

Pattern of Demand for Manufactures in Rural and Urban India 1987-88

(percentage)

Commodity groups	*Rural areas*		*Urban areas*	
	Lowest pce class[1]	*highest pce class*[2]	*Lowest pce class*[3]	*highest pce class*[4]
Edible oil	33.6	8.7	33.3	6.2
Sugar	14.6	5.4	16.2	2.5
Beverages and Refreshments	15.0	9.6	24.4	16.1
Pan, tobacco intoxicants	25.4	4.4	18.2	3.7
Clothing	8.2	30.2	5.6	21.2
Footwear	1.5	3.5	0.9	3.2
Durables	1.6	38.1	1.2	47
All manufactures	100	100	100	100
Manufactures as % total consumption	14.8	45.8	18.0	43.7

1. Below Rs. 65 per capita per month
2. Above Rs. 385 per capita per month
3. Below Rs. 90 per capita per month
4. Above Rs. 700 per capita per month

Source :Sarvekshana, July-Sept. 1991.

Within each category of manufactures, there is a further differentiation not only by types of products, but of particular products in terms of materials, quality and design. One expects rural consumers to use more of products made from traditional materials and processes; and modern manufactures figure more prominently in the urban markets. The introduction of new products, new materials and designs which has been characteristic of recent times — is likely to have brought about changes in pattern of manufactures consumption in addition to those associated with changing income level and distribution. The pace of change in patterns seems likely to be much faster in rural areas, under the influence of the spread of mass transport and communications, the widening reach of mass media, and growing economic and social integration between town and country.

Both the NAS and the NSS series point to changes in the pattern of manufacturing consumption since the early 1970s (Table 11). Estimates adjusting for changes in relative prices which are published by the NAS, suggest that the share of textile, footwear and durables have been rising at the cost of other groups especially beverages, tobacco and refreshments. But the extent of the change is by no means dramatic, at any rate at the level of commodity aggregation currently available. This may also be due in part to the omission, for want of relevant information, of petroleum products, drugs and pharmaceuticals toiletry and innumerable other products from the above comparisons. Perhaps too, the pattern changes would be more striking at a more disaggregated level. Nevertheless the fact remains that the bulk of the manufactures currently consumed consists of food, beverages and tobacco, textiles and footwear. The behaviour of demand for these products is therefore far more important in determining the rates and pattern of industrial growth than that of durables.

TABLE — 11

Household Purchases of Textiles in Rural and Urban India 1974-1987

Years	Rural areas				Urban areas				Ratio of rural to urban consumption
	Non-cotton as % of total	Unit price Rs/metre			Non-Cotton % of total	Unit price Rs/metre			
		cotton	Non-cotton	Mixed blended		cotton	Non-cotton	Mixed blended	
1974-76	26.0	4.6	15.4	17.7	51.1	6.0	22.7	23.6	79.1
1980-82	44.4	7.6	26.0	27.3	65.3	10.4	37.1	37.7	71.3
1985-87	57.4	9.8	37.2	32.9	72.1	14.1	49.9	44.1	69.9

Computed from Divatia 1990.

While evidence of structural change in overall consumption patterns in favour of manufactures is weak, there is much stronger indication of such changes in respect of some individual commodity groups; especially textiles and durables.

4.1 Textiles and Clothing

Fairly detailed tabulations of the pattern of textile consumption, by type of textiles, region and income class is available from the reports of MRW survey. They show, among other things, that (a) the rural per capita consumption has grown more slowly than urban areas, and taken together with declining share of total population, the rural share of the both cotton and non cotton textile market is falling progressively, (b) overall the share of non-cotton fabrics in total consumption has risen in both of rural and urban areas; the pace of substitution was far more rapid especially in rural areas during the latter half of the seventies than since; (c) though the consumption of non-cotton fabrics is growing everywhere, they still figure much more prominently in urban consumption accounting for over 70 per cent by value compared to less than 60 per cent in rural areas; (d) judging by the relative unit values, the rural consumers are using relatively cheaper cloth in all fabric categories and the differential is widening in the case of cotton cloth (Table 11).

4.2 Other Manufactures

The other major source of information is the market surveys conducted by NCAER and ORG. The ORG estimates, based on sample retail shops audit, are not available in sufficient detail; nor is the methodology of the survey and design published. The NCAER survey (called MISH) is reported to cover some 75 manufactured products (37 consumer expendables and 38 consumer durables[18]) accounting for most of the consumer goods other than food, textiles and fuel and power. This survey has been conducted annually from 1985-86 to 1989-90 and its results widely cited to counter the criticism that the market for many modern manufactured products (especially durables) is confined to the richer segments in urban areas. It is pointed out that the consumption of many of these (including durables) have penetrated quite deep into rural areas and down the income scale. Unfortunately published tabulations are very sketchy of and do not permit much by way of critical analysis and interpretation[19].

In practically all non-durable manufactures the share of the rural market is less and in many cases substantially less than its share in population (Table 12). This itself is not surprising because rural percapita incomes are substantially lower than those of urban areas. But one would expect pattern changes, especially in favour of "modern products", to be more pronounced in rural areas. In fact, with few exceptions (e.g. tea, soaps and hair oil) the majority of rural households did not purchase the products in 1989-90; the proportion of households reporting purchases (called the penetration rate) is invariably lower than in urban areas. In some products (e.g. tooth paste, vanishing cream, electric bulbs) the penetration rate is low in both sectors. Moreover, apart from soap and tooth paste the share of rural areas in total market is either stagnant or declining (Table 12).

TABLE — 12

Market for Selected Non-Durable Manufactured Goods, 1985-86 and 1989-90

Item	*Units*	*Total purchases*		*Rural share*		*Penetration rate (per '000 HHS)*			
						1985-86		*1989-90*	
		1985-86	*1989-90*	*1985-86*	*1989-90*	*Rural*	*Urban*	*Rural*	*Urban*
Biscuits	'000t	132	295	55	46	145	290	183	445
Vanishing cream	t	627	734	26	26	71	185	62	166
Hair Oil/ cream	t	2100	3446	48	43	530	692	658	808
Toilet soap		227	327	49	50	816	927	844	948
Washing powder	'000t	515	709	43	48	374	629	445	708
Washing cake	'000t	800	1074	61	68	704	839	930	946
Tooth paste	ns	16	30	29	32	185	541	211	579
Foot wear PVC	ns	92	139	72	64	244	242	339	393
Leather	ns	120	120	57	56	354	505	312	527
Casual	ns	127	258	64	67	313	418	579	531
Electric bulbs	ns	200	233	32	30	334	720	456	801
Electric tubes	ns	29	261	36	NA	77	372	85	413

Same NCAER :Personal communication.

ns = not specified.

The penetration rates for most products has risen from 1985 to 1989 which means that the market for manufactures is widening in rural as well as urban areas. The rural market for non-leather footwear, hair oil/cream, tooth paste and electric bulbs is widening faster than in urban areas; while in a few (e.g. some toilet products and leather footwear) the rural market seems to be narrowing. The overall rate of growth varies — from near zero in the case of leather footwear, to more than doubling (in 5 years) of the estimated purchase of biscuits and a nine-fold increase in electric tubes.

The stagnation of leather footwear consumption and the rapid growth in size and scope of the market for PVC and casual footwear is illustrative of a more general tendency for new materials to replace traditional ones. Also, though data for earlier periods are lacking, several of these products have been introduced especially in the rural market, only in the post independence period sometimes replacing traditional, home-made substitutes, sometimes catering to altogether new demands. In the former case the growth in purchases for the new products is not a net addition to the demand for manufactures, but a shift from traditional products to newer ones made for and sold in the market. The decline of handlooms, traditional footwear, food processing and earthen pottery in the face of substantial rise in the total demand for the class ot products they make, is part of reflection of this phenomenon. Traditional producers who could not or did not, adapt to these market changes have been displaced in the process.

4.3 Durables

The possession of durables has evidently become more widespread both in rural and urban areas even as their range has increased. Thus according to the NSS in 1964-65 the large majority of both rural and urban households reported owing bedsteads and metallic utensils. In rural areas one sixth of the households owned other furniture items and torchlights; one in sixteen had watches/clocks but less than 2 per cent of the households had radios, fans, and sewing machines. In urban areas one in ten households had sewing machines and fans; 13.5 per cent of households had radios and 20 per cent had a bicycle. Data on the proportion of households owing these goods are not available for more recent years but the extent of their spread can be guaged from the number of pieces of each item possessed per '00 households estimated from NCAER survey. In 1989-90, according to MISH, there were nearly 9 sewing machines per '00 households, 35 radios and nearly the same number of electric fans, 40 bicycles and nearly 80 watches (Table 13).

TABLE — 13

Percentage of Households Reporting Possession of Various Durable Goods 1964-65 and 1989-90

	NSS[1] 1964-65			*MCAER-MISH[2] 1989-90*
	Rural	*Urban*	*Total*	*Total*
Almirah	5.8	15.6	7.9	na
Bedstead	68.6	64.0	67.6	na
Radio	1.34	13.4	3.8	35.0
Metallic Utensils	79.2	78.4	78.8	na
Torch light	16.8	18.9	17.4	na
Clock, watches	6.6	35.6	12.2	80.0
Electric fan	0.3	10.7	2.2	35
Sewing machine	1.4	10.3	3.2	9
Bicycle	9.3	21.5	11.7	39
TV		not reported[3]		20
Two wheelers		not reported[3]		9

Source: 1. GOI, (1974)
2. NCAER; Personal communication
3. Probably negligible

The ISI household resurvey in rural Bengal also shows that possession of most durables has spread significantly between 1972-73 and 1985-86 (Table 14). This survey also highlights the rapid shifts from traditional to newer material; e.g. from bell-metal to aluminium and stainless steel vessels; and from metal to plastic buckets; Such shift in demand pattern in respect of established products naturally affects the pattern of domestic manufacturing industry normally to the disadvantage of traditional, small scale craftsmen.

TABLE — 14

Ownership of Selected Durable Goods by Households in Rural Bengal 1973-74 and 1985-86

Item		*Percent of Households possessing*		*No. Possessed per household*	
		1973-74	*1985-86*	*1973-74*	*1985-86*
Bedstead		30.9	33.4	0.49	0.55
Desk Table		6.2	7.6	0.08	0.10
Suit Case		54.1	64.1	1.05	1.39
Utensils:	Bell metal	48.4	50.8	2.16	2.13
	Stainless steel	5.1	20.0	0.10	0.80
	Plastic	0.2	0.9	0.00	0.01
	Aluminium	78.4	88.0	3.42	4.72
	Enamel	12.3	14.4	0.43	0.55
Bucket :	Iron	42.2	51.7	0.63	0.55
	Plastic	0.9	8.0	0.02	0.10
Lantern		47.6	57.7	0.68	0.84
Torch		29.9	49.1	0.34	0.55
Wrist watch		16.2	31.7	0.18	0.43
stove		2.4	6.3	0.02	0.06
Bicycle		19.4	34.4	0.21	0.38
Radio, Transistor		11.5	30.5	0.13	0.31

Source: Bhattacharya et.al (1987)

The spread of entirely new durable goods (such as television, two wheelers, cassette recorders, electric iron and stoves, refrigerators and kerosene and gas stoves) is noteworthy. They either did not exist or were altogether rare in the 1960s. But in 1989-90, when the total number of households was around 150 million, there were an estimated 25 million TV sets, 25 million pressure cookers, 11 million two wheelers, over 6 million refrigerators (Table 15). Their acquisition of these newer products — in so far as it is not at the cost of squeezing the consumption of other manufactures — represents an additional source of demand for manufactures. Besides the direct income and employment generated in the production of these products the maintenance of these durables has generated a rapid growth of spare parts manufacture and repairs. This has in fact been one of the most rapidly growing areas of "industry" and has contributed substantially to increased employment.

That the market for durable goods, particularly the "new" products, has grown rapidly cannot be denied, but one must guard against exaggerated notions about its range and depth. The fact of the matter is that the ownership and purchase of these goods is highly skewed. With a few exceptions (radio, fans, watches and cycles) hardly 5 per cent of the low income groups in the country own these goods. Even among the high income households, 40-50 per cent do not have pressure cookers, radios, iron or two wheelers; and 50-60 per cent do not have colour TV. The proportion of the rural households in these income categories who do not possess these goods is likely to be much, much higher.

TABLE — 15

Market for Selected Durable Manufactures 1985-86 and 1989-90

Item	*Estimated stock 1989-90*	*Penetration* rate of possession*		*Rural share of purchase*		*Penetration rates of purchase*	
		Low income	*High income*	*85-86*	*89-90*	*Rural*	*Urban*
Black & White TV 10^6	17.32	45	245	26	44	17	56
Colour TV 10^6	5.82	7	424	11	19	2.2	24
Radio 10^6	53.6	286	525	79	77	42	30
	18.2	44	246				
Electric fans 10^6	54.4	148	1652	60	58	18	45
Bicycle 10^6	59.2	327	478	82	74	41	37
Two wheelers 10^6	11.1	14	574	@	@	5.4	23.5
Electric iron 10^6	21.9	46	574	46	43	6.7	22.7
Sewing machine 10^6	13.3	41	315	60	56	2.7	5.4
Wrist watches 10^6	120	510	2384	@@	@@	106	168
Kerosene stove	na	na	na	63	58	na	na
Pressure cooker 10^6	25.4	51	815	34	37	11	48

* Per '000 households

@ The turn share in the 2 years was for mopeds 42 and 43% Motorcycles 52 51% and scooters 36 and 28%.

@@ The rural share of purchases in 2 years was 78 and 71 per cent of mechanical wrist watches and 59 and 47 per cent for quartz watches.

Source: NCAER; Personnal communication.

The NCAER survey shows that, overall, in 1989-90 the proportion of rural household purchasing durables ranges from less than 0.5 per cent (in the case of two wheelers) to a maximum of 10 per cent in wrist watches. In practically every category (except radios and bicycles) the penetration rates in urban areas are much higher than in rural areas. Also noteworthy is the fact that in many cases the rural share of total products is falling not rising. While the attraction for these products is no doubt spreading down the income scale, the majority of the poor are still in no position to afford them. If the attraction of these products is so great as to induce the poor classes to acquire them despite inadequate and meagre incomes and the cost of restricting (if not reducing) outlays on other more essential items bearing on health and well being the desirability of such a trend should be a legitimate matter of concern.

5. CONCLUSION

The main points of this empirical exploration of trend in the absorption of manufactures for consumption can be summarised as follows. First, fears that shifts in the terms of trade in favour of agriculture may have dampened the growth in the aggregate consumer demand for manufacturers are ill-founded. Quite apart from the fact that there is no secular stift in the terms of trade, an increase in relative prices of agricultural products tends to redistribute income from the urban middle and working classes to the rural middle/rich peasantry. Given that the latter have a much higher level of manufacturing consumption, better prices for agriculture may well result in a net increase in aggregate demand for manufactures.

Second, changes in the inequality of income distribution between regions and classes as well as structural changes in consumer preferences are likely to have been far more important. Evidence on income distribution is mixed though there are a number of pointers indicating a worsening of inter regional and inter class inequalities. However, there is no doubt about the rapid pace of urbanisation, the spread of education, mass media and expansion of rural-urban linkages. All of this may widen and deepen the market for manufactures, especially modern manufactures, considerably more than pure income growth, especially in rural areas.

Third, in so far as this leads to an increase in the share of manufactures as a whole in total consumption, the aggregate elasticity of consumption of manufactures relative to real incomes should be rising over time. The available evidence from the National Accounts and the National Sample Survey, however, does not seem to corroborate this; the time series elasticity of demand for manufactures implied in the NAS is actually lower for the period since 1970 than that for the preceding period. The NSS data suggest that over-time changes over 1972-1987 in manufacturing consumption are higher than cross-section elasticities, but the pattern within the period is far from consistent. Given the limitations of both sets of data, no definitive conclusion seems feasible.

Fourth, Pattern demand for manufactures has indeed changed since the early 70's but they are not as striking as one might expect given the rapid spread of commercialisation, progressive integration of rural areas into the wider market network and the introduction of many new products. Perhaps these development have led more to displacement of traditional by more modern products than to a significant deepening of the market for manufactures. Coming to specific commodities, the stagnation of textiles consumption in terms of meters per capita is not particularly significant. When allowance is made — as it should be — for changes in quality of consumption, the real consumption is found to grow at a rapid 3.5-4 per cent a year.

Fifth, Data for the latter half of the eighties — the only available at present — suggest that the market for several non-durable and durable modern products is generally widening. The share of rural areas in total purchases is understandably less than its share in total population. But the proportion of rural population purchasing selected products is much less than

50 per cent in a majority of the products covered. Somewhat surprisingly the rural market share is not increasing in all cases; some have actually fallen. The distribution of ownership and purchases of durables is highly skewed, the overall proportion of rural households possessing durables is quite low and that among the poor negligible. The popular picture of a consumer revolution sweeping the country side is grossly over drawn.

Finally, The available data base for a proper understanding of the structure and dynamics of consumer demand for manufactures clearly leaves much to be desired. Besides improving the coverage quality and comparability of official statistics (including NSS) there is a strong case for conducting, on a continuing basis, market surveys of specific categories of manufactures along the lines of MRW and NCAER. However the utility of these data will remain limited unless the results are published in reasonable detail on a regular basis and the primary data are accessible to researchers/policy makers for more detailed, critical analysis.

Notes

1. For a discussion of these issues see Chakravarty (1974), Rangarajan (1982), Rudra (1967) and Vaidyanathan (1978).

2 See also Mitra (1977) and Patnaik (1981).

3 It is worth noting that the empirical basis for most discussions on growth and structural change in industry rests on the Index of Industrial Production (IIP) and the Annual Survey of industries. The latter covers only establishments registered under the Indian Factory Act and is estimated to account for around 60 per cent of the total value added in manufacturing. The coverage of the IIP is even narrower. While the quality of data regarding unorganised industry leaves much to be desired, ignoring them gives but an incomplete picture. And given that the rates and patterns of growth between the two segments differ, the picture obtained by looking at organised industry alone is also likely to be distorted.

4 Annual surveys have been revived after 1986-87, but based on a thin sample for the years between the quinquennial enquiries.

5 Using data for 1952-53 to 1964-65 Sau (1974) estimated the share of demand for manufacture in total rural consumption to have declined and cited it as evidence of the slow growth of rural demand for manufacturers.

Roy (1987) defined manufactures to include the following categories: clothing, footwear, durables fuel and light and miscellaneous goods and services. Note that fuel and light includes firewood and cowdung cakes while the last category covers a variety of personal services which can hardly be considered manufactured goods.

6 For a discussion of these issues see Vaidyanathan (1986).

7 Minhas (1989) questions many of the criticisms concerning the validation of NSS data and believes that systematic disaggregated analysis can help to adjust for differences in scope coverage and valuation. He and his colleagues have pioneered a good deal of work in this direction. Valuable as this is, it is difficult to see how the large differences between the two estimates in respect of particular commodities (notably textiles, edible oils and sugar) reflecting differences in scope (household vs all private), sources (household inquiry vs production and disposition data from producers) and valuation and a variety of errors (sample error, non reporting, mis-reporting etc.) can be sorted out much less reconciled. As for inter temporal comparisons the fact that the NSS and NAS series show large and erratically different time patterns of change does affect the confidence with which either series can be used.

8 In so far as the index for clothing prices used as deflator relates to a fixed bundle in term of varieties, fibre and quality.

9 Note that the exclusion of Kerosene, LPG and electricity used for domestic purposes, and of drugs and miscellaneous goods from the above comparison is apt to under state the rural-urban differential in consumption of manufactures.

10 In some rounds sample households selected for consumption inquiry were asked only about consumption. Others included consumption as part of an integrated household schedule; since the early 1970's consumption and employment/unemployment schedules are canvassed on a common sample. The shift to stratified sample in recent years is another major change. There have also been changes in item classification, concept of consumption etc.

11 According to the survey, there was hardly any increase in agricultural income and that the bulk of the increase in incomes (estimated to be around 9 per cent per capita between 1970 71 and 1981-82) was on account of non-agricultural incomes and more specifically of salary incomes from non-agricultural employment.

12 The CV of per capita crop output across districts have risen from 37 per cent in the early 1960's to 54 per cent in 1977-78.

13 On this see Vaidyanathan (1988).

14 Jose (1988) Papanek (1988).

15 Total number of non-agricultural workers is estimated to have risen from 52 million in 1971 to 75 million in 1981 and 95 million in 1991. The organised sector employment as reported in the Employment Market Information data rose from 17 million in 1971 to 22 million in 1981 and 25 million in 1989.

16 GOI, Economic Survey (1991-92; s. 55) the average annual earnings (at 1960 prices) of public sector employees rose from Rs. 3083 in 1971-72 to Rs. 3551 in 1980-81 and Rs. 5107 in 1989-90. The estimates for workers in organised manufacturing are derived by deflating the average annual earnings per worker as reported in the ASI with Consumer Price Index for industrial workers.

17 The estimates of change in total consumption expenditure not indicated.

18 The product coverage of MISH in various years is not clear. Bhatty (1989) indicates that items covered by the 1986 survey account for most of the final consumption on items excluding food, textiles, fuel, power, rent, taxes, land services. According to Bhatty the expenditure on products covered by MISH in 1985-86 was Rs.13535 crores. The NAS estimate of expenditure on non-food items excluding clothing, rent, taxes, fuel and power in that year was Rs.21225 crores. The difference might be due to the fact that the scope of NAS estimates of private consumption is wider than that of NSS (which relates only to household consumption) and to non-coverage of untensils, furniture, cars etc.

19 I am grateful to Dr. S.L. Rao, Director General of NCAER for making available to me some unpublished tabulations on the break-up of consumer purchases and penetration rates for various products by region, income class and rural urban areas. These tabulations however cover only 26 expendables and 28 durables.

References

Ahluwalia, I.A. (1985), *Industrial Growth and Stagnation since the mid sixties*, Delhi, Oxford University Press.

Bhattacharya N., A. Chattopadhyay and A. Rudra (1987), *"Changes in Level of Living in Rural Bengal"*, Economic and Political Weekly, No. 33, pp 246-252.

Bhagwati J. and T.N. Srinivasan (1975), *Foreign Trade Regimes and Economic Development: India* (NBER), New Delhi, Columbia University Press.

Bhatty, I. (1989), *Rise in consumption levels in India and Consumerism, Margin*, April-June.

Chakravarty, S. (1974), *Reflections on the Growth Progress in the Indian Economy,* Hyderabad, Administrative Staff College of India.

Chakravarty, S. (1979), *"On the question of home markets and prospects for Indian Growth"*, Economic and Political Weekly.

Chakravarty, S. (1986), Aspects of India's Development Strategy in the 1980's in *Facets of Indian Development*, G.L. Mehta Memorial Lectures, Bombay, Industrial Credit and Investment Corporation of India.

Divatia, V.V. (1990), "Household purchases of Textiles 1972-87", *Journal of Indian School of Political Economy*, Vol. II, NO.2 and Vol. II No.3.

Government of India (1989), *National Accounts Statistics (New series) 1950-51 to 1979-80*, New Delhi, Central Statistical Organisation.

Government of India (1989), *National Accounts Statistics 1980-81 to 1986-87*, New Delhi, Central Statistical Organisation.

Government of India (1972), *Nineteenth Round July 1964-July 1965, Report No. 192 Tables with notes on consumer expenditure*, New Delhi, National Sample Survey Organisation.

Government of India (1990), *Report on the Fourth Quinquennial Survey of Consumer Expenditure*, NSS 43 round June 1987-June 1988.

Jain, L.R. and S.D. Tendulkar (1989), "Inter Temporal and Inter Fractile ground movements in real levels of living for rural and urban population of India 1970-71 to 1983", *Journal of the Indian School of Political Economy*, July-Dec.

Jose, A.V. (1986), "*Agricultural Wages in India*, Economic and Political Weekly", Review of Agriculture, June, No. 26.

Minhas B.S. and S.M. Kansal (1989), "Comparison of NSS and GSD Estimates of private consumption", *Journal of Income and Wealth*, Vol. II, No.1.

Minhas, B.S. (1989), "*Validation of large scale sample survey data; Case of NSS estimates of Household consumption expenditure*", Sankhya, Series B, Voll. 50, Part, 3.

Mitra, A. (1977), *Term of Trade and Class Relations: An Essay in Political Economy*, London, Frank Cass.

National Council of Applied Economic Research (1986), *Changes in Poverty and Consumption Patterns in Rural India, 1970-71 and 1981-82 A Longitudinal analysis, management*, New Delhi.

National Council of Applied Economic Research (1987), *Changes in the Structure of Household Income and Distribution of Gains in the Rural Household Sector — An All India Terminal Analysis 1970-71, 1981-82*, mimeographed.

Nayyar, D. (1978), "*Industrial Development in India: Some Reflections on growth and stagnation*", Economic and Political Weekly, special number, pp. 91-118.

Papanek Gustar, F. (1988), Poverty in India in Lucas REB and G.F. Papanek (eds), *The Indian Economy. Recent Developments and Future Prospects*, London, West view Press.

Papanek Gustar. F. (1990), *Cottage and Small Scale Industry in India Policy and Performance*, Sir Purshothamdas Thakardas Memorial Lecture, Bombay, India Institute of Bankers.

Patnaik, P. (1981), An Exploratory Hypotheses on Indian Industrial Stagnation in Bagchi A.K. and Banerjee N. (eds.) *Change and Choice in Indian Industry*, Calcutta, Bagchi & Co. pp. 65-90.

Rudra, A. (1967), *Relative Rates of Growth Agriculture and Industry*, Bombay, University of Bombay.

Rangarajan, C. (1982), *Agricultural Growth and Industrial Performance in India* Washington D.C., International Found Policy Research Institute, Research Report 33.

Roy, S. (1987), *Demand for Industrial Consumer goods in India — A Study of linkages* Ph.D. thesis, Calcutta. Indian Institute of Management.

Sundrum, R.M. (1987), *Growth and Income Distribution in India: Policy and Performance since Independence*, Sage Publishers, Delhi.

Suryanarayana, M.H. (1986), *Problem of Distribution in India's development: An Empirical Analysis* Unpublished Ph.D. thesis, Bangalore, Indian Statistical Institute.

Vaidyanathan, A. (1986), "On the validity of NSS Consumption data", *Economic and Political Weekly*, No. 3, pp. 129-132.

Vaidyanathan, A. (1978), "Constraints on Factor and Policy Options", *Economic and Political Weekly*.

Vaidyanathan, A. (1986), "Labour Use in Rural India: A Study of Spatial and Temporal Variations", *Economic and Political Weekly*, Review of Agriculture, No.12.

Vaidyanathan, A (1988), Agricultural Development and Rural Poverty in Patnaik, Gustar F. and Robert F. (eds.), *The Indian Economy: Recent Developments and Future Prospects*, London, Western Press.

9

Cottage and Small Industries in India

Policy and Performance

MOST contemporary discussions of growth and structural change in Indian industry and of restructuring industrial policy tend to assume implicitly that industry is coterminous with large industries, cottage and small industry, which currently account for nearly three fourths of total employment and close to two fifths of value added in manufacturing, hardly figure in these discussions. My intention is to correct this omission to some small measure, by providing an overview of the thrust of state policy in this sector, the extent to which it may have influenced growth and structural change in this sector as revealed by employment data and the lessons experience has for the future.

The Rationale and Strategy

The essential elements of government strategy towards cottage and small industry crystallised quite early. Even during the First Plan, a number of special boards were set up for developing specific segments of traditional industry — namely khadi and village industries, handlooms, handicrafts, sericulture and coir-along with a special organisation for the development of modern small industry. The emphasis was on removing the handicaps of village and small industry (arising from lack of access to raw material of the right quality and price, poor equipment, deficiencies in marketing and poor access to finance) by building community workshops and industrial estates, providing extension and training services, encouraging cooperatives of producers, and developing common production programmes with well demarcated spheres for large and small industry. Differential taxation of production of these two segments and preferential purchase of small industry products by the State were also introduced around this time.

This broad approach of combining protection with positive programmes to raise efficiency of cottage and small industry was endorsed by the comprehensive review of the rationale for, and means of, encouraging this segment of industry at the time of preparing the Second Plan. The Karve Committee — which was specially appointed for this purpose — suggested that the principal aims of policy should be "to avoid as far as possible, during the period of the Second Plan, further technological unemployment such as occurs in the traditional village industries"; "provide for as large a measure of increased employment as possible during the plan" and "provide the basis for the structure of an essentially decentralised society".

Mahalonobis, who looked at the issue in the context of overall development strategy, saw an important role for small industry in meeting the growing demand for essential consumer goods at a relatively low investment cost and creating in the process, a significantly larger increase in employment than would be generated by taking recourse to large scale factory production. But both Karve Committee and Mahalonobis saw this essentially as a transitional phase offering "some distinct advantages in relation to problems that need urgent solutions."

The Second Five Year Plan saw cottage and small industry as a source of immediate large scale employment; a method of ensuring a more equitable distribution of income; and facilitating an effective mobilisation of capital and skills which might otherwise remain unutilised. For this purpose a three pronged strategy was envisaged: the reservation of certain spheres of production for small industry reinforced by restrictions on expansion of capacity in large industry; measures (including differential taxation, preference in Govt. purchase and subsidies) to provide a degree of preference or assurance of market for small units; and those intended to provide positive assistance via technical assistance credit, raw material supply, and the like.

A distinction was sought to be made between sectors in which (a) small scale units have inherent advantages and not affected by large industry; (b) large industry has a predominant role but small industry is concerned with manufacture of certain parts or processes; and (c) small scale units which have to meet competition from large units. By implication, this recognised the need for a differentiated approach in framing policy. It suggested that restrictions of capacity expansion in large industry should be decided taking into account the extent to which this will enlarge the market for small sector, the volume of production required and the extent to which small scale unit can be organised to raise production. And further that the policy should be reviewed in the light of changing economic situation.

As for levies on large industry and subsidies for small industry, the plan endorsed the Karve Committee view disfavouring new subsidies and rebates, emphasising instead that "costs of protection (by these means) should be readily measurable and schemes of protection for normal economic activity should be so planned that they will be withdrawn in a reasonable period of time". These caveats however were not followed through systematically in shaping the specific content of policy.

The plan also emphasised that measure to encourage cottage and small industry should not be interpreted to suggest that "...freezing of existing techniques is at all indicated by considerations of economic or social policy. It only means that conditions have to be created in which modern techniques can be adopted and introduced more and more.... and that the transition should be orderly." Further that "It is the promotional rather than the protective aspect of policy which has to become more and more important in the adaptation and reorganisation of this sector."

The Industrial Policy Resolution of 1956 was even more explicit. While declaring a policy of "supporting cottage and village and small scale industries.... by restricting the volume of production in the large scale sector by differential taxation or by direct subsidies", it went on to say that "while such measures will continue to be taken, whenever necessary, the aim should be to ensure that the decentralised sector acquire sufficient vitality to be self supporting and development is integrated with that of large industry. The State will therefore concentrate on measures designed to improve the competitive strength of small scale producers. For this it is essential that the technique of production should be constantly improved and modernised the pace of transformation being regulated so as to avoid as far as possible technological unemployment."

One could not ask for a clearer and unambiguous statement of the rationale for state policy towards cottage and small industry. Not all the principles — and more especially the need for differentiated interventions according to the conditions of various industries and the need to view subsidies as a temporary support to be kept with in limits — were systematically followed through in practice. However the essential ingredients of intervention — namely a combination of protective measures (operating principally via discriminating in favour of cottage and small industry in respect of taxation, licensing of capacity in large scale industry, finance and government purchases) and positive measures (via. extension, credit common service facilities and the like) have remained substantially as envisaged in the First and the Second Plans.

Reservation of designated spheres of production for traditional and/or small industry has been operative on a wide range of products; banning the expansion of looms in the mill sector was one of the earliest and most important steps in this direction. There were also stringent restrictions on the installation of powerlooms outside the mill sector. In addition certain categories of cloth were reserved for the handlooms and a defined proportion of the output of spinning mills was to be in the form of hank yarn for handlooms. In the case of leather footwear, the expansion of factory production was severely discouraged to give an opportunity for production to expand in small scale units. A wide range of other products (over 800 according to the latest listing) are reserved for production by small units defined in terms of investment in plant and equipment below a specified level. Firms with investments exceeding the specified limits are not permitted to exceed their installed capacity in respect of the reserved items at the time of reservation leaving all output expansion, in principle, for the small sector.

Fiscal concessions take the form mainly of exempting certain products made by hand techniques (notable examples being khadi and village industries, handlooms and matches) from excise, lower rate of tax on a number of specified products made by small units (defined here in terms of output value), exemption from State sales taxes and price preferences in government purchase. Khadi, village industries, and handlooms not only benefit from these concessions, but also get subsidies and sales rebates. Registered small units also have some advantage in getting raw material and credit both in terms of ease of access and the terms. Small industries get bank loans at lower rates than large industry.

The total quantum of benefits accruing to cottage and small industry in these forms has not been rigorously estimated, but rough estimates for a few modern small industries show that these concessions can add up to as much as 25 to 45 per cent of output value, the excise concessions and price preference being for the most important items. The Committee on Tax measures to promote employment (which was chaired by V.M. Dandekar) estimated — and this estimate is crude and incomplete — the cost to the exchequer (in terms of revenue foregone on account of tax exemptions and concessions to cottage and small industry products, rebates on handloom and khadi, and interest subsidy on khadi) at some Rs.160 crores in 1978-79. This is indeed substantial — considering that total subsidies, according to national accounts estimates, in that year was around Rs. 2200 crores.

The "positive" programmes — aimed at improving the organisation for supply of raw materials to small industry, encouraging cooperatives, upgrading technology and constructing industrial estates with developed sites, infrastructure and common facilities — have continued to operate through the six boards dealing with different segments of traditional industry and the small industry development organisation (which attends to the whole range of modern small industry). Some limited efforts have also gone into encouraging small units as ancillaries to large scale units, especially in the public sector.

The scale of these programmes has progressively expanded with public sector outlay rising from Rs. 24 billion during 1961-66 to Rs.1965 billion in 1980-85. With the nationalisation of banks, credit supply to small industry at relatively low interest also expanded from a mere Rs.3 billion in 1969 to Rs.66 billion by 1984-85. Loans form SFCs, NSIC, SIDC and other sources which have been set up to provide investment finance have also grown but not on the same scale as bank credit. The magnitude of long-term finance is still quite small compared to short-term working capital fund provided by banks.

The Impact

What has been the overall impact of these interventions? The plethora of publications and survey reports on the subject do not shed much light on this question. We have of course some useful critical assessments of the working of policy relating to handlooms and a few on the cottage industries; but the coverage is rather thin and the empirical base generally quite inadequate. We have also several critical studies of particular aspects of small industry policy: e.g. the validity of the assumption that cottage and small industries use less capital per unit of output; the overall efficiency of resource use by small relative to large scale units; the use of fiscal policy to promote labour intensive manufacture; efficacy of industrial estates and other programmes to support modern small industry development. The contributions of Dhar and Lydall, Sandesara, IMD Little, Muzumdar and Page, and most recently, Ashok Desai, are worthy of special mention. But with the possible exception of textiles, these are hardly any studies supported by good empirical evidence of how these policies have in reality helped or impeded the growth of cottage and small scale units. Even the few which are available, tend to take a segmented view of the cottage or the more organised, modern small units per se, rather than in relation to industry as a whole.

The CSO's national income division of course does give estimates of output of factory and non factory establishments by broad class of industry. For aggregate manufacturing output, it is possible to reconstruct, with some effort, the estimated contribution of household industry, non-household non-factory industry and factories. Any one who has looked closely at the data base assumptions and procedures underlying these estimates cannot but be impressed by the ingenuity of the CSO in taking so much out of the meagre available information. But equally no one can be left indoubt about the extremely patchy and fragile data base on which they have to rely. The neglect to build a sound data base to map the characteristics (in the terms of organisation, technology, production, labour, investment etc.) of cottage and small industry and their changes over time is altogether glaring.

Large scale surveys there have been — by the NSS, the RBI, the SIDO and many others. But they are infrequent, fragmented in coverage and, when repeated, not comparable with earlier surveys. In this context the initiative of the NSS and the CSO to conduct regular quinquennial surveys of non-factory industry using the frame provided by the census of establishments should be warmly welcomed. But the more-than-normal difficulties of conducting such surveys and getting reliable information from enterprise which do not maintain regular accounts in a standard format, should not be under estimated. Besides evolving innovative methods to elicit essential information, the enterprises will need to be persuaded to cooperate in the conduct of such surveys. The industry associations have a special educative role to perform in this respect. These overall surveys need to be supplemented by more detailed industry level studies along the lines initiated by the Development Commissioner for Small Industry in the fifties and sixties but which, for reasons beyond understanding, have been discontinued since.

The situation, however, is not quite hopeless. While it is not possible to assess changes in output, technology, investment and other characteristics of small industry, we do have-thanks to the decennial census of population and the NSS — a substantial amount of information on manufacturing employment at a high level of spatial, industrial and establishment — type disaggregation. The census data, by far the most detailed, are available on a more or less comparable basis for 1961 and 1981. The NSS gives a detailed industry level estimate of employment for 1977 and 1987. This body of data has been analysed in the Planning Commission to get a picture of the structure of employment in different industries by category of establishment at different points in time since 1961. In what follows, I will draw heavily on this analysis — the details of which hopefully, will be published for wider use.

The census distinguishes between three classes of establishment in each industry: (1) Those registered under the Indian Factories Act: (2) household enterprises; and (3) the rest consisting on non-factory non-household establishments. According to the current official definition by which units with investment in plant and machinery below a specified limit are classified as "small", a sizeable segment of factory establishments will form part of "small industry". However in the absence of relevant information on this aspect, we will, in the ensuing discussion, treat "small industry" as being equivalent to the non-factory sector. This may not distort or invalidate the points made subsequently in as much as total employment in non-factory industry is several times that of small factories.

Total employment in manufacturing, according to the census, rose from 18 million in 1961 to 25 million in 1981. The National Sample Survey data suggest that workers in manufacturing rose from 23.7 million in 1977-78 to 29.2 million in 1987. These figures imply an average annual growth of total employment in manufacturing at around 2 per cent a year since 1961. While this may not seem impressive in relation to the rate of growth of total labour force, the sixties and seventies were clearly not a period of stagnation in industrial employment; nor did the eighties witness any significant deceleration in the growth of employment in industry taken as a whole.

TABLE — 1

Growth of Manufacturing Employment by category of Establishment India 1961-1987

(in million)

	1961	*1981*	*1977*	*1987*
Total	17.9	25.1	23.7	29.2
Factory establishments	3.7	7.0	6.3	7.8
Non Factory establishments	14.2	18.1	17.4	21.4
Household	9.9	7.7	NA	NA
Non Household	4.3	10.4	NA	NA

NA : Not Available

Sources : Census of India 1961, 1981

National Sample Survey

Factory Act Statistics relevant years

But more important in the context of the present discussion is the fact that between 1961 and 1981 non-factory employment grew at a considerably slower pace than in factories. And yet, in absolute terms, the additions to employment in the non-factory sector (3.9 million — See table 1) was larger than in factories (3.3 million). More recent data from the NSS suggest a considerable quickening in the growth of non-factory employment accompanied by a marked slowing down in factory sector. Between 1977 and 1987 the former is estimated to have risen from 17.4 million to 21.4 million (or close to 2 per cent a year compared to barely 1 per cent a year in the previous two decades), while factory employment growth slowed down from around 3 per cent a year during 1961-81 to 2 per cent or so a year during 1977-87. Nearly three-fourths of the additions to industrial employment during this period has thus come from non-factory industry.

To what extent can these be attributed to State policy? A definitive general answer is not possible purely on the basis of employment; we also need to know about output growth in different segments. Nevertheless employment trends in individual industries and type of establishments do give us some clues: In the first place, one can say unambiguously that one of the stated intents of State intervention — namely, to protect traditional household industries — has clearly not been achieved; Employment in household industry as a whole has declined by 2.2 million between 1961 and 1981. Eleven out of the 17 major industry groups (as per the 2 digit NJC level National Industrial Classification) recorded a fall of nearly 3.5 million in household industry employment, by far the biggest decline being in textiles, and food processing (See table 2). Between 1977 and 1987 also, industry groups where household industries dominate have continued to record relatively low growth in employment (See table 3).

TABLE — 2

Growth of Employment by Category of Industry and Establishment India : 1961-1981

(in thousands)

	1961				1981			
	Total	*Factories*	*Non-factory Non-household enterprise*	*Household Enterprise*	*Total*	*Factories*	*Non-factory Non-houschold enterprise*	*Household Enterprise*
Food & Food Products	2127	558	459	1110	2262	1047	761	454
Beverages Tobacco & products	1123	182	351	590	1824	168	642	1014
Textiles & Textile products	6552	1223	1156	4173	7433	1778	3171	2484
Wood & Wood products	2176	69	517	1590	2393	156	975	1262
Paper, Paper products and Printing	299	150	132	17	631	341	262	28
Leather & Leather products	705	26	142	537	488	54	225	209
Rubber, Plastics & petroleum products	72	39	31	2	329	178	138	13
Chemicals & chemical products	290	164	81	45	756	480	237	39
Non metallic mineral products	1504	193	462	849	1832	378	805	649
Metal & metal products	1167	312	389	466	1803	780	663	360
Machinery incld. electrical machinery	259	302		9	1270	835	377	58
Transport equipment	318	357	174	23	518	448	59	11
Repair shop	364	*		76	2435	300	1320	815
Others	951	130	379	442	1171	71	784	316
Total	17907	3705	4273	9929	25145	7014	10419	7712

Source : Reconstructed from Census of India and Factory Act Statistics. Based on unpublished working paper prepared by Haseb Drabu for the Planning Commission.

* Included in machinery and transport equipment

TABLE — 3

Estimated Employment in different branches of manufacturing, India 1977 and 1987

(in thousands)

	1977-78		1987	
	Total	*Rural*	*Total*	*Rural*
Food and Food products	2736	1670	3122	1895
Beverages tobacco & tobacco products	2308	1513	2894	2022
Bidi manufacture	2011	1335	2495	1760
Textiles & Textile products	8072	3820	9198	4939
Cotton spinning other than mills	224	139	122	93
Cotton weaving handlooms	1661	981	1636	1066
Textile products	3210	1862	4227	2430
Wood and paper products	468	94	732	167
Leather and leather products	569	326	581	265
Rubber, plastic & coal products	264	48	403	104
Chemical and chemical products	723	195	987	346
Non metallic mineral products	1959	1445	2575	1910
Manufacture of earthen ware	881	778	866	731
Metal and metal products	1508	493	2201	721
Machinery and electrical machinery	1109	425	1432	446
Transport equipment	401	70	595	81
Others	982	449	1219	532
Total	23725	12526	29245	16005

Source: National Sample Survey

The fall in household sector employment in all these groups is concentrated in the traditional industries (notably non-mill spinning, handlooms, khadi, hand printing, grain milling, oil crushing, gur making, leather and leather footwear and earthenware). Substantial expansion of household industry activity (creating an additional 1.2 million jobs) has taken place in a few industry groups notably beverages and tobacco (mostly in bidi making) and repair services. The former is eminently suited for household production on a putting-out basis and this advantage has been reinforced by the policy of differential excise taxation of the factory and non-factory production. But the growth of household enterprises in repairs is largely a spontaneous process owing little to State intervention or support.

The decline of household enterprises in the above mentioned traditional industries — which seems to have continued in the eighties — in part reflects a shift to non-household enterprises which have in most cases recorded significant increases, especially in urban areas. With the widening and integration of the markets, which is a generalised and ongoing process, a shift to superior forms of organisation in urban locations is to be expected. But the expansion of non household non-factory enterprises in traditional industries has been inadequate to compensate for the reduction in several segments of traditional industry — notably food products, handlooms and leather. Consequently overall employment in most segments of traditional manufacture have remained constant or declined inspite of wide ranging protective and positive interventions by the State. The reach of these interventions seem to be limited and, at any rate their impact has been blunted by their piecemeal character and lapses in implementing declared policy.

The most striking instance of this is handlooms which have

suffered from a calculated ambivalence of State policy regarding power looms and the failure to evolve a comprehensive policy covering different fibres and different segments of the weaving industry. Even in respect of cotton fabrics-which has traditionally been the sphere of handlooms– the restriction on the expansion of the powerloom sector was never seriously enforced even though the State could easily have contained it simply by, denying power connections. The concerned State agencies also failed to enforce the regulations regarding the production and distribution of hank yarn for handlooms. On the other hand, the grant of fiscal concessions to powerlooms-in respect of excise duty — gave them an added disadvantage over the handloom sector. Moreover instead of encouraging handlooms to become more resilient and aggressive in exploiting the changing patterns of demand, the state focussed more on subsidising them for producing low quality fabrics for mass consumption. All this, combined with rapid growth of non-cotton fabrics, contributed to a phenomenal expansion of powerlooms thus defeating the declared intent of State intervention.

In the case of bidi and leather products the policy of exempting output of non-power using sector from excise duty has given a decisive advantage to the small enterprises. Most of the leather footwear is now reported to be produced outside factories. This policy stimulated a rapid growth of employment in non-factory bidi units. But total employment in non-factory leather footwear industry has declined largely, it would seem, due to the emergence of cheaper substitutes in the form of rubber and plastic footwear. Other traditional industries in agricultural processing, coir and earthenware are not much affected by protective measures; the "positive" promotional measures largely implemented through the KVIC have clearly not been successful in preventing a decline.

In many other non-traditional industries also the decline in household industry is noticeable but this is more than offset by the expansion of employment in non household forms of small industry. The growth of total non-factory employment in non traditional industries is indeed impressive both in terms of range of industries and of magnitude. By far the largest increase is under repair services — 1.8 million additional workers or nearly 45 per cent of the increment to employment outside the factory sector — is accounted by this sector. Textile products as a whole, with an increment of close to one million workers, is the other striking area of expansion in small industry. Within this sector, garments, carpets and embroidered products have added close to 1.2 million jobs; while some (coir and manufacture of threads) have suffered an absolute decline. The other major area of expansion in small industry is in metals, metal products and machinery. Moderate increases in employment has also occurred in paper (including printing), chemicals, rubber and plastic products and non-metallic mineral products (notably brick making).

The growth of small enterprises in non traditional industries is of different types. Firstly in industries like repairs and bricks, small scale production close to the market is economically more advantageous to the producers and demand has grown rapidly. Secondly, over a wide range of industries small industry would appear to be manufacturing more or less similar products in a competitive market. But in point of fact the products of the two segments are often differentiated by quality, specifications, design, brand names and such other dimensions; also they cater to the demands of consumers who are highly differentiated in terms of tastes, preferences and incomes. Even casual observation shows that the market for commodities like textiles, garments, footwear, furniture, plastic goods and household equipment are indeed segmented by quality and price with small enterprises concentrating on lower quality/price segment. Therefore, the fate of traditional small industry is as much a function of their "efficiency" as the changing character of the market shaped in part by the flood tide of new materials product and high styles.

Thirdly, there is sub-contracting. There is a basis for the widespread impression-from various scattered, partial studies — that sub-contracting arrangements between large and small industry has grown rapidly in recent years. Several large textile firms are known to get their cloth woven and/or processed in the decentralised sector; a number of durable consumer goods (like air conditioners, fans, sewing machines and electronic equipment) carrying brand names associated with large companies are known to be fabricated in the small scale sector; and production of components and parts for machinery and transport equipment is quite widespread.

There have been significant changes in the rural-urban as well as the spatial distribution of small industrial activity over this period. The share of rural areas in total employment in non-factory industry has declined sharply pointing to a tendency for greater concentration of small industry in urban areas. But if we consider only the non household small industries — which is the more modern, better organised and rapidly growing segment — there has been a shift in favour of rural areas. The latter's share in total non-household non factory industrial employment has risen from a little over 30 per cent in 1961 to nearly 35 per cent in 1981. There is reason to believe that this tendency has quickened in the 1980's. The extent of inter-state variation in both total non-factory employment and non household, non-factory employment as a proportion of total work force also seems to have declined appreciably during this period. This would suggest a greater spatial diffusion of small industry. Both are significant development, the character of which merits systematic interpretative study.

Governmental policies and programmes for development of non traditional small industry are likely to have benefitted primarily the second and the third categories. The considerable price advantage deriving from differential taxation and price preference in government purchase should in principle enable the small units to compete more effectively with large units; even as the restriction of further expansion of designated lines of production in large industry enlarges the space for growth of small units. The policy of promoting ancillary production must have helped the expansion of small industry activity of the third category but being largely focussed on public sector units its impact was probably limited. At a more general level the expanded flow of industrial credit at rates well below prevailing in the informal credit market and the fact that minimum wages and the legislation concerning benefits are not applicable or are not enforced on the small sector gives the latter a generalised advantage in relation to large industry.

However small industry has still to get a relatively higher proportion of its funds from the high cost informal credit market; atleast some segments have higher capital costs per unit of output than large units; and suffer from less efficient use of raw materials and poor quality control. The net balance of advantages on all these accounts naturally differs with industry. The available information does not give even an approximate picture of the relative shares of factory and non factory sector in different industry segments, leave alone their dynamics or the role of above mentioned factors in shaping growth and structural change in this sector.

Lamentably, information on the reach and coverage of even the government's own programmes is either not available (at any rate in a published, accessible form) or is hopelessly outdated. Two recent studies dealing with modern small industry (one by Little and Associates and the other by Ashok Desai) report that the latest data on the extent of output produced by registered small units which fall in the reserved list relates to 1972. It suggests that less than a quarter of the output of selected product categories items comprise of reserved items. The impact may be larger to the extent that unregistered small firms also benefit from reservation. This would be the case, for instance, in leather footwear. But reservation has not been particularly effective in the case of textile weaving which, in quantitative terms, is one of the most important segments of unorganised industry. Preferential purchase by government which accounted in 1972 for barely 2.7 per cent of the sales of registered small industries; no data for any subsequent year is available! — could not be a major force in stimulating small industry. The extension services and District Industrial Centres are on the face of it quite widespread. The network of small Industry Service Institutes and their branches (some 59 in all), the extension centres (39), field testing centres (20) and training and research institutions (7) is estimated to cover one fifth of the small firms. But there has been no systematic evaluation of the quality of the services provided, or their impact on assisted units. The industrial estate programme also benefits only a small fraction of the small firms and evaluations have highlighted a number of defects in their operation.

State Intervention

State intervention in favour of cottage and small industry has been informed by two main concerns. (i) to prevent technological unemployment in traditional industries; (ii) promoting labour intensive techniques in manufacturing as a means of generating larger, more diffused employment in the economy. In reality the first objective has not been achieved; employment in most traditional industries have in fact declined. However there has been a significant net expansion of employment in small industry as a whole with signs of it outstripping employment growth in large industry during the eighties. In view of this one may ask whether protection of traditional industry, on ground of employment, should continue to be a major concern of policy.

The answer to this question would be in the negative in so far as workers engaged in traditional industry, who lose their employment due to competition from large industry/substitutes are able to benefit from the expansion of employment in other areas. Some of this is no doubt happening — eg. handloom weavers shifting to powerlooms, traditional potters shifting to brick making — but not on a sufficiently large scale. This is especially true of many handloom weavers and leather workers who are large in number and who are drawn mostly from socially disadvantaged lower castes, scheduled castes and minorities. Though precise information is lacking, scattered studies and impressions gathered by persons with intimate first hand knowledge of these industries, suggest that a large mass of workers who are displaced, along with new entrants to the labour power from these communities or who cannot find employment in these sectors, are forced into casual labour in agriculture. In order to get an index of the dimensions involved, consider handlooms and leather work. The employment in these two sectors in 1961 was 2.8 million and in the normal course the number of workers in this class would have exceeded 4 million in 1981. But actual employment available in 1981 in these industries was barely 1.9 million implying a displacement of over two million workers over the two decades. Given these magnitudes the social case for intervention to prevent further reduction in employment in some of the large traditional industries and to the extent possible enabling them to expand is very strong indeed.

But, as experience shows interventions to help traditional industries are apt to fail if they ignore potential sources of competition from producers of the same product using modern techniques — in the case of textiles powerloom is a good case in point — and from competing products using altogether different material and techniques. (eg. Synthetics vs cotton fibre; leather vs rubber/plastic, earthenware vs metalware/plasticware). Past government policies in respect of traditional industry can be faulted on both counts. In some cases, as with powerlooms, the policy explicitly recognised the first problem and provided for checks, but these checks were not implemented.

The disadvantages faced by traditional industry can be mitigated substantially if only the State enforced minimum wage and other labour legislation on the modern small industry competitors; taxed the latter' output more effectively and charged them reasonable prices for electricity and other utility services they consume. But the problems faced by the emergence of alternative materials and products which can be used in place of traditional products, are of a different order. The modern substitutes for traditional products are in several cases preferred by consumers because the former are more durable and/or easier to maintain and therefore effectively cheaper. Of course, the demonstration effect of mass media and advertising may have helped shift the peoples preferences away from traditional products without regard to cost consideration. These can be counteracted only to a limited extent by taxing the modern products very heavily; often times even this does not work. Nor is it obvious that modern substitutes for traditional products should always be severely restricted. We have also to consider whether the supply of traditional products and the material needed to produce them (eg. cotton and leather) can be expanded on a scale consistent with the growing demand.

Under these circumstances policy should address the question of how far and through what means the rapid shifts in peoples preferences away from traditional products can be contained, if not reversed. Economic measures (operating via prices) can go only a limited way; they need to be combined with a sort of mass counter — campaign to generally restrain the mindless drift to "modernity" and at the same time selectively cultivate demand for traditional products among particular segments of the population. From the producers end the exploitation of opportunities created by such a strategy would call for greater resilience in seeking out promising avenues in a fast changing market and in adapting production (in terms of designs, variety and other attributes of the product). Such resilience cannot be achieved by traditional industry without a massive collective effort. Cooperatives in their present state have shown themselves incapable of playing this role. A revitalised, democratically controlled and professionally run cooperative system could make a difference. This reform must in any case be done. But perhaps one should not rely only on formal cooperatives — alternative organisational forms should also be given ample room to evolve and develop.

Many of these comments apply to non-traditional small industry as well. The general case of encouraging small entrepreneurs on the ground that they are capital saving and therefore economically more efficient has long been contested. Several studies have shown that there is no evidence of capital output ratios being generally lower in small compared to large enterprises; there is in fact no systematic general relation between size and capital output ratios or for that matter total factor productivity. Such advantages as small firms may have in terms of saving on investment could be offset by more than proportionately lower labour productivity and efficiency in use of material and other inputs. On the other hand the quality of products made by small and large units and by different segments of small industry vary and often they cater to different markets.

No generalisation therefore is possible as to where the balance of advantages lies for small enterprises. This is apt to vary across industries. Policy intervention would be more effective if these differences are explicitly taken into account in designing interventions. The broad categorisation suggested as early as the Second Plan — namely industries where large and small industry cater to the same market and are therefore competitive; where they cater to quite distinct markets; and the sub-contracting type situations where two are in a complementary relation — is a good starting point. At the same time policy should recognise that small scale sector itself is not homogeneous; the existence of quality differences and segmentation of markets for products of large and small industry and the fact that competition for the product of one industry is often from products of other industries (using different materials) should be taken into account in formulating industry specific policy.

An integrated intervention policy tailored to the differentiated needs and circumstances of various industries is of course more demanding and will not be easy to accomplish. Apart from this there is a more general question about the desirability of a general discrimination in favour of small industry without knowing what it costs the exchequer, who its real beneficiaries are and the extent to which it promotes healthy development of small enterprise. While it is possible to get a rough idea of the fiscal cost of protecting traditional industry, the cost of tax exemptions and concessions of other segments of small industry in terms of revenue foregone cannot be estimated in the absence of even halfway reliable estimates of the value of production benefitting from these concessions.

Moreover fiscal concessions combined with the reluctance of the state to enforce legislation in respect of wages, benefits and safety on the modern small enterprise sector and subsidised electricity and utilities and the fact that this segment gets more of the institutional credit, confer unfair advantages on larger, better equipped and modern small scale sector in relation to the traditional industries and the so called "tiny" sector generally. One should remember that in several cases (textiles particularly) the two segments are competing with each other. In so far as larger industries set up small units or fragment large units into small units in order to take advantage of the concessions, this policy does not benefit genuine small entrepreneurs. On the other hand it may have a deleterious effect on the efficiency of industry generally.

Improved access to credit is potentially a powerful 'positive' intervention. Following bank nationalisation a conscious effort has been made to enlarge the flow of bank credit to the small industries. While the quantum has recorded impressively large increase, some important weaknesses have also emerged. One is the imbalance between flow of short term and medium/long term loan funds; the latter being abysmally low. The creation of SIDBI is meant to correct this. The benefit of institutional credit appears to accrue disproportionately to the larger units within the small sector. Increasing the flow to the really small units probably runs into resistance because of the large numbers involved, the relatively high cost of administering small loans and the higher risks involved. The attempt on the part of the government to pressure banks into lending more to the tiny sector may have made some difference but it also greatly adds to the risk of politicising decisions about who the specific beneficiaries should be and possibly in pursuing recoveries as well. The apprehension is that this tendency is becoming widespread to a degree which is inimical to sound management of more financial institutions. According to informed opinion the standard of scrutiny and appraisal of loan applications leaves much room for improvement. The phenomenon of widespread and growing sickness among assisted small units surely has something to do with this. All these are important problems which need to be addressed by the banking community and the government. It is the prerogative of the government to lay down general policy and guidelines. While the banks are bound to implement the policy guidelines, they should be free to apply the general principle and guidelines to specific loans objectively and with due regard for the soundness of the borrower.

The effect of existing interventions on the capacity and willingness of small firms to grow also needs greater attention. There is no obvious inhibition for small units to grow upto the unit of investment/employment beyond which their entitlements to fiscal and other concessions cease. But evidence suggests that enterprises are reluctant to expand beyond a level where they will be subjected to the provisions of the factories and associated laws, and forfeit other benefits as small enterprises. There is also a fear that growing beyond a certain size will invite organised union activity adversely affecting both wage rate and ability to control labour. Scattered studies point to a widespread tendency for proliferation of units under the same ownership to avoid these problems. This is clearly inimical to growth of firms and technical progress. Moderating the fiscal gradient between large and small units and better enforcement of minimum wages combined with positive assistance should make for a healthier and a more dynamic small sector.

There is clearly much room for improvement in the positive assistance programmes aimed at raising the productive efficiency, technological dynamism and growth potential of the non-household segment of small industry. By now this sector probably has a couple of million establishments with over 10 million workers. This is the ground where entrepreneurs are getting experience in organising and managing modern industry; and the labour force is acquiring industrial skills. Much of this happened without any significant government involvement. But if these enterprises are to hold their own in the market, and grow, they need to improve efficiency and quality by upgrading skills, better product design, more efficient use of materials and improved marketing organisation. These are par excellence areas where State assistance can make a significant positive contribution. Though they do figure in the existing government programmes, the scale of the effort and the way it is implemented cannot make more than a marginal impact.

Here again, larger, more innovative and industry specific programmes are essential. It is far from obvious that such differentiated flexible programmes tailored to the needs of specific industries can be mounted solely by the state through its machinery. Greater consultation with industry and industry associations and, over a period of time, greater involvement of these bodies in shaping and managing the assistance programmes is essential. Associations of small industry — as indeed similar organisations in other sectors — need to change their role from merely lobbying for this or that concession from the State to the more positive type of collective effort for promoting a healthy, dynamic small scale sector.

Sir Purshotamdas Thakurdas Memorial Lecture, 1990, The Indian Institute of Bankers.

Section – II

Poverty, Inequality and Development Policy

10

Poverty and Development Policy

I

BACKGROUND

THE idea that eradication of abject poverty must be a central concern of public policy has gained wide currency in current academic and public discourse on development. Time was when the focus used to be on the rate and pattern of growth, and on inequalities in distribution of income and wealth. Even as these continue to be important concerns, increasing attention is being given to the extent to which people in individual countries and the world at large are deprived of the minimum requirements for a long, healthy and fulfilling life.

The idea is not new. In India it dates well back into pre-independence era – recall Naoroji's book *Poverty and UN British Rule* – and was prominent in the deliberations of the Congress Party. The National Planning Committee report in fact spelt out in concrete terms the concept and content of minimum living standard. The 15th Indian Labour conference which deliberated on the basis for fixing fair wages also spelt out the constituents of a living wage. A committee on economic policy (headed by Nehru) appointed by the AICC suggested that assurance of a national minimum standard in respect of "all the essentials of physical and social well-being" to every family within a reasonable period of time" should be the practical goal of all schemes of development. The Constitutional provisions on the Directive Principles of State Policy specifically enjoined the government to ensure adequate livelihood and employment, health and nutrition, education and security to the citizens.

However it took a long time for government to define its developmental objectives and policies with reference to these principles. The first three Five-Year Plan documents saw sustained high rates of growth as the principal means to alleviate malnourishment, unemployment, illiteracy and other manifestations of poverty. There was much talk in political rhetoric and in policy pronouncements about reducing inequalities of income and wealth through land reforms, public ownership and control of key sectors, and progressive taxation. But with actual growth proving to be much slower than expected, and redistributive measures proving to be ineffective, the appalling conditions in which the bulk of the population continued to live and the necessity to address their problems seriously came into sharp relief. The late Ram Manohar Lohia dramatised it by calling attention of parliament to the fact that more than half the population subsisted on less than 6 annas per head per day!

In 1962, an unofficial seminar,[1] in which several leading economists, political figures and social activists participated, gave a fresh impetus to the idea that planning should aim at ensuring a minimum standard of living to every one within a reasonable period. They suggested that the national minimum should include a time-bound target of minimum income (Rs. 20 per capita per month in rural areas and about Rs. 25 in urban areas); expenditure on education and health to be provided by the state according to the Constitution[2] transfers and social welfare expenditure to ensure minimum for the poorest 20 per cent of the population who are not likely, for various reasons, to benefit automatically from growth.

Soon thereafter the implications of planning for this minimum living were worked out in a paper[3] prepared by the perspective planning division of the Planning Commission and further elaborated entitled "Notes on Perspectives of Development India's 1960-61 to 1975-76" [GoI, PC, 1964]. The latter was considered but not formally approved by the Planning Commission. In the event, for a variety of reasons (including Nehru's death, the aftermath of military engagements with China and Pakistan, and the droughts) it was shelved. The Fourth Five-Year Plan did not even mention minimum living standard or basic needs!

The late 1960s witnessed a spurt of interest among economists in the study of poverty both at the conceptual and empirical levels. At the conceptual level, questions began to be raised about the validity of using per capita GDP or per capita consumption as a satisfactory measure of well-being. A strong case was made for a much broader concept of 'quality of life' which would include nutritional status, life expectancy and literacy. Attention was also focused on the possibility – based on the example of Kerala in India and Sri Lanka – that the quality of life in the broader sense is not necessarily contingent on high level of income. The factors – largely social and political – which made this possible have attracted much attention and discussion [United Nations 1975; Sen 1981; Bhalla 1988; Streeten and Burki 1978].

The findings of the Mahalanobis Committee [GoI, PC 1964, 1969] and Hazári's study (1967), as is well known, found no reduction in inequalities in consumption, incomes or in concentration of economic power. A number of researchers took up empirical and theoretical studies focused on absolute poverty and strategies to eradicate it. Dandekar and Rath's (1974) well known monograph 'Poverty in India' argued for defining the poverty line on the basis of the minimum income required for nutritional diet and other essentials, provided estimates of the number of people who fell below this line, and outlined a strategy (based on a massive public works programme) to give them the needed additional incomes to reach the minimum. Around the same time a number of others discussed estimates of inequalities in income distribution, incidence of and trends in poverty, conceptual and measurement problems involved, and strategies for tackling poverty.

This research highlighted significant differences in estimates of mean incomes and consumption, inequality indices and poverty incidence obtained from different sources. There was a major controversy over whether or not poverty incidence had declined during the 1960s. This stimulated serious investigation into theoretical aspects of concepts and measurements, the merits and weaknesses of different sources of relevant data, the interrelation between growth, distribution of assets and income, employment and poverty; and different strategies for rapid reduction of poverty.[4] All these themes continue to figure prominently in the ever growing literature on this subject both nationally and internationally. The discussions have of course become more detailed, technically more refined and wider in scope.

By the early 1970s, development economists, both within the country and abroad as well as in international agencies, had veered round to the view that overall growth, while necessary, would not by itself be able to take care of the needs of the poor. The pace of growth is unlikely to be uniform across regions; all segments of the economy and sections of the population are not integrated into the wider economy; and large sections are not equipped (for a variety of reasons) to take advantage of the opportunities arising from growth. Therefore programmes for 'direct attack' on poverty came to be accepted as desirable even by agencies like the World Bank.

This perception did not long remain a matter of academic interest. In India, the set back to the economy during the late 1960s, (slow growth, cut back in investment, inflation), heightened apprehensions of increased inequalities, growing unemployment and worsening of poverty. It happened to coincide with the struggle for political power in the (then dominant) Congress Party. 'Radical' measures, (like bank nationalisation and abolition of privy purses) ostensibly meant to contain the rich, were tried but they were limited in scope and did not mean much to the poor. In this conjuncture, Indira Gandhi sought to broaden her political base by adopting the 'Garibi Hatao' slogan and launching a number of poverty alleviation schemes.

Apart from a Minimum Needs Programme, a number of other initiatives – notably special schemes for small and marginal farmers (later replaced by Integrated Rural Development, IRDP for short), rural employment schemes, mid-day meals for school children, and subsidised public distribution of food and other essential commodities – were launched. Some were new; others essentially were refurbished versions of older schemes. That they did not remain slogans, but were backed by substantial financial allocations made them politically credible. That it struck a positive chord among the people is evident from the resounding electoral success of Congress Party under Indira Gandhi's leadership.[5]

For the first time, assurance of basic minimum needs found an explicit and prominent place in the Fifth Plan. The concept included not only an assurance of purchasing power sufficient to procure a collection of basic items of consumption deemed to constitute 'basic' or 'minimum' collection, but also elementary education for all children up to 14 years of age; minimum public health facilities integrated with family planning and nutrition for children; protected water supply; amenities for landless labour and slum improvement in larger towns; and rural roads and rural electrification.

The idea of direct, targeted poverty alleviation programmes quickly took root and gained widespread acceptance across the entire political spectrum.[6] Governments, at the centre and in the states, have since vied with each other in increasing allocations and devising new schemes (or the same schemes under different names) under this rubric. Along with the number and variety of schemes, financial allocations have also increased progressively. Motivations were of course not as high minded as the slogans made out. They reflect cold political calculations. That the programmes provided opportunities for large-scale, widespread and diffused patronage as well as opportunities for personal gain for political leaders and cadres obviously made them highly attractive to parties in power.

Having reviewed, briefly, the evolution and acceptance of minimum living standard among the objectives of policy in the agenda of political parties as well as governments, we now turn to a consideration of some important issues concerning concepts and measurement of poverty as well as the design and implementation of policies to tackle the problem.

II

CONCEPTUAL ISSUES

In India, there is a broad consensus that the minimum should include (i) a nutritionally satisfactory diet, a reasonable standard of clothing, housing and other 'essentials'; and (ii) access to a minimum level of education, health care, clean water supply and sanitary environment. Norms for specific elements under both categories have been specified. The income necessary for people to afford the elements constituting the first category defines the 'poverty line'. Ensuring the minimum standards for various social services and amenities are deemed to be the responsibility of the state. These concepts as well as the specific content of the minimum standard have gained wide currency in public discourse on development policy. Minimum living standards and poverty are however deceptively simple notions. Complex and contentious issues are involved in deciding the basis on which the minimum bundle is to be determined and valued; whether the status of individuals or households is to be judged in relation to affordability of the bundle as a whole or on the basis of actual consumption/use relative to the norms for individual items; whether the bundle should be uniform or allowances be made for differences in need and circumstances across space and between classes.

Of the various ingredients entering minimum income consumption, food has received the most attention. The emphasis on food is obviously justified. The fact that nutrition experts have worked out the level of nutrients (calories, proteins, fat, etc) necessary for healthy, active functioning of human beings would appear to give an objective basis for determining minimum norms. The normal practice has been to work out the per capita norm for a reference population of specified composition (in terms of age, sex, body size and activity) in rural and urban areas. The appropriateness of a uniform per capita calorie norm has been questioned on the grounds that the relevant characteristics of the population (age and sex composition, body mass and activity) vary across and even within regions and that there are biological mechanisms which enable individuals to adapt to lower intakes, over a sizeable range, without any adverse effects on health or activity.[7] Nevertheless, there is a strong case for such a uniform norm and it rests basically on three grounds:

(1) The purpose of the norm is to help define a standard of consumption which is socially accepted as the minimum desirable. This standard covers not only food but also other items.

(2) A uniform standard provides a common yardstick for comparisons across regions and of directions and relative rates of its change over time. It is also essential for meaningful discussion of the public policy for poverty alleviation and their effectiveness in different regions. This consideration acquires added force when poverty incidence (or the numbers of poor) is used – as it has come to be used – as an important criterion in deciding the sharing of central tax revenues, central government assistance for state plans and also of allocation for poverty alleviation between and (increasingly) within the states.

(3) A standard basket of food products corresponding to the calorie norm also helps comparability. One could in principle estimate the minimum cost food basket taking into account food habits and prices prevailing in different regions. But the practical problems (in terms of information requirement and computational complexity) make it difficult to do so. Reasons of both comparability and convenience therefore argue for using a uniform commodity composition for determining the poverty line. The current practice in India is to use the NSS data on commodity composition of food basket of people whose calorie intake is equal to the nutritional norm. This is done separately for rural and urban area using national level data.[8]

(4) The levels and composition of non-food items included in the minimum standard are taken to be whatever happens to go along with the fulfilment of the calorie norm at the national level. Together they also used to determine the value of per capita consumption expenditure which defines the national poverty line for rural and urban areas. This procedure for determining the non-food components of the minimum is obviously quite arbitrary. Hardly any thought has gone into working out norms for clothing, housing and other elements under this category. The necessity to consider explicitly and systematically the basis for determining levels and components of non-food consumption to be included in the minimum and the need to review and revise the specification of the minimum bundle at periodic intervals hardly needs emphasis.

While there are good reasons for adopting a standard commodity basket comprising the national minimum, there are no good reasons to ignore differences in level and structure of prices between states (and also between rural and urban area) as well as their behaviour over time. On the contrary there is a strong case for taking these into account in as much as the income necessary to afford the minimum consumption bundle is a function of price level and structure. There may also be a case for taking regional differences into account in fixing norms for social amenities. Following the recommendations of the Lakdawala Committee [GoI, PC 1993], the earlier practice of using a single national level poverty line and deflator (to adjust for price changes) for state level estimates has been given up. Instead state level poverty lines, adjusting for differences in base year price levels and deflated on the basis of state-specific price indices, are used.

Ensuring that households have sufficient incomes to acquire

the minimum consumption standard and that norms for publicly provided schools health care and water supply and connectivity are met, does not automatically ensure that people actually obtain and consume the bundle of goods and services or use the amenities as envisaged in the standard. Actual consumption patterns depend on individuals' decisions which are influenced by numerous personal, familial, environmental and cultural factors. If they choose not to acquire the normative minimum bundle the state can do little about it. Furthermore, consumption data, which usually are obtained for the households do not tell us much about what individual members get and whether it meets the minimum standard for them. The extent to which the poor and the underprivileged actually use and benefit from social services and amenities to be provided by the state also depends to a considerable degree on the decision of individual households which in turn is influenced by the economic circumstances and socio cultural attitudes as well as by the quality and cost of services provided by these public facilities. Because of these factors, the actual position of households, including poor households, may differ substantially from the potential for achieving to minimum living standard even where growth and state policies enable them to do so. Such deficiencies cannot be attributed to failure of government policy except insofar as they are the result of deficiencies in design and implementation of government programmes.

At a more fundamental level, minimum incomes and minimum standards of social amenities are not all desired solely or even mainly for their own sakes but for what they do to peoples' well-being.[9] Amartya Sen, who has done so much to clarifying the complex issues involved in the assessment of well-being and suggesting ways to deal with them in a practical way, has strong and persuasive arguments to show that well-being of persons cannot be judged only on the basis of their incomes or access to education and other amenities or of the volume and composition of goods (and services) they have. While these are indeed important, goods and services are not sought for their own make but as means to achieve desired states of what he calls 'being and doing' (such as leading a well nourished, healthy and long life, being well clothed, mobile, able to take informed part in community life, etc). The particular combination of functionings which individuals choose depends on the resources (income) available to them, the different combinations of goods from which they can choose and the kinds of functioning they make possible. Together they define the domain of choice effectively available to individuals which Sen calls 'capabilities'.

The choice within this domain reflects the valuation which individuals place on different kinds of functioning which in turn depends on their personal and social characteristics. Choices are constrained not just by resources at their command but also by social conditioning. The availability and quality of education, healthcare, sanitation, transport/communication networks and other facilities – which are not determined solely by individuals but depend, to an important degree, on the efforts of society and community, governments and non-government organisations – have a direct bearing on peoples' well-being, the choices open to them as well as their perception of the choices. One must also bear in mind that people often have a tendency to restrain their aspirations within limits of what they consider realistically feasible.

The assessment of well-being in a society needs to take into account not only individuals' choices but also assess different social states. The problems involved in doing this are at the heart of the continuing debate among economists and social philosophers. This debate has highlighted the limitations of the market as the arbiter of social states and the difficulties in arriving at a generally acceptable consensus on desirable social states based on a consistent and complete evaluation of available alternatives.

A satisfactory general solution to this problem remains elusive. However, this is much less of a problem in the context of poor countries where large sections do not have adequate and nutritious food, are prone to disease and relatively low life expectancy and are not equipped to access the knowledge and skills needed to function in a complex economy, take advantage of economic opportunities and participate in community life. Under these conditions, it is not surprising that assurance of adequate food (in quantity and quality), basic education and healthcare facilities and connectivity with the outside world figure prominently in the concept of 'minimum living standard' in India and other similarly placed countries. Though, as noted earlier, concretising this and relating it to well-being is a difficult task.

Moreover, if our concern is 'well-being', conventional indicators such as the proportion of population below the poverty line, mean calorie intake, mortality rates, literacy and school enrolment are inadequate basis to assess progress towards poverty eradication. Important as these are, one needs to supplement them with assessments of nutritional and health status, duration of education as well as quality aspects, and gender and group disparities. This calls for considerably wider and more detailed information through surveys to ascertain people's perceptions of their state as well as direct, non-market observations of access to basic goods and functionings at the individual level. There is also a good case to broaden the scope of 'well-being' to cover such aspects as freedom, fresh air, absence of crime, child and women abuse, social peace.

Broadening the notion of well-being and the indicators used to evaluate it has gained currency thanks to the United Nations' Human Development Reports put out by the UNDP. Even those, like the World Bank, who have reservations about preoccupations with poverty and minimum standard of living as the main focus of policy, now include them in their list of development indicators. Increasingly researchers outside government are also broadening the scope of their investigations. However devising objective and measurable indicators for this purpose is daunting and fraught with great difficulties.[10]

III

MEASUREMENT ISSUES

Conceptual problems are compounded by problems of empirical measurement. The Indian statistical system generates an extraordinarily vast and rich amount of data on different aspects of economy and society. The most important and richest source for assessment of poverty and levels of living is the National Sample Survey (NSS). The NSS, which has been in existence for nearly 50 years, has conducted large-scale sample surveys on a variety of subjects relevant for this purpose (ownership of land and other productive assets, household consumption, employment, educational levels, school enrolment, morbidity, health care, access to and the benefit from various programmes meant for the poor and the underprivileged, disability, housing, water supply sources and sanitation). Several of these surveys, particularly those relating to employment and consumption, have been repeated periodically. Published reports provide estimates of mean value of key characteristics and their distributions, as well as their composition for rural and urban areas of the country as a whole and in most cases at the state level. Until recently these were the principal basis for estimation and analysis outside the government. The recent policy decision to make primary household level data available for researchers makes possible vastly more intensive and detailed analyses.

Large-scale sample surveys of household incomes and consumption, education and health have also been done by the National Council of Applied Economics Research (NCAER),[11] though at a lower frequency. The National Nutrition Monitoring Board (NNMB) has been conducting for over 20 years detailed surveys of actual food intake and nutritional status of individuals on a small sample basis in several States.[12] The National Family Health Survey (NFHS) provides detailed information especially on children and women.[13] The ICRISAT survey of 26 villages in semi-arid tropical regions of the country, and a common set of households, for a period of 12 years provides a rare and rich body of panel data on practically every aspect of rural economy.[14] In addition, there are a large number of micro studies assessing the impact of government's poverty alleviation programmes and exploring particular aspects of nutrition, health education and social amenities.

Published reports on NCAER surveys are generally less detailed and give less information on design, concepts and comparability compared to NSS. Far more detailed information and analyses based on them is available for the ICRISAT survey and the NFHS. The primary data from both of them are also freely accessible to researchers. The ICRISAT survey data in particular have been extensively used for exploring – in a degree of detail and depth not feasible with published NSS (and more so NCAER) reports – the characteristics of the poor, adaptations to fluctuations and shocks, transient and permanent poverty, participation and impact in employment schemes and other related issues. Of late the NSS has greatly liberalised access to its primary data which can now be purchased at nominal cost on cd-roms and diskettes. NCAER is also giving researchers access to its primary data.

On the whole, the use of these data have, until recently, tended to focus heavily, if not exclusively, on definition of the poverty line and estimating poverty incidence and its trends. Factors underlying regional and temporal variations in these respects and policy interventions have also been explored but not to the extent one would expect. Other aspects such as gender discrimination, educational participation and attainment, health and nutrition are beginning to greater attention among scholars but do not figure at all in official assessments of the poverty situation.

The methodology of poverty estimates has long been the subject of debate. The first time this came into prominence was in the context of sharply divergent estimates of trends in poverty incidence during the 1960s: one estimate pointing to a significant rising trend in the headcount ratio and another to a falling trend. It was apparent that much of this difference was traceable to the different estimates of mean consumption used by them: one relying on the NSS and the other National Accounts estimate. Systematic differences between the two sources in the estimated consumption expenditure, both overall and for major commodity groups, as well as their time profiles was brought out in the course of that debate.

This led to a critical scrutiny of the assumptions and procedures underlying NSS and official estimates of consumption per head [Kansal 1965; Srinivasan et al 1974; Vaidyanathan 1986; and Minhas 1988]. Significant differences in scope, coverage, data sources and basis of evaluation were identified. Minhas and Kansal (1989) attempted a systematic assessment of the effect of these differences and more importantly the relative merits of estimates for various specific items from these two sources verifying them in some cases with other independent data sources. They also offered several important suggestions to reconcile the differences and for ensuring greater comparability in future. Useful as these are, problems remain.

For one thing the differences in scope of methodology and basic data sources are too large to permit reconciliation or even reasonable degree of comparability. To the extent this is possible, it can be done at best for aggregate private consumption for the country as a whole; nothing can be done about rural-urban or state level estimates.[15] Assessing the relative merits of the two-time series in capturing changes over time is problematic; the scope, concept and assumptions underlying NAS and NSS have both changed over time; and both are prone to errors of observation and estimation of unknown magnitudes.

There have been significant changes in the scope, design and procedure of NSS consumption surveys. The 1950s were a period of experimentation about sampling, questionnaire design, reference periods and the relative merits of single versus multipurpose surveys, which continued into the 1960s when consumption data were for a while compiled through integrated household surveys. There is much greater comparability after the early 1970s when NSS switched to quinquennial consumption-cum-employment surveys. But as we shall see presently, some changes in sampling design and reference periods have raised doubts about comparability of more recent data.

Changes have also been made in the NAS estimates. The changes were no doubt implemented after discussion with experts with a view to ensure firmer empirical base and minimising arbitrary assumptions. While the general consensus is that these have led to significant improvements, serious gaps and weaknesses in basic data remain: the system for obtaining output data for agriculture and even organised industry has visibly deteriorated. State-level estimates suffer from even more serious deficiencies in basic data. The basis for back-casting the series for earlier periods at every revision, though transparent, can hardly be called robust. The arbitrary manner in which estimates for agriculture have been revised recently hardly helps to increase confidence. In view of the above, the revised NAS series cannot be accepted without question and there is certainly no basis to assume that they are better than the NSS.

During the 1970s the Planning Commission – which puts out the official estimate of poverty – reviewed and revised the poverty line essentially by refixing the calorie norms, but did not address the problem of discrepancy between NAS and NSS estimates.[16] Instead it used NAS estimates of consumption expenditure, and NSS estimate of the distribution of population by level of consumption to estimate poverty incidence. That the NAS does not provide separate estimates of consumption for rural and urban areas at the national level, or estimates of even total consumption expenditure of the state level, did not deter them from providing disaggregated estimates of poverty. The highly arbitrary and questionable assumptions underlying this procedure were highlighted by the Lakdawala Committee [GoI, PC 1993].

This committee examined the possibilities of cross validation of NAS and NSS estimates. They noted that even if one could find a satisfactory procedure for reconciling the differences in estimates of aggregate consumption and making appropriate adjustments to in the estimate of size distribution, problems arising from '...differences in coverage, time period classification schemes and implicit prices...' will remain. Adjusting NAS to get state-level estimates and estimates for rural and urban areas would involve far too many arbitrary assumptions. They noted that the NSS gives statewise estimates of size distribution and commodity composition of consumption for rural and urban areas separately derived from surveys which are carefully organised, use uniform concepts and procedures across the country and sampling is rigorous. While NSS data are not free from errors and sustained efforts to improve their quality is essential, it remains the best available source for assessing poverty incidence and characteristics of the poor across space and time. They therefore suggested that "if estimates of incidence are to be made with minimum recourse to adjustments based on arbitrary assumptions, the best course would be to base them entirely on the NSS". The Planning Commission has since accepted these recommendations and official estimates of poverty are based entirely on the NSS.

During the 1970s and 1980s the NAS and NSS showed similar, though not identical, time profiles of change in mean consumption at the national level. Using NSS estimates of inequality, both showed a declining trend in the headcount ratio. However, the NSS, whose estimate of mean consumption was lower and its rise considerably slower than the NAS, showed poverty incidence to be higher and declining much more slowly than the official estimate.[17] But since both showed a decline, the relative reliability of the two sources did not figure prominently in the debate.

But after 1987-88 the NSS began providing annual estimates of mean consumption as well. This shows no significant trend in either inequality or mean per capita consumption in rural areas, and therefore in the incidence of poverty. In urban areas, according to NSS, poverty has declined largely because of an increase in per capita real consumption. Overall poverty incidence in the country has not changed significantly. That this happened during the decade of major changes in economic policy and despite the relatively high rate of overall growth indicated by NAS is cited by critics of the reforms as evidence of its anti-poor character. The reliability of NSS data in capturing changes in consumption levels and distribution has, therefore, again become an issue.

While the NAS estimate of consumption no longer enters poverty estimation, the striking difference between the time profile of consumption growth during the 1990s obtained from it and that of the NAS deserves notice. This comparison, which is possible only at the national level, shows that while according to NAS, per capita real consumption expenditure increased progressively at an average annual rate of over 2 per cent during the 1990s, the NSS showed an erratic trend and a much smaller rise.[18] However, using the same deflation procedures, the movement of the two series based on the quinquennial data from 1973-74 to 1993-94 turn out to be more or less similar. Therefore the divergence between two in the 1990s seems unlikely to be due to deflation procedure. We have to look for other explanations, in terms of changing designs, procedures and biases in the NSS itself.

One aspect of the post 1988 NSS series which has attracted notice is that, except for 1993-94, they are based on so-called thin samples. In the quinquennial surveys, whose primary focus is consumption and employment, the sample size is large enough to provide state level estimates at an acceptable margin of sampling error. In other years consumption and employment data are canvassed on a much smaller sample, and subsidiary to the main theme which varies each year. Sampling and survey design being the same, the smaller size of the sample in the annual surveys by itself should not make any difference to the reliability or comparability of their national estimates with those of large samples. The fact that the primary focus of annual surveys is on other subjects could however affect the quality of consumption data obtained through them: Being secondary themes the investigators and their supervisors may not give as close an attention to this part of the survey as for the primary theme.

While this may increase the scope for non-sampling errors, there is no basis to suppose that they would affect the nature or extent of such bias NSS data may be generally prone to. There is a widespread belief that richer households tend to be less cooperative and tend to underestimate their consumption more than the poor. But we do not have information to test the validity of this supposition and how large its magnitude is. Unfortunately, despite repeated suggestions, NSS does not provide information on the relative incidence of non-response or the characteristics of non-responding households, nor the investigator's impressions about the cooperativeness of the respondents and their willingness to provide information. Unless the under reporting bias of richer households in the thin sample rounds is higher for either of these reasons, and has increased over time, there is no reason to question comparability of the series on this ground.

It is also arguable that the underestimates of consumption by the rich does not affect the poverty estimates so long as the not-so-well-to-do people report their consumption correctly. The rich may have an incentive to understate much more than the poor. While this is true, it needs noting that if NAS estimate is correct, and the poor accurately (or at least far more accurately than the better off) report their consumption to NSS, the degree of underestimation by the rich, and therefore inequalities, must have increased. But this is pure conjecture.[19]

Changes in sampling, reference periods, questionnaire design, and interview procedures can however make a difference. A significant change in sampling design allowing for stratification of households according to broad income class, and a higher sampling fraction of richer households, did take place in the 1980s. But this should not affect the comparability of the series from the late 1980s through 1998 unless – let me repeat – the degree of non-response or non-cooperation of the better-off can be shown to have increased.

Another source of non-comparability is changes in reference period. That the length of the reference period affects the respondents' estimate is well known. After some initial experimentation, the NSS decided on a uniform 30-day reference period for all items of consumption and kept to this practice for nearly 30 years. In the 1980s this aspect was again reviewed. The effect of changing reference period from 30 days to one year on the responses regarding consumption of clothing and durables was tested by canvassing two independent sets of sample households. The differences were expectedly substantial. Subsequently, from 1991, this experiment was extended to all commodities getting information from two independent subsamples one on the basis of a 30-day reference period for all commodities and another using different reference periods for different commodity groups. This was expected to assess the direction and magnitude of difference in reported consumption with different reference periods. Reference periods did indeed make a difference, more in some commodity groups and less in others. The difference in reported consumption of food, drink and tobacco based on a 30-day reference and seven-day reference period turned out to be quite large, the latter being much higher. In the case of clothing and durables, the figure reported with 30-day reference period was lower, and substantially lower in the case of durables, than for the 365-day reference period. Such exercises are essential to provide a basis, after systematic analysis and, if need be, further experimentation with different sets of reference periods, to improve the survey design. So long as this is done on independent sub-samples we get a comparable series using the prevailing practice and the difference changes make to the magnitude. When the prevailing practice is changed we also have a clear basis to link the earlier and the new series without losing comparability.

While these precautions were taken care of up to 1998,[20]

the large sample survey of 1999-2000 made a significant departure by canvassing information on consumption using two different reference periods, on all sample households. This, it has been rightly pointed out, vitiates the estimates obtained from the latest survey and makes it difficult to compare them with those of earlier surveys including the 1993-94 surveys. Those, like me, who believed that a comparison of the 1999-2000 results with those of 1993-94 ratio provide a better basis to assess the impact of reforms on consumption levels, inequality and poverty at the national and state levels are understandably dismayed!

As already mentioned large-scale surveys of household income, consumption and several other aspects have also been done by NCAER. Estimates of mean consumption, inequalities and poverty incidence reported on the basis of these surveys differ significantly from the ones widely in use: For instance 1968-69 survey [Bhatty 1974] found per capita consumption close to the official estimates, but there were large differences compared to NSS rankings of states by levels of consumption expenditure and inequalities. Based on panel survey of rural households at 2 different time points (1970-71 and 1980-82), NCAER concluded that incomes have grown considerably across all classes; (and more so at the lower end) and that poverty had declined substantially more than shown by NSS [NCAER 1987]. There are obvious and large differences in scope, aims design and methods between NSS and NCAER surveys [Bhatty 1974] and between NCAER surveys at different points of time [Bhalla 1988; Pradhan et al 2000].[21] These differences have not attracted the degree of critical scrutiny which one would have expected.

That different sources, using different methods, give quite different estimate is confusing. Much greater attention must be given to assessing the purposes, concepts and methods underlying different data sets, their reliability and suitability for generating reasonably comparable estimates of mean consumption and inequality. The scope for confusion could be reduced if these details were available for critical scrutiny by scholars and informed analysis of the reasons for differences in the estimates. Better still if different survey organisations get together and agreed on minimum degree of comparability in scope and concepts in the conduct of such surveys.

With the best of efforts, however, these issues cannot be fully resolved. The fact is that here is nothing like perfectly accurate and reliable data. The challenge is to make ingenious use of imperfect, incomplete information subject to sizeable, and often unknown, margins of error and to squeeze such insights as we can legitimately extract from them. Plurality of data sets is useful as cross checks. If independent sources reveal the same or similar patterns we can be more confident of the patterns they indicate. But it is necessary to recognise and allow for defects and non-comparability and to maintain pressures to ensure the integrity and transparency of the statistical system.

An equally important lesson to be drawn is not to be preoccupied exclusively, or even primarily, on poverty incidence as the sole index of well-being. It is necessary to broaden our inquiries to cover other aspects which affect and reflect well-being; and to pay much more attention to the characteristics of those at the bottom of the socioeconomic pyramid, how their conditions are changing and how effective public interventions are in improving their conditions and opportunities.

It is for these reasons that the Lakdawala Committee recommended that, apart from estimates of the proportion and number of poor, a fuller picture of the living conditions and well-being of the poor must cover the following aspects:

(i) The composition of the poor population in terms of

dominant characteristics, i.e., their distribution by region, social group, family characteristics (e g, size, education, age, sex of household head, dependency ratio) and the way this is changing over time. Much of this can be done by appropriate tabulation of NSS employment and consumption survey data.

(ii) Nutritional status of the population; levels of intake of principal nutrients, incidence of malnourishment, anthropometric measurements and activity patterns by age, sex and socioeconomic categories. This can be done by the National Institute of Nutrition.

(iii) Health status: mortality (overall, infant and child, maternal); morbidity; access to and use of health services (public and private) and costs. The quinquennial surveys of public consumption as well as mortality indicators based on the Sample Registration System and the morbidity surveys of NSS need to be put on a systematic and continuing basis.

(iv) Educational status: school enrolment by region, sex and age group and by economic social class; reach and quality of public education services and costs. Here again information from the NSS social consumption enquiries and the all-India Education Surveys suitably restructured would provide the basic data.

(v) Living Environment: distribution by density of settlement: living space per head; type of houses; access to safe drinking water and sanitation; access to amenities (post office, telephones, railway, pucca road, markets, etc).

The committee further suggested the preparation of a 'State of Poverty' report every five years covering the above aspects and highlighting the condition of the poorest 30 per cent of the country's population. Unfortunately there area as yet no signs of these suggestions being implemented by the Planning Commission.

IV

CORRELATES AND DETERMINANTS

Having discussed the problem of data and measurement at length and cautioned about assessments of changes in overall poverty incidence, I would like now to turn to what we have learnt from the available data, and from studies based on them, about incidence of poverty, its characteristics and determinants.

It is indisputably clear that a large proportion of the country's population cannot afford the bundle of good and services including food, education, health which constitute the currently accepted norms of minimum living standard. The deficiencies both in absolute and relative terms are considerably larger in rural India than in urban areas. It is also evident that in rural India asset-poor households, those dependent mainly on wage labour, and those with relatively large families and a high proportion of children relative to adults figure far more prominently among the poor than those with land (especially those with relatively large holdings), self employed in non-agricultural activities and those with better education. Scheduled castes/tribes households, being disadvantaged on all these counts, have a considerably higher incidence of poverty then other groups [Visaria 1978, 1979; Lipton 1981].

Poverty incidence shows large variations across states. In 1993-94, rural poverty incidence varied from about 2 per cent in the Punjab to 58 per cent in Bihar. Broadly speaking the proportion of rural population living below the poverty line is higher than the national average in east and central India and well below the average in the southern states. About two-fifths of the country's rural poor are concentrated in Bihar, Orissa, MP and West Bengal. The NSS data also show the rate of poverty reduction in these states to be much slower than in others. This implies an increase in the geographical concentration of poverty.

Overall poverty incidence in rural areas seem to be largely a reflection of differences in mean per capita incomes across states and less to inequalities within states [Bhattacharya et al 1988]. More detailed analysis using household level data from an NCAER survey [Gaiha 1988] suggests that the likelihood of a household being poor is influenced by the social and economic infrastructure of the village they live in, some characteristics of agricultural technology and the demographic and other feature of the household. The effect of agricultural technology being the largest followed by household characteristics. Both are seen to have a more marked influence on poverty incidence among cultivator households than other categories. The relative importance of factors varies between different groups.

Tendulkar and Sundaram (1988) constructed and estimated a model to assess the impact of demographic pressure on land (the principal productive resource of rural areas), value of productive assets per head and inequality in their distribution, productivity of land, wage labour incidence, employment and interactions among them in accounting for variations in rural poverty. Estimates of the reduced form of the model showed that poverty incidence tends to be lower (to a statistically significant extent) in regions with relatively low demographic pressure (low land man ratio), higher productive assets per head and more equal distribution of these assets. Other things being the same, the higher productivity per unit of land goes with lower poverty incidence. This line of approach to understanding determinant of rural poverty, with refinements to take into account price differentials, the determinants of land productivity, diversification of employment and such other elements seems promising. But not much further work on these lines has been done since.

Attempts to explain trends in rural poverty incidence in terms of trends in agricultural production and prices have given some useful insights. The factors underlying them have also been extensively examined but for reasons already cited the conclusions are much less robust. An early attempt along these lines [Ahluwalia 1978] found that at the all- India level there was a significant negative relation between the value added by agriculture per head of rural population and rural poverty ratio; and that there was also a significant element of secular decline over time on account of other (unspecified) factors. Subsequently Ahluwalia (1986) showed that the price index for the poor relative to the average for the population also has a significant bearing on rural poverty trend: the higher this index, the higher the poverty. But in this case there is no time trend independent of production and prices. At the state level the inverse relation between agricultural production and poverty was found to hold in several but not all states.[22]

The rationale for inclusion of price and its specification has evoked a lively debate [Mellor and Desai (eds) 1988]. The argument for taking the overall inflation rate as an explanatory variable is not clear. Presumably it would impact on poor via the wage rate. But this depends on the extent and rapidity with which rural wage rates adjust to changes in the general price level. Very little is however known about this. Moreover, as many have pointed out, changes in consumer price index for the poor relative to that of the better off may be more relevant than the general rate of inflation. A better specification (and one used in several recent studies)[23] would be the relative price of food to non-food items in as much as food dominates the poor's consumption and accounts for a much higher proportion of expenditure than the better off.

Till recently the debate on rural poverty focused mainly on agriculture and has been marked by an underlying concern that emerging patterns of technology and production tend to increase inequalities and that therefore agricultural growth may not automatically reduce poverty. The HYV-fertiliser-irrigation centred strategy was, and to some degree still is, widely believed to be biased against small and marginal farmers and the growing class of wage labourers. Relatively small farms cannot afford the resources needed to make effective use of the new technology. Also the new technology does not generate fast enough increase in employment opportunities to absorb the growth of labour force particularly for the burgeoning class of wage labourers. This led to predictions of increased unemployment, reduced real wages and worsening inequalities in rural areas. And in the context of relatively slow growth in the rest of the economy, this tendency was expected to spill over into the non-agricultural sector and urban areas as well. The evidence from actual experience is mixed.[24] Access to irrigation has traditionally been relatively higher among small holdings compared to large ones. But during the last three decades irrigated area has increased much faster than average among larger farms. This would tend to accentuate inequalities. There is also evidence of increased inequality in the distribution of operational holdings in some areas due to dispossession of tenants and the spread of 'reverse' leasing. On the other hand the adoption ratio of HYV and fertilisers, which used to be relatively low on small farms compared to large farms in the early stages of their spread, is no longer so. This narrowing difference in adoption of bio-chemical technology offsets the impact of large farmer bias in irrigation, though to what extent remains an open question.

Agricultural employment has increased much slower than agricultural output partly because of the spread of mechanisation. Over time this tendency seem to have intensified. While the share of wage labour in total rural labour force has increased rapidly, agricultural employment has remained virtually stagnant. However, the expected worsening in rural unemployment and in real wage rates has not materialised. On the contrary, non-farm employment has risen at a surprisingly rapid rate during 1970s and 1980s and real wage rates have everywhere risen.

This has led to broadening the scope of the explanatory hypotheses regarding determinants of rural poverty to include the extent of non-agricultural employment (which captures differences in the degree of diversification in the rural economy), commercialisation, real wage rates and public development expenditure. But specifications vary in terms of the variables included without a convincing a priori basis to choose between them. Most of them do well in terms of the proportion of variance explained (R squares exceeding 85-90 per cent) in both national time series and pooled state cross section and time series. The coefficients for individual variables have the expected signs and are statistically significant [Ravillion and Datt op cit and Abhijit Sen op cit].

It is noteworthy, however, that inequality in distribution of productive resources or determinants of labour supply and demand do not figure in these exercises in the manner attempted by Tendulkar and Sundaram. There are also data problems arising from the marked deterioration in the system for compiling official agricultural statistics. The levels and, more importantly, time profiles of change in agricultural output per rural person and NSS estimates of real consumption per capita are often dissimilar. Also as noted earlier, changes in scope, methods and basis of estimation, which affect both NSS and Official estimates, vitiate comparability across different periods and raise questions about the validity of time series analysis especially for long periods as done in some world bank studies.

Poverty studies deal mostly with rural areas. Urban poverty has received comparatively less attention even at a descriptive level.[25] Available surveys show urban areas to have a higher level of mean per capita consumption as well as higher inequality. Mean per capita consumption in urban areas is higher and more unequally distributed than in rural India. Regional variations in both respects are marked: poverty incidence being higher than average in Bihar, MP and Orissa and less than average in Assam, Punjab, Haryana and West Bengal.

There seems to be no significant association, across states, between poverty incidence and mean consumption. However, states where urban poverty incidence is persistently higher than the national average, price levels as well as inequalities are higher than average; the contrary being the case in those where urban poverty rate is persistently below national average. In both cases differences in inequality are more important than price differentials [Minhas et al 1988].

NSS data point to a progressive decline in urban poverty since the early 1970s reflecting a modest rising trend in mean per capita consumption without any significant change in the inequality index [Datt 1999]. The trend towards urban poverty reduction is noticed in all states but in varying degrees. The differences largely reflect differences in the pace of increase in mean per capita consumption; there seems to be no significant urban trend in inequality in most states.

Factors underlying regional and temporal variations in urban poverty have not been explored even to the limited extent attempted in the case of rural areas.[26] Very little is known about the characteristics of the urban poor. There are isolated location specific studies of the informal sector, slum and pavement dwellers. But these need to be considerably expanded in scope and integrated into a wider framework to better understand urban poverty. Here perhaps the focus of comparative studies could be on towns of different sizes and different degrees of economic dynamism. Understanding urban poverty naturally would also require greater attention to the migration patterns and more generally to the nature of rural – urban linkages in terms of commodity, income and labour flows.

Refinement in mapping and analysis of income poverty is necessary but not sufficient. Their scope needs to be widened to include different aspects of the poor's well-being in its broader sense. Also deeper investigations are necessary to understand how the poor and the underprivileged cope with vicissitudes how they adapt to reduction in employment and incomes, how far they are able to take advantage of opportunities opened by the growth of the economy and various poverty alleviation and affirmative action policies of the government.

Some aspects – notably food intake and nutrition, transient and chronic poverty, gender disparities, literacy and educational levels, and access to health care – have been the subject of study based both on macro data and in depth micro-level studies. But there is much room for extending and refining such work and making them an integral part of the effort to better understand the nature and role of socio-economic deprivation. Trends in level and composition of food intake, both overall and for different fractile groups, intra-family allocation of food (especially between males and females), the effectiveness of special nutrition programmes and subsidised food supply and the relation between food intake and nutritional status have attracted much attention.[27] Despite their limitations, the mean level of calorie intake and the proportion of population with intakes below the calorie norm continue to be widely used as an indicator of nutritional status of the population. The NSS data show a trend of decline in calorie intake of the better off and the very low elasticity of calorie consumption even among the poorer groups, whose calorie intake remains well below the norms. There have also been significant shifts in the pattern of consumption, including (especially among the poor) from food to non-food items, from cereals to more costly non-cereal foods and, within cereals, from cheaper to more expensive grains.[28] But there has been hardly any serious investigation of the factors underlying these changes or their impact on health and nutritional status.

If the data on food consumption trends of the poorer segments is correct, one must explain why, despite near stagnation of calorie intake, there are no signs of deterioration in height, weight, health or activity indicators even in states, which, by all indicators are very poor.[29] Surprisingly this apparent puzzle has not attracted much attention.

Nutritional status obviously cannot be judged by food intake levels alone. Education, safe drinking water, hygiene, incidence and control of infections – all of which have a bearing on how efficiently food is utilised – must be taken into account. While the standards in all these respects are no doubt far below desired levels, improvements have taken place partly as a result of public policy and partly the spread in availability and use of antibiotics. Both may have contributed to an overall improvement in nutritional status despite stagnation in calorie intake at low levels. This is only a conjecture whose validity (especially for the poorer socio-economic groups) needs much closer investigation.

On other aspects of living standards – eg, clothing, housing, education, water supply/sanitation, and health facilities – considerable amount of information is available in numerous surveys and studies based on them. Literacy rates, enrolment and intention of children in school, mean years of schooling, costs, inter-group disparities and other aspects of education are well documented [PROBE Team 1998; Vaidyanathan and Nair (eds) 2001]. So are mortality rates, morbidity, availability and use of public and private health care facilities in different regions and socio-economic groups. We know that, while considerable improvement has taken place in most of these respects, they are generally inadequate and highly uneven with rural areas and poorer sections of the population invariably reporting lower access and use the facilities and at a higher cost relative to their incomes, than the rich.[30] These data sources, and analytical studies to interpret factors underlying spatial and temporal variations, need to be given a much more prominent place in the study of poverty and well-being. Another example relates to the attempt at differentiating between different types of poverty (seasonal and annual; transient and persistent; poor and ultra poor).[31] Macro surveys can tell us little, if at all, on these matters or of the process underlying them. Only detailed micro-level inquiries and panel type surveys can provide the needed information. We do have some micro studies which give an idea of diverse strategies that poor people adopt to tide over bad years and lean seasons. They include maintaining emergency reserves, borrowing, sale of assets, migration, changing nature, and intensity of activity and altering intra-fairly food allocation. Panel surveys have been used to focus on households who are persistently below the poverty line [Gaiha 1988].

The role of formal and informal social security mechanisms to take care of the aged, disabled and widows among the poor is attracting increasing attention in research and policy discourses. The coverage, organisation and scale of arrangements for the organised sector are best documented. Descriptive accounts of informal and traditional social mechanisms (family, kin networks, charitable institutions) as well as of various government sponsored pension and insurance schemes for the poor are available.[32] But critical studies of their working and impact have not received as much attention.

The nature, extent and manifestations of persistent gender disparities in access to family resources for food, education and health care have been extensively documented and commented on.[33] The deprivations and disadvantages suffered by underprivileged social groups (especially scheduled castes and tribes, artisans) are also well documented. That they figure prominently among the poor and are prone to various forms of 'exclusion' which handicaps them in taking advantage of opportunities generated by growth and that they are specially vulnerable to the introduction of new products and processes is well known.

There is compelling evidence that the position of these groups in terms of practically every indicator of well being remains much below the average. However the evidence also shows that there have been substantial improvements and, in some respects at least, a substantial narrowing of the gap between them and the rest of the population.[34] The extent of this phenomenon however varies considerably between and within regions. The reasons for these variations in the extent and manner in which some segments of this excluded groups are able to improve their condition while others continue in chronic deprivation; the way affirmative action and other government interventions meant to mitigate their disadvantages actually work; and the reasons why, even when basic amenities are in place, some groups do not make effective use of them deserve far more attention than they have received so far.

V

POLICY

Some people – especially among those who see rapid overall economic growth as both a necessary and sufficient condition for eradicating poverty and who see excessive state intervention as the major impediment to growth – consider this obsession with poverty, and counting the number of poor, as distracting attention and resources from growth promoting policies. The government according to them should confine itself to ensuring law and order, enabling markets to function freely, facilitating free trade and capital movements and providing universal elementary education, health care, water supply, sanitation and essential infrastructure. On the other hand they question the efficacy of various poverty alleviation programmes and, by implication, the justification for spending huge amounts on social programmes. These arguments are fundamentally flawed.

Growth – necessary as it is – does not 'benefit' automatically and in equal proportion to all regions and sections of the population. For a variety of reasons – historical factors, resource endowments, social and political conjunctures and, of course, government policy – growth happens to be very uneven across regions. This fact is beyond dispute. It also happens that regions which are poorly developed to begin with have also grown at a slower rate than average. This tendency cannot be dismissed as an inevitable but transitional phase which will get corrected over time. Nor can one accept the proposition that so long as there is no decline in level of development in any region and all record some improvement, there is no need for intervention. Such a proposition, apart from being questionable on merits, is politically unacceptable in a democracy. Concern for equity and political necessity are compelling arguments for government intervention to correct the imbalance.

This argument acquires even greater force in relation to people: both as a proportion of the population and in absolute terms, those who do not have and cannot afford even the quite modest minimum living standard currently accepted as the norm in the Indian context are very large. And they happen to be concentrated in the poor regions, among sections of the population who suffer the cumulative consequences of systematic exclusion and the attendant social and economic disadvantages. That basic needs and minimum living standards figure so prominently not only in rhetoric of all political parties, but also in the sizeable public resources committed for this purposes is a reflection of both moral and political compulsions.

The evolution of policies and programmes meant to tackle this problem may be haphazard and in some respects even incoherent. Nevertheless one can see a clear pattern in the way they seek to recognise and address differing needs of backward areas with special problems, and of different segments of the poor and underprivileged. Broadly they can be divided into the following groups:

(1) Affirmative action by way of reservations for scheduled castes and tribes in elected bodies, public sector jobs and educational institutions supplemented by special programmes, with earmarked allocations, for their development and welfare.

(2) Programmes (notably IRDP, TRYSEM, DWACRA) designed to help poor segments to acquire or add to their productive assets and enable them to make more productive use of such assets.

(3) Various special programmes to provide additional employment to the poor.

(4) Schemes to ensure that all villages have access to a minimum standard of educational and health facilities, safe drinking water and roads.

(5) Various forms of direct transfers by pension and insurance schemes for aged, disabled and widows, school feeding and child nutrition programmes and subsidised distribution of foodgrains and other essential commodities to the poor.

(6) Special programmes for the development of production potential for hill tracts, deserts and drought prone areas.

For the most part these programmes are conceived and funded by the central government which determines the criteria for allocation between states (and in some cases within states). Actual implementation is left to the state government agencies subject to guidelines (sometimes quite detailed) regarding the scope and content of schemes, and their targeting and implementation procedures. Only a few (notable being the Maharashtra Employment Guarantee Scheme and Tamil Nadu's Midday Meals Programme for school children) have been taken up entirely at the initiative of states.

Over the years the functioning of these programmes and their impact on the poor has attracted a great deal of attention. Numerous studies - several under the auspices of the government, and many more based on independent surveys, micro studies and analyses of available macro data - have highlighted their achievements as well as weaknesses.[35] A healthy and wholesome feature is the extraordinarily free and open discussion of deficiencies of particular schemes, the relative merits of different interventions and suggestions for restructuring and reorientation.

Official claims of the number of beneficiaries, works carried out, additions to productive assets and employment generated are unreliable and exaggerated. Poor targeting is reflected in the high proportion of non-poor and other non-eligible persons among the beneficiaries. Leakages due to inappropriate works, inefficient implementation and corruption are high. Quality of assets provided/created under these programmes is poor and their impact on income level of beneficiaries dubious. Assets and schemes are frequently not appropriate to the needs and potentials of particular regions or groups. There is little consultation with, not to speak of involvement of local communities generally and target groups in particular, in deciding and implementing schemes. Lack of accountability remains a major problem. The structure, content and funding of these programmes remain mostly in the hands of the central government. There is considerable overlap among these schemes as well as between them and development schemes included under the normal state plans. Typically each programme is administered by a separate agency, each with its own line hierarchy and operating independently. These features, taken together with the rigidity of central guidelines, make for fragmentation and duplication of schemes. Coordination is difficult; so is monitoring of accomplishments in terms of efficacy of targeting, quality of works actually completed and impact on the beneficiaries.

The programmes tend to emphasise loans and subsidies and provision of current wage employment rather than ensuring that they are used to augment productive capacity for achieving a higher level of employment and income on a sustained basis. The selection of beneficiaries, the distribution of loans and subsidies, and the recovery of loans offer much scope for patronage and corruption at the political and bureaucratic levels.

The public distribution system (PDS) does not accomplish its ostensible aim of ensuring essential consumer goods to the poor at reasonable prices. Large parts of the country (especially states which have the largest concentration of poor) simply to not have a distribution network to reach the supplies where they are most needed. In states (Kerala, West Bengal, Tamil Nadu) which have such networks, the coverage is not limited to the poor. And attempts to ensure better targeting have been thwarted by administrative difficulties and political opposition. The efficiency of PDS as a poverty alleviation measure and the desirability of continuing it in the present form is being questioned. Supporters of PDS, who see it as a major instrument for ensuring food security for the poor, strongly oppose this prescription even as they recognise the need for restructuring the programme.[36]

These widely known and documented deficiencies have given poverty alleviation programmes a bad name. Critics argue – some explicitly and more by implication – that the effective contribution of these schemes to sustained poverty reduction is not commensurate with the resources spent on them. That given the high level of fiscal deficits and the severe shortage of resources for infrastructural investments needed for overall growth, the country can ill afford this luxury.

It is certainly true that outlays on targeted poverty alleviation programmes have increased rapidly both in absolute terms and relative to total public sector plan outlay. Prior to 1970, these were limited to special schemes for nutrition scheduled castes and tribes, social welfare, backward areas, and a minuscule rural works programme during the Fourth Plan (1969-74). Total outlay for these was Rs 6 billion, or less than 4 per cent of public sector plan. During the Eighth Plan (1992-1997), the outlay on a vastly larger and more varied poverty alleviation programme amounted to Rs 460 billion (about 11 per cent of the total public sector plan).[37] Also, outlays on PA programmes have grown considerably faster than total plan outlay in a period marked by severe infrastructure shortage and bottlenecks. However large these figures might seem, the fact remains that they account for barely 1 per cent of the GDP, and barely a sixth of the gross fiscal deficit of the centre and the states put together. The public sector resource crisis cannot be laid at the door of PA programmes. The more important and deeper causes lie in the falling tax to GDP ratio, the inability to contain runaway increase in revenue expenditures and the huge and burgeoning deficits incurred in providing public services.[38] All of these are due to policies – be it taxation, salaries and allowances of public sector employees, subsidised supply of water and power – which largely benefit the better off segments in fact the top quintile of the population. A disproportionate share of the food and fertiliser subsidies also accrue to the better off. Under these conditions cutting back the allocation for poverty alleviation is no solution to the fiscal problem; and it is certainly not justified morally or politically.

This is not to deny the need and immense scope for improving the efficacy of poverty alleviation programmes by better targeting, reducing waste and corruption, making the programmes more meaningful in terms of relevance to local needs and priorities, and creating institutional conditions for greater accountability. The focus should be on rationalising the approach, organisation and priorities of the PA programmes rather than on cutting back the outlays.[37] The number of PA programmes can, and should, be drastically reduced and streamlined to minimise duplication and fragmentation. We need distinguish only between 3 and 4 basic PA programme categories: (1) Those which are meant to ensure that all communities in the country have a minimum standard of school, primary health care, water supply, sanitation and connectivity. (2) Those which are meant to enable resource poor segments of the population to acquire productive assets and to use them effectively. (3) Programmes to provide additional employment opportunities to those poor who do not have productive assets and depend on wage employment. And (4) programmes to enable scheduled castes and tribes to take advantage of educational and health facilities so that they are better equipped to take advantage of growing opportunities.

There are already accepted norms of minimum standards mainly in terms of distance of each community from each facility as well as physical facilities and personnel at delivery points. The norms may in some cases need review and redefinition. Once this is done, a comparison between existing ground situation and the norms would provide an objective basis for identifying, fairly precisely, the areas and locations which are deficient, as well as quantify the extent and nature of the deficiencies. Investment in physical facilities to make up these deficiencies should of course be part a national Minimum Needs Programme. But creating physical facilities will not suffice. The tasks of ensuring that the prescribed staff are in position, that they function regularly and well, that the underprivileged segments can readily access them and get proper attention are equally important. These will need action in the sphere of administrative reform and social mobilisation.

Category 2 covers the present IRDP and also special area programmes: The former, which provide loans and subsidies for purchase of non-land assets by the poor, has proved to be wasteful and far less effective than expected. The latter are meant to develop productive resources in drought prone, desert and hill areas to facilitate more effective use of resources and open up opportunities for increased production in a variety of activities. These two have not been effective partly because they overlap with schemes which are part of the sectoral programmes and also because of poor design and implementation. All these schemes are in need of drastic change.

IRDP in its present form deserves to be scrapped.

Identification of poor, the kinds of assets to be provided, ensuring the back up needed for their programme cannot, as experience has shown, be managed efficiently by government. The difficulties are compounded when they involve heavy subsidies and are implemented by a bureaucracy open to political interference. Instead, public investment ought to concentrate on providing infrastructure to facilitate overall development in each region according to its resource potential thereby opening up greater and more diverse opportunities for employment and entreprenurial activity.

The poor of course need special help by way of information, technical advice and training to take advantage of growing investment opportunities. The government has a key role in providing this help. But it is neither necessary nor desirable for the government to decide what assets are to be provided, to whom and on what terms. These tasks are better left to individual's choices. Those who want to invest in any enterprise can seek credit from financial institutions who must be left free to judge the viability of the loan and the borrowers. The government's role here would be essentially to lay down guidelines (such as priority sector lending) and providing interest subsidies or insurance of loans given to the poor.

There is also a strong case for including land among the assets eligible for institutional credit for the rural landless and land poor. Redistribution of land through conventional approach to land reforms has not worked and seems unlikely to make much headway. However, the spread of education among the bigger farmers is leading to increasing migration to urban areas; they are also seen to be investing their surplus in non-agricultural activities. The resulting weakening of their economic stake as well as their power in the village communities is creating a situation where they are willing to sell their land. This process has already occurred on a significant scale in several parts of the country and seems to be spreading. In such a situation, asset poor households wanting to acquire land – the most important productive resource in rural areas- deserves as much emphasis in poor-oriented credit programmes as for the acquisition of other assets or setting up other enterprises.

The rationale for special area programmes as a separate category is also questionable. Practically all the components of these programmes figure in the sectoral programmes. Scrapping the special area programme and merging them into sectoral and area development programmes will make for more effective use of public funds by eliminating dysfunctional and wasteful fragmentation of resources and effort. From the view point of poverty alleviation, agriculture and related activities are the most important. The scale and content of these programmes should however be tailored to the diverse resource potentials in different regions and constraints impeding their realisation. This is the rationale for watershed development and planning on the basis of agro-climatic regions. But these are at present no more than in name. If these are pursued seriously and the organisational arrangements for planning are recast on that basis, there is really no need for special area (or for that matter special crop specific) schemes.

In implementing integrated regional resource planning, it would be perfectly legitimate to earmark allocations, and even provide special extra funds, for use in regions which rank low in terms of per capita income and employment. The distribution of funds between regions must however be based not only on needs, but also potential for development of land, water and livestock resources as part of integrated area development plans.

Employment schemes can all be merged into one and allocations between and within states determined on the basis of the magnitude of poverty incidence, magnitude of unemployment and development potential. There is considerable room for refinement to get disaggregated estimates of poverty and unemployment (which is feasible with available NSS data by pooling central and state samples and in some cases pooling across years). Information available in the population, agricultural and livestock censuses together with studies of the kind which the agro-climatic regional plans can provide indications of potential for development and interventions needed to exploit them. This would however call for a shift from the current pre-occupation with generating additional employment in the present as the over-riding objective to giving much greater emphasis to creating assets which by augmenting production and improving socio-economic infrastructure can lead to a sustained higher level of employment and incomes.

Within the framework of the above broad approach, it is possible to provide earmarked allocations for schemes to ensure minimum standard of amenities and acquisition of assets for scheduled castes and tribes; and for assistance (by way of subsidies or loans) to enable them to finance higher education and skill acquisition. These would make better sense and be more effective when they are part of an overall regional plan.

Targeting

The other, and in many ways more important, issue is targeting. The search for ways to reduce chances of mistargeting has largely focused on more effective monitoring of beneficiary selection; creating credible checks against mistargeting; and creating incentives for 'self selection'. Incomes are notoriously difficult to ascertain. And once it is known to determine eligibility for benefits, there is a strong general incentive to understate incomes. It is better to rely on more easily verifiable attributes (family size, land holding, caste, etc) associated with poverty. Though this does not eliminate scope for falsification, it certainly reduces the scope for it compared to the income criterion.

Clearly, targeting errors can be reduced if conditions of eligibility and/or the scale of benefits are so defined as to reduce the incentives for those above the poverty line to get into the programme. Insisting on a certain portion of beneficiaries being drawn from poor/vulnerable groups (SC, ST, women) and providing wage employment in employment schemes at wages somewhat below the market/minimum wage rate and at locations away from the residence would be a more effective way of reaching target population than relying on discretionary authority. The reservation idea is now incorporated in the guidelines for all ministry of rural development projects. But the idea of lowering wage rates on works programmes below the legal minimum is not favoured: The government cannot violate its own laws!

Targeting has not only a class/individual dimension, but also a spatial aspect. The poor being unevenly distributed between regions, spatial targeting is an important, but relatively neglected, aspect. Except in Jawahar Rojgar Yojana, allocations of PA programme outlays between and within states are not systematically related to poverty, unemployment or deficiency in basic amenities. Richer states generally tend to have larger resources and plan outlays per capita. One would expect the PA programme allocations to correct this imbalance at least to some degree. Data for the early 1980s [Subbarao 1992] suggest that, if anything, states with low incidence of poverty had higher outlay on PA programmes both in absolute per capita terms and as a proportion of total state plan outlays.

There is thus a strong case for rationalising the criteria for spatial allocation along the following lines. Allocations for all employment and production oriented PA schemes should be pooled and distributed between states, and within states, in proportion to the absolute number of poor or preferably, income deficit and the number of unemployed. Funds for programmes to ensure a minimum standard of basic amenities (elementary education, health care, water supply and access to roads) can be similarly pooled and distributed in proportion to the magnitude of deficiency in relation to the accepted minimum levels of facility. This would greatly add to the transparency of the programme and its effectiveness.

Accountability

Public accountability for ensuring proper choice of beneficiaries and proper use of funds remains a serious problem. Efforts to publicise the scale and nature of PA programmes in a particular block or district, the criteria by which beneficiaries are selected, the specific benefits to which they are entitled under each programme, and the procedures for availing of them have not been effective. Even when the information is available, there are no institutional mechanisms for making complaints or seeking redressal of grievances. Involvement of MLAs, MPs and other local leaders – whether formally as members of advisory committees or because of their ability to exert informal pressure – has not helped. On the contrary, irrespective of their party affiliation, politicians tend to use the opportunity to influence choice of schemes, locations and beneficiaries under these programmes as a source of power, and as instruments for consolidating their political base and often for personal gain. Surprisingly, neither elected representatives nor local cadres of political parties (even when they belong to the opposition) have shown much interest in taking up these issues.

Non-governmental organisations do take up such issues, but they are far too few to make more than a localised impact. Though numerous, they differ greatly in terms of focus, motivation, effectiveness. Some are concentrated on particular activities like education, social welfare and watershed development. Some are concerned with development activities covering several sectors. Funding sources differ. Most use their contacts with sympathetic government officials to secure support and resources for activities in their area. Some get funding from institutional agencies and foreign foundations. Several have innovative programmes to mobilise beneficiaries and building local institutions to make more effective use of government programmes.

NGOs also play a role in making people aware of the various PA programmes and benefits available under them; and interceding with concerned government agencies to secure benefits for eligible people. Some have taken the role of mobilising public opinion to assert people's entitlements under various PA programme or to press the government to allocate more resources and permit greater flexibility in programming to adapt scheme to local conditions. NGOs have played an active role in lobbying for freedom of information concerning details of public development schemes, entitlements to their benefits and the beneficiaries.

All this has contributed to raising people's consciousness of entitlements under government programme, including PA programmes. There is also growing awareness, especially among the poor, of their importance in influencing the outcome of electoral politics. There is greater assertiveness on their part in articulating general demands in the political arena. But there is as yet no organised attempt to see that the choice of beneficiaries and implementation of local programmes in particular communities is improved. This does not seem likely unless both the power and the resources for local development are fully devolved to elected representatives of local governments.

The necessity and the wisdom of democratic decentralisation

has been a recurrent theme of debates on the structure of government in India. The Constitution did not recognise or provide for representative local government institutions. By the late 1950s a review of the experience of the community development programme emphasised the need for democratically elected local governments for vigorous and equitable development in rural areas. Legislation to create panchayati raj bodies were passed by most states soon thereafter. However, few are keen to devolve powers and resources, and there was no legal or political compulsion to do so. Many did not even hold regular elections.

But some states (notably Karnataka and West Bengal) have tried to make it work. After a promising start the Karnataka experiment has stuttered. West Bengal's record in holding regular elections is the longest and most sustained though the devolution process has not gone as far as expected. Nevertheless both experiences have demonstrated the benefits of consultation and participation of local communities in making schemes more relevant to local felt needs, reducing duplication, ensuring that schemes are completed on schedule (often below estimated costs) and also in terms of the functioning of schools and PHCs.

The passage of the 73rd and 74th Constitutional Amendments which provides for a three tier system of local government, mandatory elections every five years and devolution development functions with authority and resources from the state to these bodies, has created a space and opportunity for decentralised participatory local development effort with in-built pressures for accountability. Implementation of these provisions is far from complete. Several states have not held local body elections as required by the Constitution. Even those which have, show a strong unwillingness to hand over to the elected bodies the authority and the resources to decide and implement local development. They have no power over the staff assigned to them nor the flexibility to hire any personnel on their own; schemes continue to be decided and implemented by the government and its bureaucracy; practically everywhere opposition state- and central-level politicians and the bureaucracy are resisting the process vigorously and in most places successfully.

This is evident even in Kerala which has made by far the most serious and determined effort to implement the spirit of the 73rd and 74th Amendments in all its essential respects. Legislating a statutory transfer of 40 per cent of state plan resources to local bodies – Kerala is the only state to have done so – is a revolutionary step. Efforts to prepare elected members of local bodies for their new role through mass mobilisation and public education training programmes and innovative ways to promote active and meaningful people's participation have been as impressive as they are unprecedented. The process, however, is being impeded at every step by strong rearguard opposition from those with a vested interest in the current dispensation.[39] That this is being increasingly contested by local leaders cutting across party lines and insisting on effective devolution of resources and power to them gives basis for optimism that this opposition will be overcome in due course.

A number of reasons are advanced to justify the opposition. One is the argument that given the highly stratified and unequal socio-economic structure of Indian villages, the dominant landowning caste elites would effectively control power and that they are unlikely to be concerned about the welfare of the poor and the women. Reservation of a specified, substantial proportion of elected positions for SC/STs and for women is meant to give a secure space for the disadvantaged to articulate their needs in the decision-making bodies. Sceptics doubt whether this space can and will in fact be used effectively in all cases and soon. However pessimism on this account seems unwarranted, at any rate exaggerated, for several reasons.

The growing political consciousness of the so-called lower castes as well as the scheduled castes and tribes is bound to express itself in local government as well. Secondly, villages/ blocks differ greatly in caste/class composition: Some villages are no doubt dominated by better off upper castes, but this is by no means the case everywhere. One must expect the outcome of decentralisation will be far from uniform. Even if initially only a fraction of elected local bodies do well, their superior performance will over a period of time act as spur to improvement in others.

The growing economic differentiation of rural society, the rapid diversification of activity and its commercialisation have loosened traditional social structures. The process will if anything intensify and lead to a significant realignment of the power structure in substantial parts of rural India favouring the disadvantaged groups. Such realignments will not of course to occur in all cases spontaneously and in a manner which gives effective voice to the poor and promote their interests. The process initiated by PR and the potential for change created by it are much more important than the immediate outcomes. Interventions in the process must therefore focus on creating conditions which will facilitate and encourage, the realisation of its potential. In this context three aspects deserve special attention.

First, a great deal of knowledge and expertise is needed to assess local resources and their potential, different ways of exploiting the potential, the costs involved and raising resources. This knowledge, much of it technical in nature, is often not available locally. Strong support from state agencies and/or non-government organisations (including educational institutions) is necessary to make it accessible to the communities and their leaders. A major change in the role of government agencies is also necessary. Instead of planning, deciding and implementing schemes on their own, as they now do, the agencies will have to play a supportive role by providing expertise, helping elected bodies to take informed decision and facilitating coordination between related schemes of different communities and in the larger regional context.

Second, the creation of democratic institutions of local government and assured representation for disadvantaged groups are necessary, but not sufficient conditions to ensure that the latters' interests are safeguarded. The determination of priorities, in the context of limited resources, inevitably involves a process of bargaining between different groups. In order for this to work in favour of the poor/vulnerable, the latter have to articulate their needs and actively persuade and/or pressure the relevant forums to take necessary action to meet their needs. None of these occur easily or automatically. Conscious measures to encourage and strengthen institutions of civil society are essential.

Non-governmental and voluntary organisations have a particularly key role in obtaining and disseminating information on the working of government (including local government), making people aware of their entitlements and obligations, and enabling them to vent their grievances and seek redress. Besides interceding with the concerned authorities to secure benefits for the eligible and minimise leakages, they have a role in motivating and organising local communities to take active interest in the working of specific programmes and persuading bureaucracy to work with the community for improving the effectiveness of programmes. Over time they can help promote a process of more broad-based changes in institutional mechanisms for funding/managing local development activities to meet the specific local conditions. Active encouragement of NGOs and giving them ample public space is therefore highly desirable for healthy evolution of local government.

Third, rising expectations and assertiveness of the people vis-a-vis government and bureaucracy increases pressures on the latter to perform. But better performance often requires a significant change in the relative roles of the three elements involving, among other things, reduced power and increased accountability of bureaucracy. It also involves shifts in the relative power of those who hold political office at different levels and of different segments of the bureaucracy. Reform therefore invariably encounters resistance. Moreover if the elected panchayat raj institutions merely generate demands for larger devolution of resources from the state and central governments there is little stake or incentive for them to address the task of efficient use of resources. It is therefore imperative that local bodies should be required to mobilise their own resources to meet a significant part of the costs of their programmes and given greater control over their staff engaged in various activities.

All this implies a basic change in the relations between the state and local governments, the role of the bureaucracy and the attitudes of local governments. There are no standard blue prints for accomplishing the change. A great deal of experiment and learning from experience is inevitable. The upsetting of existing power balances between the various groups involved creates an opportunity for engineering desirable changes through a combination of sustained pressures on the system as a whole via the general political process along with grass roots efforts to initiate and sustain a discussion of the problem of restructuring among the concerned groups (namely the local and state level politicians, the bureaucracy and its trade unions and non-government organisations).

Notes

[Kale Memorial Lecture delivered at Gokhale Institute of Economics and Politics, Pune, December 10, 2000.]

1 It merits noting that the late Pitambar Pant, who was then personal assistant to Nehru in his capacity as chairman of the Planning Commission, was the moving spirit behind the seminar on Planning for Minimum Living and, as head of PPD, the preparation of a perspective plan based on its recommendations.

2 Interestingly this was followed by a phrase 'in the light of its other commitments' which in effect diluted the force of this commitment.

3 This paper, titled 'Perspective of Development 1961-1976: Implications of Planning for a Minimum Level of Living', is reprinted in Srinivasan and Bardhan (eds) (1974).

4 Much of the work of this period is published in Srinivasan and Bardhan (eds) (1974).

5 Notable subsequent collections include Bardhan and Srinivasan (eds) (1988); Harris et al (eds) (1992); Drese and Sen (1995); Krishnaswamy (ed) (1990); Bhattacharya et al (1990); Rao (ed).

6 For a review of the evolution of these programmes and their problems see Vaidyanathan (1994a).

7 For a comprehensive and detailed discussion of the complex issues involved see Srinivasan (1981); Osmani (ed) (1992); and Sukhatme (ed) (1992).

8 For a detailed and critical discussion of this procedure see Rudra (1974, 1978); Dandekar (1996).

9 The ensuing summary of Sen's arguments is based on Sen (1985).

10 The theoretical and measurement problems involved are discussed in the Development Reports and their background papers published by the UNDP.

11 Noteworthy among these being the All India Household surveys of income, savings and consumption conducted in 1967-68 and 1975-76; panel surveys of sample rural households in 1970-71 and 1981-82; Market Information Surveys of Households (done more or less regularly since 1985); a survey of social indicators (1998); and a household survey to assess macro impact of macro adjustment policies.

12 Reports of NNMB's annual nutrition surveys, which are being conducted more or less regularly since the mid 1970s, are published by the National Institute of Nutrition, Hyderabad. Unfortunately these reports, not to speak of the primary data, are not easily accessible.

13 International Institute of Population Studies 1995.

14 A description of the scope, aims and methodology of the surveys is available in Walker and Ryan (1990).

15 One could compare SDP per capita estimates and per capita weighted mean consumption from NSS at the state level. But output originating is not a

good proxy for incomes accruing to the population in a state, which is more relevant for determining consumption. In the case of rural areas SDP in agriculture may not be a good indicator of even total output originating (let alone income accruing) in rural areas. At the all India level, there seems to be a significant positive correlation between official estimates of agricultural GDP per head of rural population and NSS estimates of per capita real consumption (both at constant prices) in the post 1973 period. But at the state level in many cases agricultural GDP per rural population is not strongly correlated with per capita real consumption.

16 For details of these revisions see GoI PC (1993) Ch 3.

17 According to official estimates poverty incidence fell progressively from 51.5 per cent in 1972-73 to 29.9 per cent in 1993-94; while the NSS based estimate showed a decline for 54.9 per cent in 1972-73 to 39.3 per cent in 1993-94 [GoI PC 1993].

18 A point-to-point comparison shows that the mean per capita consumption (in real terms) during the triennium ending 1997 was about 14 per cent higher than during 1989-91 according to NAS and only 3 per cent higher according to NSS.

19 If the conjecture is valid, the criterion that the reforms have accentuated inequalities would stand vindicated.

20 These points are discussed at length by Abijit Sen (2000) and Visaria (2000) and in an as yet unpublished note by Deaton.

21 The aims, scope and design of these surveys vary. Some were focused primarily on household incomes, other or market for branded manufactures and yet others on social indicators. This and the fact that, in some cases, two different surveys give very different estimates raises serious questions as to their comparability and reliability especially for assessing changes in inequality and poverty incidence. Even in the case of the panel survey of 1970-71 and 1981-82, more than one-fourth of the 1970-71 sample could not be traced in 1971-72; and not all the panel responded. The characteristics of the missing households is not indicated.

22 Significantly during the period covered by his study, the rate of decline in poverty is not significantly correlated with the rate of agricultural growth. Punjab and Haryana, which recorded among the highest growth rates in this period, showed no significant fall in poverty.

23 Two recent examples being Ravillion and Dutt (1995) and Abijit Sen (1996).

24 The relevant data are summarised in Vaidyanathan (1994, 1996).

25 For a recent overview see Rakesh Mohan and Pushpa Thottan (1988) and Minhas et al (1988). Also GoI PC 1993.

26 Abhijit Sen's (1996) attempt to explain trends in urban poverty incidence at the all India level in terms of changes in agricultural incomes per head of rural population, per capita non-agricultural incomes, commercialisation, etc, are not as convincing as in the case of rural areas both in terms of the underlying logic and the consistency, significance and stability of the estimated coefficients.

27 On the nature and extent of these shifts use Radhakrishna and Ravi (1992); Suryanarayana (2000) and Meenakshi (2000).

28 State level time series for education and mortality indicators compiled from official sources are collated in Nayyar 1992. Information on morbidity and access to medical care is available from the social consumption surveys conducted by the NSS in 1986-87 and in 1996-97. NNMB surveys give data, for small but representative sample of households in major states, of measured food intake, anthropometric measurements and assessment of clinical signs of nutrition deficiencies. There has been little analysis of the NNMB data. For analysis of nutrition data from the ICRISAT village surveys see Walker and Ryan 1990.

29 See Visaria and Gumber 1996 for a comprehensive and comparative analysis of NSS data on morbidity and health care utilisation and expenditure pattern in different states in 1986-87.

30 See for example Lipton (1983); Chambers (1988); and Sahn (eds) (1989).

31 Notable and pioneering works on this subject include Guhan (1988); Chen (ed) (1998); Dreze and Sen (1989).

32 See for example Lipton (1983); Sen (1988); Bardhan (1988); Walker and Ryan (1992); Kumar and Stewart (1992); Agarwal (1994); Vaidyanathan (1986, 1994).

33 The censuses and the NSS collect and publish data separately for scheduled castes and tribes in respect of demographic features, education, vital rates, employment and land ownership. They show that while their position in all these respects remain well below the average, there have been substantial improvements both in absolute and relative terms. The large variations in these respects between and within regions and in particular the underlying factors (including the effect of affirmative action policies) have received surprisingly little attention.

34 The literature on effectiveness of policy interventions is vast. For useful summaries of current debates and bibliographies on IRDP see Copestake (1988); on employment, Mahendra Dev (1993) and Gaiha (1997), on nutrition, Subba Rao (1988), Osmani (ed) (1992).

35 For a recent and thorough discussion of issues See Krishnan and Krishnaji (eds) (2000) and Swaminathan (2000).

36 The estimate for the Fourth Plan includes outlays on area development, village industries, backward areas, slum improvement, social welfare and special area programme. That for the Eighth Plan includes rural development, scheduled caste and tribes, social welfare, nutrition and village industry. Including outlays on minimum needs programme, for which separate for as figures are available the total is substantially higher bringing the total outlay on targeted PA programmes to 17 per cent of the public sector plan outlay.

37 In 1994-95 unrecovered costs of publicly provided goods and services are estimated at Rs 1,370 billion which exceeds the public sector plan outlay by 30 per cent and overall fiscal deficit by 40 per cent.

38 The subsequent arguments draw heavily than earlier paper of the author, Vaidyanathan (1998).

39 For a detailed, illuminating and self-critical assessment of the Kerala experience see Isaac (2000).

References

Agarwal, Bina (1994): *Field of One's Own: Gender and Land Rights in South Asia,* Sage, New Delhi.

Ahluwalia, M S (1978): 'Rural Poverty and Agricultural Performance in India', *Journal of Development Studies.*

——— (1986): 'Rural Poverty, Agricultural Production and Prices: A Re-examination' in Mellur and Desai (eds).

Bardhan, Pranab K (1988): 'Sex Disparity in Child Survival in Rural India' in Srinivasan and Bardhan (eds).

Bhalla, Surjit (1988): 'Is Srilanka An Exception? A Comparative Study of Living Standards' in Srinivasan and Bardhan (eds).

Bhalla, Surjit and Prem Vasishta (1988): 'Income Distribution in India: A Re-examination' in Srinivasan and Bardhan (eds).

Bhattacharya, N D Coondoo, P Maiti and R Mukherjee (1991): *Poverty Inequality and Prices in Rural India*, Sage, New Delhi.

Bhatty, I Z (1974): 'Inequality and Poverty in Rural India' in Srinivasan and Bardhan (eds).

Chen, Martha Alter (ed) (1998): *Widows in India,* Sage, New Delhi.

Copestake, James (1992): 'The Integrated Rural Development Programme' in Harris et al (eds).

Chambers, Robert (1992): 'Poverty In India; Concepts, Research and Reality' in Harris et al (eds).

Dandekar, V M (1996): The Indian Economy 1947-1992 Vol 2: *Population, Poverty and Employment*, Chapter 6, Sage, New Delhi.

Dreze, Jean and Amartya Sen (1989): 'Public Action for Social Security: Foundations and Strategy', *STICERD, No 20,* London School of Economics.

Gaiha, Raghav (1988): 'On Measuring the Risk of Rural Poverty in India' in Srinivasan and Bardhan (eds).

——— (2000): 'Rural Public Works and the Poor: A Review of the Employment Generation Scheme in Maharashtra' (mimeo).

GoI, Planning Commission (1962): *Report of the Committee on Distribution of Income and Levels of Living,* 2 Volumes, New Delhi.

——— (1964): *Notes of Perspectives of Development, India: 1960-61 to 1965-66,* New Delhi.

——— (1993): *Report of Expert Group on Estimates of Poverty and Number of Poor,* New Delhi.

Gopala Krishna Kumar and Frances Stewart (1988): 'Tackling Malnutrition: What Can Targeted Nutritional Interventions Achieve?' in Harris et al (eds).

Guhan, S (1988): 'Social Security in India: Looking One Step Ahead' in Harris et al (eds).

Harris, Barbara, S Guhan and Robert Cassen (eds) (1992): *Poverty in India:. Research and Policy*, Oxford University Press, New Delhi.

Hazari, R K (1967): *The Structure of the Corporate Prive Sector - A Study of Concentration, Ownership and Control,* Asia Publishing Home, Bombay.

International Institute of Population Studies (1995): *National Family Health Survey, 1992-93*, Mumbai.

Issac, Thomas and Richard W Franke (2000): *Local Democracy and Development: Peoples Campaign for Decentralised Planning in Kerala,* Leftword, New Delhi.

Kansal, S M (1965): 'Preliminary Estimate of Total Consumption Expenditure in India 1950-51 to 1963-64', Indian Statistical Institute Planning Unit, Discussion Paper 5, Delhi.

Krishnaji N and T N Krishnan (eds) (2000): *Public Support for Food Security: The Public Distribution System in India,* Sage, New Delhi.

Lipton, Michael (1983): 'Poverty, Undernutrition and Hunger', World Bank Staff Working Paper, P 23, Washington, DC.

——— (1983): *The Poor and the Ultra Poor: Characteristics, Explanation and Politics,* Development Research Department, CDS, Survey.

——— (1985): 'Poor and the Poorest', World Bank Discussion Paper 25, Washington DC

Mahendra Dev, S (1995): 'India's Maharashtra Employment Guarantee Scheme: Lessons and Experience' in Frederick Von Braun (ed), *Employment for Poverty Reduction and Food Security*, International Food Policy Research Institute, Washington, DC.

Mellor John and Gunvant Desai (ed) (1986): *Agricultural Change and Rural Poverty,* Oxford University Press, Delhi.

Meenakshi, J V (2000): 'Food Consumption Trends in India: A Regional Analysis' in Krishnajis and Krishnan (eds).

Minhas, B S (1985): *Validation of Large-Scale Sample Survey Data in Case of NSS Estimates of Household Consumption Expenditure*, Sankhya: A series B Vol 50 - Part I.

Minhas, B S and S M Kansal (1989). 'Comparison of NSS and CSO Estimates of Private Consumption: Some Observation Based on 1983 Data', *The Journal of Income and Wealth,* Vol III-November 1.

Minhas, B S, S M Kansal and L R Jain (1988): 'The Incidence of Urban Poverty in States 1970-71 to 1983 in Harris', Guhan and Casen (eds).

National Institute of Nutrition - Annual Reports on the NNMB Nutrition Surveys.

Nayyar, Rohini (1991): *Rural Poverty in India: An analysis of Inter State Differences,* Oxford University Press, Mumbai.

NCAER (1987): *Changes in the Structure of Household Income and Distribution of Gains in the Rural Household Sector: An All-India Inter Temporal Analysis 1970-71, 1981-82.*

Osmani, S (ed) (1992): *Nutrition and Poverty,* Clarendeon, Oxford.

Parikh, K S and T N Srinivasan (1990): 'Poverty Alleviation Policies in India:

Food Consumption Subsidies, Food Production Subsidies and Employment Generation', mimeo, Indira Gandhi Institute for Development Research, Mumbai.

Pradhan, Basant K et al (2000): 'Rural Urban Disparities, Income Distribution, Expenditure Pattern and Social Sector', *Economic and Political Weekly.*

Probe, Team (1999): *Public Report on Basic Education,* Oxford University Press, New Delhi

Rakesh Mohan and P Thottan (1992): 'The Regional Spread of Urbanisation, Industrialisation and Urban Poverty' in Harris et al (ed).

Rao, C H H and H Linneman (eds) (1996): *Economic Reforms and Poverty Alleviation in India*, Sage, New Delhi.

Radhakrishna R and C Ravi (1992): 'Effects of Growth, Relative Prices and Preferences on Food and Nutrition', *Indian Economic Review.*

Ravillion, Martin and Gaurav Datt (1995): 'Poverty in India', Background paper to the 1995 World Development Report, working paper series 1405, World Bank, Washington DC.

Rudra, Ashok (1974): 'Minimum Level of Living: A Statistical Examination' in Srinivasan and Bardhan (ed).

——— (1978): *The Basic Needs Concept and Its Implementation in Indian Development Planning,* ILO, ARTEP, Bangkok.

Sahn, David E (ed) (1989): *Seasonal Variability in Third World Agriculture: The Consequences for Food Security* John Hopkins University Press, Baltimore.

Sen, Abijit (1996): 'Economic Reforms, Employment and Poverty: Trends and Options', *Economic and Political Weekly.*

——— 2000: 'Consumer Spending and its Distribution...', *Economic and Political Weekly,* December.

Sen, Amartya (1985): *Commodities, and Capabilities,* North Holland, Amsterdam.

Sen, Amartya K and S Sengputa (1988): 'Family and Food: Sex Bias in Poverty' in Srinivasan and Bardhan (eds).

Srinivasan, T N (1981): 'Malnutrition: Some Measurement and Policy Issues', *Journal of Developing Economics.*

Srinivasan, T N and P K Bardhan (eds) (1988): *Rural Poverty in South Asia,* OUP, Delhi. Srinivasan, T N, P N Radhakrishnan and A Vaidyanathan (1974).

Streeten, Paul and S J Burki (1978): 'Basic Needs: Some Issues', *World Development.*

Sundaram, K and Tendulkar S D (1988): 'Towards an Explanation of Inter Regional Variations in Poverty and Unemployment in India' in Srinivasan and Bardhan (eds).

Subba Rao (1992): 'Interventions to Fill Nutrition Gaps at the Household Level' in Harris et al (eds).

Sukhatme, P V (ed) (1992): *Newer Concepts in Nutrition and Their Implications for Policy*, Maharashtra Association for Cultivation of Science, Pune.

Suryanarayana, M H (2000): 'How Real is the Secular Decline in Rural Poverty',

Economic and Political Weekly.

Suryanarayana, M H and N S Iyengar (1986): 'On Reliability of NSS Data', *Economic and Political Weekly.*

Swaminathan, Madhura (2000): Weakening Welfare: *The Public Distribution of Food in India*, Leftword, New Delhi.

UNDP (2000): 'Human Development Report'.

——— (various years): 'Human Development Papers'. United Nations, Department of Economic and Social Affairs, 1975

Vaidyanathan, A (1986a): 'On the Validity of NSS Consumption Data', *Economic and political Weekly.*

——— (1986b): 'Food Consumption and the Size of the People: Some Indian Evidence', Economic and Political Weekly.

——— (1992): 'On Measurement of Nutrition and Health Status'.

——— (1994a): 'Political Economy of the Evolution of Anti Poverty Programmes' in Sathyamurthy T S (ed).

——— (1994b): 'Second India Series Revisited, Food and Agriculture', mimeo, MIDS, Chennai.

——— (1996): 'Employment Situation: Some Emerging Perspectives', *Economic and Political Weekly.*

Vaidyanathan, A and P R G Nair (eds) (2000): *Elementary Education in Rural India: A Grass roots View,* Sage, New Delhi.

Visaria, Pravin (1978): 'Size of Holdings, Living Standard and Employment in Western India, 1972-73', World Bank Staff Working Paper.

——— (1979): 'Poverty and Development in India: An Analysis of Rural Evidence', World Bank Staff Working Paper.

Visaria, Pravin and Anil Gumber (1996): *Utilisation of and Expenditure on Health Care in India 1986-87,* Gujarat Institute of Development Studies, Ahmedabad.

——— (2000): 'Alternative Estimate of Poverty in India', *The Economic Times,* June 29.

Walker, Thomas S and James Rayan (1990): *Village and Household Economics in India's Semi Arid Tropics*, Johns Hopkin University Press, Baltimore.

R.R. Kale Memorial Lecture delivered at the Gokhale Institute of Politics and Economics, Pune, December 10, 2000.

11

The New Economics of Poverty

THE discussions of development policy reflect deep concern at the massive dimensions of poverty in India and the slow pace of improvement in the conditions of the poorer segments of the population. This concern is of course not new. As early as 1962, the Perspective Planning Division (PPD) of the Planning Commission drew pointed attention to the fact that the large majority of Indians do not have and cannot afford nutritionally satisfactory diet and minimum standard of clothing, housing and other necessities. It went on to argue that

> Such widespread poverty is a challenge which no society in modern times can afford to ignore for long. It must be eradicated both on humanitarian grounds and as an essential condition for orderly progress. No programme or policy which fails to alleviate the conditions of the poor appreciably can hope for the necessary measure of public co-operation and political support in a mature democracy. The central concern of our planning has to be the removal of poverty as early as possible. The stage has now come when we should sharply focus our efforts on providing an assured minimum income to every citizen of the country within a reasonable period of time. Progressively this minimum itself would be raised as development goes apace.[1]

I am grateful to M.S. Ahluwalia, Jagdish Bhagwati, P.K. Bardhan, Ashok Mitra, Raj Krishna, S.K. Singh and T.N.Srinivasan for comments on an earlier draft of the paper. The paper expresses my personal views and not necessarily those of the institution for which I work.

The issue under debate relates to the strategy appropriate to achieving this objective. The PPD paper cited above, as indeed the successive five year plans,[2] ruled out drastic changes in the existing distribution of incomes as inconsistent with the accepted Constitution. Nor was it considered particularly desirable because of the very low average incomes and because a certain degree of inequality was deemed as an essential part of the incentive structure. That the pattern of income distribution appeared to be remarkably similar in countries with very disparate social and economic systems was seen by the PPD as a further corroboration of the judgement that very little could be done to alter the pattern of income distribution at the point of origin. Under these circumstances, the rate at which the incomes and living standards of the poorest segments of the population could be raised was seen fundamentally as a function of the rate of over-all economic growth, together with a gradual increase in public ownership of reproducible wealth, and a purposive policy of taxing the rich to finance health, education and other programmes for the benefit of the poor as instruments for progressively reducing inequality of incomes and opportunity.

This strategy is being seriously questioned on the ground that it has not, and is incapable of, solving the problem of low-end poverty. That actual production achieved has persistently fallen short, and considerably short, of targets in most key sectors of the economy is an established fact. What is more, despite the substantial increase in the rate of investment, the over-all growth rate shows no sign of acceleration. The investment rate rose from 6-7 per cent in the early fifties to 15 per cent by 1965-66, but throughout the period the trend growth rate of gross domestic product remained constant at round 4 per cent a year. Since then the rate of real investment has actually declined and, not surprisingly, the growth of output has also decelerated. This admittedly disappointing record has shaken the faith in rapid growth as the solution for mass poverty. Some consider an appreciable acceleration in the rate of growth to be unfeasible or at any rate unlikely. Others feel that if we were to rely on growth alone, it will take an unacceptably long time to provide a decent life to everyone. Yet others argue that in the normal course the benefits of development do not flow to the poor and that rapid growth may actually worsen income distribution. Hence the emphasis on immediate and direct measures to raise the living standards of the poorest 30-40 per cent of the population.

A further source of disenchantment is the widespread belief that whatever little increase in real incomes has taken place has only made the rich richer, and the poor poorer. It has been argued that the proportion of the population below a normative minimum has, in fact, increased in recent years,[3] that the real wage rates of agricultural labourers, who are among the poorest classes of the population, have declined over large parts of the country,[4] and that bigger farmers have benefited more from investment and incentives provided by Government than smaller cultivators. The evidence in support of the contention about agricultural wage rates is indeed compelling, but we do not know enough about changes in the number of working days per annum. The data on the relative increase in income of different classes of farmers is limited to a few regions so that one has to be cautious in making generalizations. In any case, the behaviour of inter-regional disparities is just as important — and on this we have insufficient evidence. Whatever data we have on distribution of total population by level of consumption do not indicate any aggravation of inequalities. It is the slow pace of growth rather than worsening distribution which explains the persistence of mass poverty.[5,6]

It is tempting to conclude from this evidence that the

growing importance of public ownership of capital and of tax-financed public expenditures has neutralized any aggravation in the inequalities of private income. The public sector's share in total reproducible wealth and aggregate national expenditure has indeed risen sharply since 1951. But since surpluses generated by the public sector are negligible, it is very doubtful whether expanded public ownership has had a favourable impact on overall income distribution. Nor can it be unambiguously established that the net effect of taxation and public expenditure policy has been to reduce inequalities to any appreciable extent.

The meagre results of the growth-public ownership-fiscal policy strategy has led many economists to seek other avenues of action for tackling poverty. A common ground for this quest is the belief that the poor are getting more and more restive and unless something is done to provide them a tolerable living standard within a reasonable period of time, their frustrations will rapidly and inexorably reach the point of explosion.

At one extreme are those who see no salvation for the poor except in revolutionary transformation of society, its institutions and its power structure. That some countries, notably China and Cuba, seem to have succeeded in eliminating abject poverty by such means adds to their appeal. But it is often forgotten that the Chinese and the Cuban revolutions were the product of a particular conjunction of historical and political events which do not exist in India and cannot be made to order. It is also arguable whether failure to provide a specified minimum by a specified date will inevitably lead to disaster. There is no simple equation between intensity of poverty and prospects of political upheaval. The sheer number of the poor, staggering as it is, gives no measure of their political strength. Effective power, whether one likes it or not, rests with a few privileged classes (large landholders, traders, unionized labour, educated urban elite, and the like). The prevailing atmosphere of tension and violence is more due to the clamour of these classes to maintain, and if possible improve, their relative positions than to any massive revolt of the poor. Agricultural labourers, small peasants and others belonging to the poorest strata of society are simply not organized to effectively press their claims, much less to alter the balance of power in their favour. This does not imply that the problem of the poor is irrelevant or that it can be ignored with impunity. It simply means that instead of waiting for revolution, we ought to find ways of serving their needs better within the confines of the existing order.

Land ceilings, tenancy reform, unionization of landless rural labour and other direct measures to increase the real poor's share in total income, though desirable, do not seem to have much chance of success, at any rate in the immediate future and on a significant scale. Experience during the last twenty-five years shows how difficult it is to enforce meaningful land reform. Radicalist pressures did succeed in forcing political parties to accept land reform as part of their programme. Many statutes were also enacted. But the realities of power being what they are, the laws are all too frequently riddled with loopholes and tend to get further emasculated in the process of implementation. The result has been that the reforms have made hardly any impact on rural inequalities. On the other hand, they have created vast uncertainties and a state of enervating tension. One expects that unionization of landless labour, which constitutes a rather large segment of the country's electorate, would have attracted the radical parties for its potential political dividends, if not its benefits to the poor. That this has not happened on any significant scale is among the more puzzling aspects of the Indian political scene.

There is a school, and it has some powerful advocates, who argue that the 'relevant radicalism' does not lie in the path of revolution, and that it is possible to eradicate abject poverty speedily if only planners would give more attention to evolving a strategy for wider diffusion of additional incomes, and for directly increasing employment and incomes of the poor. Specifically, it is being suggested that these objectives could be achieved by (a) encouraging labour-intensive techniques of production; (b) a change in the composition of investment in favour of agriculture and rural sector generally; and (c) a massive works programme designed to provide guaranteed full-time employment at reasonable wages to the unemployed and the underemployed. To anyone familiar with the debate on Indian planning none of these ideas are novel. Nevertheless, in the context of the greatly heightened concern for the poor, and the growing clamour for a reorientation of development strategy, a reconsideration of the validity of these solutions is in order.

Increasing Labour-Intensity of Production

For any given growth rate, the quantum of employment would be larger, and the additional incomes more widely diffused, if relatively labour-intensive forms of production were adopted. This is the argument advanced for greater emphasis on agriculture over industry, light industry as against heavy industry and on dispersed small-scale enterprise. This is also the argument for choosing quick-yielding, small irrigation projects rather than large projects which take several years to complete, and for labour-intensive construction techniques. These are much-debated questions. The potential conflict between better income distribution made possible by labour-intensive production in the short run and the problem of raising savings to support long-term growth are well known. What is perhaps not as well recognized are the limits to increasing employment intensity of a development programme by manipulating the product- and the technology-mixes.

Product-Mix

The nature of products required to sustain economic growth constraints the possibility of increasing the employment content of a given aggregate income target. Part of the reason is the unequal distribution of income. If the projected pattern of consumer demand and the nature of technology require large supplies of energy, mass transportation, modern machinery, metals and chemicals, the investments necessary to produce them have to be provided in the plan. The major part of investment is currently absorbed by these sectors. They are inherently capital-intensive and the margin for substituting capital with labour is strictly limited.

The need for such investments can in principle be reduced under one of two conditions: (1) More efficient use of energy, reducing the steel and cement content of construction, more austere standards of housing and factory, buildings, could reduce the demand for capital-intensive inputs. But often such economies can be obtained only with larger inputs of skills and, in some cases, of investment, both of which are scarce resources. (2) If export possibilities were unlimited, one could expand production of labour-intensive goods and services for export and use the proceeds to import the more capital-intensive products. It could be argued that the possibilities have not been given sufficient attention in Indian development, partly because of a strong streak of export pessimism and partly perhaps of the difficulties, real or imagined,of making the necessary policy adjustments. Nevertheless, given that barely 5 per cent of the country's input is exported, the potential of an export-oriented development strategy appears to be relatively limited. Several studies have demonstrated that within a fairly wide range of export assumptions, the scope for economizing capital-intensive investments is not significant.[7] Unless we are thinking of an economy which can wholly reject modern technology and a system of production which uses little energy, metals, chemicals and machinery, there is simply no escape, at any rate for India, from investing in the production of these inputs. The possibility of building such a system may be a worthy subject for speculation but hardly a basis for immediate policy.

Limits to Technological Choice

The complex nature of technology and the factors limiting the range of choice can be illustrated by reference to agriculture.[8] While in some operations like ploughing and harvesting the choice is real, there are others, for example, irrigation pumps, which are essential to increasing productivity, and, far from displacing labour, may in fact increase employment. Again the notion that minor irrigation should always be preferred to large projects on grounds of shorter time-lags and lower cost represents too simplistic a view. Whether or not a particular source of water can be harnessed by larger or small works is often determined by technical considerations. The lack of adequate knowledge of ground water resources is frequently a constraint on the capacity to invest in minor works. Even if the knowledge were available and a large enough portfolio of projects exists, considerations of inter-regional balance and the need to ensure a sustained expansion of facilities over a longer period often dictate simultaneous investments in both types of projects.

Further, it has to be recognized that labour-using techniques are often 'inferior' in the sense that capital required per unit of output is not reduced by using more labour.[9] In many instances, modern techniques are more attractive from both the private and the social points of view because of strong economies of scale and because they make more efficient use of raw materials. One could, in theory, promote research to develop so-called intermediate technologies better adapted to the factor proportions obtaining in India. But even if we knew how to go about developing such techniques and the efforts were successful, they are of little practical relevance in the immediate future.

Finally, much of the discussion on technological choice is confined to manufacturing and construction, which account for less than 8 per cent of total employment and almost one-fourth of non-agricultural employment. Over the greater part of the economy and particularly in trade and services, there is a considerable flexibility, and the relative factor endowments as reflected in the market have, more or less spontaneously, led to the choice of labour-intensive techniques.

All this is not to suggest that there is no room for extending the use of labour-intensive techniques to attain a given pattern of production. The outstanding success of the policy of limiting production of large integrated mills to provide opportunities for expansion of the decentralized weaving industry clearly shows such possibilities exist. Nor can one claim that everything possible has been done to exploit all the significant possibilities for increasing efficient labour-intensive techniques. It is just possible that the relatively high wage rates in the unionized sectors may have encouraged enterprises to use techniques with a higher capital-intensity than is socially desirable. The point is that even if such distortions could be corrected, the area of choice is far more limited than is usually believed.

Rural Development

One of the persistent criticisms of Indian plans has centred on their alleged excessive preoccupation with industry, especially heavy industry, to the neglect of agriculture and rural development. A major shift of emphasis in favour of the latter is often recommended as the most effective way of improving the conditions of the poor, the majority of whom live in villages and depend on agriculture. Though the protagonists of 'new economics' do not always advocate this view explicitly, their arguments often imply that such a reorientation is desirable.

The level and composition of investment is a function of the desired level of income in the target year and the rate of growth over the longer run, the technical input-output relations among the various sectors, and the constraints imposed by the supply of savings and foreign exchange. The composition of investment could be changed without jeopardizing the over-all growth objectives by encouraging labour-intensive techniques to reach output targets in particular sectors and/or by greater emphasis on expansion by labour-intensive exports. But, for reasons discussed earlier, the possibilities in both these directions are limited.

For any given level of aggregate income, the demand for agricultural products would be larger, and the requirements of manufactures smaller, as the distribution of that income becomes more egalitarian. In so far as the consumption of energy, transportation, metals and other capital-intensive inputs per unit of production is lower in agriculture compared to other sectors, a more egalitarian distribution of income would, other things being equal, also reduce the demand for these inputs. Altogether this would mean an increase in the proportion of investment allocated to agriculture for achieving a given growth of aggregate income. If the incremental capital-output ratio in agriculture were less than in industry, it would also mean a reduction in the over-all investment needed to sustain the targeted growth rate. Note, however, that a redistribution of income is an essential precondition to sustain this line of approach. While a change in income distribution has a direct and predictable impact on the pattern of demand and hence of output, changing the output-mix in favour of food and other essential consumer goods does not automatically result in a more egalitarian distribution.

Since the incidence of mass poverty is most acute in rural areas, it might seem plausible that the problem could be solved more speedily by giving agriculture a much larger share in investment and additional output than visualized by the planners. This would be the case if (a) larger investments automatically lead to faster growth of agricultural production; (b) the distribution of additional agricultural production is not such as to result in an aggravation of inequalities; and (c) there are no adverse effects on the terms of trade of the rural sector. There are strong grounds to believe that none of these conditions are likely to be met.

It is doubtful if, in fact, the shortage of investment is the critical constraint on agricultural growth. Much of the increase in agricultural production depends on the use of better seed, fertilizers and other yield-raising techniques which do not require a great deal of fixed investment. It is true that the potential for using these inputs and techniques is determined by soil conditions and the availability of assured water supply. But, if available experimental and demonstration data are to be believed, there is considerable unexploited scope for increasing production by the use of these techniques even at the existing endowments of soil and irrigation. Investment in irrigation, soil conservation, rural roads and other similar works are of course important, but they are essentially in the nature of long-term improvements to ensure a sustained expansion of production potential. In any event, the explanation for slow growth of agricultural production in the short and medium terms has to be sought at least as much in the reasons for slow spread and inefficient use of known improved techniques as in the shortage of investments for basic improvement in land and water.

Even if it were true that larger allocations to agriculture

would accelerate the growth of farm output in the aggregate, it does not follow that the increases will be evenly distributed. So long as the inequalities in the distribution of land remain uncorrected, the distribution of income is bound to be unequal. Moreover, there is a general impression that larger farmers are better placed, both by virtue of their superior command over resources and their political power, to adopt improved techniques and that they tend to get a disproportionately larger share of the benefits of public investment and supporting services (credit, inputs, etc.). To the extent this is true — one cannot be categorical on the basis of available evidence — the distribution of income may actually become more unequal.

If income distribution remains as unequal as it was to begin with, or becomes more unequal, an increase in the agricultural sector's share in the targeted total output will necessarily lead to imbalances between the composition of supply and of demand. Specifically the supply of farm products will tend to outstrip, and that of manufactures will fall short of, demand. Unless these imbalances could be corrected through foreign trade, the terms of trade would shift against agriculture and the real incomes of the rural sector would grow slower than agricultural output. Since the poor generally, and the rural poor in particular, spend a much larger proportion of their incomes on farm products, a relative cheapening of the latter would of course improve the distribution of real incomes. A substantial shift in terms of trade would however dampen the incentives for sustained growth of farm output over the long run. And if the increased agricultural investments are accommodated at the cost of other sectors, the long-term potential for expansion of non-agricultural activities — which everyone agrees to be essential for sustaining a satisfactory growth of employment at rising levels of productivity — will also be reduced.

All these arguments are of limited practical interest because the feasibility of increasing agricultural production much faster than planned is far from established. The fact is that, despite massive investments and the much-advertised high-yielding varieties and other harbingers of the green revolution, the rate of agricultural growth (around 3 per cent a year) has stagnated at levels far below the plan targets. Though we may be reluctant to admit it, the ingredients of a programme to significantly improve on past trends in agricultural performance remain elusive. The relevant question therefore is whether we can do more for the poor within the constraints of a 3-3.5 per cent rate of agricultural growth. One way would be to try and compensate for slow agricultural growth by a faster expansion of industries thereby raising the over-all growth rate. This would, however, mean a substantial change in the mix of new industrial investments with a greater weight to manufactures which can be exported in exchange for larger agricultural imports. Considering that foreign trade in manufactures is a minuscule fraction of total output, it is rather doubtful whether this course would make a substantial difference to the over-all growth. To the extent it relaxes the foreign exchange bottleneck and permits a more liberal import, such a shift may significantly improve the efficiency of resource use. But the benefits would primarily consist in improving the over-all growth rate; it may not have any significant, direct impact on the conditions of the poor.

Another possibility would be to scale down the targets of over-all growth rate while maintaining the effort at resource mobilization at the planned level. A lowering of the over-all growth target, on grounds of feasibility, would necessarily mean smaller investment allocations for industry, particularly those producing capital goods, energy and transportation. Together with improvements in project formulation, implementation and operation, this could mean substantially lower investments in productive sectors. If at the same time the Government policy were successful in mobilizing savings on the scale visualized by the planners, there would be a 'surplus' of investible resources. This surplus could then be used for providing basic improvements in rural infrastructure and better essential amenities in areas with high concentrations of the poor. The crucial question here is one of resource mobilization and capacity to so manage the economy that the impact of the potential inflation on the poorer segments is effectively kept in check.

Works Programmes

Many argue that, irrespective of the efficiency aspect of investment allocations, a massive rural works programme offers the only effective way of increasing the living standard of the poor. The proximate cause of poverty, as the argument goes, is unemployment and under-employment; if only the poor could be guaranteed full-time employment at a reasonable wage, the problem of low-end poverty could be solved directly and within an acceptable period of time.

Dandekar and Rath's *Poverty in India* is a good illustration of this approach.[10] On the basis of the National Sample Survey data, and a normative standard of minimum consumption, they estimate that approximately 40 per cent of the rural population and about half the urban population are below the poverty line. While the extreme poverty of the poorest decile might reflect special circumstances like destitution, disability and excessively large number of dependents per adult, the condition of the others below the poverty line must, in their judgement, be attributed to lack of adequate employment to its working members. They estimate that these sections of the population would need an additional annual increase of the order of Rs. 800 crores to enable them to afford the minimum standard. A works programme which will guarantee adult members of this class full-time employment at a daily wage rate of Rs. 2.50

per male and Rs. 1.60 per female would directly raise them above the poverty line.

Such aggregative calculations may have some value for illustrating the dimensions of poverty, but they are far from an adequate basis for policy. In the first place, the notion that poverty is basically a reflection of unemployment and underemployment is too simplified a view of reality. It is true that a large proportion of the poor consists of landless labourers who suffer from low wages and underemployment. But the ranks of the poor also includes a not inconsiderable number of families with land, some with fairly large-sized holdings. It is also significant that the incidence of poverty seems to be strongly associated with the size of the family.[11] Clearly a generalized works programme is not the appropriate remedy in all cases. It can benefit families with very little land and whose adult members do not have year-round employment. For those with some land, measures to augment their productivity are more important. And where poverty is the result of large family size and high proportion of infant, aged and the disabled, extra wage employment cannot make any difference. An anti-poverty programme must, therefore, distinguish between different categories of the poor. As Raj Krishna puts it,

> Poverty of the employed, unemployed, the self employed and the unemployable receive different treatment.The unemployable need simple income transfers; the self-employed need additional input, credit and knowledge; the employed need more effective unionism and the unemployed need work and a means of production.[12]

The need for a discriminating approach is evidently recognized by the planners. They distinguish between rural works programmes to provide additional work for the underemployed, programmes designed to increase productivity of viable smallholders and those aimed at providing supplementary occupations to marginal farmers. The focus of the small farmer and marginal farmer schemes is essentially to provide easier access, at a lower cost than is possible under existing arrangements, to inputs required for increasing productivity. The problem here is essentially one of building an organization capable of effectively reaching the supplies and credit to small farmers on a large enough scale and ensuring smooth turnover of loans. But it should also be recognized that, beyond a point, the productivity of small farmers cannot be increased without basic improvements in the quality of land and water. And such improvements have to be planned on an area basis rather than for particular classes of farmers. Even where works programmes have a role, several important questions remain: should they seek to provide work for the underemployed in the slack season or should they seek to provide full-time employment in construction activity? In the former case, works will have to be near the locations of the underemployed and should be organized on a seasonal basis. In the latter, works could be undertaken on a year-round basis and need not necessarily be located near the concentrations of the poor/underemployed. But then it would involve a major effort to organize full-time construction workers corps and move them from one project area to another.[13] If this course is preferred, as some do, what would be the effects on the supply of labour and the costs of labour for agricultural operations? If supply falls and/or costs rise, would the prospects of increased production be seriously affected? What would be the effect on the capital-intensity of farming? So long as one is conceiving policy in the existing institutional framework, rather than in the context of a major reorganization of the rural economy, these are very relevant questions.

Moreover, since the potential beneficiaries of the works programmes are unevenly distributed in space, one has to consider how the benefits can be made to reach them. If all that we need is to generate a certain magnitude of aggregate wage incomes from construction work, the problem is relatively simple. For instance, the current level of investment (Rs. 4,000 crores) gives rise to wage incomes equal to, if not greater than, the amount (Rs. 800 crores) which Dandekar and Rath estimate to be necessary for abolishing abject poverty. But unless the distribution of construction activity coincides with that of the poor or, alternatively, the poor freely migrate to areas where the works are being constructed, there is no guarantee that it will raise the incomes of the poor. Works programmes designed for the benefit of the poor must therefore be discriminating in the spatial dimension as well. This leads to the question: what kinds of works?

In general, given the scarcity of savings, and given that sustained growth of incomes is desirable, it would be wise to so choose such investments in the backward areas as will increase their productive potential and leave behind a permanent increase in employment and incomes. To rely solely on works, without bothering about their productivity, means that the State has to maintain a relatively high level of construction activity year after year in the poor areas so that the employment and incomes of the poor can be maintained at the desired level. The extent to which the requirement of the productivity of investments coincides with the aim of providing work to the poor where they are depends, however, on whether the areas where the poor happen to be concentrated also have potentials for investment which sooner or later can be expected to increase production.

To the extent regions with low per capita incomes offer scope for increased production, the constituents of an action programme are known and have been worked out in requisite operational detail, a conscious redirection of investment to such areas would clearly help redress inequalities. Precisely to what degree and over how long a period depends, however, on the magnitude of the production potential and on the time required for output to respond to investments. It does not always happen that the poor regions have large potentialities capable of being realized quickly. In any event, such a strategy would call for a great deal of definitive knowledge of production possibilities and the measures needed to exploit them, organisations to work out and implement concrete projects, and above all a clear sense of priorities.

At present none of these conditions is fulfilled. There are indeed a number of special programmes for backward areas, drought-prone areas and the like. But, in general, these are not tailored to the needs and possibilities of specific areas; they are often conceived and implemented in an uncoordinated manner. Nor is there any indication that the locations of these programmes were selected on the basis of an objective determination of the intensity of poverty, unemployment and future production potential. There is the further problem that in an effort to satisfy as many constituents as possible, the limited resources tend to be spread thinly among regions and projects: far too many schemes are started in far too many areas with the result that all of them get delayed, and their effectiveness greatly reduced. Even if all these defects were removed, one faces the problem that, under the existing rules of federal finance, there is relatively little freedom to ensure adequate resources flow to the regions with a high concentration of the poor.

These lacunae, however, do not vitiate the essential soundness of the idea. Rather they point to the directions in which improvements are needed so that the strategy can, over a period of time, make a significant impact on rural income distribution. First, we should clearly recognize the diverse characteristics of the poor and their uneven spatial distribution. Second, the programmes should, to the maximum extent possible, be designed with a view to generating a lasting increase in production and employment in the poor areas. Third, districts/talukas should be classified according to the incidence of poverty and the characteristics of the poor. This would help identify areas with the largest concentrations of the poor, and the type of programmes appropriate to each. Fourth, there should be a proper assessment of the potentials for agricultural development in different regions both in the near future and over the long run. Finally, a long-term action programme should be worked out with priorities determined on the basis of the incidence of poverty, the known potential for growth and the state of readiness for absorbing productive investment. The spatial allocation of rural investments should be governed to the maximum extent possible by the priority so defined. In particular, the temptation to start schemes haphazardly and in piecemeal fashion should be avoided.[14] Progressively integrated long-term programmes of rural development should be drawn up for all regions.

The mobilization of resources to finance a massive works programme also presents a formidable problem, and one which tends to be underestimated. For instance, Dandekar and Rath argue that in order to increase the income of the poorest 40 per cent to the desired minimum all that is needed is to get the richest decile of the population to reduce their consumption by 5 per cent. Put this way, the task sounds deceptively simple. But clearly exhortation and preaching about the moral and political imperative of eradicating abject poverty will not persuade the rich to reduce their consumption. The reduction has to be forced by deliberate policy. The real challenge is to devise concrete fiscal measures by which we can generate the necessary additional resources in a manner which ensures that its incidence is on the richest 10 per cent and that it does not affect savings. In order to appreciate the magnitude of the task, one has only to remember that the normal development programme already calls for nearly as large an effort at additional resource mobilization. And there is the further problem of ensuring that the resources so mobilized in fact flow into programmes for the relatively poor areas and poorer classes. The implications of this for the rules of resource transfers from the Centre to the States can be far-reaching.

Moreover, a reduction in aggregate consumption of the rich by the desired amount is not enough. The consumption pattern of the rich happens to be very different from that of the poor. Thus, while the richest 30 per cent spends 30-35 per cent of their consumption expenditure on foodgrains, the corresponding proportion for the poorest three deciles is 55 per cent. A transfer of income from the former to the latter means a substantial increase in the demand for food and a reduction in the demand for manufactures and services. It is possible that the excess supply of manufactures could be traded; but since services cannot, the redistribution would reduce income and employment from services. To this extent, the net employment effect of the income transfer would be less than the employment created by the works programme financed by such a transfer. The second and more important problem comes from the imbalance between the supply of and the demand for food created by the redistribution of income. Unless the additional food demand can be met by increased domestic production and/or imports, or the Government is prepared to take effective steps to ensure equitable distribution of the available supplies, the resultant increases in the price of food will neutralize at least part of the effects of the additional money incomes accruing to the poor.

In sum, therefore, a major shift in development strategy in favour of labour-intensive modes of production and a greater emphasis on rural development seems unlikely to make a significant and early impact on income distribution. The scope for expanding labour-intensive production is limited. A relatively faster growth in the incomes and employment of the rural poor is not just a matter of diverting a larger share of total investments for rural development. These investments have to be planned with due regard to the heterogeneous character of the poor and their uneven distribution in space. The identification of the poor, the formulation of concrete programmes appropriate to increasing the productivity and employment of different categories of the poor in different areas, and the creation of appropriate organizations to implement them effectively will necessarily take time. Such a discriminating programme aimed specifically for the benefit of the poor should therefore be viewed essentially as a long-term effort and as a complement rather than as a substitute for programmes to stimulate over-all growth. Indeed, to a large extent, a more systematic and rational planning of rural development along the above lines could, over a period of time, help increase the efficiency of investment. To this extent, the interests of growth and equity coincide.

Apart from knowledge and organizational capacity, the scale of rural development programmes is limited basically by the ability to mobilize resources and by the supplies of essential consumer goods. If agricultural production increases at barely 3 per cent a year, fiscal management remains as weak as it has been in recent years, and the shortage of foreign exchange persists, there is precious little room for manoeuvre. Relaxation of these constraints is as important for growth as it is for facilitating larger programmes specifically meant to provide employment and increase the productivity of the poor. Massive anti-poverty programmes launched without adequate preparation and in neglect of these above constraints could easily become counter-productive. And even if the constraints are relaxed, one has to accept the fact that so long as the deeper causes of inequality remain uncorrected and the poor are not properly organized, it is unrealistic to expect any dramatic or speedy improvement in income distribution.

Notes

1. Government of India, Planning Commission, Perspective Planning Division, Perspective of Development; India — 1960-61 to 1975-76: *Implications of Planning for a Minimum Level of Living*, mimeographed, 1962.

2 The plan documents themselves do not spell out, systematically and at a single place, the economic and political rationale of development strategy. But individual elements of the argument are discussed at different places in different plan documents. The broad thrust of the argument is faithfully captured in the PPD formulation.

3 P.K. Bardhan, '*On the Minimum Level of Living and The Rural Poor*', Indian Economic Review, April 1970.

4 P.K. Bardhan, *'On the Incidence of Poverty in Rural India'*, Economic and Political Weekly, February 1973.

5 A. Vaidyanathan, *'Some Aspects of Inequalities in Living Standards in Rural India'*, mimeographed, 1970.

6 B.S. Minhas, *'Rural Poverty, Land Distribution and Development'*, Indian Economic Review, April 1970.

7 See for example, PPD, *Notes on Perspective of Development, India, 1960-61 to 1975-76* (New Delhi, 1964).

8 For a lucid exposition of some of the complexities, see Raj Krishna, *Measurements of Direct and Indirect Employment Effects of Agricultural Growth with Technical Change* (forthcoming).

9 See, for example, A.K.Sen, *Choice of Techniques*, Blackwell; P.N. Dhar and H.F. Lydall, *Small-Scale Industries in India*, Institute of Economic Growth, Delhi; V.M. Dandekar and N.Rath, *Poverty in India*, Indian School of Political Economy, 1971; and PPD, *Village Industries in the Perspective of Indian Development, 1961-1976*, mimeographed.

10 V.M. Dandekar and N. Rath, op. cit.

11 See A. Vaidyanathan, *'Some Aspects of Inequalities in Living Standards in Rural India'*, op. cit.

12 Raj Krishna, *Unemployment in India*, Presidential Address, Indian Society of Agricultural Economics, 1973.

13 For a discussion of the organizational aspect of works programmes, see Dandekar and Rath, op. cit.

14 The outline of an operational programme for integrated rural development is outlined in B.S. Minhas, op. cit. His approach, together with an objective determination of spatial priorities determined on the basis of the incidence of poverty and development potential, can have far-reaching consequences for the approach to rural development programmes.

Economic Theory and Planning, (ed.) Ashok Mitra, Essays in Honour of A.K. Dasgupta (1994) OUP, Delhi.

12

The Political Economy of the Evolution of Anti-Poverty Programmes

Raising the Standard of Living of the Poor: The First Four Plans

THE notion that the state should intervene on behalf of the under-privileged is embedded in the Directive Principles of State Policy and in the mandatory provisions for positive discrimination in favour of Scheduled Castes (SCs) and Scheduled Tribes (STs) in the Indian Constitution. While the former was no more than a declaration of intent, the concerns it embodies have been invoked in the formulation of state policy and are reflected in the Five Year Plans. In the case of SCs and STs, as well as a reservation of quotas for admission to educational institutions and government jobs, the Five Year Plans include special programmes to provide financial assistance for education, water supply, housing, and other welfare programmes. The Five Year Plans have consistently addressed the problems of poverty and inequality by attempting to achieve sustained expansion and diversification of economic activity.

The First Five Year Plan stressed that:

The elimination of poverty cannot, obviously, be achieved

> merely by redistributing existing wealth! Nor can a programme aimed only at increasing production remove existing inequalities. The two need to be considered together..... The problem is not one of merely rechannelizing economic activity within the existing socio-economic framework. That framework has itself to be remoulded so as to enable it to accommodate progressively those fundamental urges which express themselves in the right to work, the right to adequate incomes, the right to education and a measure of insurance against sickness, old age and other disabilities. [Government of India 1953:8].

Nor is full employment (with rising wages) possible without growth:

> A programme for full employment with assurance of at least the current level of real wages to the newly employed can get into swing only as the capital formation in the community goes up [Government of India, 1953:8].

Socialism, and later 'socialistic' patterns of society, were, of course, highlighted in the political rhetoric of the Indian National Congress. But, apart from land reform, no serious effort to alter the distribution of existing wealth was ever contemplated in any radical way. The land reform programme itself was not really pursued, then or subsequently, with conspicuous vigour or success. The expansion of public ownership through fresh investment, public sector control of 'the commanding heights', and regulation of private sector activity were seen as the means of containing the concentration of wealth, income, and power in the private sector.

This broad approach informed Indian planning well into the '60s. The Mahalanobis strategy was explicitly designed to rapidly expand the capacity of the Indian economy to achieve and sustain a high rate of growth on a self-reliant basis. Apart from reiterating the role of land reform, cooperatives and the public sector, the conflicts between growth and employment were seen as essentially transitional and containable by encouraging labour-intensive techniques in construction and light industry (especially in the production of mass consumer goods). Specific programmes — both protective and positive — were designed to help traditional and small industry. But in terms of allocation, these were relatively small, adding up to a mere 5 per cent of total public sector plan outlay.

Even as the overall development strategy was crystallizing, the '50s witnessed significant new initiatives for promoting rural development with the involvement of the people. The early years after Independence saw a great deal of interest in reviving the village panchayats and gram sabhas as a means of encouraging participation in local development. The first Plan referred to the need to establish village panchayats which would, amongst other things, be concerned with civic and economic activities in the community. Some States passed legislation for this purpose. Meanwhile, the central government sponsored a nationwide community development programme to encourage the rural population and enlist its cooperation in development.

Under the community development programme, a complement of staff was appointed specifically to carry out comprehensive development works in each block — the basic administrative unit for development. A substantial amount of state funds was placed at the disposal of the block development staff. The use of these funds was to be decided in consultation with local leaders through nominated committees. But the committees were rarely 'representative' enough of different sections of the rural population to generate the expected broad-based popular enthusiasm and participation. Also, the block level programmes throughout the country had to conform to a standard, schematic budget specified by the Centre, leaving little room for adapting the content of programmes to specific local conditions.

Dissatisfaction with the way the community development programme was evolving led to the appointment of the Balwantrai Mehta Study team in 1957 to review the working of the programme and suggest ways in which it could be made more effective.[1] The team came to the conclusion that administrative decentralization was essential for the effective implementation of the development programme and that elected bodies should control a decentralized administrative system. They recommended the early establishment of statutory elected local bodies and devolution to them of the necessary resources, power, and authority.

The recommendations had Nehru's support. The National Development Council (NDC) passed a resolution accepting them. The late '50s and early '60s saw a spate of Panchayati Raj legislation. By the mid -'60s, Panchayati Raj was in place in most States, but mostly in name only. From the beginning, it was clear that the members of the State legislatures, the State-level leaders and the bureaucracy were reluctant to devolve power and resources upon the elected local bodies. The latter were not enthusiastic about mobilizing resources on their own initiative and consequently depended almost wholly on the State and central governments for their resources. Once the intensive phase of community development (lasting five years) was over, the quantum of resources available for use by the panchayats declined significantly.

In some cases — e.g. Maharashtra and Gujarat — the initial enthusiasm for Panchayati Raj was dampened once the State-level politicians and the bureaucracy realized that their 'influence' would be greatly reduced if local bodies were given substantial resources and the freedom to allocate them. So, the role of panchayats was curtailed by making them responsible only for the implementation of projects, with an advisory body comprising ministers, MLAs, MPs, and officials actually making decisions. The launching of the Intensive Agricultural Development Programme in 1960 and, subsequently, the Small Farmer Development Programme, the Drought Prone Area Programme, and others outside of the Community Development projects, further eroded the fledgling experiment with Panchayati Raj and strengthened the hold of the line departments on development at district level.

Criticisms of the development strategy, voiced even at the time of the Second Plan, began to find stronger political articulation in the early '60s. The draft Third Plan was criticized for not paying sufficient attention to the unemployment problem on the ground that, despite a decade of planning, the majority of Indians did not earn even as much as 6 annas per head per day, and that, if anything, the rich were getting richer and the poor poorer. The immediate response of the government was to assuage such criticism by incorporating a special employment programme as part of the Plan; appointing an expert Committee to review trends in the distribution of income and wealth; and ascertaining the extent to which the operation of the economic system may have resulted in concentration of wealth and means of production.

The Plan document stated that until the economy was strengthened, it would be difficult to provide work at an adequate level of remuneration to the entire labour force. In the meantime, the government would follow a strategy of maximizing the employment potential of the Plan programmes; speeding up and even enlarging programmes under the Plan with large employment potential 'especially in areas with heavy pressure of population and in which there is considerable underemployment'; and introducing a special rural work programme (RWP) to provide 100 days of employment per year for 2.5 million people. Programmes for village water supply and local development works were accelerated and later developed into the 'minimum needs programme'.

At the same time, a section of the Planning Commission put forward its view that accelerated growth is the best means of resolving the problem of poverty and employment. This viewpoint was articulated in a Perspective Planning Division (PPD) paper which outlined a long-term plan whose central aim was to assure a specified minimum standard of living within 15 years to everyone (Government of India, 1964). The paper ruled out as impractical any drastic redistribution of existing wealth and focused instead on using progressive taxation and public expenditure policies, along with an expanding and efficient public sector — all in a context of rapid overall growth — to bring about better distribution of incremental income and wealth.

The PPD view did not survive the droughts of the mid-'60s and the Indo-Pakistan conflict of 1965. The emphasis had shifted significantly by the time the final version of the Third Plan was completed. The latter part of the '60s saw a period of low investment, high inflation, and persistent balance of payment problems. Several studies highlighted the failure to check increased concentration of industrial activity among big business houses, and the skewed-off benefits from various rural development programmes.

Strategies such as the Integrated Agricultural District Programmes (IADP) and the use of High Yield Variety (HYV) seeds were allegedly aggravating inequalities (Das Gupta, 1977; Frankel, 1971). Confidence in growth-centred strategies (among economists and politicians) weakened. Interventions aimed more directly at particularly 'vulnerable' segments came to the fore. The Rural Credit Survey of 1960 had argued for special programmes to help small and marginal farmers increase their asset base and productivity (Reserve Bank of India, 1969). An incipient RWP was launched in the Third Plan, which also recognized regional disparities as an important problem calling for, among other things, special programmes for backward regions.

The planners continued to maintain that no significant reduction in disparities could be effected by redistributive fiscal, pricing and other policies; that surpluses derived from the rich were needed for investment; and that socio-economic goals had to be pursued through overall growth. But they were also forced to respond to the growing perception that the pace of alleviation of mass poverty and unemployment was unacceptably slow and needed to be addressed more directly.

At one stage, the requirements of rapid growth and those of speedy redressal of mass poverty and unemployment were thought to be reconcilable. The Planning Commission paper setting out the approach to the Fourth Plan (Government of India, 1972; Minhas, 1974) outlined a strategy consisting of two key elements. One was the proposal to launch a basic minimum needs programme which would earmark part of the Plan funds to ensure that all parts of the country had a specified minimum level of education, public health, transportation, and water supply facilities. The other was an integrated local works programme centred around improved land and water resource utilization, which would generate additional employment opportunities in rural areas so as to augment the production potential of agriculture and related activities.

The idea of 'basic minimum needs' was incorporated in the Fourth Five Year Plan and also figures in all subsequent Plans. It was not, however, backed up by adequate resources. Such resources as were made available were, however, not distributed (either to the States or eventually to the districts) in accordance with local needs.

If the Minimum Needs Programme existed only in name, the concept of an integrated land and water development programme for employment does not even figure in the Five

Year Plans. Both would have called for major changes in the way rural development programmes were planned, funded, and implemented. Evidently no one was eager to confront the thorny issues which this would have raised; they were side-stepped in favour of a variety of programmes to benefit particular regions and classes of people who were poor, backward, or underprivileged.

Political Pressures Impinging on Poverty Alleviation Programmes

Developments in the political arena gave a powerful impetus to the movement towards targeted poverty alleviation programmes. The split in the INC, and the subsequent internal struggle for control over the party, saw Indira Gandhi using a 'radical' platform in order to seek popular support. Bank nationalization and abolition of privy purses were the initial moves in this strategy, but they proved to be of limited usefulness. Prior to the 1972 general elections, Mrs Gandhi had adopted Garibi hatao as the main plank of her manifesto. The persistence of unemployment, the slow pace of improvement in living standards, and the fact that poor and unemployed people comprised a large part of the population compelled the politicians to pay attention to their problems.

It has been pointed out that the last 30 years have witnessed a major transformation in Indian politics. Large numbers of illiterate and impoverished people have become active participants in the political arena. They are aware of their political rights and, increasingly, have become more capable of wielding political power. Even conservative parties, if they are to remain committed to a competitive electoral political system, will have to satisfy new criteria based on the promise of eradicating mass poverty in the foreseeable future (Frankel, 1977:550).

The growing emphasis on poverty alleviation programmes has also been interpreted as a sign of 'elites competing for political power', seeking to exploit the situation created by the decline of the Congress party as a relatively stable and dominant party based on a measure of political consensus. This decline was in part a reflection of the process of disintegration set in motion by commercialization, by the rapid growth of wage labour, and by vertical dependency in a traditional society on which the Congress party organization and patronage networks had depended heavily. Reinforcing the decline of the Congress party was a parallel process of politicization of the lower rural classes, which also contributed to the weakening of traditional vertical ties. Indira Gandhi's Garibi hatao slogan can thus be interpreted as an integral part of the strategy for mobilizing mass support in this changed situation (Kohli, 1987: 84-8).

Indira Gandhi's resounding success in the 1972 elections helped place poverty alleviation programmes firmly on the national agenda. From the Fourth Five Year Plan onwards, the scope and scale of these programmes were progressively extended.

The Fourth Plan declared that area development plans were to be prepared for tribal areas, whilst SCs were to be better integrated within the rural communities in which they lived. The planners found it necessary, however, to emphasize that in both cases the special programmes were meant to supplement the allocations under the normal Plan. Evidently there was a fear that the States might divert resources allocated for SC/ST welfare, provided under the regular programme, to other uses.

Initially, a distinction was made between marginal farmers and landless labourers, on the one hand, and potentially viable small farmers, on the other. For the former, the emphasis was to be on encouraging activities such as animal husbandry and on expanding employment opportunities on a sustained basis through area development programmes by improving local infrastructure and developing natural resources. For small farmers it was felt that measures (including subsidized credit) to enable them to gain better access to irrigation and other yield-augmenting inputs would be more appropriate. In addition, there were to be special programmes for problem areas — notably drought-prone districts, desert regions, and hill areas.

Faced with criticisms of the Emergency, Indira Gandhi went to the electorate with a 20-point programme which was no more than a refurbished version of the Garibi hatao package. The opposition was highly critical of the centralization of power and the authoritarianism of her regime, and argued for a different approach to development, based on decentralization of power, participation of the people, full employment, and poverty alleviation as the central themes.

The Janata government set up a committee to provide a blueprint for decentralization (Government of India, 1978). The new Planning Commission pleaded for active state support to organize the poor (Government of India, 1978) in order to enable them to press their interests more effectively in the political process. These ideas were not pursued seriously. However, the revised Fifth Plan, prepared under the Janata government, provided a substantially larger allocation for rural development and employment programmes. After Indira Gandhi's return to power, the scale of poverty alleviation programmes was enlarged, even though they had paid her such poor political dividends earlier. The Sixth Plan (1980-5) nearly trebled the allocation for rural development and employment programmes. All this underlines the enduring political appeal of these programmes and their becoming an accepted part of the discourse and agenda of practically all political parties and consequently of the Five Year Plans.

Indira Gandhi's second tenure witnessed some changes in her government's approach to poverty alleviation programmes. The minimum needs programme continued, but there was still no attempt to ensure that the allocation of resources between State and districts, for various basic needs, was designed to create a minimum standard of facilities everywhere. The creation of national technology missions for rural water supply and immunization constituted the only major departure from the earlier pattern. The three major area-based programmes (namely, drought-prone, desert, and hill areas) were also continued on an enlarged scale without much change in concept. Others went through significant changes in organization and process along with an expansion of the scale of outlays.

The small farmer and the marginal farmer/agricultural labour programmes were discontinued and replaced by the Integrated Rural Development Programme (IRDP) from 1977 onwards. Two types of employment-generating programmes were launched. The National Rural Employment Programme (NREP), which commenced in 1980, was designed to utilize the accumulated food stocks to create employment, and improve the nutrition of the rural poor. Subsidized supply of foodgrains was an essential part of this scheme. It was distinguished from earlier food-for-work programmes by its emphasis on creating specified durable community assets, with detailed guidelines as to the category of people who were to be benefited and also as to the kinds of assets which were to be created. Three years later, another programme, the Rural Labour Employment Guarantee Programme (RLEGP), was aimed primarily at providing additional employment to landless labourers, without laying any special emphasis on the creation of durable assets.

In 1982, a programme for the Development of Women and Children in rural areas was undertaken to help women increase their income opportunities and provide support services (including child care facilities) to enable them to take up economically viable activities. The scheme of Training Rural Youth for Self Employment (TRYSEM) was started in 1977. It was intended to help young people from poor rural families to set up production units of their own in both agricultural and non-agricultural sectors. The target group for all these programmes was to be families with incomes below a specified level; quotas were also specified for sub-categories among the poor, especially SCs, STs, and women. The total allocation for IRDP and employment programmes in the Sixth Plan (1980-5) exceeded Rs. 40 billion —- compared to Rs. 15 billion in the Fifth Plan.

Significantly, the political initiative, as well as the funding of targeted poverty alleviation programmes, came for the most part from the Centre. There were, however, important exceptions. The most notable of these was the Employment Guarantee Scheme (EGS) of Maharashtra; the Midday Meals Programme of Tamil Nadu, and some other States; Andhra Pradesh's Rice for the Poor at Rs. 2 per kilogram; and a variety of social security programmes.

Maharashtra's EGS, started in 1972 and given statutory form in 1979, undertook to provide gainful and productive employment on approved works for all unskilled persons in rural areas who were prepared to take up manual labour. The guarantee was limited to manual, unskilled work in the vicinity of the worker's residence, with payments consistent with prescribed minimum wages. The original intention was to take up only schemes which created durable community assets; but this has been gradually relaxed to include works benefiting individuals. The programme was started entirely at the initiative of Maharashtra State and has not lost its identity among the numerous anti-poverty and employment programmes sponsored by the Centre. The cost of the EGS has also risen rapidly (from approximately Rs. 210 million in 1975-76 to Rs. 3180 million in 1988-89) and is several times larger than the cost of the centrally sponsored NREP. Significantly, despite the fact that the EGS was a highly innovative programme conceived in a Congress-ruled State, it was not accepted as a model for the centrally-sponsored national employment programmes. It is only recently, in the context of discussions about the 'Right to Work', that the EGS model has been considered seriously as an alternative to a constitutional guarantee.

The central government has sponsored a special programme for supplementary feeding of children below six years of age and for mothers. In addition, a number of States have introduced special nutrition programmes. The most important of these is the mid-day meals programme introduced in Tamil Nadu, Gujarat, Maharashtra and West Bengal, with substantial financial support. The Tamil Nadu programme, which seeks to provide one meal a day throughout the year to all pre-school children registered with balwadis, and all school-going children up to the age of ten years, was estimated as benefiting 8 million children (as at 1984) at a cost of Rs. 2240 millions (met entirely by the State from the proceeds of special levies). This outlay accounted for nearly 10 per cent of the Tamil Nadu budget (Harriss, 1991). Arguments about whether the State can afford such a large subsidy have not made much impact because of its evident popularity among the mass of the people and the beneficial effects on childrens' health and school attendance.

Similarly, the 'rice at Rs. 2 per kilogram' scheme of Andhra Pradesh provides direct consumption subsidies to the poor. This scheme also carries an extremely high financial burden, borne entirely out of the State's own resources (Radhakrishna and Indrakant, 1987). Expensive as it is, none of the successive governments have found it politically expedient to curtail the programme or the magnitude of subsidies to it.

Several States have introduced social security schemes of widely varying design. Commencing with the introduction of old age pensions, the tendency has been to extend such schemes to other categories, e.g. accident relief, maternity assistance, support for destitute and disabled people. One of the most comprehensive schemes is in operation in Tamil Nadu. The annual cost, currently, is approximately Rs. 700 million, again borne entirely by the State budget (Guhan, 1989).

Most States do not have a strong enough resource base to sustain such programmes on a significant scale. The few which do, e.g. Maharashtra, Tamil Nadu, and Andhra Pradesh, are in a relatively strong fiscal position and can afford to ignore the Planning Commission's disapproval. The Planning Commission has, indeed, been forced to accept the necessity of allocating substantial resources for targeted poverty alleviation programmes. It has also acquiesced, however reluctantly, in a variety of subsidies for the benefit of the poor. However, the Commission has sought to discourage States from setting up their own subsidy programmes, partly because they divert resources from productive investment, and also because there is a strongly held belief at the Centre that the enhancement of asset base and employment opportunity is a far more effective way of ensuring a sustained improvement in living standards. Hence, the emphasis is on programmes targeted towards regions with special problems.

The scale and range of such programmes has expanded considerably and currently account for perhaps as much as a sixth of the public sector plan outlay. The allocation of the outlay is a matter for central decision-making. The States resent this and complain about excessive centralization and rigidity in the design of the programmes. Nevertheless, they have seldom opposed, or rejected, the expansion of the centrally sponsored anti-poverty programmes. Apart from their obvious political appeal, these programmes provide a means for the States to receive additional central funds. Moreover, because monitoring and accountability are weak, the programmes encourage elaborate and extensive networks of patronage, reaching out to every corner of the country. It is a network in which State functionaries (political and bureaucratic) can participate, as well as ruling party workers at grass roots level. The role of professional intermediaries who mediate between the village and the State has also expanded considerably. At the same time, criticisms about duplication, waste and corruption have simultaneously intensified.

Organizational Problems Facing Poverty Alleviation Programmes

A number of evaluation studies (carried out by the government as well as by independent researchers) have drawn attention to the many deficiencies in the working of these programmes (see, e.g. Government of India, 1985a; Godbole, 1990).[2] Among the main points repeatedly made, the following are the most common:

1. The benefits of the programmes are not reaching the intended beneficiaries because it is easy for the better-off, by virtue of their superior connections with local bureaucracy, to appropriate a sizeable part of the benefits.
2. Even when the beneficiaries are part of the target groups, their selection is often biased, and intermediaries tend to siphon off a substantial part of the resources.

3. The intended beneficiaries lack knowledge/information about the programmes under which they could seek assistance, or about its form and terms.
4. Intended beneficiaries are not organized to press their claims, to correct biased selection and other defects.
5. The fragmentation of effort and lack of integration of various anti-poverty programmes cause much waste.

The pros and cons and organizational problems of different types of anti-poverty programme have also been discussed extensively.

Such deficiencies as there are have evoked two different strands of response: one emphasizing the need for decentralization of power and the other focusing on improving administration. The former derives from the view that the root of the problem lies in the centralization of resources and power. Indira Gandhi's (Mark I) regime, which culminated in the Emergency, carried the process of concentration of power into the hands of the central government— and that too into the hands of a small group of individuals — to an extreme limit. A major plank of Jayaprakash Narayan's Nav Nirman movement was the need to reverse this process and take active steps to devolve more power not only from the Centre to the States, but also from the States down to the representative level government institutions below. One of the first actions of the Janata Government after assuming office was to set up a Committee on Panchayati Raj Institutions (PRIs). The Resolution appointing that Committee declared.

> The Government accords the highest priority to rural development ..... The Government considers that the maximum degree of decentralization both in planning and in implementation is necessary.... It has accordingly decided, in consultation with the State governments and Union Territories, to set up a committee to inquire into the working of Panchayati Raj institutions and to suggest

> measures to strengthen them and enable a decentralized system of planning and development to be effective. [Government of India, 1978b].

The Committee found the activities of the PRIs to be unsatisfactory. By way of explanation, the Committee referred to the frequent tendency of some States to override one or other of the tiers of the system; the failure to hold elections as provided by the law; the lukewarm attitude of the high level political elite — including MLAs and MPs — to the need to strengthen the democratic process at grassroot level, and the perception of the Panchayati Raj leadership as a threat to their own position; factionalism, corruption, and political interference in the functioning of PRIs; and the tendency of economically and socially privileged segments to dominate decision-making.

The Committee reiterated the view of the Balwantrai Mehta team that

> establishment of democratic bodies below the state level is imperative from the political and socio-developmental perspectives. Democratic institutions with periodic elections at all levels will provide a forum for the assertion of their strength in large number by the weaker segments. With... adequate opportunities to exercise power at various levels national energy in political recrimination will yield to constructive competition and worthwhile cooperation. [Government of India, 1978b].

They recommended a three-tier system of Panchayati Raj with both development and some regulatory functions (through Nyaya Panchayats); periodic elections supervised by the State election officers (with reservation for SCs/STs); devolution of substantial powers from States to local bodies; constitution of State level Finance Commissions to determine the devolution of resources from the states to the PRIs; and the establishment of development staff under the Chief Executive Officer of the district, answerable to the elected Zilla Parishad.

This report was neither placed formally on the table of the Parliament, nor discussed with the states. But some states, notably Karnataka and West Bengal, made a serious effort to resuscitate PRIs as instruments of decentralized development. In West Bengal, the Left Front government has shown a consistently positive attitude to decentralization since the late '70s. Elected representatives of the PRIs have been actively involved in decision-making and implementation of local development programmes; and, increasingly, the responsibility for local planning, along with the allocation of resources, is being devolved upon them. This process has been helped by several circumstances. Thus, for example, the same coalition has been voted back to power in four successive general elections; the implementation of a substantial land reform programme which has secured the rights of a large number of bargadars (small tenants) over land they cultivate; and the ruling party has been elected to a large majority of PRIs in three successive elections.

Likewise, Karnataka passed a Panchayati Raj bill — substantially along the lines recommended by the Asoka Mehta committee — soon after the Janata government was elected. But, because of a delay in the grant of presidential assent, the law became effective only in 1985. Under the Janata and later under the Janata Dal, a serious effort was made to devolve substantial powers and resources to the zilla parishads and PRIs, and to confront the many difficult political and administrative issues which the process entails. But, unlike in West Bengal, the party in power at the State level has changed during the last 10 years: inter-and intra-party conflicts, and conflicts between the PRIs and the bureaucracy have impeded the progress of the reforms. The recent action of the State government seeking to restrict the freedom of PRIs and, more importantly, the decision to postpone elections to these bodies have been decisive setbacks.

Kerala also has gone through a similar experience; the Kerala District Councils Act took nearly 10 years to pass, reflecting the reluctance of the State legislature to devolve power. Even after the law came into effect the State government has been slow to transfer resources to the PRIs, leaving them in an economically difficult situation.

The other approach focuses on administration. The Planning Commission issued a series of guidelines on district planning as early as 1969, in which the need for building up capabilities in terms of organization and expertise was emphasized. In 1977, a committee on Block Level Planning made a number of suggestions for strengthening the machinery and processes of local development planning. But progress was slow, and the problems of fragmentation and waste increased in the wake of the proliferation of rural development and anti-poverty programmes. A comprehensive review of the problem was undertaken by another committee set up by the Planning Commission in 1984. This committee recognized that

> For decentralized planning to be making headway, [the] institutional mechanism has to be made broad-based with active involvement of local representatives, and endowed with greater degree of autonomy in local decision-making. But a full fledged transfer of power to decide all sectoral allocation can be achieved only 'at some distant point of time'. [Government of India, 1984].

Various initiatives and improvisations (necessary to bring about much needed technical and administrative changes and changes in attitudes) should be introduced cautiously. Adequate time should be allowed for assimilating them.

While District Panchayat Authorities should have adequate representation for elected representatives, representatives of economic/occupational and social groups and voluntary agencies, it should be coordinated by the District Collector. The development officials at district level and below should be deputed and answerable to the District Panchayat Authorities. There is a great deal of emphasis on upgrading technical expertise, training of planning personnel, and building professional planning organizations for expert scrutiny and evaluation of projects. The role of elected PRIs was thus relegated decisively in to the background. The committee suggested that a certain portion of local development funds may be given to District Panchayat Authorities to be spent at their discretion.

Underlying this view is a deep scepticism about the efficacy of PRIs. Criticisms have been made along the following lines:

1. There is no strong grass roots pressure for decentralization.
2. Under the existing social structure and property relations, the rural elite dominate these institutions and appropriate much of the benefits of development.
3. Weaker segments are sceptical about decentralization without 'basic changes in property relations'.
4. State level leaders, involved in a struggle for their political survival, use the opportunity provided by the rapid growth of plan outlay for consolidating their own power by controlling the allocation of funds for schools, hospitals, roads, and other essentially local works (Rao, 1989).

In the meantime, the trend towards the expansion of poverty alleviation programmes, largely sponsored by the Centre, has continued, indeed gathered further momentum. Rajiv Gandhi saw them as a means of mobilizing the electoral support of the poor. At the same time, several changes were made in the design and organization of these programmes, in an attempt to ameliorate deficiencies.Interest in political and administrative decentralization revived during the '80s, partly because of the strong plea made by the Rao Committee (which investigated the organization and management of poverty alleviation programmes) and the Economic Advisory Council to the Prime Minister; and partly because of the popularity and apparent success of the West Bengal and Karnataka experiments.

The Seventh Five Year Plan recognized the need to combine administrative improvement with political decentralization, whilst leaning heavily towards the former. It proposed a three pronged strategy whereby 'poverty alleviation programmes will be formulated and implemented in a decentralized manner with the participation of local people at the grass roots level through village panchayats, panchayat samitis' in a gradual fashion; the existing administrative arrangements would be restructured in order to ensure that rural development and poverty alleviation are planned in an integrated way and implemented effectively; and emphasis would be placed on group-oriented activities for beneficiaries.

Recent Shifts in the Debate on Decentralization

In 1987-88 Rajiv Gandhi organized a series of workshops to discuss with the District Magistrates from all over India ways of creating 'responsive administration'. On the basis of the deliberation of these workshops, the Chief Secretaries of the governments of various States produced an overall report in 1988. Its thrust was to make the District Magistrate the focal point of district planning. Besides being in charge of law and order, (s)he was to be the chief executive of the zilla parishad with elected representatives playing a distinctly secondary, if not passive, role. The distrust of the political process is made quite clear in the following passage from the Chief Secretaries' report:

> The Presidentship of Zilla Parishads proving such a glittering prize, furious contests will develop with money and communal/caste influences overriding considerations of

> competence and commitment to social justice among the candidates leading to the capture of the top position by undesirable elements. This may be contrasted with the existing position where the bureaucracy may be sluggish but tries to be fair in its dealings as a rule. And making the collector CEO of ZP will bring knowledge, experience and influence of the Collector and enhance its effectiveness.

The entire exercise of drawing a blueprint for a restructuring of administration in areas which constitutionally fall in the States' domain was undertaken without consulting or involving the Chief Ministers of States. Even the participation of District Magistrates was not cleared through the State governments. In 1989, the Centre decided to deal directly with the Panchayats in implementing the Jawahar Rozgar Yojana (JRY). The funds available under the JRY were transferred directly to panchayats, which were empowered to utilize them (subject to certain guidelines on the categories of works/beneficiaries) for local development. This move was widely seen as an attempt on the part of the Centre to bypass the States and establish control over the district administration and even panchayats by passing on substantial funds directly to them.

Around the same time, the Centre introduced a Constitutional Amendment Bill on Panchayati Raj. The bill reflected the general consensus among political parties about giving constitutional status to Panchayati Raj, making periodic elections to their bodies mandatory, as in the case of the States and the Centre. Other provisions included reservations in order to ensure adequate representation for SCs, STs, and women on local government councils; the creation of a State level Finance Commission with a view to determining the devolution of resources to the PRIs. However, the bill was far too detailed in spelling out the distribution of the powers between States and the PRIs, leaving little flexibility for the States to work out the specific allocation of functions, procedure, etc. in the light of their own particular circumstances.

The feeling that the bill encroached widely on the power of the States was reinforced by the parallel moves, described above, for the Centre to establish direct channels through the district administrations and the panchayats. That the bill was vague on the role of the district administration and its relation to PRIs deepened such suspicion. In the event, a general election was called. The Parliament was dissolved, and the amendment lapsed.

The Janata Dal government introduced a fresh amendment which recognized the States' power to legislate details within the broad principles outlined in the Constitution. The bill tabled in Parliament in 1991 follows broadly the same approach. It is now before a Select Committee.[3]

The introduction of an amendment to the Constitution, and the declarations of support for its objectives from virtually all parties, reflects a general recognition that democratically elected local government institutions have not been given a fair chance; that the system has become far too centralized to cater to the diverse needs of different regions; and that the various anti-poverty programmes implemented by the state bureaucracy, besides being wasteful, are not effective in reaching the target groups.

At the same time, the leisurely way in which the amendment is being processed is indicative of continued hesitation and doubts about its implications. The view that elected PRIs are inherently incapable of using funds wisely for the benefit of the poor is still prevalent, not only among officials but also in non-official circles. PRIs, according to this view, will be dominated by the upper castes and substantial landholders, who are unlikely to work in the interests of the weaker segments or the unemployed. The higher levels of the state and its functionaries must, therefore, ensure that the resources for local development meant for the poor do, in fact, reach them. An extreme version of this view sees the District Collector as a better custodian of the interests of the poor than elected representatives.

It is altogether naive to suppose that under the existing dispensation the District Collector acts autonomously and is not influenced by pressure from the upper castes and classes. Despite central control and implementation through the bureaucracy, inefficiency, wastage and corruption are the rule rather than the exception. Restructuring the developmental bureaucracy at the district level, itself by no means an easy task as experience has shown, is not enough. Making people better aware of their rights/entitlements under various programmes; insisting on greater information about the benefits of specific programmes in a particular locality; allowing the village assembly to decide who are the eligible beneficiaries on the basis of well-specified criteria; and monitoring the distribution of benefits are all features that are essential in helping generate political pressure in order to ensure more effective implementation of the programmes.

If political pressures must be brought into the process, the case for an institutionalized framework based on representative bodies (subject to the discipline of mandatory periodic elections) becomes very strong. The experience of Karnataka and West Bengal would suggest that the effect of political decentralization is contingent upon the willingness of the State and the Central government to transfer resources and responsibilities to the PRIs. At a rough estimate, 30-40 per cent of the State plan outlays comprise programmes which, by their nature, have to be planned and implemented locally. The proportion may be even higher if the employment programmes were included.

An essential precondition for the success of decentralization is that these programmes should be transferred to the elected local bodies and the allocation used without interference from the State government. Once this is done, local self-government will acquire the necessary political credibility and become truly effective. The real hurdle is the reluctance of State level politicians to shed control over the dispensation of any substantial part of plan resources and the opposition of the bureaucracy to decentralized administration.

These changes will clearly not take place without considerable political effort. But the passing of the constitutional amendment would be a big step forward. Once PRIs, periodic elections and statutory mechanisms for the devolution of resources are made mandatory, those interested in promoting greater decentralization (including local leaders) will have a better chance of succeeding in their struggles.

Notes

1. This review of the Balwantrai Mehta team's recommendations and its implementation is largely based on the report of the Asoka Mehta Committee (Government of India, 1978a).
2. For an interesting micro-study of the relation between politics at the grassroots level and the working of IRDP, see Gebert (1989).
3. When this volume was going to Press, the Constitutional amendments were passed.

References

Chandrasekar, B.K., 1989: 'Panchayati Raj Bill: The Real Flaw', Economic and Political Weekly 24 (1 July): 26, pp. 1433-5.

Das Gupta, B., 1977: *New Agrarian Technology and India* (New Delhi: Macmillan).

Frankel, F., 1971: *India's Green Revolution* (Princeton: Princeton University Press).

—, 1977; India's Political Economy 1947-1977 (Delhi: Oxford University Press).

Gebert, R., 1989: 'Poverty Alleviation and Village Politics in Tamil Nadu — whose interests first?' Economic and Political Weekly 24 (28 Jan.): 4, pp, 197-202.

Godbole., M., 1990: *Rural Employment Strategy: A Quest in the Wilderness* (Bombay: Himalaya Publishing House).

Government of India, 1953: *First Five Year Plan* (New Delhi: Planning Commission, Government of India).

———, 1961: Third Five Year Plan (New Delhi: Planning Commission, Government of India).

———, 1964: 'Notes on Perspective of Development India 1960-61 to 1975-76: Implications of Planning for a Minimum Level of Living' (Planning Commission, Government of India, New Delhi). (mimeo.).

———, 1972: *Towards an Approach to the Fourth Five Year Plan* (New Delhi: Planning Commission, Government of India).

———, 1978: *Draft Five Year Plan 1978-83* (New Delhi: Planning Commission, Government of India).

———, 1978a: *Report of Working Group on Block Level Planning* (New Delhi: Planning Commission, Government of India).

———, 1978b: *Report of the Committee on Panchayati Raj Institutions* (New Delhi: Ministry of Agriculture and Irrigation, Government of India).

———, 1984: *Report of the Working Group on District Planning* (New Delhi: Planning Commission, Government of India).

———, 1985: *Sixth Five Year Plan 1985-90, Vol. II* (New Delhi: Planning Commission, Government of India).

———, 1985: *Evaluation Report on IRDP* (New Delhi: Planning Commission, Government of India).

Guhan, S., 1989: *'Social Security Initiatives in Tamil Nadu 1989'* (Working paper 96) (Madras Institute of Development Studies, Madras) (mimeo.).

Harriss, B., 1991: *Child Nutrition and Poverty in South India — Noon Meals in Tamil Nadu* (New Delhi: Concept).

Kohli, A., 1987: *The State and Poverty in India: The Politics of Reform* (Cambridge: Cambridge University Press).

Mathew, G., (Ed.)., 1986: *Panchayati Raj in Karnataka Today: Its National Dimensions* (New Delhi: Concept).

Minhas, B.S., 1974: *Planning and the Poor* (New Delhi: S.Chand).

Radhakrishna, R. and S. Indrakant, 1987: *'Effect of Rice Market Intervention Policies in India: The Case of Andhra Pradesh'* (Hyderabad: Centre for Economic and Social Studies) (mimeo.).

Rao, C.H.H., 1989: *'Decentralised Planning: An Overview of Experience and Prospects'*, Economic and Political Weekly 24 (25 Feb.): 8, pp.411-16.

Reserve Bank of India, 1969: *Report of the All India Rural Credit Survey Committee* (Bombay: Reserve Bank of India).

Glossary

bargadar	Sharecropper.
benami	Literally, without name. It refers to the system of holding land or property nominally in the name of another person while the actual owner retains the right to usufruct.
bhoodan	Land gift.
Operation Barga	The LF government's massive drive (1978) to record the names of sharecroppers.
pucca	Solidly built.
taluqdar	Owner of a revenue estate—taluq.
zamindar	Tax farming proprietor of land who paid a fixed revenue to the state.

Modern Indian Politics (Volume 2): Industry and Agriculture in India Since Independence (ed.) Satyamurthy, (1995) OUP, New Delhi.

13

Restructuring Poverty Alleviation Programmes

THAT assurance of a basic minimum living standard for everyone should be a central concern of development policies has been a recurrent refrain of Indian plans for over 3 decades. During the first three plans (1951-1965) the emphasis was on measures to quicken the pace of overall growth, diversify the economy and reduce inequalities in private wealth and income. But there was a growing feeling that land reforms, expansion of public sector, checks on growth of big business and other measures meant to reduce inequalities were tardy and ineffective.

There were apprehensions that inequality may in fact be increasing. In this context, it is significant that the outline of a 15 year plan (covering the period 1961 1975) prepared in the Planning Commission, and published in 1964, shifted the focus from relative inequalities to absolute poverty. Noting that more than half of the country's population lived in abject poverty, the document declared "....such widespread poverty is a challenge which no society in modern times can afford to ignore for long.... The stage has come when we should sharply focus on providing an assured minimum income to every citizen of the country within a reasonable period of time."

The continued slow pace of overall growth during the sixties and seventies, along with the growing skepticism about the efficacy of the so called 'trickle down' process to speedily eradicate mass employment and poverty, made Indian policy makers (and indeed many aid agencies including the World Bank and the SIDA) veer more and more towards targetted Poverty Alleviation (PA) programmes aimed at directly raising incomes and living standards of poor people.

In India measures meant to help particular social groups to overcome the cumulative disadvantages of centuries of discrimination have a long history. "Affirmative action" programmes favouring Scheduled Castes and Tribes as well as special programmes for their welfare have been in operation from the early 1950s. The big increase in general poverty alleviation programmes however came much later. The phenomenal expansion in the scale and coverage of these programmes and their growing diversity is one of the most significant features of Indian planning over the last 25 years. By mid 1990's perhaps as much as one sixth to a fifth of the public sector plan outlays was being allocated to PA programmes, broadly defined.

Main Characteristics

The latest Annual Report of the Rural Development Department lists some 17 Poverty Alleviation Programmes. These can be divided into 5 broad groups.

1. Those (of which IRDP is by far the most important) which seek to help the poor households to acquire/augment their productive assets and/or enable them to make more productive use of their assets.

2. Programmes meant to develop production potential of areas with special problems leading to backwardness

(eg. hill areas, desert and drought prone areas).

3. Various special employment programmes culminating in the Jawahar Rozgar Yojana.

4. Special programmes to ensure that people everywhere have access to a minimum standard of educational and health services and water supply.

5. Social security programmes for the aged, widows, disabled etc.; subsidised supply of essential commodities to the poor through the Public Distribution System, school feeding programmes and the like which, in effect, directly supplement current incomes of the target groups.

Of these, social security schemes are as yet relatively limited and uneven in coverage. In terms of scale and reach, the IRDP and special employment programmes are by far the most important, with special area programmes coming a distant third.

Some of the programmes are targetted at particular regions, and some at particular classes/groups of people (like programmes for SC/ST). But most combine both. Thus IRDP, JRY and area programmes have guidelines stipulating that certain groups (namely women, SCs and STs) should be given priority in the choice of beneficiaries. Some cases (e.g. IRDP) even indicate the proportion of outlays to be allocated to the specified groups.

The schemes taken up, or assisted, under these programmes include expansion/improvement of essential social services (education, health, drinking water, housing); and infrastructure (roads); development of irrigation, social forestry, watershed development and other schemes meant to enhance production potential; and assistance to individuals to acquire productive assets. Some of these activities figure under more than one PA programme: eg., irrigation and soil conservation works are included in JRY, IRDP, DPAP, and DDP. Most of them also figure under normal plan programmes of concerned line departments (like Agriculture, PWD, Minor Irrigation, Education, Women's welfare, health, SC and ST welfare, etc.). Activities included in the PA programme are supposed to be in addition to these normal plan schemes.

The other major characteristic of the PA programmes is their top - down character. Most of the programmes are conceived and largely funded by the central government. There are relatively few instances of programmes being taken up wholly by states on their initiative and with their resources. Employment Guarantee Scheme in Maharashtra and Chief Ministers' Noon Day meals for school children in Tamilnadu being the outstanding examples.

The criteria for distribution of funds under these programme to different states, and in the case of JRY between districts within each state, are decided by the centre. The content of each programme in terms of nature of activities which can be taken up and the categories of people who are to benefit are also subject to detailed central guidelines. This leaves hardly any freedom for the states to shift funds from one programme to another or determine their content in the light of local needs and possibilities. The states do have considerable scope to decide on distribution of the funds under particular PA programmes - other than JRY - across different districts/blocks. But hardly any seem to have used this flexibility to evolve rational criteria for deciding the intra-state allocations.

The third feature is the relatively soft nature of the programmes manifest in their emphasis on subsidies and loans and providing wage employment without being overtly concerned whether the works create facilities which augment productive capacity and continuing employment. Laxity in recovering of loans, which has over the years become more or less state policy, has encouraged popular perception of these programmes as handouts. Securing the benefits of these handouts often involves access to political patronage and/or corruption.

Deficiencies

Poverty alleviation programmes have grown in scale and diversity. Prior to 1970, these consisted mostly of special programmes for scheduled castes and tribes, social welfare, and a limited rural works programme. But since then a wide variety of new programmes differentiated in terms of targetted region and classes have come into operation. The total outlays on these programmes (including water supply but excluding education and health) have risen from Rs. 28 billion (7 per cent of total public sector plan outlay in the Fifth Plan) to Rs. 757 billion (or 17.5 per cent of public sector plan outlay in the Eighth Plan). This is an eloquent testimony to the political appeal of PA programmes. That this happened without the poor exerting any organised public pressure is largely on account of the compulsions of electoral politics; The poor happen to constitute nearly half the country's electorate. And Mrs. Gandhi demonstrated in the early 1970s that appealing to them through the 'garibi hatao' slogan could bring in a lot of votes. Since then PA programmes have caught and held the imagination of practically every party. In fact parties have vied with each other in starting new schemes under different labels in an effort to woo different regions and segments of the poor. There has been no opposition to increasing the outlays on such programmes. Recent experience in the wake of the recent structural reforms initiated by the central government shows that any attempt at whittling down outlays on such programmes provokes sharp political criticism. Fiscal problems notwithstanding outlay on PA programmes in the last 2 years have been stepped up substantially and with fanfare.

The scale of outlays is not as much of the problem as their efficacy. The employment programmes (EGS, JRY) are perhaps the most effective. Those who work under these schemes are unemployed or under-employed wage laborers. EGS, is perhaps the largest in terms of scale and evaluation studies suggest that it has contained rural unemployment in Maharashtra; provided more even seasonal distribution of work; and helped reduce gender differences in wage rates. The national employment programme (JRY) has also generated sizeable employment (estimated at around 1 billion person days in the early 1990s). Though this is not as large in relation to total employment as in Maharashtra, it is still substantial. The emphasis on creation of employment without concern for nature and quality of assets; the neglect to create productive assets which will provide the base for continuing employment; leakages and corruption; and the rate of wages paid under these programmes are among the features which have attracted considerable criticism.

Numerous evaluation studies — by government agencies and independent researchers — of IRDP have shown that substantial part of the benefits (both in terms of number of beneficiaries and quantum of benefits) accrue to people who are not eligible in terms of the poverty criterion; that the proportion of women and SC/STs assisted generally falls short of targets; that the beneficiaries do not get the full extent of assistance (by way of subsidies/loans) because of corruption; and the projects are poorly designed, badly executed and costly. Moreover assets obtained under IRDP are often found to be inappropriate, of poor quality and/or too costly; the record of repayment is poor; and a significant proportion of beneficiaries soon give up the assets acquired under the programme.

The other major problem is the relation of the poverty alleviation schemes to other 'normal' development programmes; one concern (discussed later) is whether outlays on poverty alleviation bear any systematic relation to the incidence of poverty and unemployment; whether they supplement or substitute normal programmes in particular region and the extent of duplication and overlapping of activities under the two. It is widely known that even where the funds are to be used for investments to create amenities and augment productive capacity, effectiveness is impaired because similar activities are taken up by different departments under different programmes; and related activities (eg. extension, credit marketing processing) bearing on the success or failure of a particular intervention are typically not taken into account in planning/implementation. Weak monitoring compounds the problems.

The line departments, not surprisingly, are very reluctant to part with their resources and control over their schemes to other agencies; there is no mechanism for monitoring at any level the progress of schemes relating to a particular activity under different programmes, or for verification of the veracity of progress reports by different programme agencies. Under these circumstances, it is difficult to keep track of the outlays and achievements of similar activities under different schemes and ensure proper coordination between different line departments involved in similar activities.

Ensuring that resources flow to areas and in measure needed, and that the available resources are put to effective use remains an extraordinarily daunting task. Except in the case of JRY, it is impossible to judge whether the allocation of PA programme resources across districts/blocks within each state is tailored to the magnitude of deficiencies/needs, and how much of impact they make in correcting the deficiencies. It is difficult to get information even on the quantum of resources spent in different districts under different PA programmes leave alone their impact!

Lack of public accountability is thus a serious weakness of PA programmes. With a few exceptions (notably West Bengal) all important decisions on the design and implementation of scheme as wcll as the choice of location and beneficiaries are taken by the bureaucracy. Elected representatives (MLAs, MPs, and executives of local bodies) are usually part of the advisory committees which are supposed to have a role in these decisions. But, even if they are interested in these larger issues, non-officials do not have much of a say on the scale, content or priorities. For the most part, they are content to use their membership of the Advisory Committees to cultivate their local support bases by influencing the choice of individuals and locations benefiting from the schemes and the choice of contractors for various works taken up as part of the PA programme. They rarely evince much interest in ensuring that the selection of beneficiaries conforms to the specified criteria or that the schemes are managed efficiently. Instead their role often tends to aggravate mistargetting, leakages and inefficiency.

These deficiencies, repeatedly highlighted by several evaluation studies, have provoked widespread discussion of remedial measures. Broadly speaking the corrective measures thrown up by the debate focus on the following:

1. Preparation of integrated area development plans for district and blocks to serve as a framework for deciding the priorities of PA programmes and minimising the scope for duplication.
2. Ways to improve the efficacy of targeting.

3. Encouraging greater involvement of non governmental organisations in local development. And
4. Handing over the responsibility for planning and implementing local development works to democratic decentralised institutions of local government.

Integrated Local Area Planning

Integrated area planning has figured prominently in the rhetoric of the plans for a long time. Several committees have gone into the modalities for preparing such plans. A number of district plans have also been published. Elaborate guidelines for this purpose have been issued by the Planning Commission and the Ministry of Rural Development (the latter in the context of IRDP) but these have not yielded any significant results.

Local level planning does not consist in merely enumerating the resources, social amenities and infrastructure facilities available in a district/block. In some cases (education, health) it is possible to quantify deficiencies to be made up to reach accepted minimum standards. But increasing the potential for income generation by making more and better use of local natural resources calls for a great deal of information on the volume and quality of resources, the available technology and the costs of harnessing these resources. Programmes of development in any given region cannot always be meaningfully considered without taking account of development in contiguous blocks/districts and sometimes other regions. In many cases especially transport/marketing infrastructure — investments in a particular block/district cannot be planned in isolation from what is happening in the neighbouring blocks/districts. Development possibilities based on materials and inputs from outside the region are often important. But these are not within the control of local bodies;

they depend on the growth of the economy at the state/national level and on location decisions of the public enterprises and the private sector. Local governments can however play a role by being alert to such possibilities and taking steps to make their regions attractive to investors.

The organisation and the competence for grappling these complex tasks of local planning do not exist in the district agencies; they are often inadequate even in higher level planning agencies. Nor is such expertise at present available in any significant measure from outside the government. A conscious attempt to encourage involvement of NGOs, universities/colleges, research institutions and consultancy firms in the process of local development is necessary to fill this gap. Apart from building local knowledge and expertise for planning development specific to each area, these institutions can play a major role in organising and facilitating participation of village communities in systematic collection and interpretation of data on local resources, identify potential for improvement specific to each community; and deliberating on action needed to exploit the potential.

The effectiveness of PA programmes can, ofcourse, be substantially improved even without integrated local area plans. This will be facilitated if resources available under normal as well as PA programmes for a particular district/block are viewed as part of a pool and if the agencies responsible for local development works (be it the bureaucracy or the elected executives of local government) have the discretion to decide on the content of the programmes in the light of local needs and possibilities.

This would require that allocations for all development activities in each district be placed under the control of elected local bodies where they are in place or, pending their constitution, with the District Rural Development Agency

(DRDA). Line departments should be required to implement schemes decided by the District authority and be accountable to it. The relative powers of elected bodies and the district officials in charge of development is a much debated issue. But once elected bodies are in place, it is only proper that the bureaucracy functions under their control, subject of course to monitoring, reviews and audit in a transparent manner.

Targeting

The other, and in many ways more important, issue is targetting. The search for ways to reduce chances of mistargetting has largely focused on more effective monitoring of beneficiary selection; creating credible checks against mistargetting; and creating incentives for "self selection". Experience has shown that once eligibility is defined in terms of income, there is a strong general incentive for understatement of incomes. And verification of incomes is notoriously difficult. Assessing vulnerability in terms of other, more easily verifiable, attributes (family size, land holding, caste, etc.) is in principle a better procedure but chances of bias and falsification remain high. In fact even if the eligibility is in terms of caste — which in principle is well known to everyone in the village and is easily verifiable — false certificates of caste can be got for a fee!

Clearly it is preferable to have the conditions of eligibility and/or the scale of benefits so defined as to reduce the incentives for those above the poverty line to get into the programme. Insisting on a certain portion of beneficiaries being drawn from poor/vulnerable groups (SC, ST, Women) and providing wage employment in JRY at wages well below the market/minimum wage rate and at locations away from the residence could improve targetting through self selection rather than through the exercise of discretionary authority. The reservation idea is now incorporated in the guidelines for all

Ministry of Rural Development projects. But the idea of lowering wage rates on works programmes is resisted especially if it means paying less than the legal minimum. The government cannot violate its own laws!

Targeting has not only a class/individual dimension but also a spatial aspect. Since the poor are unevenly distributed in space, the latter is an important, but relatively neglected, aspect. Except in JRY, allocations of PA programme outlays between and within states are not systematically related to poverty, unemployment or deficiency in basic amenities. Richer states generally tend to have larger resources and plan outlays per capita. One would expect the PA program allocations to correct this imbalance at least to some degree. There is doubt whether this in fact happens. Some data for the early 1980's show that, if anything, states with low incidence of poverty had higher outlay on PA programmes both in absolute terms per capita and as a proportion of total state plan outlays.

The position can be substantially improved by rationalising the criteria for spatial allocation. Specifically, the funds set apart for all employment and production oriented PA schemes should be pooled and distributed between states, and within states, in proportion to the absolute magnitude of poverty (in terms of the head count or, preferably, the Sen index) and the number of unemployed. Funds for basic amenities can be similarly pooled and distributed in proportion to the magnitude of deficiency in relation to the accepted minimum levels of facility for elementary education, health care, water supply and access to roads. With such an approach it is possible to do away with the needless proliferation of PA programmes by combining them into just 3 types! Employment generating schemes; augmenting the productive assets of the poor; and ensuring minimum basic amenities. This simplification would greatly add to the transparency of the programme and its effectiveness.

Accountability

There remains the problem of public accountability. Attempts to achieve this goal by creating advisory committees with MLAs, MPs and other non official members or encouraging NGO involvement have not been particularly effective. Information on the scale and nature of PA programmes in a particular block or district, the criteria by which beneficiaries are selected, the specific benefits to which they are entitled under each programme, and the procedures for availing of them is not easily accessible to the public. Even if the information is available, there are no institutional mechanisms for making complaints or seeking redressal of the grievances. Neither the elected representatives nor, surprisingly, the local cadres of political parties (even opposition parties), show much interest in taking up these issues. Non governmental organisations do take up such issues, but they are far too few to make more than a localised impact.

The NGOs have grown in number; but they vary greatly in motivation, the role they play and their effectiveness. Some are focussed on particular activities (eg. education, health, agriculture); some on overall development. Some have access to non government resources to sustain their activities. Most use their contacts with sympathetic government officials to secure resources for activities in their area and intercede with the government agencies to adapt programme content and design to be to local conditions. A few have innovative programmes to mobilise beneficiaries and building local institutions to make more effective use of government programmes for education, health, and resource development (especially irrigation, watershed development and social forestry). NGOs also play a role in making people aware of the various PA programmes and benefits available under them. Often they intercede with concerned government agencies to secure benefits for eligible people. Very few have taken the role of mobilising public opinion to assert peoples entitlements under various PA programme or to press the government to allocate more resources and permit greater flexibility in programming.

Consciousness of entitlements under government programmes, including PA programmes, is however growing as is the awareness of their importance in influencing the outcome of electoral politics. This has led to greater assertiveness in articulating general demands in the political arena, but not to an organised attempt to see that the choice of beneficiaries and implementation of local programmes in particular communities is improved. This does not seem likely unless both the power and the resources for local development are fully devolved to elected representatives of local governments by the centre and the states.

Role of Panchayat Raj Institutions

The experience of West Bengal — where elections to PR have been held regularly for the last 15 years — shows that representative local government bodies empowered to decide and execute local development projects can make a significant difference to the quality and efficacy of local development. The transfer of resources along with responsibilities is far from complete in West Bengal. The officials still seem to have a key role in approval of projects and release of funds. Nevertheless, the system does seem to have a better arrangement for keeping track of the resources available/ committed to various activities under different programmes. This helps to reduce the incidence of fragmentation and duplication in PA programmes thereby improving effectiveness on the use of resources.

More importantly, the panchayats play an active role in selection of beneficiaries, indicating the kinds of schemes which the village consider to be of high priority and, often, in organising and supervising the construction of works. Decisions and their implementation are under closer and more constant public scrutiny. There is a forum to vent grievances and, being elected bodies, the Panchayats are also more responsive. There is some evidence that costs of local development works in West Bengal are lower and quality of construction better. Bengal's experience suggests that democratic decentralisation will make a significant difference to the relevance, quality and efficiency of local development works.

The necessity and the wisdom of democratic decentralisation has been a recurrent theme of debates on the structure of government in India from the time of Constituent Assembly. By the late 1950's a review of the experience of the Community Development programme emphasised the need for democratically elected local governments for vigorous and equitable development in rural areas. Legislation to create Panchayati Raj bodies were passed by most states soon thereafter but they lacked constitutional sanction. The state governments were then — as they are now — reluctant to devolve powers and resources to these bodies; and in due course even elections were not held regularly.

Nearly three decades later, interest in decentralisation revived at the political level leading eventually to the passage of the 73rd Amendment to the Constitution. For the first time, the Constitution provides for a three tier system of local government based on mandatory elections every 5 years, and the states are required to devolve specific powers and resources to these bodies. This is a major landmark which opens up space for potentially meaningful, and creative, local development effort with in built pressures for accountability.

There are nevertheless apprehensions. Perhaps the most

widespread is the fear that, given the highly stratified and unequal socio-economic structure of Indian villages, the dominant landowning caste elites would effectively control power and that they are unlikely to be concerned about the welfare of the poor and the women. Recognising this, the constitutional amendment provides explicitly for reserving a substantial proportion of elected positions for SC/STs and for women. This reservation is essentially enabling in nature: it gives a secure space for the disadvantaged to articulate their needs in the decision making bodies. Skeptics doubt whether this space can and will in fact be used effectively in all cases, and soon. However pessimism on this account seems exaggerated for several reasons.

In the first place, the growing political consciousness of the so called lower castes as well as the scheduled castes and tribes is bound to express itself in local government as well. Secondly, villages/blocks differ greatly in caste/class composition: Some villages are no doubt dominated by better off upper castes, but by no means all the growing economic differentiation of rural society, the rapid diversification of activity and its commercialisation loosen traditional social structures. All this suggests that, while the outcome of decentralisation will be far from uniform, it opens up the possibility of significant realignment of the power structure in substantial parts of rural India favouring the disadvantaged groups.

It is unrealistic to expect such realignments to occur in all cases spontaneously and in such a manner as to give effective voice to the poor and promote their interests. The process initiated by PR and the potential for change which it creates are much more important than the immediate outcomes. Interventions in the process must therefore focus on creating conditions which will facilitate, and encourage, this potential to be realised. In this context three aspects deserve special attention.

First, a great deal of knowledge and expertise is needed to assess local resources and their potential, different ways of exploiting the potential, the costs involved and raising resources. This knowledge, much of it technical in nature, is often not available locally. Strong support from state agencies and/or non government organisations (including educational institutions) is necessary to make it accessible to the communities and their leaders. This implies a major change in the role of government agencies. Instead of planning, deciding and implementing schemes on their own, as they now do, the agencies will have to play a supportive role by providing expertise, helping elected bodies to take informed decisions, and facilitate coordination between related schemes of different communities and in the larger regional context.

Second, the creation of democratic institutions of local government and assured representation for disadvantaged groups are necessary but not sufficient conditions to ensure that the latters' interests are safeguarded. The determination of priorities, in the context of limited resources, inevitably involves a process of bargaining between different groups. In order for this to work in favour of the poor/vulnerable, the latter have to articulate their needs and actively persuade and/or pressure the relevant forums to take necessary action to meet their needs. None of these occur easily or automatically especially to the under-privileged segments. Conscious measures to encourage and strengthen institutions of civil society are essential.

Non governmental and voluntary organisations have a particularly key role in obtaining and disseminating information on the working of government (including local government), making people aware of their entitlements and obligations, and enabling them to vent their grievances and seek redress. Besides interceding with the concerned authorities to secure benefits for the eligible and minimise leakages, they have a role in motivating and organising local communities to take active interest in the working of specific programmes and persuading bureaucracy to work with the community for improving the effectiveness of programmes. Over time they can help promote a process of more broad-based changes in institutional mechanisms for funding/managing local development activities to meet the specific local conditions. Active encouragement of NGOs and giving them ample public space is therefore highly desirable for healthy evolution of local government.

Third, raising expectation and assertiveness of the people vis-a-vis government and bureaucracy increases pressures on the latter to perform. But better performance often requires a significant change in the relative role of the three elements involving, among other things, reduced power and increased accountability of bureaucracy. It also involves shifts in the relative power of those who hold political office at different levels and of different segments of the bureaucracy. Reform therefore invariably encounters resistance. Moreover if the elected Panchayat Raj institutions merely generate demands for larger devolution of resources from the state and central governments there is little stake or incentive for them to address the task of efficient use of resources. It is therefore imperative that local bodies should be required to mobilise their own resources to meet a significant part of the costs of their programmes and given greater control over their staff engaged in various activities.

All this implies a basic change in the relations between the state and local governments, the role of the bureaucracy and the attitude of local governments. There are no standard blue prints for accomplishing the change. A great deal of experiment and learning from experience is inevitable. The upsetting of existing power balances between the various groups involved creates an opportunity for engineering desirable changes through a combination of sustained pressures on the system as a whole via the general political process along with efforts to initiate and sustain a discussion of the problem of restructuring among the concerned groups (namely the local and state level politicians, the bureaucracy and its trade unions and non government organisations). As already noted non government organisations can play a valuable role in this process.

CONCLUSIONS AND SUGGESTIONS

What inferences can we draw from the above on specific issues concerning design and implementation of PA programmes raised in the TOR?

Design

In general, the tendency for proliferating PA programmes differentiated by region and target groups impedes their effectiveness. They should be collapsed into two, or at best three, broad categories: (a) those that aim at increasing employment and income of the poor; (b) those that ensure a minimum basic services to everyone, everywhere; and (c) those aimed at helping the poor to acquire or enlarge their productive asset base. This will greatly sharpen the focus of the programme and help increase their effectiveness.

Schemes taken up under different PA programmes in particular areas are decided and implemented wholly by government agencies. There is a proliferation of agencies, considerable duplication and little flexibility to adapt schemes to specific local conditions. There is little consultation, and even less participation, by the communities in deciding programme content or beneficiary selection. Hardly any attention is paid to the functioning of the institutions at the interface between them and the people they are meant to serve. Several improvements are needed; getting rid of unnecessary proliferation of agencies and programmes and rationalising criteria for spatial allocation is one. Another aspect is to make the public institutions accountable for the services they provide; and the third is to ensure that benefits in fact flow in full measure to the target groups.

Democratic decentralisation will go someways in furthering community participation and ensuring greater accountability. But the impact is likely to be limited unless the local communities are given effective command over use of resources allotted to PA programmes; and freedom to decide the content of local development programmes. At the same time, it is necessary that they acquire greater stake and responsibility and have powers to control the staff of the institutions which serve them. All of these no doubt raise difficult political issues. But they need to be confronted if genuine progress is to be made and sustained. Perhaps it is well to recognise that progress will be uneven and focus initially on areas/villages/towns where the socio economic configuration and attitudes are favorable to such change. Successful transformation in such select areas will have a significant demonstration effect on other communities.

Project design must also pay much more attention to institutional aspects. This is particularly important in the case of micro water shed plans, social forestry, local irrigation and other projects to develop common pool resources. The complex and multifaceted character of the problem is not adequately appreciated, and certainly not reflected, in the projects reviewed. The focus is usually on government agencies who are supposed to implement the project. The arrangements and procedures for ensuring effective unified planning and coordinated implementation by the concerned government agency is of course important. But the success of these types of projects require the forging of a consensus among the affected groups in each community about the rules on maintenance and use of facilities; the sharing of costs and benefits; and the ability to enforce rules. This aspect needs far greater emphasis and attention in project design.

At a more general level, it is necessary to create or strengthen support structures — NGOs and voluntary organisations — to help the communities concerned to acquire the knowledge and understanding to assess the programme, develop and consider alternatives and effectively present their view point. Creating conditions to ensure that institutions at the local community level give voice to the poor/ underprivileged and are responsive to their interests is the other important task. The best conceived, and so far the best implemented, example of this is the Rajasthan education project; the social forestry projects, the worst. There is much to be learnt from the successes and the failures of these, and other similar, experiments.

Monitoring and Evaluation

Projects are for the most part monitored on the basis of reporting of the number of beneficiaries, no. of wells constructed, area covered, loans issued and such other indicators for which targets are usually specified. Comparison of the achievements relative to targets is used to assess performance. This is problematic partly because there is hardly any independent check on the veracity of reporting by implementing agencies. Even 'independent' evaluations tend to rely far too much on data provided by implementing agencies. Evaluation studies usually lack time and resources needed for conducting their own surveys, to undertake an indepth assessment of achievements and analyse reasons for successes and failures. More importantly, an excessive concern for targets detracts attention from important substantive aspects like the quality of the work, the efficacy of targetting, leakages, the processes of deciding and implementing schemes, community participation, the impact on the living conditions of the areas and population segments benefitting from the schemes. The dangers of preoccupation with targets and the importance of focussing more on processes of decision making and implementation, and of outcomes (in terms of the coverage and quality of services provided) have been highlighted by SIDA evaluation reports on the Social Forestry and the Durgapur projects.

There is a strong case for revamping the monitoring/evaluation systems for PA projects. First, the top management of the programmes (at the central and the state level) should pay greater attention to monitoring processes, outcomes and impact rather than physical programme targets alone. In the case of the latter, independent sample verification of reporting under the direct control of the state/central authority is essential. There need to be more evaluations of the type attempted in JRY and IRDP. However apart from substantially improving scope and design of the surveys, more intensive, sustained and critical analysis of performance, especially of differences in performance within a given programme.

Such a monitoring-evaluation system cannot be effective it is were to be essentially within government. Non Government research organisations should be encouraged and supported to build up and sustain high quality data collection and analyses. The scope and methodology of surveys and the issues on which analyses is to be focussed can be decided by the agencies with expert advice. But thereafter the researchers should have the freedom to report their findings for discussion and review. This will cost more, but it would be more than justified by the insights and lessons it can offer. It is also important to bear in mind that the impact of many interventions take time to manifest and that meaningful evaluation is not always possible within the duration and timeframe of funding. A longer term perspective is necessary.

Targeting

Ensuring proper spatial targetting of allocation under PA programmes is as important as ensuring that non poor do not take advantage of the programme. It is possible to devise reasonable and objective criteria for spatial allocation.

Targeting by class of beneficiaries by the poverty criteria has given rise to numerous problems arising in part from difficulty of determining whether or not a particular individual meets the poverty criteria. Use of verifiable attributes (like landholding, occupation, education, size and other family characteristics, and in some cases caste) associated with poverty would reduce, but not eliminate problems.

Targeting for SC/ST as a group would be necessary especially in district/blocks where they are not numerically dominant. In order to implement this special guideline, intra-district (esp. inter-village) allocation may be needed. The mere fact of allocating more resources to a particular block or village where there is higher concentrations of such groups would ease the problem. Whether in fact they have access to opportunities will continue to depend critically on the way village society and its institutions function.

The ability of these vulnerable groups to press their interests can grow only as their consciousness of the need and their knowledge of the opportunities available increase; and as this consciousness translates itself, through an essentially political process, into effective pressure on the system to provide them better access to resources and services. NGOs and democratic decentralisation have a potentially crucial role in this process.

Women are a special category in that they suffer a general disadvantage vis-a-vis men in accessing education and health; they have special problems arising out of their limited control over family income, and their multiple responsibilities, among other things for rearing children, fetching fire wood and water and homecare. Participation of women is essential both to create demand for a variety of services related to their welfare and the welfare of children, and to exert pressure for delivery of more and better services. To accomplish this transformation, the kind of approach adopted in Siksha Karmi, Lok Jumbish, and in some womens' health programmes, whereby NGOs actively mobilise opinion and are given the opportunity and space to devise flexible ways of accomplishing health education goals adapted to particular local circumstances, and organise women more effectively must be given a great deal more attention. For this reasons projects like Lok Jumbish and Siksha Karmi needs to be encouraged and supported.

The reservation of a sizeable proportion of elected posts in local bodies for SC/ST/and women creates a secure space in the decision making forums, but does not automatically ensure that they will use it. There is, and will continue to be, a great deal of variation in this respect. A systematic study of the factors responsible for these variations within the same or similar social-institutional — policy environment will be rewarding for design of more effective interventions.

This essay is extracted from "Poverty Alleviation Programmes: The Indian Experience" published in Vatsala Sahai (ed.): *Sharing Challenges: The Indo Swedish Development Corporation Programme*, Ministry of Foreign Affairs, Sweden, 1996.

14

Some Aspects of Inequalities in Living Standards in Rural India

Introduction

THE existence of large disparities in living standards between regions and between classes of people is widely believed to be an important cause of prevailing social tensions and unrest. Many hold the view that inequalities are growing and that this trend, if unchecked, would aggravate tensions and endanger the country's stability. The precise relationship between economic inequalities and socio-political tensions may be debatable. But there can be no denying that the prevalence of inequalities constitutes a major problem. Practically every shade of political opinion is exercised about it. Development policies of the Government are increasingly judged not merely by their success in achieving a rapid expansion of aggregate real output but also in terms of how the fruits of development are distributed between different classes and regions. It is in this context that a proper understanding of the nature and extent of inequalities, the manner in which they change, and the specific factors underlying these phenomena assume practical importance.

Review of Recent Literature

Over the years a considerable body of quantitative

information on inequalities in living standards has been accumulated. The most important source is the National Sample Survey (NSS) which provides data on the average per capita consumption and its distribution in rural and urban areas and by States. It also gives valuable information, for some years, on various aspects of economic activity which have a bearing on the distribution of income and consumption. The NCAER Surveys of rural and urban savings conducted in the early 1960's give estimates of income distribution at the national level. These surveys have been extensively utilised to assess the degree of income inequalities and the changes in inequalities over time.

Available estimates of income distribution for the country as a whole are summarised in Table 1. The differences are striking: The Lorenz Ratio (LR), which is the commonly used measure of inequality, varies from less than 0.29 to 0.47. Except for the NCAER study, which differs from other surveys in sample design and concepts, estimates of income inequalities in India are derived from NSS data on the distribution of consumption expenditure adjusted for savings and direct taxes. Apart from the fact that the estimates do not refer to the same year, there are significant differences in the basis of estimation reflected in the assumptions regarding the distribution of savings, adjustments of the NSS data for biases, differences in period of references and valuation, and the procedure for pooling of rural and urban data to arrive at the all-India distribution. It is nearly impossible to sort out the effect of these differences to permit a confident estimate of the precise degree of income inequality in India.

TABLE — 1

Different Estimates of Income Inequality: All India

	1952-53 to 1956-57	*1953-54 to 1956-57*	*1956-57*	*1962 rural*	*1960 urban*	*1951-52 to 1959-60*
(0)	*(1)*	*(2)*	*(3)*	*(4)*	*(5)*	*(6)*
share in total income of:						
top 10%	25%	28%	37%	32.8%	42.4%	43%
bottom 20%	9%	8%	6%	5.9%	5.3%	4%
Lorenz ratio	0.29	0.36	0.44	0.41	0.48	0.47

Sources : Col.(1): Iyenger, N.S. and Mukherjee, M. (1961): A Note on the Derivation of Income Distribution from a Given Distribution of Consumer Expenditure, Paper presented to the Second Indian Econometric Conference.

Co.(2): Ojha, P.D. and Bhatt, V.V. (1964): "Pattern of Income Distribution in an Undeveloped Economy — A Case Study of India", American Economic Review.

Col.(3): Ahmed, M. (1961): Size Distribution of Personal Income and Saving, Paper presented to the Third Indian Conference of Research on National Income.

Cols.(4) and (5): NCAER, (1965): All India Rural Household Survey, 1962, Occasional Paper 13.

Col.(6): Subramanian Swamy, Structural Changes and the Distribution of Income by Size: The Case of India (mimeographed unpublished).

Changes in the distribution of income and consumption over the period 1950-65 have been explored in two recent papers[1], one by Mukherjee and Chatterjee[2] and another by Swamy.[3] Both seek to assess trends in inequality on the basis of NSS data as well as the behaviour of inter-sectoral disparities as revealed by national income estimates. Mukherjee and Chatterjee conclude that "...reckoned at current prices, there appears to be some reduction in the disparity of the distribution of consumption expenditure during the period covered both within urban and rural areas and for the country as a whole". However, in real terms, they found a tendency for disparities to increase : "Roughly there appears to be relative stability within both rural and urban areas. The all-India figures, however, exhibit a higher level of disparity during the Second and Third Plan periods". The estimate of inequalities in real consumption is derived by deflating the per capita expenditure in several expenditure classes by the price index of cereals for each of these classes obtained from the NSS. This procedure is open to criticism on two grounds : First, it implicitly assumes that prices of non-cereal items change in the same direction and by the same proportion as that of cereals. This is obviously an untenable assumption. Second, changes in the average prices of cereals obtained from NSS reflects changes in the prices of individual cereals as well as shifts in the composition of cereals. The latter, which appears to have been a significant factor, must be adjusted to get at a proper index for deflation purposes.

Swamy also uses NSS data but, unlike Mukherjee and Chatterjee, adjusts them for differences in valuation and reference period biases. His conclusion, however, is that even at current prices inequalities in consumption in the second plan were larger than in the first plan. His estimate suggests that inequalities remained more or less stable in rural areas, but increased in urban areas. The rural-urban disparities increased. Since the proportion of urban population rose, overall inequalities also tended to increase. However, full details of the procedures and rationale for adjusting NSS data are not readily available to permit an informed comment on the analysis.

Mukherjee and Chatterjee, as well as Swamy, have sought to substantiate their conclusion about changes in income distribution on the basis of LR of income for various periods computed from CSO estimates of income and employment by sectors. The basis for estimating changes in sectoral employment is notoriously weak. A large per cent of income originating in trade, commerce and services is based on the rather unreliable projections of employment levels. Moreover there is some doubt whether changes in income inequality among working population accurately reflects the changes for the population as a whole.

Recently, a number of authors have attempted to assess the change in the incidence of poverty between 1960-61 and 1967-68. Following very different procedures, Ojha[4] and Bardhan[5] concluded that the proportion of population falling below a specified minimum consumption standard has increased sharply. Minhas' analysis however led him to the opposite conclusion. He found that the proportion of population below a specified minimum has consistently declined over that past decade.[6] The divergent conclusions would appear to be partly a reflection of differences in the methods of adjusting for price changes, but primarily due to divergent estimates of changes in real consumption. This is discussed more fully in the last section of the paper.

Regional variations in degree of inequality[7] have been explored by Mukherjee and other workers in the Indian Statistical Institute. These studies reveal that the degree of inequality is not uniform as between states. Since per capita consumption also varies widely, the incidence of poverty, measured as the proportion of the State population falling in the poorest 10 per cent of the national population is uneven. Comparisons of disparity in 1960-61 and 1963-64 suggest that the degree of changes and to a lesser extent even the direction of change, in inequality is again not uniform as between States. These are significant findings but their utility is limited because the underlying causes have not been analysed.

The Scope of the Present Study

The intention of this paper is to carry the analysis of disparities in living standards a bit further. The focus is limited to rural areas. On the basis of data drawn primarily from the National Sample Survey, it explores three major aspects of the problem:

(a) The pattern of inequalities in per capita consumption levels at the national level by principal occupational and land holding categories and by household size.

(b) Inter-State variation in the degree of inequality in consumption and the extent to which these can be explained by inequalities in the distribution of the principal productive resource of rural areas, namely, land and livestock.

(c) Changes in degree of consumption inequality by States and All India over the period 1958-59 to 1967-68.

The Pattern of Inequality : All India

The estimated shares of rural households and population at different levels of per capita consumption expenditure in aggregate[8] rural consumption are given in Table 2.

Broadly speaking, in 1960-61 the poorest 10 per cent of the rural population accounted for approximately 3-3.5 per cent of total consumption expenditure of all rural households. The richest 10 per cent on the other hand account for 25 to 30 per cent of the total. In other words the average per capita consumption of the top decile is nearly 8-9 times that of the lowest decile. This is one measure of the extent of inequality in rural living standards. An alternative and more satisfactory index is the Lorenz ratio (LR) which measures the extent to which the actual distribution deviates from a perfectly egalitarian distribution of consumption. The LR for rural households was 0.288 in 1960-61. Since households with relatively high per capita consumption tend to be smaller, the LR for the rural population is somewhat higher at 0.323.

TABLE — 2

Distribution of Households, Persons and Total Consumption by Levels of Per Capita Consumption
Rural India : 1960-61

monthly per capita expenditure class	*percentage share of*		
	households	*persons*	*total consumption*
(1)	*(2)*	*(3)*	*(4)*
0-8	5.46	6.38	1.94
8-11	10.23	11.95	5.34
11-13	9.19	9.88	5.58
13-15	9.85	9.82	6.44
15-18	13.97	13.79	10.58
18-21	12.13	11.44	10.39
21-24	9.44	9.03	9.47
24-28	8.27	7.72	9.25
28-34	8.14	7.66	11.00
34-43	6.19	5.93	10.47
43-55	3.66	3.12	6.95
55 and above	3.47	3.28	12.59
all classes	100.00	100.00	100.00

An independent estimate of consumption inequality in rural areas can be obtained from the Rural Savings Survey of the NCAER (Table 3). This survey which relates to 1962, gives estimates of the distribution of rural households by different income classes as well as the average annual income and net savings for each class. Consumption expenditure is obtained as the difference between income and savings. On this basis the LR of consumption for rural India is 0.39 which is considerably higher than the figure derived from NSS data.

TABLE — 3

Estimated Number of Households, Average Net Consumption Per Household and Total Consumption by Income Class, Rural India, 1960-61

income class (Rs.)	*estimated no. of households (000 nos.)*	*cumulative percentage*	*average net consumption (Rs.)*	*total consumption (Rs. million)*	*cumulative percentage*
(1)	*(2)*	*(3)*	*(4)*	*(5)*	*(6)*
upto	4286	6.52	235	1007	1.21
361-480	4680	13.44	462	2162	3.81
481-600	6356	23.31	571	3629	8.18
601-720	6488	33.18	687	4457	13.54
721-900	8821	46.60	814	7180	22.17
901-1200	10530	62.62	1046	11014	35.42
1201-1800	12450	81.56	1424	17729	56.75
1801-2400	5436	89.83	1954	10622	69.53
2401-3600	3786	95.59	2634	9972	81.52
3601-4800	1512	97.89	3705	5602	88.26
4801-7200	809	99.12	4639	3753	92.77
7200 and above	579	100.00	10377	6008	100.00
total	65733		1265	83135	

Source: NCAER — All-India Rural Household Survey : Volume II, New Delhi (1965). Derived from Table 12 (page 52) and Table 33 (page 96).

Part of the explanation might be in the conceptual differences between the two surveys. The NCAER estimate of saving excludes saving in the form of currency and precious metals. It also makes no adjustment for direct taxes paid by rural households in calculating consumption. Since both these elements are likely to be more unevenly distributed than income, it is to be expected that the NCAER index of inequality will be higher. A third factor is the basis of evaluating consumption. In the NSS, cash purchase and consumption out of gifts and kind receipts are valued at rural retail prices and consumption out of homegrown stock at farm harvest prices.[9] The NCAER on the other hand valued income uniformly at farm harvest prices.[10] Since poorer households cereal consumption tends to have a higher proportion of cash purchase,[11] the NSS procedure would, other things being equal, show a lesser inequality in consumption than the NCAER procedure.[12]

We are in no position to assess the quantitative significance of these conceptual differences in explaining the divergent value of LR obtained from the two sources. Nor can we categorically say which of the two provides a more accurate measure of inequalities in living standards in rural areas. It may however be pointed out that the NSS figures of both average per capita consumption and of inequality appear to have a small margin of error. In 1960-61, the average per capita consumption expenditure in the sub-samples differed from the average for the whole sample by no more than ±4 per cent. The LR for the two sub-samples was 0.318 and 0.329, the average being 0.323. For the purposes of the present study, we shall use NSS data only because it provides by far the most detailed and comprehensive information over a sufficiently long period of time.

Distribution of Land Holdings and Consumption Inequality

Since the bulk of the rural population is dependent on agriculture, inequalities in living standards within the rural sector are largely a reflection of the uneven distribution of land. Data from the 17th round of the NSS show that nearly 42 per cent of rural households had operational holdings less than one acre and accounted for 1.3 per cent of total area operated. At the other extreme, 4.5 per cent of households operated holdings in excess of 20 acres and their share in total area was nearly 35 per cent (Table 4). Significantly however, the overall inequality coefficient (LR) for land holdings is much higher than for consumption. In other words the disparities in living standards are appreciably less than the disparities in operational holdings. There are several reasons for this phenomenon.

TABLE — 4

Distribution of Households, Area Operated, Irrigation And Milch Animals by Size Class of Household Operational Holdings — All India : 1960-61

		size class of household operational holdings (acres)							
sl. no.		*upto 1.00*	*1.00 -2.49*	*2.50 -4.49*	*5.00 -9.99*	*10.00 -19.99*	*20.00 -49.99*	*over 50.00*	*total*
(0)	*(1)*	*(2)*	*(3)*	*(4)*	*(5)*	*(6)*	*(7)*	*(8)*	*(9)*
1.	households	41.96	15.63	16.17	13.83	7.95	3.81	0.65	100.00
2.	area operated	1.30	5.77	12.74	21.03	23.81	24.26	11.09	100.00
3.	area irrigated	2.12	8.80	16.84	25.17	23.84	17.31	5.92	100.00
4.	cattle in milk	15.55	11.55	19.25	22.24	16.96	11.18	3.27	100.00

Source : National Sample Survey — 17th Round, Report No. 113.

Small holdings are generally better irrigated, more intensively cropped and yield more per unit area than large holdings. It is estimated, on the basis of data given in Table 4, that nearly 30 per cent of the area held by holdings below 2.5 acres is irrigated compared to about 14 per cent in holdings exceeding 20 acres. The Farm Management Surveys conducted in selected districts all over the country also show that smaller holdings have a higher cropping intensity, superior crop patterns and higher yield per unit area. In general there appears to be an inverse relation between the size of holding and the value of output per acre.

There is also striking evidence that the output of animal husbandry, another important source of rural income is more evenly distributed among different sections of the rural population than land.[13] In consequence the disparity in the gross value of output as between small and large holdings is likely to be smaller than the disparity in area operated would suggest. Since the purchased inputs (including hired labour) as a proportion of gross production tends to increase with farm size and bigger cultivators have larger families, the disparities between small and large land holders reckoned in terms of per capita income tend to get further dampened. Furthermore, the rate of savings being a positive function of per capita income, it is to be expected that inequalities in consumption will be less than inequalities in income.

The Influence of Family Size

A closer study of the data suggests that although, on the average, households with large holdings have a relatively high level of per capita consumption, the converse is not true. The rich households do not consist exclusively of big land holders nor are all big land holders 'rich'. Thus the 11th round of the NSS shows that 1.34 per cent of rural households possessed more than 50 acres. Of these only a third had per capita consumption of Rs. 21 per month or more, which represents barely 5 per cent of all rural households with per capita consumption in the above range. It can be seen from Table 5 that the rich households are drawn from practically every land holdings class. Naturally, the proportion of rich households rises as one moves up the scale of holding size.

TABLE — 5

Distribution of Rural Households by Size of Land Holding and Per capita Consumption, India : 1956-57

land possessed (in acres)	*per capita household-expenditure levels in rupees*								
	0-7	*8-10*	*11-12*	*13-14*	*15-17*	*18-20*	*21-27*	*28 & above*	*total*
(1)	*(2)*	*(3)*	*(4)*	*(5)*	*(6)*	*(7)*	*(8)*	*(9)*	*(10)*
0.00	0.02	0.05		0.01		0.04	0.09		0.21
0.01-0.49	2.01	2.80	1.18	0.36	0.84	0.21	0.23	0.10	7.75
0.50-0.99	1.56	2.79	1.09	0.62	0.44	0.29	0.31	0.22	7.32
1.00-1.49	1.61	2.69	1.30	0.39	0.82	0.33	0.22	0.09	7.37
1.50-2.49	2.47	4.59	2.30	1.40	1.51	0.93	0.43	0.21	13.84
2.50-3.49	1.78	3.71	1.59	1.11	1.63	0.78	0.40	0.17	11.17
3.50-4.99	1.32	3.17	2.32	1.39	1.58	1.14	0.55	0.32	11.79
5.00-7.49	1.40	4.44	2.01	1.49	1.46	0.99	0.84	0.39	13.02
7.50-9.99	0.63	1.91	1.25	0.61	1.04	0.61	0.36	0.25	6.66
10.00-14.99	0.77	2.58	1.26	0.85	1.37	0.69	0.73	0.24	8.49
15.00-19.99	0.55	1.11	0.75	0.38	0.64	0.37	0.31	0.29	4.40
20.00-29.99	0.44	0.84	0.69	0.42	0.50	0.54	0.40	0.22	4.05
30.00-49.99	0.12	0.48	0.39	0.34	0.54	0.31	0.22	0.19	2.59
50.00-99.99		0.10	0.21	0.12	0.14	0.06	0.11	0.22	0.96
100.00 & above		0.02	0.03	0.14	0.06	0.03	0.04	0.06	0.38
total	14.08	31.19	16.38	9.63	12.57	7.32	5.26	2.97	100.00

Source : The Cabinet Secretariat, Govt. of India, The National Sample Survey : 11th round-1956-57, Number 140. Tables with Notes on Consumer Expenditure.

Much the same is true of the "poorer" households as well. While the proportion of poor households is relatively high among small land holders, not all "poor" households are drawn from this category nor are all small holders 'poor'. Thus, according to NSS 11th round data, households with less than one acre accounted for no more than 20 per cent of all households with per capita consumption of less than 10 rupees per month. Roughly a fifth of all households with less than an acre had per capita monthly consumption exceeding Rs. 15. This picture is also corroborated by data from the 14th round of the NSS[14] (Table 6).

This apparent anomaly can be explained by taking into account family size along with land holdings as a factor determining per capita income and consumption. As mentioned earlier, since average family size increases with size of holding, the per capita income differences between small and large holdings will be smaller than difference in aggregate income. Moreover, within each land holding class, family size varies a great deal around the average for the class. It is therefore conceivable that a small holder with a very small family may have a per capita income greater than that of a large landholder with a very large family. The importance of family size in determining per capita consumption is vividly brought out by the fact that average family size is seen to be smaller as one moves up the scale of per capita consumption. There is a marked concentration of small sized families in the upper end of the consumption distribution. For instance in 1958-59, single member households which accounted for barely 6 per cent of the sample households, constituted nearly one sixth of households with per capita consumption exceeding Rs. 34 per month. Significantly, two thirds of them had less than half an acre of land. At the lower end of the distribution, on the other hand, there is a concentration of relatively large households though this is not as marked as the dominance of small sized families in the higher per capita consumption category. Again in 1958-59, households with eight or more members made up nearly a sixth of sampled rural households, but accounted for over 20 per cent of households with per capita monthly

TABLE — 6

Distribution of Sample Rural Households by Size of Land Holdings and Per Capita Consumption, India : 1958-59

household operational holdings (acres)	*per capita consumption expenditure (Rs.)*												
	0-8	*8-11*	*11-13*	*13-15*	*15-18*	*18-21*	*21-24*	*24-28*	*28-34*	*34-43*	*43-55*	*55 & above*	*total*
(1)	*(2)*	*(3)*	*(4)*	*(5)*	*(6)*	*(7)*	*(8)*	*(9)*	*(10)*	*(11)*	*(12)*	*(13)*	*(14)*
upto .49	242	369	254	234	263	178	144	124	114	92	56	57	2127
0.50-0.99	41	57	51	34	53	36	33	25	23	14	7	1	375
1.00-2.49	107	174	160	130	201	161	120	113	108	64	35	29	1402
2.50-4.99	65	161	128	140	227	152	116	137	120	81	33	40	1400
5.00-7.49	38	56	57	71	94	76	68	63	53	55	30	32	693
7.50-9.99	22	45	28	35	38	48	39	24	37	37	17	9	379
10.00-12.49	14	31	24	33	38	21	39	23	31	28	16	16	314
12.50-14-99	4	5	7	7	15	17	10	12	14	14	8	9	122
15.00-19.99	5	16	22	17	23	18	28	26	22	25	19	22	243
20.00-24.99	7	4	8	3	23	14	11	12	11	11	9	17	130
25.00-29.99	2	2	3	7	5	7	6	8	6	7	7	7	67
30.00-49.99	2	7	4	11	11	9	15	12	9	17	11	14	122
50.00 and above	—	2	1	1	4	3	4	5	8	5	6	12	51
total	549	929	747	723	995	740	633	584	556	450	254	265	7425

Source: Special tabulation by NSS 14th round data

consumption below Rs. 11 (Table 7). A Similar picture is revealed by 19th round data relating to 1964-65 (Table 8).

TABLE — 7

Distribution of Sample Households by Monthly Per Capita Expenditure and Household Size
India : 1958-59

household size	*no. of households by per capita expenditure (Rs.)*				*% to the total no. of households in each household size*			
	0-11	*11-34*	*34 and above*	*total*	*0-11*	*11-34*	*34 and above*	*total*
(1)	*(2)*	*(3)*	*(4)*	*(5)*	*(6)*	*(7)*	*(8)*	*(9)*
1	37	228	166	431	8.6	52.9	38.5	100.0
2	61	488	159	708	8.6	68.9	22.5	100.0
3	131	678	141	950	13.8	71.4	14.8	100.0
4	231	865	130	1226	18.8	70.6	10.6	100.0
5	261	825	106	1192	21.9	69.2	8.9	100.0
6	284	629	76	989	28.7	63.6	7.7	100.0
7	173	442	60	675	25.6	65.5	8.9	100.0
8	131	292	33	456	28.7	64.0	7.3	100.0
9	74	181	32	287	25.8	63.1	11.1	100.0
10	39	120	18	177	22.0	67.8	10.2	100.0
11	15	69	8	92	16.3	75.0	8.7	100.0
12	12	55	13	80	15.0	68.8	16.2	100.0
13	8	29	4	41	19.5	70.7	9.8	100.0
14	8	16	8	32	25.0	50.0	25.0	100.0
15 & above	12	60	15	87	13.8	69.0	17.2	100.0
total	1477	4977	969	7423	19.9	67.0	13.1	100.0

Source : National Sample Survey, 14th Round

The relative influence of land holdings and of family size on per capita consumption was also examined with the help of data from the 14th round of NSS. We could obtain detailed information on occupation, land holding, family size and per capita consumption in respect of 7416 sample households. These were grouped into 4 occupational categories namely,

TABLE — 8

Distribution of Sample Households by Monthly Per Capita Expenditure and Household Size and Their Percentage — All India : 1964-65 (NSS 19th round)

household size	no. of households by per capita expenditure group (Rs.)				% to the total no. of sample households in each household size			
	0-13	13-43	43 and above	total	0-13	13-43	43 and above	total
(1)	(2)	(3)	(4)	(5)	(6)	(7)	(8)	(9)
1	23	244	179	446	5.2	54.7	40.1	100.7
2	31	532	142	705	4.4	75.5	20.1	100.0
3	79	680	110	869	9.1	78.3	12.6	100.0
4	161	891	111	1163	13.8	76.6	9.6	100.0
5	179	920	86	1185	15.1	77.6	7.3	100.0
6	193	817	61	1071	18.0	76.3	5.7	100.0
7	147	564	34	745	19.7	75.7	4.6	100.0
8	103	404	24	531	19.4	76.1	4.5	100.0
9 and above	114	609	65	788	14.5	77.3	8.2	100.0
all size	1030	5661	812	7503	13.7	75.5	10.8	100.0

Source : Indian Statistical Institute; The National Sample Survey 19th round July 1964-June 1965. Draft Report No. 207. Tables with Notes on Household Consumer Expenditure and Enterprise for Rural and Urban areas.

farmers, farm workers, administrative and professional workers, and all others. In all these categories, multiple regression analysis showed (a) a positive correlation between land holding size and per capita consumption; and (b) a negative correlation between family size and per capita consumption. All the regression coefficients for family size are statistically significant at 1% level (Table 9).

TABLE — 9

Results of Multiple Regression Analysis of Per Capita Consumption Against Landholdings and Household size
India : 1958-59

occupation group	*regression coefficients of*	
	land holdings	*family size*
(1)	*(2)*	*(3)*
1. farmers	0.422	-1.204
2. farm workers	0.335	-1.377
3. professional and administrative workers	0.782	-1.523
4. others	1.11	-2.338

The importance of family size in determining per capita consumption is partly due to the fact that large holdings tend to be less productive in terms of output per unit area and have to support larger families. It is also possible that differences in the composition of large and small families may be a contributory factor. There is some evidence that the proportion of dependents (as distinguished from earners) tends to significantly higher in larger households.[15] The variation in family composition by age, sex and activity status and their relationship to the income earning capacity of households merit much closer analysis.

If the foregoing analysis of the relation between land distribution and family-size on the one hand and inequalities in rural living standards on the other is valid, some important policy implications follow. One of the widely used instruments for reducing rural disparities is to impose a ceiling on the size of land holdings and to redistribute land in excess of the ceiling among the poor classes. In both cases the basis generally seems to be "family holding". Our analysis suggests that in order to be effective, it is necessary (a) to define ceiling in terms of some 'standard acre' which would make allowance for quality variations; (b) to fix the ceiling in terms of standard acres per capita rather than in terms of the size of family holding; and (c) to relate eligibility for redistribution of surplus land with the per capita area, in standard acres, held by the claimants. Fixing ceilings in per capita terms has the added merit in that it is far more difficult to evade.

Occupation and Consumption Inequality

The analysis so far was focussed on the pattern of inequality for the rural population as a whole, its relation to the distribution of land holdings and the influence of family size. It might be useful to examine the pattern of inequalities as between different occupational groups and within each occupational group. Published data bearing on this aspect of rural inequalities is available only for 1964-65.[16] They suggest that nearly four fifths of the rural population are in households whose principal occupation is agriculture, forestry and fishing. The per capita consumption of this group is nearly the same as the average for the rural population as a whole. Households in the occupational category of craftsmen and production process workers account for slightly over 8 per cent of the population and their per capita consumption is below the overall average. The remainder, including professional and administrative workers and service occupations, appear to be appreciably better off than the rest of the rural population (Table 10). The degree of inequality as between the agricultural and the non-agricultural households does not appear to be significantly different.[17]

The bulk of the population with a relatively low per capita consumption is drawn from agricultural households. The proportion of craftsmen in the poor classes is somewhat higher than their share in total population. The higher incidence of poverty in this group is probably a reflection of the relatively

TABLE — 10

Percentage Distribution off Estimated Number of Persons by Monthly Per Capita Expenditure and Major Occupation Division for Rural India : 1964-65

	major occupation division	*monthly per capita expenditure groups (Rs.)*														
		0-8	*8-11*	*11-13*	*13-15*	*15-18*	*18-21*	*21-24*	*24-28*	*28-34*	*34-43*	*43-55*	*55-75*	*75 & above*	*all level*	*per capita monthly consumer expenditure (Rs.)*
	(1)	*(2)*	*(3)*	*(4)*	*(5)*	*(6)*	*(7)*	*(8)*	*(9)*	*(10)*	*(11)*	*(12)*	*(13)*	*(14)*	*(15)*	*(!6)*
1	professional, administrative, clerical and sales workers	0.95	3.[illegible]1	4.20	5.33	5.73	6.54	6.21	7.38	7.00	7.20	8.84	10.51	12.06	6.24	28.66
2	farmers, fishermen, hunters, loggers and related workers	81.82	82.27	80.98	80.52	77.20	80.27	80.29	79.66	81.79	81.75	78.96	80.99	74.52	80.18	24.81
3	miners, transport, craftsmen and labourers n.e.c	11.42	10.55	9.92	10.20	12.61	10.46	9.42	9.73	8.01	7.48	7.40	6.51	3.23	9.68	22.11
4	services and workers not classifiable by occupation	5.81	3.77	4.90	3.95	4.46	2.73	4.08	3.23	3.20	3.57	4.80	1.99	10.19	3.90	25.62
5	all occupations	100.0	100.0	100.0	100.0	100.0	100.0	100.0	100.0	100.0	100.0	100.0	100.0	100.0	100.0	24.83

Source : The National Sample Survey : 19th Round July 1964-June 1965, Draft Report 207: Tables with Notes on Household Consumer Expenditure and enterprise for Rural and Urban Areas of India. (Indian Statistical Institute — April 1969).

low average per capita consumption. In the case of non-agricultural households since per capita consumption is higher than the average, a smaller proportion of them fall in the poor category.

The above picture is corroborated by a more detailed analysis of the incidence of poverty in different occupational categories on the basis of 14th round data (Table 11). Over 80 per cent of the sample households and a similar proportion

TABLE — 11

Distribution of Sample Households by Major Occupation and Selected Range of Per Capita Consumption, Rural India : 1958-59

sl no.	*occupation*	*per capita monthly consumption*		
		less than Rs. 11	*more than Rs. 34*	*total*
(0)	*(1)*	*(2)*	*(3)*	*(4)*
1	professional, technical, managerial, clerical and sales workers	86 (5.8)	91 (9.4)	511 (6.9)
2	farmers	609 (41.2)	718 (74.3)	4469 (60.3)
	up to 1 acre	46 (3.1)	34 (3.5)	279 (3.8)
	1 to 2.5	152 (10.3)	101 (10.5)	947 (12.8)
	2.5-5.0	167 (11.3)	140 (14.5)	1222 (16.5)
	5.0-10.0	147 (10.0)	172 (17.7)	1003 (13.5)
	10.0 and above	97 (6.5)	271 (28.1)	1018 (13.7)
3	farm workers	610 (41.3)	56 (5.8)	1649 (22.2)
4	mining, transport draftsmen etc.	128 (8.7)	84 (8.7)	605 (8.1)
5	Others	44 (3.0)	17 (1.8)	182 (2.5)
6	total	1477 (100.0)	966 (100.0)	7416 (100.0)

Source: NSS, 14th round.

of low income households is accounted by farmers and farm workers. However, within the latter group, the incidence of poverty is strikingly different as between farmers and farm workers. The latter, being worse off on the average, account for 41 per cent of households with per capita consumption below Rs. 11 per month. While 35-36 per cent of farm workers households belong to the poorer categories in the above definition, the comparable proportion for the farmers is only 13-14 per cent. Among the farmers the incidence of poverty is somewhat but not significantly greater among small landholders.

Consumption Inequalities : Inter-State Variations

State-wise estimates of the average per capita consumption and the degree of inequalities in its distribution are given in Table 12.

Average per capita consumption is below the national average in seven states, the lowest being Orissa. The richest state by this criterion is the Punjab with per capita consumption nearly 50 per cent above the national average. In a majority of states, the LR for persons is greater than the LR for households. This is in line with the all-India picture which shows an inverse relation between per capita consumption and household size. However in the case of Bihar, Mysore and West Bengal, the two LR's do not differ much. In Punjab the LR for persons is actually lower than the LR for households which suggests a tendency for average household size to increase with per capita consumption. The more striking, though by no means original, conclusion emerging from the table is that the degree of inequality in living standards is not uniform as between states. The value of LR (persons) varies between 0.241 in Assam to 0.394 in Bihar. Broadly speaking consumption seems to be more evenly distributed in Assam, Jammu & Kashmir, West Bengal, Gujarat and Maharashtra than in the country taken as a whole. Inequalities appear more pronounced in Bihar and the Punjab.[18]

TABLE — 12

Relative Per Capita Consumption and Inequality in Different States of India : 1960-61

sl. no.	*State*	*average per capita consumption (Rs.)*	*index of inequality*		*percentage of poor population**
			households	*persons*	
(0)	*(1)*	*(2)*	*(3)*	*(4)*	*(5)*
1.	Andhra Pradesh	19.50	.261	.323	18.74
2	Assam	24.00	.168	.241	1.20
3	Bihar	25.51	.381	.394	15.17
4	Gujarat	23.46	.208	.254	8.43
5	Jammu & Kashmir	25.62	.193	.273	3.44
6	Kerala	18.12	.269	.323	23.18
7	Madhya Pradesh	18.04	.230	.295	20.64
8	Madras	18.57	.244	.306	21.65
9	Maharashtra	19.13	.201	.279	15.93
10	Mysore	21.42	.267	.285	15.22
11	Orissa	14.54	.216	.322	32.62
12	Punjab	31.40	.410	.345	1.23
13	Rajasthan	23.17	.240	.314	11.24
14	Uttar Pradesh	20.11	.249	.300	16.40
15	West Bengal	22.81	.252	.252	6.34
16	All India	21.44	.288	.323	15.65

* Defined as population with per capita consumption below Rs. 11 a month, which is roughly half the national average.

Source: The National Sample Survey, Tables with Notes on Consumer Expenditure (Preliminary): Sixteenth Round, July 1960 - June 1961 (Draft Report No. 113) ISI, Calcutta - 1963.

Differences in average per capita consumption and its distribution account for the large variations in the incidence of poverty between States as measured by the proportion of their respective population with per capita consumption below a specified level. In the country as a whole, a little under a sixth of the rural population appear to have less than half the average per capita consumption. The proportion is much higher in Orissa, Kerala, Madras and Madhya Pradesh all of which have an average per capita consumption appreciably below the average. In Punjab, on the other hand, the average per capita consumption is high relative to all India that the proportion of poor on the above definition is very small.

The degree of inequality seems to bear no consistent relation to the level of per capita consumption. The 16th round data show practically no correlation between the two variables. Data from the 18th and the 22nd rounds suggest a negative association between the LR of consumption and per capita consumption expenditure but the coefficients are not statistically significant.[19]

Since agriculture is the dominant economic activity of rural areas, one would expect differences in the pattern of land distribution to be an important cause of variations in consumption inequality. The frequency distribution of households by size of ownership and operational holdings is available for 1960-61.[20] The LR's for land holdings estimated from these data, were correlated with LR's for consumption relating to the same year. The results confirm the expectation that greater inequality in distribution of land will be associated with more uneven distribution of consumption. However, the association is not strong : the correlation coefficient for operation holdings (0.38) is in fact statistically not significant. The coefficients for ownership holdings (0.48) is significant at 10 per cent confidence level but explain less than 25 per cent of the variation in consumption inequality. It is significant that the pattern of land ownership is more important than the pattern of land operation in determining the degree of consumption inequality.

The LR of land holdings used in the above correlations make no allowance for the variation in land quality. For reasons mentioned earlier, the disparities in total area owned (or operated) do not accurately reflect the differences in productive capacity of the land. In an attempt to allow for variations in land quality as between different size classes of holdings, the proportion of area irrigated was introduced as an additional element. A multiple regression of LR of consumption against LR of land holdings and irrigated area did not appreciably improve the explanation. Contrary to expectation the coefficient for irrigated area was positive though insignificant.[21] Possibly the intensity of irrigation is too crude a correction for quality differences. One has to use a measure which allows for the large inter-regional variation in average land quality as well as in the distribution of unirrigated area as between size class of holdings. Essentially what we need is a measure of distribution of holdings in terms of some "standard acre". This is a direction in which further research could be fruitful. One possibility is to use the farm management survey data on land revenue per acre in different size classes for getting a crude correlation factor for quality. Alternatively the hypothesis being explained here could be tested with data from the farm management survey itself.

Cultivation of land is the most important means of livelihood in rural areas but by no means the only source. A substantial part of rural incomes is derived from animal husbandry and from non-agricultural activities. The inequalities in aggregate income and consumption is therefore likely to be influenced by the manner in which income from these sources is distributed. State-wise estimates of the income generated in animal husbandry and crop production are available.[22] Assuming that these activities are mostly located in rural areas, it is possible to get a measure of the relative importance of animal husbandry as a source of rural income in different states. Similar estimates of rural non-agricultural income are not available. The next best index, though not a very satisfactory one, is the proportion of non-agricultural workers in total rural working population. This can be readily obtained from census reports.

A multiple regression of LR of consumption against LR of land holdings, proportion of total agricultural income contributed by animal husbandry and proportion of non-agricultural employment was attempted. The coefficient for animal husbandry was in fact higher and statistically more significant than for LR of land holdings. One possible interpretation is that income from animal husbandry, though more evenly distributed than land area, is less evenly distributed than income from crop production. If this were so, the larger the proportion of income derived from animal husbandry the larger will be the inequality in income (consumption). Non-agricultural employment is not a significant factor in explaining the variations in consumption inequality. By excluding it from the regressions the proportion of variance in LR of consumption explained is not affected appreciably and the coefficients are statistically more significant. It would appear that inequality and land holdings and the relative importance of animal husbandry in rural economy would explain about 55 per cent of the variance in consumption inequalities.

One would expect that inequalities in distribution of land, the proportion of irrigated area and the contribution of animal husbandry would provide a fuller explanation of inequalities among farm households than of inequalities among all rural households. Data from the 14th round do not seem to bear out this expectation. While the importance of the distribution of land holdings is corroborated, the analysis suggests that (a) difference in the proportion of income from animal husbandry is not a significant factor explaining inter-state variations in consumption inequality among farmers; (b) the proportion of area irrigated tends to be negatively associated with consumption inequalities, and (c) inequalities in land ownership and irrigation explain only 40 per cent of the variation in consumption inequality among farmers. However, since the data used in the analysis are incomplete and the distributions are unweighted, these findings cannot be considered conclusive. Further analysis is clearly necessary.

Behaviour of Inequalities Over Time

The LR's of nominal consumption, that is consumption uncorrected for price changes, in rural India for different rounds of the NSS are presented in Table 13. Since the sample size, the time coverage, reference period and methods of imputation have been changing from round to round the indices prior to 1960-61 are not strictly comparable. Thereafter, the concepts and coverage have been standardised and more valid comparisons are possible. The inequalities in nominal consumption seem to have remained more or less stable upto 1957-58. Since then, they have fallen appreciably. Though LR in 1967-68 was higher than in 1963-64, it was still lower than in 1960-61.

The picture at the state level presents a mixed pattern. The LR of nominal consumption in Andhra, Assam, Madras, Jammu & Kashmir and UP show a consistent decline from 1960-61 to 1967-68. In a majority of the remaining states, LR in 1967-68 was lower compared to 1960-61. But there does not seem to be a uniform trend. Rajasthan, Gujarat, MP and Mysore show an increase in inequalities in the period though here again, except for Mysore, the behaviour is not consistently in the same direction.

TABLE – 13

Lorenz Ratios of Consumption, Rural India : 1957-58 to 1967-68

sl. no.	state	1957-58 SS_1	1957-58 comb.	1957-58 SS_2	1960-61 SS_1	1960-61 comb.	1960-61 SS_2	1963-64 SS_1	1963-64 comb.	1963-64 SS_2	1967-68 SS_1	1967-68 comb.	1967-68 SS_2
(0)	(1)	(2)	(3)	(4)	(5)	(6)	(7)	(8)	(9)	(10)	(11)	(12)	(13)
1	Andhra Pradesh	.310	.327	.339	.258	.323	.363	.285	.302	.318	.263	.284	.300
2	Assam	.238	.252	.252	.253	.241	.249	.208	.220	.224	.178	.205	.235
3	Bihar	.294	.312	.331	.315	.334	.415	.288	.289	.290	.294	.300	.301
4	Gujarat	.279	.293	.306	.198	.254	.279	.286	.295	.304	.249	.278	.289
5	Jammu & Kashmir	.256	.268	.271	.254	.273	.287	.228	.243	.272	.199	.214	.227
6	Kerala	.328	.345	.357	.284	.323	.352	.296	.299	.302	.296	.314	.343
7	Madhya Pradesh	.369	.402	.426	.282	.295	.306	.320	.341	.359	.289	.314	.347
8	Madras	.311	.316	.320	.299	.306	.306	.305	.306	.305	.268	.275	.283
9	Maharashtra	.279	.293	.306	.259	.279	.299	.278	.289	.300	.247	.262	.287
10	Mysore	.300	.374	.421	.278	.285	.280	.267	.287	.306	.245	.300	.356
11	Orissa	.289	.313	.332	.308	.322	.332	.274	.276	.275	.270	.301	.356
12	Punjab	.290	.317	.337	.285	.345	.368	.286	.297	.309	Pb..276	.295	.306
											H. .243	.276	.324
13	Rajasthan	.380	.393	.396	.307	.314	.318	.300	.302	.305	.284	.338	.362
14	U.P.	.282	.293	.303	.291	.300	.307	.287	.295	.302	.274	.282	.288
15	West Bengal	.246	.265	.280	.248	.252	.250	.244	.261	.274	.237	.250	.255
16	India	.330	.334	.337	.318	.323	.329	.292	.287	.302	.284	.293	.301

Note : (1) SS1 and SS2 give the lowest and highest values as obtained from various sub-samples.
(2) 1967-68 estimates are based on results of Quick Tabulation of 22nd round. These are instant issued data.
(3) The figures for Gujarat and Maharashtra in 1957-58 relate to undivided Bombay state.

The period since 1960-61 was one of rapid increase in prices. The NSS data have to be adjusted for these price changes in order to get an idea of the inequality in real consumption. This requires (a) data on rural consumer prices by commodities; and (b) an index of consumer prices for different classes of rural consumers.

Data on retail prices of consumption goods in rural areas are very scanty. The rural price index published by the Labour Bureau relates only to rural labour households. The NSS provides time series data on unit prices of major cereals for different classes of rural population. Similar data for other commodities are presently available only in respect of the 17th and 19th rounds. A number of consumer price indices are available but they relate to particular classes in urban areas and may not accurately reflect the situation in rural areas. The only other source is the official index of wholesale prices. In the absence of adequate information, we have used the NSS prices wherever available and the wholesale prices for analysing changes in real consumption and its distribution.

Since the pattern of consumption for different segments of the rural population is not uniform, it would be misleading to use a single overall index to deflate nominal consumption expenditures of all classes. A better procedure would be to construct a separate index for each fractile or per capita expenditure class on the basis of its consumption pattern. The weighting diagram for the present exercise is based on the proportion of total expenditure going to different categories of commodities in each fractile prevailing in 1964-65 (19th round of NSS).

The nominal expenditure in each fractile was deflated by an index reflecting the price changes for the bundle of goods and services consumed by that fractile. This formed the basis for estimating the inequality in real consumption at different points of time. In order to test the sensitivity of the results, a number of alternative deflators were tried :

Case 1 : In this case the total expenditure in each fractile group was divided into the following groups of commodities (i) cereals and cereal substitutes; (ii) milk and milk products; (iii) edible oils; (iv) meat, egg and fish; (v) sugar and gur; (vi) salt; (vii) other food; (viii) clothing; (ix) fuel and light; and other non-food. The expenditure on each of these groups was deflated by the corresponding wholesale price index (with base 1952-53 = 100). The sum of the deflated expenditures by commodity in each fractile gave the total expenditure at constant prices. From this the LR's were calculated.

Case II : The commodity groupings are the same as in case I, but instead of commodity-wise deflation, the average per capita expenditure in each fractile is deflated by a single price index. Fractile-wise price indices have been constructed using the official wholesale price series (1952-53 = 100) for each commodity group, weighted by the pattern of consumption in each fractile as revealed by the 19th round of NSS.

Case III : The procedure here is the same as in the previous case with the difference that the deflators are computed with 1957-58 as base instead of 1952-53.

Case IV : This is the same as case III except that the aggregate consumption is divided into only five groups namely; rice, wheat, other cereals and cereal substitutes, other food and non-food.

Case V : The commodity groupings and fractile-wise weighting patterns are as in case IV, but in calculating deflators the fractile-wise data on average prices of different cereals obtained from the NSS have been used. For other commodities the wholesale price index forms the basis of calculations. The base year in this case as in cases III and IV is 1957-58.

The results summarised in Table 14 suggest that in rural India taken as a whole, the behaviour of inequalities in real consumption has been roughly similar to that of inequalities in nominal consumption. Both appear to have declined between 1957-58 and 1967-68. However, the reduction in inequalities in real consumption appears to be less than the reduction in inequality of consumption valued at current prices. This is due to the fact that the prices of commodities consumed by the relatively poor groups has risen appreciably more than the prices of goods consumed by the relatively rich. The Lorenz curve of real consumption in 1967-68 is also found to be uniformly interior to the curve for 1960-61.

TABLE — 14

Lorenz Ratio of Consumption Under Different Assumptions, Rural India

		rural India Lorenz ratio					
NSS round no.	*period*	*at current prices*	*Case I*	*Case II*	*Case III*	*Case IV*	*Case V*
(1)	*(2)*	*(3)*	*(4)*	*(5)*	*(6)*	*(7)*	*(8)*
13	Sept. '57-May '58	.328	.321	.324	.328	.328	.328
16	July '60-June '61	.321	.305	.309	.313	.312	—
17	Sept.'61-July '62	.314	.300	.303	.307	.305	.309
18	Feb. '63-Jan. '64	.297	.286	—	—	—	—
19	July '64-June '65	.294	.291	.294	.208	.298	.299
22	July '67-June '68	.293	.297	.293	.297	.294	—

While the NSS data suggest that the degree of inequality in real consumption has declined appreciably in the last decade, they also reveal a significant reduction in the average real consumption standards during the sixties. On the basis of a fractile-wise deflation of nominal consumption expenditure (see

Table 15), the overall average per capita consumption in rural India (valued at 1960-61 prices) is estimated at Rs. 20.3 in 1964-65 and a little over Rs. 18 in 1967-68, compared to Rs. 21.5 in 1960-61. In other words, according to NSS data, per capita real consumption in 1967-68 was about 16 per cent

TABLE — 15

Fractilewise Estimates of Per Capita Consumption (Rs. per 30 days) At Current and Constant Prices, Rural India : 1960-61, 1964-65, And 1967-68

	1964-65				1967-68		
fractile group	*per capita expendi-ture at 1960-61 prices*	*per capita expend-iture at current prices*	*price index 1960-61 = 100*	*per capita expendi-ture at 1960-61 prices*	*per capita expendi-ture at current prices*	*price index 1960-61 = 100*	*per capita expendi-ture at 1960-61 prices*
(1)	*(2)*	*(3)*	*(4)*	*(5)*	*(6)*	*(7)*	*(8)*
0-5	6.28	8.00	132.93	6.02	9.86	191.13	5.16
5-10	8.35	12.00	133.00	9.02	13.45	191.57	7.02
10-20	10.30	14.00	132.75	10.55	16.68	190.96	8.73
20-30	12.45	16.40	132.62	12.37	20.25	190.68	10.62
30-40	14.46	17.60	132.46	13.29	23.62	190.36	12.40
40-50	16.41	20.00	132.13	15.14	27.07	189.66	14.27
50-60	18.81	23.00	131.67	17.47	30.94	188.56	16.41
60-70	21.43	29.00	130.76	22.18	35.56	186.26	19.09
70-80	25.14	31.00	130.50	23.75	41.49	185.66	22.35
80-90	31.72	39.00	129.24	30.18	50.45	182.27	27.68
90-95	40.92	46.00	128.41	35.82	62.40	180.23	34.62
95-100	72.19	82.59	125.66	65.72	88.18	172.98	50.98
0-100	21.46	26.43		20.32	33.30		18.04

Note : (1) The price index (1960-61 = 100) has been computed according to case (3) as explained on page 25.

(2) The per capita expenditure in 1967-68 at 1960-61 prices is obtained by deflating col. (6) by col. (7).

lower than in 1960-61. Because of this sharp fall in the average, the proportion of rural population with per capita consumption below Rs. 20 per month (at 1960-61 prices) estimated wholly on NSS data show an appreciable increase during the sixties even though the degree of inequality in distribution declined.

The NSS estimate of changes in per capita consumption, however, differs sharply from that derived from the official national income series. According to NSS, per capita consumption at current prices in 1964-65 was about 23 per cent higher and in 1967-68 56 per cent higher than in 1960-61. The official series on the other hand suggests an increase of 32 per cent between 1960-61 and 1964-65[23] and nearly 80 per cent between 1960-61 and 1967-68. The level of per capita consumption in 1967-68 implied by the official series is thus about 16 per cent higher than the NSS figure. If the official estimate of consumption growth were taken along with the pattern of inequalities revealed by the NSS, the proportion of rural population below the poverty line as defined earlier shows a mild fall from about 59 per cent in 1960-61 to about 58 per cent in 1967-68.

TABLE — 16

Proportion of Rural Population with Per Capita Consumption Below Rs. 20 per month at 1960-61 prices

	1960-61	*1964-65*	*1967-68*
NSS	59.5	60.4	67.8
official series	58.8	56.9	57.8

The use of NSS distributions along with the average derived from official data can be questioned because of the appreciable divergence between the NSS and the official estimate of average per capita consumption. In other words, the validity of the distribution obtained from NSS cannot be considered independent of the validity of the average obtained from NSS. Some persons have in fact suggested that not only is the NSS figure of consumption in 1967-68 an underestimate but the underestimation is mostly, if not wholly, in the upper income groups. This proposition is, however, not backed by any objective evidence. Even assuming that NSS estimates are biased, there is no basis to believe that these biases have been changing systematically over time. It seems reasonable to go on the presumption that the direction and degree of bias in NSS data, if any, relating to different classes has remained more or less the same at different points of time. Given this it is legitimate to use the NSS distributions along with the official average for making valid inferences about the relative changes in the incidence of poverty. Obviously to the extent the degree of bias in NSS data is not uniform between different fractiles, the absolute proportions of the poor obtained from them will not be accurate.

The more important question seems to be : which of the two available series gives a more accurate measure of the real consumption and of changes in it over time. A comparison of the two series reveals the following :

(a) Aggregate nominal consumption expenditure from the two sources are more or less in agreement upto 1962-63 but they diverge quite sharply thereafter.

(b) Even during the years when the aggregates were in close agreement, there are significant differences in the composition of consumption.

(c) The time trends in the consumption of particular items shows a mixed picture. In some cases the two series are in close agreement while in others there are sharp divergences.

Much more work at the detailed commodity level is necessary before the relative accuracy of the two sources of information can be confidently assessed.

Notes

1. Some of the other studies on this problem are, Bhattacharya, N. And Iyenger, N.S : Changes in the pattern of distribution of persons by monthly per capita expenditure. ISI, Planning Division Working Paper, No. 218 (Mimeographed).

   Iyengar, N.S. (1964) : Contribution to Analysis of Consumer Expenditure, Doctoral Thesis, ISI, (Calcutta (1964). Iyengar N.S. (1967): A Study of Differential Price Movements and Consumer Behaviour. Indian Economic Review, October 1967.

   Datta Mazumdar, D.K. (1969) : Changes in the size distribution of Income and consumption expenditure in India during the First Two Plans. Ninth Indian Econometric Conference, Patna, 1969.
2. Mukherjee, M. and Chatterjee, G.S. (1967) : Trends in Distribution of National Income 1950-51 to 1965-66. Economic and Political Weekly, July 15, 1967.
3. Subramanian Swamy (1967) : Distribution of Income in India. Economic and Political Weekly, Annual Number, Feb. 1967.
4. Ojha, P.D. (1970) : A configuration of Indian poverty : Inequality and levels of living, Reserve Bank of India Bulletin, January 1970.
5. Bardhan, Pranab (1970): The so-called green revolution and agricultural labourers. Economic and Political Weekly, Special Number, 1970.

   Bardhan, Pranab (1970): On minimum level of living and the rural poor. Indian Economic Review, Vol. V. (New Series), November 1, 1970.
6. Minhas, B.S. (1970): Rural poverty, land re-distribution and development. Indian Economic Review, Vol. V (New Series) November 1, 1970.
7. Mukherjee, M. (1969): Size and area distribution of the level of living in India. Sankhya Series, B Vol. 31, Parts 3 and 4.
8. The estimate of the absolute level of consumption expenditure obtained from the NSS do not always agree with figures derived from the official national income statistics. Since there is not easy way of explaining the difference or assessing the relative accuracy of the two estimates, a considerable measure of caution is needed in using the absolute figures. For most of the subsequent analysis, we are not so much concerned with the absolute level of per capita consumption as with its distribution and with relative levels of consumption between different groups.
9. See, National Sample Survey, 19th Round : Instructions to Field Workers, Section 8, p.23.
10. "The prices used to value agricultural production in national income statistics

are the average wholesale prices during the harvest months. Quantities retained for home consumption are also valued at the price at which the marketed portion is sold. It appears logical to value home consumed produce at the same price that is used in national income statistics so that income estimates from the Survey can be compared with the latter, particularly income originating in the agricultural sector", NCAER, All India Rural Household Saving Survey 1962 : Vol I, Methodology (New Delhi, 1964) p. 33.

11. See NSS, Draft Report 207, p.66.

12. The two surveys also differ in the treatment of improved rental value of own houses. The NCAER includes it as part of income while NSS excludes it. This difference however seems to make no appreciable difference to the value of LR of income.

13. Apart from the evidence presented in Table 4, we have also some information from earlier rounds of NSS to corroborate this. The 5th and 6th rounds of the NSS collected data on level of milk output in different classes of households. On this basis, the LR of milk production is estimated at 0.47-0.48. The LR of operational holdings in 1953-54 (8th round of NSS) is estimated at 0.72.

14. A word of caution about 14th round data used in this paper is in order. The data are incomplete; out of the 7589 households surveyed, we could obtain information only for 7416 households. The bulk of the missing households appear to be in the lower income group. A second limitation that our analysis is generally based on crude distributions. A more accurate picture can be had only by estimating weighted distributions. This could not be attempted for want of the relevant information. We have nevertheless used the data because it is available in a form which permits far more detailed analysis of consumption inequalities by occupation, land holding, household size than any other available information.

15. See NCAER, All-India Rural Household Survey : Vol. III (New Delhi - 1965).

16. NSS, Draft Report No. 207.

17. NSS data for 1963-64 also suggest that the degree of inequality among cultivator households is nearly the same as in the rural population as a whole. However, the consumption disparities in the non-agricultural households seems to be slightly less and in the agricultural labourer households significantly less than the average for rural areas.

    See, Mukherjee, M : Size and area distribution... op.cit.

18. This statement is based on 17th round data. The relative degree of inequality in State varies appreciably as between different rounds (see Table 13). Thus while in almost all years for which data have been analysed, LR for Assam and West Bengal are well below national average, the LR for Punjab and Bihar was roughly equal to or below the All-India figure in 1957-58, 1963-64 and 1967-68. The converse is true of Rajasthan and Madhya Pradesh where the LR was higher than national average in all years other than 1960-61.

See also Mukherjee, M. "Size and area distribution of level of living in India" op.cit.

19. The correlation coefficients for different rounds are

    13th round (—) 0.06

    16th round (—) 0.09

    18th round (—) 0.38

    22nd round (—) 0.25

20. Though a similar survey was conducted in 1956-57, the data have apparently not been tabulated by states. It might be pointed out that the analysis for 1960-61 is based on inequality indices for households and not for persons. In the absence of data on average family size by class of holdings in different states, it is not possible to compute LR of land holdings with reference to population.

21. Since irrigation improves productivity of land and smaller holdings have a large proportion of irrigated area, one would expect, opinion that a higher degree of irrigation development would be associated with a lower degree of inequality in incomes.

22. See NCAER "Agricultural Income by States, 1960-61".

23. The official series give an estimate of per capita consumption for the population as a whole. The actual figures are taken from Radhakrishnan's computations. The corresponding figures for rural areas is estimated on the basis of projected rural-urban distribution of population and the ratio of per capita consumption in rural to per capita consumption in urban areas. The latter is taken from the relevant rounds of NSS.

15

The Validity of NSS Consumption in Rural India

FOR nearly three decades the National Sample Survey (NSS) has been collecting, every year upto 1973-74 and at five year intervals thereafter, data on the level and pattern of consumption from a representative sample of households in rural and urban areas of different parts of the country. It is by far the most comprehensive source of information on the subject. No other source provides such detailed continuous and apparently comparable data over as long a period. Naturally they have been used extensively for studying a variety of questions such as the sources of variation in per capita consumption levels (Visaria, 1980); responsiveness of consumer demand patterns and demand for particular commodities to changes in incomes and prices (see among others Ganguly et al, 1960; Iyengar, 1967; Rudra, 1972); inter-regional disparities in living standards (Bhattacharya and Chatterjee, 1974); inequality in consumption, incidence of poverty and changes therein (see, e.g., Srinivasan and Bardhan, eds, 1974; Dandekar and Rath, 1971; Rajaraman, 1974; Ahluwalia, 1978). While these studies provide many valuable insights, the question of the validity of the NSS data keeps surfacing in the discussion particularly in the context of the debate on trends in incidence of poverty.

Several important questions concerning the quality of NSS consumption data have been raised in the literature, prominent among them being: the chances of systematic understatement of consumption by upper income groups arising from the relatively small number of rich households in the sample (Dandekar and Rath, 1971); the possibility of inaccuracies in the information obtained from the sample households (Bhattacharya and Chatterjee, 1975); the appropriateness of current NSS design to get a reliable estimate of frequency distribution (Murthy, 1977); comparability of estimates over time (Mukherjee, 1981; Bhattacharya and Chatterjee, 1975); and the reasons for and significance of divergence between the NSS and the official estimates in respect of level and composition of consumption (Kansal, 1965), their behaviour over time (Mukherjee, 1969; Mukherjee and Chatterjee, 1972; Srinivasan et al, 1974) as well as its implication for inferences on changes in the incidence of poverty (Vaidyanathan, 1974). Discussion of these questions has, however, been rather fragmentary and inconclusive. Considering their importance for the on-going debates on various aspects of growth and distribution, it seems worthwhile to review systematically the various possible sources of 'bias' and 'error' in the NSS data on consumption expenditure and its distribution by classes and examine, with such evidence as is available, whether and in what manner they in fact affect the reliability of NSS estimates. This is what the present paper seeks to do. While we are in no position to settle all the questions definitively, the evidence suggests that there is strong reason for being circumspect in using NSS estimates as the basis for judging trends in consumption and in the incidence of poverty.

SOURCES OF INACCURACY IN NSS DATA

The reliability of NSS data on consumption (in the aggregate and by particular commodity groups) at a given point of time has to be judged basically in terms of how closely they correspond to the 'true value' of these characteristics. The sample survey estimate may differ from the true value because of sampling error, defects in sample design, inaccuracies in the information obtained from sample households or a combination of these. For a study of changes in consumption, the magnitude of the sampling error in the estimate relative to the true rate of change is clearly relevant: The larger the former is relative to the latter, the less reliable the sample estimate for assessing change. Other biases and errors need not vitiate use of sample data for this purpose and for assessing changes in inequality so long as their magnitude relative to the true value in different regions/classes does not change systematically over time.

Sampling Errors

Any attempt at estimating the 'true value' of a characteristic of a population from observations relating to a sample thereof is necessarily subject to a 'sampling' error. The NSS reports seldom give the sampling error of its estimates for consumption and its components. However, until the mid-seventies, the NSS design had inter-penetrating sub-samples and the reports invariably gave sub-sample-wise estimates which provide a rough indication of the sampling error for various estimated magnitudes.[1] On this basis it would seem that the all India estimates of per capita consumption (in the aggregate, by major commodity groups and also by expenditure classes) were subject to a relatively small margin of sampling error.[2] The errors are naturally larger in the case of state level estimates and estimates for detailed commodity groups. For this reason, and given the relatively slow pace of change during the last 2-3 decades, even if the information were otherwise accurate and unbiased, the NSS is likely to be less reliable for measuring the magnitude of differences in levels of expenditure (aggregate and even more by commodities) across regions and classes and of the magnitude of changes in them. However it is not always essential to have accurate estimate of levels or of percentage change; useful insights on several questions can be obtained with information on relative positions of regions/classes in respect of total consumption, consumption of particular commodities and the composition of consumption.

Sampling Design

Sample households for consumption enquiries are selected essentially on the basis of probability proportional to population without reference to the level of their income or consumption. In this process the number of "rich" households likely to be included in the sample is necessarily small and consequently the estimate of the upper income groups consumption will have a higher margin of sampling error compared to lower incomes groups. For this reason some people have questioned the suitability of the present NSS design to get a reliable estimate of frequency distribution. Murthy (1977: 192) observes:

> Since the NSS estimates are based on general purpose design with emphasis on point parameters, the estimates of tails, in which the users are specifically interested, are subject to larger sampling error and hence not amenable to deeper analysis.

If we are interested in measures of relative inequality, this is indeed a serious limitation. However it has been shown (Srinivasan et at, 1974) that the larger sampling error (or for that matter non-sampling errors and bias) in the upper tail does not necessarily vitiate estimates of the incidence of poverty in the population or changes therein.[3]

Over the years the size of NSS sample for consumption enquiries has progressively increased[4] and so the sampling errors must have fallen. However even as the NSS sampling design has remained basically unchanged, the basis for defining the strata, the number of strata, the procedure for selecting the sample households and the size of the sample for the consumption survey have all undergone changes. Thus the number of regions, which defines the strata for selecting sample villages, has risen from 48 in the early 1960s to 66 in 1972-73. The number of sample households surveyed for consumption expenditure has risen from one per sample village between 1958-59 and 1960-61 to two in 1961-62, six in 1970-71 and twelve in 1972-73; in 1973-74 it was again reduced to two per village (Gupta and Ramaratnam, 1975). It seems likely that these changes affect only the variance of the estimates without affecting comparability in any other way. However, the NSS also stratifies households within each sample village by household size and means of livelihood or land possessed before sample selection. The basis of stratification and the number of strata vary (in 1964-65 there were as many as six while in 1970-71 there were only three).[5] It is not clear how this stratification enters into, and affects, the selection of sample households for canvassing the consumption schedule especially in years (e.g. 1960-61 and 1961-62) when the number of households per village is less than the number of strata. Nor is it clear whether and to what extent these changes may affect the comparability of the estimates over time. These are technical questions which can best be clarified by specialists in sampling.

Bias in Sampling

Then there is the question of 'bias' in the NSS design. It has been alleged that the NSS has an in-built 'bias' to underestimate the true value of consumption per capita and the extent of inequality in distribution because (a) the sample has relatively few households from the 'rich' classes who account for a disproportionately high percentage of total consumption; and (b) it does not fully capture seasonal variations in consumption. Both these propositions are erroneous. As Srinivasan et al (1974) have pointed out the fact that the NSS sample has few 'high' income households essentially increases the variance of the estimate of the average for the population and for the upper "tail"; it does not imply any in-build 'bias' in the sampling procedure toward systematic over or under estimation of the true value in any class. Again the practice of spreading the collection of data relating to the sample households over the year effectively captures seasonal variations in consumption. Some have argued however that the present procedure of canvasing different sets of households during each sub-round may exaggerate the degree of inequality.[6] There is hardly any other basis to expect 'bias' in the sampling design itself.[7] Systematic errors can arise for reasons independent of sample designs: For instance a higher proportion of upper income sample households may refuse to respond; informants, or some sections of them, may systematically over-or under-state their actual consumption; and inaccurate reporting of information[8] could arise from recall lapses, the way questions are framed and communicated or simply negligence.

Non-Sampling Errors

The incidence and magnitude of these 'non-sampling errors' could be randomly distributed among the sample households in which case their effect on the estimate is similar to that of sampling errors though the magnitude of overall error in the estimate will naturally be larger than sampling error. Much the same would be the case even when the non-sampling errors are systematic so long as all households tend to over-or under-state the true value of the characteristic to a uniform degree. In both cases, the errors in the estimates are affected but, subject to the caveat mentioned by Murthy, the estimated distribution around the mean should not be affected. However, when the magnitude of non-sampling errors relative to the true value varies systematically in the sample — this would be the case for instance when the degree of over or under reporting is greater in the upper income households than in poorer classes — the accuracy of both the average and its distribution are affected.

The nature and incidence of non-sampling errors may also change over time due to changes in concepts, the way questions are framed, or in the investigation procedure. Clearly if the systematic errors in different classes can be shown to have no particular trend over time, the sample data can be used with greater confidence to speak about changes in per capita total consumption and its distribution. On the other hand any evidence that these errors themselves vary in some systematic way over time would throw doubt on the usability of NSS data for evaluating changes over time. The rest of our discussion is largely concerned with the nature and direction of non-sampling errors in NSS consumption data. (Questions concerning sampling design are left to the specialists.) It is based partly on a comparison of the NSS estimates of per capita consumption levels (in the aggregate and by major product categories) with corresponding estimates of the CSO and partly on evidence internal to the NSS. In both respects this paper seeks to extend earlier work by using more recent information.

COMPARISON OF NSS AND CSO ESTIMATES

More than a decade back, Mukherjee (1969) had emphasised the close correspondence between CSO and NSS estimates of per capita consumption as a basis for confidence in the NSS data. The force of this argument was however weakened by the increasing divergence between the two estimates from the early 1960s (Mukherjee and Chatterjee, 1972, Srinivasan et al, 1974). Since then the CSO has published a detailed time series of consumption (aggregate and by commodities) at current and constant prices. The CSO series differs markedly from those of the NSS not only in the aggregate but also in respect of the major categories of consumption; more importantly the two series show quite disparate trends.[9] (The basic data are given in Table 1). Thus the divergent trends between the two series of per capita total consumption noticed in first half of the sixties has been reversed after 1967-68 when the difference has progressively narrowed. However while the NSS shows a significant decline of PCE upto 1967-68 and a steep rise thereafter, total PCE in 1973-74 was no higher than in 1960-61. The CSO series on the other hand shows a sustained rising trend over the entire period, the level of PCE in 1973-74 being some 13 per cent higher than in 1960-61.

In the case of food other than foodgrains, though the CSO estimates are considerably higher than NSS, the two series move more or less together; the degree of difference shows but a mild tendency to rise over time. Neither series shows any significant rise in per capita real consumption level over the period as a whole. The CSO estimates of per capita consumption of non-food items as a group are not only higher than NSS but show a strong rising trend. The NSS shows a decline upto 1967-68 followed by a rise. While this has brought the two series closer, the level of per capita consumption in 1973-74 was only marginally higher than in 1961-62 according to the NSS, while CSO series show a 19 per cent rise. But the most dramatic difference is in respect of foodgrains. Between 1960 and 1970, the NSS shows a sustained decline of nearly 13-14 per cent, but estimated consumption rose sharply in 1972 and 1973 bringing it close to the 1960-61 level. The CSO on the other hand records erratic fluctuations

TABLE — 1

Per Capita Consumption Expenditure Estimates by Major Commodity Groups, India 1960-61 to 1973-74

Rs. per annum in constant (1960-61) prices

	1960-61	*1961-62*	*1963-64*	*1964-65*	*1965-66*	*1966-67*	*1967-68*	*1968-69*	*1969-70*	*1970-71*	*1972-73*	*1973-74*
Total												
CSO	276	270	273	291	278	282	294	299	303	314	302	313
NSS	279	273	254	270	265	257	246	257	256	263	272	286
Food-grains												
CSO	78	77	75	82	69	72	81	83	83	88	78	81
NSS	110	113	104	103	106	105	98	97	96	98	101	111
Food excluding foodgrains												
CSO	88	87	86	91	88	85	87	85	91	96	92	97
NSS	74	71	67	80	69	65	61	65	70	75	68	73
Non Food												
CSO	110	106	112	119	120	125	126	131	129	126	132	134
NSS	94	90	84	85	83	79	78	83	87	86	97	94

Notes : (1) CSO estimates taken from National Accounts Statistics 1960-61 to 1974-75 (New Delhi, October 1976). The publication gives estimates at current price and at 1960-61 prices. The implicit deflator for each category of consumption is used to derive per capita consumption at 1960-61 prices corresponding to the NSS series. The deflation is done for total consumption and for each of the categories separately. Therefore, the sum of deflated expenditure in component categories do not always add up to the figure under 'total'.

(2) The NSS estimate have been taken from publication entitled 'Tables with notes on consumer expenditure' for various rounds. The reports, identified by numbers, from which the figures have been estimated are listed below.

	1959-60	1960-61	1961-62	1963-64	1964-65	1965-66	1966-67	1967-68	1968-69	1969-70	1970-71	1972-73	1973-74
NSS Report No	104	101	135	142	192 & 196	209	230	216	228	235	231	284	240

The figures relate to total population and have been estimated as the weighted average of rural and urban per capita figures using the proportion of population in the two sectors as weights. These proportions are based on the Census data for 1961 and 1971 with the values for other years obtained by linear interpolation.

upto 1970 followed by a steep decline in 1972 and 1973. In relative terms the difference between the two estimates fell during the sixties but has again increased in the early seventies.

There are of course well known reasons why the two estimates of private consumption cannot be expected to agree. In the first place the NSS estimates of private consumption relate strictly to direct consumption by households while those of the CSO are derived by deducting estimated usage for intermediate inputs in the process of production, for capital formation, public consumption and exports from the estimated total availability of each commodity and service (production plus imports). The residual measures not only the direct consumption of households, but also 'consumption' by institutions (hostels, temples, charities, etc). However, the effect of this should be to make the CSO estimate generally higher than that of NSS. The second reason is that the CSO estimate is derived from estimates of availability and of absorption for uses other than private consumption all of which are subject to errors. Errors in the estimate of any of these magnitudes (which arise in part from lack of reliable data and in part to errors in data) necessarily affect the accuracy of the estimate of private consumption. Indeed for several items the CSO estimates are based on such weak data that one would be inclined to rely more on the NSS whose estimates are based on direct enquiry from consumers. This is especially the case where 'household consumption' is relatively easy to define in clear terms and the informants are not required to remember a great many details.

Nevertheless it is instructive to compare the NSS estimate for specific commodities which are mostly used by households for consumption with corresponding CSO estimates especially when the latter are known to be based on data collected systematically and independently of NSS. If the NSS estimate is lower and if the two series move more or less parallel to each other, confidence in the reliability of NSS data for evaluating trends would be strengthened. The CSO and the NSS estimates of per capita real consumption of cloth, sugar and gur, edible oil are set out in Table 2. In all these cases the NSS estimate in most years is lower than that of the CSO; but they show quite dissimilar patterns of change over time. In the case of edible oil and clothing the two series often differ even in the direction of year-to-year change; the overall trend is also dissimilar in the case of sugar and gur and even more in the case of clothing. In the latter case the NSS series point to a steep decline upto the mid-sixties followed by a

TABLE — 2

Indices of Per Capita Real Consumption of Selected Items as Estimated by CSO and NSS

(1960-61 = 100) *(Rs per capita)*

	1960-61	*1961-62*	*1963-64*	*1964-65*	*1965-66*	*1966-67*	*1967-68*	*1968-69*	*1969-70*	*1970-71*	*1972-73*	*1973-74*
Edible Oils												
CSO	10.9	95.3	94.5	104.6	92.7	91.7	100.9	93.6	98.2	115.6	98.2	97.2
NSS	8.3	106.6	118.1	108.6	104.1	89.1	84.3	110.6	95.7	89.0	107.5	93.7
Sugar and Gur												
CSO	13.7	100.1	102.2	105.1	108.0	100.0	83.9	95.6	106.6	107.3	102.9	111.7
NSS	8.1	102.2	77.2	85.9	94.6	84.6	68.9	94.8	101.2	99.2	89.0	98.3
Clothing												
CSO	18.3	99.5	115.3	130.1	121.3	135.0	135.5	139.9	132.2	134.4	137.2	139.9
NSS	22.1	107.5	94.7	96.7	86.0	78.8	80.5	84.4	87.7	98.3	98.4	96.9

Source : See Table 1.

rise with the per capita consumption in the early seventies being somewhat below the 1960-61 level; the CSO series points to a more or less steady rise of some 35 per cent over this period.

In the case of foodgrains, we have already noted the disparate time pattern of change in per capita real consumption (i.e. value of consumption at constant prices). A more direct comparison of the differences in terms of quantities consumed is possible in the case of the three major cereals. Table 3 gives estimates of the per capita consumption of rice, wheat and other cereals and total cereals derived from three different sources namely, (i) the official estimates; (ii) the estimates from the NSS consumption surveys; and (iii) estimates based on the NSS Land Use and Crop Cutting Surveys. Since the relevant data are not available for all years in the case of NSS, we have compared averages for groups of years at different points between 1958 and 1973. They show that in all three estimates the direction of change in respect of total cereals as well as individual cereals is generally similar. For instance all three series point to a progressive rise in wheat consumption per capita over the period and a general decline in the case of rice and other cereals. However the two NSS based estimates show a much steeper and more sustained decline (or a much slower rise) than the official estimates.

TABLE — 3

Alternate Estimates of Per Capita Consumption of Different Cereals in India

(Kg per annum)

	1959-61[1]			*1963-64*[2]			*1966-1968*[3]			*1970-73*[4]		
	Off (P)	*NSS (C)*	*NSS*	*Off (P)*	*NSS (C)*	*NSS*	*Off (P)*	*NSS (C)*	*NSS*	*Off (P)*	*NSS (C)*	*NSS*
Rice	70.6	82.3	93.5	71.0	74.2	93.0	60.8	56.8	NA	68.3	NA	78.6
Wheat	28.7	37.6	36.2	31.0	37.4	38.1	34.3	40.0	NA	42.4	NA	43.8
Others	44.0	62.6	71.2	41.6	46.5	63.0	42.0	47.3	NA	36.2	NA	53.1
All Cereals	143.4	181.1	200.9	143.5	158.0	194.1	137.1	144.2	NA	146.8	NA	175.7

Notes : 1 1959-60, 1960-61, 1961-62

2 1963-64, 1964-65

3 1966-67, 1967-68, 1968-69

4 1970-71, 1972-73, 1973-74

Off — Official Estimates.

NSS(P) — Estimates based on NSS LU-CCE Survey.

NSS(C) — Estimate based on NSS Consumption Surveys.

Source: Various NSS Reports.

NATURE OF NON-SAMPLING ERRORS IN NSS

The mere fact that NSS estimates diverge significantly from the official figures does not tell us much about the relative reliability of either. However there are independent reasons to believe that NSS estimates in respect of foodgrain and clothing are subject to rather large non-sampling errors, that these errors have been changing systematically over time, and further that the incidence of these changes is not the same in all classes.

The NSS rightly defines 'household consumption' of foodgrains (and of other items) in terms of the consumption of the members of the household; it explicitly excludes any payments in grain for production activities, payments in exchange for consumer service (priests, barber, washermen, etc) as well as transfers and gifts. The instructions to field workers for the 25th round (1970-71) states:

> The data.... should be strictly restricted to the non-productive consumption of the household including that of pet animals... While recording entries for household consumption care should be taken not to include any transfer payments in kind like loans advanced, charities, gifts and other payments in kind... But any consumption out of transfer receipts in kind like borrowings, gifts, charities, perquisites received by the household free collection and other receipts in kind if any will have to be considered. (GOI, NSS, 1970).

Payment in the form of grains or cooked food to hired workers for farm or non-farm enterprises of the household should thus be excluded from the estimate of its consumption. Consumption out of receipts in kind as wage must however figure in the schedule of the recipient household as part of its consumption. As for payments in grain for consumer services (priest, barber, etc) the instructions require that such payments should be shown in terms of imputed value against the appropriate item under 'Miscellaneous goods and services'.[10] Payment for services in cooked meals is to be recorded at their imputed value against the particular service in the schedule of the paying household and as consumption of cooked meals in that of the recipient household.[11] However, the quality of the data actually reported in the schedule depends on whether investigators attempt to get, and succeed in getting detailed information on these aspects.

The 'consumption' of foodgrains by a household in a given period consists of the quantity cooked at home and eaten by members of the household as well as cooked food obtained from employers or as gifts, transfers and loan. The grain used in the former may have been obtained from several sources namely past accumulations of grain stocks, fresh receipts in the form of uncooked grain for wages or as gifts, and fresh purchases. But since part of available grain may be used for other than household consumption, the estimation is complex.

Total quantum of grain consumed = Quantum cooked at home + Quantum received as cooked food from others — Quantum of cooked food given to others.

Quantum of grain cooked at home = Opening stock of the grain + Kind receipts (own farm, payment for services, gifts) + Purchases — Payments of uncooked grain for wage, gifts, etc. — Sales — Closing stock.

Given that few households keep any systematic accounts and that the foodgrain block in the NSS schedule lists 25 to 40 items, getting reliable information on these aspects is a formidable task even for the best of investigators. That the schedule is not designed to reconstruct the sources and disposition of foodgrains in a systematic manner with built in checks on internal consistency, adds to the difficulties. Thus the foodgrain block seeks information only on total consumption, consumption out of home-grown stock, purchase, and in some years, receipts in kind in exchange for goods and services. Consumption in the form of cooked meals is treated separately. Stocks are beyond the scope of the schedule and value of payments in exchange for goods and services are left to be recorded against the latter items.[12]

Under these circumstances, there is clearly considerable scope for errors in estimating household consumption of foodgrains. The most obvious possibility is the failure to fully capture cooked food received from others as part of the consumption of the recipient household and from failure to fully net out payment in cooked and uncooked grains under various categories listed above. The former seems likely to be relatively more important in poorer households (especially wage labourers and service castes) than among the rich and payments (of both cooked and uncooked food) on the other hand are apt to figure more prominently in the richer households who after all are the principal employers of attached labourers, domestic help and service castes. Much the same is true of food consumed at feasts. There is thus a real possibility of double counting of foodgrain consumption and a systematic tendency for the NSS estimate to be higher than the true value of consumption.[13] Not only does the NSS tend to over-state the consumption of foodgrains but, if as seems plausible, the quantum of kind payments for wages and services and by way of transfer, gifts and loans relative to household consumption among upper income households is higher than among the poorer classes, the incidence of the overestimation is likely to be greater among the former. This may well be the explanation for the improbably high level of foodgrain consumption in the top deciles of the population.[14] It would also mean that NSS would tend to over-state the inequality, in foodgrain consumption.

These problems would also affect estimates for other items but to a lesser degree because they do not figure as prominently as cereals in payments to workers and artisans and because a larger proportion of household consumption is purchased. On the other hand, the use of these products outside the household sector (mostly by restaurants, eating houses and manufactures of prepared food and, in the case of edible oil, for non-food users) seems likely to be much larger than in foodgrains.[15] In the case of clothing, since non-household consumption is relatively small one should expect a much closer correspondence between the two estimates. But they differ partly because of the difficulties in getting accurate data on receipts and payments in kind and gifts (especially at marriage and other ceremonial occasions) and partly from the differences in the concept of consumption. Unlike the CSO, the NSS defines clothing consumption in terms of the time when a piece of clothing is brought into use rather than in terms of purchase. These factors could lead to NSS estimate being lower than the CSO.

Changes in Non-Sampling Errors

There are also reasons to believe that the magnitude of non-sampling errors has not remained constant over time and may well be changing systematically. One indication of this is that both in the aggregate and in all the commodity groups reviewed, except foodgrains, there is a growing divergence between the two series upto the mid-sixties followed by a sustained tendency to converge. In the case of foodgrains the pattern is reversed. A second indication is the apparent change in the incidence of non-response. In 1959-60, the number of households actually surveyed was reported to be 1.5 per cent fewer than the number allotted according to the sample design; in 1960-61, this difference was less than 1 per cent. Thereafter there seems to be no difference between the number of allotted and surveyed households. Third, the NSS has changed its method of enquiry from 1964-65. Upto that point schedules relating to different socio-economic aspects of households were canvased in relation to different sets of sample households. Thereafter, until 1970-71, the procedure was replaced by the Integrated Household Survey (IHS) whereby information on all socio-economic and demographic aspects selected for enquiry in a particular round were collected from the same set of sample households. The IHS provided the means to incorporate closer checks on the internal consistency of responses. This could have made a difference to the estimates of both the level and the pattern of consumption expenditure.[16] But to our knowledge no attempt has been made to ascertain whether in fact this change made any significant difference to the data compared to those obtained by the earlier method.

There have also been significant changes in the level of detail of item classification under various categories of consumption. Thus in the case of cereals, schedules of the early sixties listed 31 items; the IHS schedule for 1964-65 lists 26 in the detailed version and 10 in the abridged version; the 1973-74 schedule lists 10 items under this category. In the case of clothing the consumer expenditure schedule in 1960-61 and 1961-62 listed 56 items under clothing; in 1964-65, when consumption enquiry was merged into the integrated household survey, the number was reduced to 18; and subsequent rounds listed 23 items including footwear. The number of items under miscellaneous goods and services was also reduced from 95 in 1960-61 and 1961-62 to 59 in 1964-65. Thereafter 66 items are listed. The level of aggregation and the names used to denote various items seems likely to make a difference to the response. The more detailed the itemisation, the lesser the chances of omission and the more accurate the estimate of total consumption which is obtained by adding expenditure on individual items. In view of the evidence of systematic inaccuracies in the reported consumption of such important items as foodgrains and cloth, we cannot take it for granted that recall and reporting errors for various items are random in nature and tend to cancel out. These aspects however, have not been systematically investigated.[17]

The format for recording data on consumption of food and clothing has undergone marked changes. For all items under these two categories the 16th-17th round schedules sought information separately in respect of (a) receipts in exchange for money; (b) receipts in exchange for goods and services; (c) consumption out of home-grown stock; and (d) consumption out of gifts, loans, etc. The 19th-20th round schedules distinguish only two categories, namely cash purchases and consumption out of home grown stock. The category of receipts in exchange for goods and services was reintroduced in the 25th round for all cereals and cereal substitutes only to be given up again in 1973-74. In the case of clothing this category was apparently not reintroduced. As for durables, where again the concept is 'purchase', the 17th round included value of second hand purchases in total consumption; the 1965-66 schedule did not even seek the information while in 1967-68 the information is obtained but it is not clear whether it is counted as part of total consumption; the item on second hand purchase was dropped in 1970-71 only to be reintroduced in 1973-74, again, however, without clarifying whether or not it is to be counted as part of consumption.

EFFECTS OF NON-SAMPLING ERRORS

We have no way of knowing exactly what effect these changes may have had on the estimated level of per capita consumption and its composition. However it seems likely that the estimates of foodgrains and clothing would be significantly affected especially by the changes indicated earlier and, insofar as investigators try to balance total consumption against the sum of the quantities and values by source of supply, also by those mentioned in the previous para. There are in any case independent reasons to believe that there have been significant and systematic changes in the extent of error in the NSS estimates. That there is a pattern in the relative profiles of the two series in most cases is one indication of this.

In the case of foodgrains we have two further reasons for this surmise. Firstly, unlike in NSS Consumption surveys, the techniques of estimation underlying the official series of foodgrain production have remained by and large constant over the last two decades, at any rate between 1960 and 1973 to which our comparisons relate. These estimates also seem more in the line with the recorded increase in cropped area and in the major inputs (namely irrigation, fertilisers and HYV).[18] Secondly, close examination of the NSS series shows that the decline in the per capita food intake is not uniform across all segments of population. In fact, between the late fifties and early seventies, the NSS estimates suggest that the per capita intake of cereals of the poorest quartile of the rural population has been more or less stagnant while that of the richest quartile shows a sustained and steep reduction (Table 4). This seems altogether implausible.

TABLE — 4

Per Capita Cereal Consumption of Poorest and Richest Quartiles of Rural Population All India

(Kg/capita/30 days)

	1958-59	*1959-60*	*1960-61*	*1961-62*	*1964-65*	*1965-66*	*1970-71*	*1972-73*	*1973-74*
First Quartile									
Total	11.29	11.97	12.20	12.77	11.25	10.30	11.61	10.99	11.14
Rice	4.45	5.04	5.17	5.61	5.49	4.47	4.24	4.66	4.91
Wheat	1.09	0.79	0.87	1.03	1.21	1.35	1.33	1.96	1.63
Other	5.75	6.14	6.16	6.13	4.55	4.48	6.04	4.37	4.60
Fourth Quartile									
Total	23.30	23.55	22.26	22.26	21.05	20.00	19.04	19.27	18.91
Rice	10.35	9.97	10.64	10.75	10.08	8.87	8.97	7.77	8.58
Wheat	4.58	4.83	5.80	5.15	4.97	5.19	4.61	6.40	5.65
Other	8.37	8.75	6.14	6.36	6.00	5.94	5.46	5.10	4.68

Note : Estimated by interpolation from estimated per capita intake of total cereals rice and wheat in different per capita expenditure class.

Source : Various NSS reports.

In the case of clothing the official statistics are based on a fairly elaborate system of direct reporting of production, inventories and foreign trade, show a steady rise. As mentioned earlier, the definition of consumption in terms of the time when they are brought into use might lead to an underestimation in the NSS. The omission of receipts by way of gifts since the 20th round could account for the steep drop in reported consumption in the mid-sixties. These two factors would probably result in the reported aggregate expenditure on cloth being lower than 'consumption' (in the usual sense of purchase plus that net imports less inventory changes). But it is not obvious why the NSS estimate was much higher than the CSO's in the early sixties nor why they should lead to a divergence of the two series in the earlier half of the period and a convergence in the second half.

CONCLUSION

The above discussion points to the following conclusions on the reliability of NSS consumption data:

(1) It is not possible to say anything definite on the accuracy of the NSS estimate of the level of per capita consumption. While the sampling error seems to be quite small, and the sampling design unbiased the scope for non-sampling errors is considerable. There are indications that NSS generally overstates foodgrain consumption and that the degree of overestimation is higher in the upper income group. In the case of clothing it is difficult with available evidence to be sure of the direction of the error. While we have no basis for evaluating the direction of non-sampling errors in respect of other items; the scope for such errors here would seem to be generally less than in foodgrains and clothing; in any event the NSS data, being based on direct enquiry would seem superior in many cases to the official estimates. There is no basis to assume that non-sampling errors in individual items will tend to cancel out. Therefore to the extent that a major

item like foodgrains is over-stated, the estimate of total consumption is also likely to be overstated. And insofar as the degree of over estimation is greater in the upper income groups, it would also tend to over-state the disparities in consumption.

(2) There is however more compelling evidence of systematic changes in the degree of non-sampling errors of estimates relating to foodgrain and clothing arising from identifiable changes in the design of schedules and in concepts. In both cases, there is reason to believe that the official estimates (which point to a mild rising trend) are much more reliable indicators of changes in consumption than the NSS (which shows a significant reduction during the sixties). Consequently even if we assume that the NSS estimates for other items are more reliable than the official series for assessing changes, the NSS series would tend to underestimate the growth (or exaggerate the decline) in per capita total consumption.

(3) There is reason to believe that the NSS tends to overestimate the consumption of foodgrains and cloth at the beginning of the period and that the degree of overestimation has fallen during the sixties. The incidence of this phenomenon seems to be much more pronounced in the upper income groups than among lower income sections at least in the case of foodgrains. If this surmise is correct, the NSS would tend to understate the extent of deterioration (or exaggerate the improvement) in inequality in the distribution of consumption.

(4) Insofar as the NSS understates the growth in average PCE, (or exaggerate its decline), it would tend to exaggerate the extent of increase in incidence of poverty (measured by the proportion of population falling below specified poverty line). However, its tendency to understate the worsening in inequality (or overstate the improvement) would have the

opposite effect. It is not possible to say, with the evidence at hand, what the relative strength of the two effects are.

All this suggests the need for far greater awareness among analysts of the various sources of error and non-comparability in NSS data while using them for studying consumption levels, inequalities in living standard, incidence of poverty and changes in all these respects. Given the circumstantial and patchy nature of evidence available, the above inferences are necessarily tentative. But it is hoped that they will provoke persons with first hand knowledge of NSS and its working as well as persons who have made use of the data to corroborate or to join issue with the arguments, evidence and conclusions presented here so that the uses and limitations of NSS consumption data for the above purposes may be better understood by users. Hopefully it will stimulate greater interest in, and concern for, improvements in the design of the schedules, the methods of enquiry and ensuring comparability over time.

Notes

[This is a revised version of a draft prepared some two years back. In revising it, I have greatly benefited from discussions and comments from Nirmal K Chandra, N Krishnaji, Chandan Mukherjee, T N Srinivasan and S D Tendulkar. While acknowledging my debt to them, responsibilities for any errors remain mine].

1 This practice was given up after the NSS was reorganised into a separate agency under the government. Sampling errors of estimates under the revised system have not been published.

2 For instance the standard error of the 13th round estimate for per capita total consumption in rural India has been calculated at barely 1 per cent, for food 1.2 per cent, and non-food 2.5 per cent. Gupta and Ramaratnam (1975).

3 More specifically, their conclusion was:

> ...for the limited question of estimating the incidence of poverty all one needs to be concerned with is the degree of bias (and its variation over time) at the chosen normative poverty line provided that stated consumption is an increasing function of true consumption is satisfied. But if one is interested in quantifying the magnitude of income transfers from the rich

to the poor required to reduce the incidence of poverty, it is essential to know the extent of bias at all levels of consumption (Srinivasan et al, 1974: 161)

Note that the word 'bias' is used here in a loose sense to cover both 'sampling bias' and inaccuracies in information.

4 The number of sample households surveyed for consumption has risen substantially. Thus in rural areas it rose from 2,600 in 1958-59 to 8,400 in 1969-70, 16,800 in 1971-72 and over 1,00,000 in 1972-73. See Gupta and Ramaratnam, 1975: 88 for details.

5 For a general description of the evolution of NSS design see Bhattacharya, (1981). Tendulkar in a personal communication refers to a change in the definition of household: Upto the 25th round, the size of the HH was defined as normal residents plus temporary guests less temporary stay aways. Since the 25th round it is defined as normal residents less temporary guest plus temporary stayaways. Whether this has any effect on the comparability of averages and/or distribution is again unclear.

6 For instance Bhattacharya and Chatterjee (1975: 103) argue:

... the programme of field work of any NSS round is organised in the form of sub-rounds so that the dates of interview for individual sample households are evenly spread over the duration of the round. This eliminates the effect of seasonality almost completely as far as the averages of consumption based on the entire round are concerned. But as different households are interviewed on different dates seasonal variation is superimposed on the true variation between households and the distribution of population by size classes of PCE exaggerates the true extent of inequality. What is more serious, seasonality may be distorting the Engel curves and Engel elasticities based on NSS budget data.

7 If non-response is systematically more in some classes than others, the estimated average and distribution would be affected. Unfortunately there is little information on the magnitude of non-response or the characteristics of the non-responding households.

8 Chatterjee and Bhattacharya (1975: 105-6) note that there are "a good number of absurd entries" in the schedules, in terms of absurdly low (or high) consumption level and/or prices arising from errors in conversion from local units to standard units, difficulty of finding true measures of local units, confusion between number and length (in the case of some items of clothing) and failure to distinguish between purchase and consumption. They advocate systematic editing and even rejection of "absurd entries" from the estimates.

9 Srinivasan et al (1974) also attempted to compare the behaviour of NSS series of consumption for a few selected commodities (namely foodgrains, clothing, edible oils and sugar) with a series constructed from official estimates of per capita availability of these adjusted by their respective wholesale price index. This was necessary because detailed commodity break down of the National accounts estimate of private consumption were not available at that time.

10 The treatment of payment made in kind to priests, domestic servants, barbers, etc. for consumer services rendered by them to the sample household is however not simple. Thus Instruction 5.8.1 stipulates that "the imputed value of the items offered should be entered under column 4 of the block 8 against the particular service consumed in cases where the payment is made in terms of items for blocks 5, 6 and 7 (where the concept is that of consumption). When such payments are made in terms of block 8 (miscellaneous goods and services) or 9 (durable goods for domestic use) (where the concept is that of purchase) the payment in kind should not be shown in block 8 against the service consumed. In this case, the value of purchase of items offered (provided such purchase was made in the reference period) should be entered in block 8 or 9 against the items themselves." (Instructions to field staff, 25th round, mimeo 1970.)

It may be noted that household consumption is supposed to exclude any transfer payments in kind like loans advanced, charities, gifts and other payment in kind.... But any consumption out of transfer receipts in kind like borrowings, gifts, charities, perquisites received by the household, free collections and other receipts in kind, if any, will have to be considered (Instruction 5.5.6).

11 The 25th round instructions (No 5.6.15) to investigators says:

Meals received by an employee as perquisite from an employer's household should be accounted for in the employers household in terms of their constituent items like cereals, pulses, vegetables, etc. The same meal should be accounted for in the employee household an item 96, i.e., cooked meal.

This seems somewhat ambiguous about the treatment of the item in the schedule of paying household. Obviously ingredients of cooked meals given to workers should be netted out in estimating the household consumption of employers in order to avoid double counting.

12 The instructions in fact do not say whether total consumption of foodgrain is to be estimated independently or as the sum of the purchases, use of own stock, kind receipts for goods and services, and transfers. In either case there are difficulties of ensuring internal consistency in the foodgrain receipts and disposition accounts.

13 The following observations by Chatterjee and Bhattacharya (1975: 101), who have intimate knowledge of NSS organisation and procedure, are relevant to this context:

We feel that employees may not be excluding such meals, etc, when reporting their respective household consumption so that there is risk of double counting as well as a tendency to exaggerate the consumption standards of the rural rich. This may be partly responsible for the high figure of cereals consumption obtained from the NSS. Ceremonials may also provide a partial explanation; while the host household reports the entire quantum of cereals needed for the feast in its budget, most, if not all, the invitees may forget that they had a meal outside when reporting for their respective households.

They feel that a similar problem may exist in respect of animal feed where household consumption is supposed to include only what is fed to pet animals but not the amount given to livestock used for productive purposes.

14 In 1960-61, the top decile of the population was estimated to consume 28 kg of cereals per head per month or nearly one kg per head. The corresponding figure for 1972-73 is estimated at 21 kg.

15 If CSO estimates are 'reliable' (or at least as reliable as the NSS), this means that private consumption derived from the former should be generally larger than household consumption obtained from the latter. While this seems to be the case, the levels of intake of non-cereals items in the top income levels seems implausibly high as can be seen from the following estimate of calorie content of different sources of food in 1972-73 (Table A). Note that in the highest expenditure group, the average daily calorie intake from non-cereal sources is over 3,000 per consumption unit; in per capita terms it will be considerably higher. The desirable intake from a nutritional view point is said to be 2,300 calories per capita from all sources.

16 According to Chatterjee and Bhattacharya (1975: 99) the incorporation of the consumption questionnaire as part of a comprehensive questionnaire covering productive activity employment and other aspects, was a major change. They also refer to some differences between the consumption block of IHS and earlier schedules.

17 The following estimates of per capita consumption in 1964-65 based on the detailed and the abridged schedules (IH 15 and IH 17 respectively) suggests that aggregation could make some difference:

	RS./30 Days Rural	
	IHS16	*IHS17*
Foodgrain	12.87	12.26
Other food	6.42	5.56
Non-food	7.15	7.01
Total	26.44	24.83

Source : GOI, NSS, 189: 8.

The sub sample estimates for IHS 16 (26.2-26.66) are closer than for IHS17 (24.2-25.5).

18 On this see among others Vaidyanathan (1978), Sarma et al (1979).

TABLE — A

Per Expenditure Rs/30 Days	*Total*	*Calorie Intake/Cons Unit/Day, 1972-73*				
		I	*II*	*III*	*IV*	*V*
0–15	1493	1300	51	30	49	63
15–21	1957	1672	81	50	72	82
75–100	4574	2820	316	450	395	596
110	6181	3167	441	808	620	1145
All	2924	2078	187	217	191	251

Notes : I — Cereal, Cereal substitutes, Potato, sugar jaggery.
II — Pulses, nuts and seed
III — Milk, meat, egg, fish
IV — Edible oil
V — Fruits, Vegetable, Processed food.

Source : Sarvekshana, Vol II No. 3, January 1979: 116-7

References

Ahluwalia M S *(1976): 'Rural Poverty in India 1956-57 to 1973-74', "India: Occasional Papers", World Bank Staff Working Paper No. 279.

Bardhan P K (1974): 'Pattern of Income Distribution in India', in Srinivasan T N and Bardhan P K (1974: 103-138)

Chatterjee G S and Bhattacharya (1975): 'Some Observations on NSS Household Budget Data' in Dandekar V M and Venkataramiah P, ed (1975: 97-113)

Bhattacharyya A K (1981): 'Evolution of the Sample Design of the National Sample Survey', Design of the National Sample Survey', Sankhya, Series C, Vol. 38.

Dandekar N M and Rath N (1971): "Poverty in India", Indian School of Political Economy, Lonavala.

Dandekar V M and Venkatramiah P. ed (1975): "Data Base of Indian Economy II, Role of Sample Survey", Statistical Publishing Society, Calcutta.

Gupta S K and Ramaratnam D S (1975): 'Consumer Expenditure Surveys and Family Budget Enquiries', in Dandekar and Venkataramiah eds (1975).

Ganguly A, et al (1960): 'Studies on Consumer Behaviour", Asia Publishing House, Bombay.

Government of India, National Sample Survey: Reports Numbers 101, 104, 135, 142, 191, 192, 209, 216, 226, 230, 231, 235, 240, 284 (Draft).

Government of India, CSO (1976): "National Accounts Statistics 1960-61 to 1974-75", New Delhi.

Iyengar N S (1967): 'Some Estimates of Engel Elasticities Based on National Sample Survey Data', JRSS A, 130.

Kansal S A (1965): "Preliminary Estimates of Total Consumption Expenditure in India; 1950-51 to 1963-64", ISI, memeo.

Mukherjee M (1969) "National Income of India: Trends and Structure", Statistical Publishing Society, Calcutta.

Mukherjee M and Chatterjee G S (1972): 'On the Validity of NSS Estimates of Consumption Expenditure', Arthavijnan, July.

Murthy M N (1977): 'Use of Empirical Studies in Evaluating Sample Design for Estimating Frequency Distribution', Bull International Statistical Institute, XLVII, 3.

Rajaraman, I (1975): 'Poverty, Inequality and Economic Growth: Rural Punjab 1960-61 to 1970-71', Journal of Development Studies, July.

Rudra, A (1972): 'Relative Rates of Growth: Agriculture and industry', in Pramit Chaudhury ed "Readings in India Agricultural Development", George Allen and Unwin, London.

Srinivasan T N, Radhakrishna P N, and Vaidyanathan, A (1972): 'Data on Distribution of Consumption Expenditure in India: An Evaluation' in Srinivasan and Bardhan eds (1972).

Sarma J S, Roy Shyamal and George P S (1979): "Two Analyses of Indian Foodgrain : Production and Consumption Data", IFPRI, Washington DC.

Vaidyanathan A (1974): 'Some Aspects of Inequalities in Living Standards in Rural India', in Srinivasan and Bardhan ed (1974).

Visaria, Pravin (1980): 'Poverty and Living Standards in Asia', Population and Development Review, Vol 6, No. 2.

Economic and Political Weekly, Vol. 21, No.3, January 18, 1986.

16

Asset Holdings and Consumption of Rural Households in India

A Study of Spatial and Temporal Variations

THE impact of development programmes, especially the new agricultural technology on different classes of rural population has been the subject of a continuing debate (Kurien, 1981; Frankel; 1971). A strong and vocal school of thought maintains that the new technology (high-yielding varieties (HYVs) and cross-bred cows) is inherently biased in favour of the larger farmers and that on the whole the distribution of benefits of such development as has taken place is skewed in favour of the better-off-segments of the rural population. The argument is that, even if one grants that the new technology is technically scale-neutral (in the sense that there is nothing inherent in these techniques which would make the small farmer get a lower level of productivity than the larger farmers at comparable levels of input), the distribution of benefits will favour the larger, better endowed farmers. This bias is believed to arise partly because the small farmers do not have access to complementary resources (such as water and credit) to the same extent and on the same terms as the large farmers. Moreover, the significant increase in productivity and incomes

I am grateful to P. Anbazhagan and Asha Krishna Kumar for computational assistance and to D. Jayaraj, K. Nagaraj and S. Subramanian for discussions which helped to clarify some substantive points.

made possible by the new technology may induce changes in the distribution of land and irrigation in favour of the better-off (through resumption of leased land for self-cultivation, reverse leasing, purchase of land by the large from the small farmers and differential investment in ground water).

There is an extensive literature on trends in inequalities in rural income and consumption, and in the incidence of poverty (Bardhan and Srinivasan, 1974; 1988; Mellor and Desai, 1986). The available data from the National Sample Survey (NSS), as well as other national surveys conducted by the National Council of Applied Economic Research (NCAER), do not show any systematic trend in inequality of consumption and certainly there is no relationship between agricultural growth and inequality in consumption. The trends in the distribution of land has attracted some attention but here again, there is no evidence of a trend deterioration in the inequality of landholdings. If anything the NSS data points to a mild fall in the concentration of land-ownership since 1961.[1] Studies of the relation between the level and distribution of assets on the one hand and the level and distribution of consumption on the other are even rarer. The few that are available (Sundaram and Tendulkar, 1988) concentrate on variations across states regions at a point of time.

No systematic study of the trends in asset holdings and their distribution or of their relation to the changes in the level and distribution of consumption is available though the National Sample Survey Organisation (NSSO) has been systematically collecting the relevant information over nearly four decades.[2] Surveys of private consumption expenditure have been done regularly by the NSSO — almost every year from 1960-61 to 1970-71 and on a quinquennial basis since 1973-74. The All India Debt and Investment Surveys (AIDIS) conducted by the NSSO provide a wealth of information, down to the state level (and, at least for one year, to the regional level), on the level, composition and distribution of assets in rural India at three points of time, namely, 1961-62, 1971-72 and 1981-82.[3] Much care has gone into designing these surveys in order to gather comprehensive and detailed data on the asset holdings of a representative sample of rural households. And the design, concepts and procedures of successive surveys are by and large comparable. While the Reserve Bank of India (RBI) has published fairly extensive tabulations based on their data, very little is available by way of analyses or interpretation.

This paper is a small first step in filling this gap. It brings together the salient features of rural asset holdings and its regional and temporal variations; and examines whether any systematic patterns can be seen in these variations and in the relation between assets and consumption. As it turns out, the data raise more questions than they answer. Nevertheless, we hope that our discussion will stimulate interest in a deeper examination of this (and other similar) bodies of data both from the viewpoint of assessing how well they capture the reality and for exploring the insights they may have to offer on several important questions regarding trends in the rural economy.

Level and Composition of Assets of Rural Households

As of June 1981, a rural household in India had, on the average, physical assets valued at Rs.36,000.[4] The major part (63 per cent) of it consists of the value of owned land; buildings account for about 21 per cent, durable consumer goods 7 per cent, livestock 5 per cent and machinery and implements 3.8 per cent. Land, livestock and machinery equipment, which together constitute the productive asset base of the rural community, account for 72 per cent of the total value of physical assets held in rural India (Table 1).

TABLE — 1

Distribution of Total Physical Assets of Rural Households by Class of Assets, All-India

(Per cent)

Type of Assets	*1961-62*[1]	*1971-72*[2]	*1980-81*[2]
(1)	*(2)*	*(3)*	*(4)*
Productive Assets	72.6	76.6	71.8
Land	62.3	67.3	62.9
Livestock	7.5	6.5	5.1
Machinery and Equipment	2.8	2.7	3.8
Building	21.1	18.6	21.0
Durable Household Goods	6.2	4.6	7.2
	100.00	100.00	100.00

Source : 1. Estimated from RBI (1965, p.810).
2. RBI (1987, p.133).

Both the average value of assets per household and its composition show, not surprisingly, wide regional variations. Average total assets per rural household in 1981 ranged from Rs. 17,600 in Orissa to over Rs. 90,000 in the Punjab and Haryana. The share of productive assets in the total varies from a low of 58 per cent in Tamil Nadu to 82 per cent in the Punjab (Appendix 3). There is no systematic relation between the relative share of productive assets and the level of asset holdings. However, holdings of productive assets per household show a somewhat larger variation across states (as measured by the coefficient of variation) than total assets per household.

Land everywhere is by far the largest single component of productive assets; livestock and machinery/equipment in most cases comprise less than 15 per cent of the total productive assets. However, in a few states, notably Gujarat, Madhya Pradesh and Rajasthan, non-land productive assets are somewhat more important and account for as much as one-third of the total in Rajasthan. Nevertheless, all these states are important cattle breeding tracts.

A little under a fourth of the rural households have assets less than Rs.5,000 but they account for a mere 1.5 per cent of the total assets held by the rural population. Households with assets exceeding Rs.50,000 constitute nearly a fifth of all rural households and account for nearly two-thirds of the total rural assets. The share of productive assets in total assets increases as we move up the scale of total asset holdings (Table 2).

TABLE — 2

Distribution of Households and Total Assets in Rural Area by Size of Total Assets Holdings, 1981-82

Asset Group (Rs/per household)	*Percentage of*		*Proportion of Assets of Different Kinds*			
	Estimated Household	*Estimated Assets*	*Productive assets*	*Land*	*Livestock and poultry*	*Machinery and equipment*
(1)	*(2)*	*(3)*	*(4)*	*(5)*	*(6)*	*(7)*
<1,000	5.7	0.1	25.5	15.9	4.8	4.8
1,000-5,000	18.2	1.4	41.4	29.2	9.1	3.1
5,000-10,000	14.6	3.0	52.1	40.2	9.4	2.5
10,000-20,000	18.7	7.5	60.1	48.7	8.9	2.5
20,000-50,000	23.8	21.0	66.1	56.5	6.9	2.7
50,000-1,00,000	11.1	21.4	70.3	62.1	5.1	3.1
1,00,000-5,00,000	7.6	38.3	73.9	68.5	3.1	4.3
>5,00,000	0.3	7.3	84.0	74.9	2.3	6.8
All	100.00	100.00	70.9	62.1	5.0	3.8

Source : RBI (1987, p.25, S-3)

Overall the Gini coefficient of concentration (GCC) for total assets in rural India is estimated at 0.635. Productive assets (GCC 0.674) seem more unevenly distributed than total assets; and among productive assets, land (by value) is rather more unequally distributed (GCC=0.687) than livestock (GCC=0.481).

The degree of inequality in the distribution of all assets across different classes of rural population is again seen to vary across states. Judging by the Gini coefficient, asset distribution is least unequal in Rajasthan (GCC=0.526) and most unequal in Andhra Pradesh and Tamil Nadu (GCC=0.661 and 0.666 respectively).[5] In general, peninsular and east India (excluding Assam) are seen to have relatively more unequal distribution of assets than the central and northern parts. There is, however, no systematic relation between the level of assets per household and the degree of inequality in their distribution.

Relation between Assets and Consumption

The NSS also collects data on consumption of rural households and provides states-wise estimates of mean consumption expenditures and the distribution of the population around the mean. Unfortunately, consumption and asset data are generally not collected for the same year. For instance, while the last survey of assets was done in 1981-82, consumption surveys were done in 1977-78 and in 1983. In the context of changing prices, and given the greater volatility of rural consumption (due to year-to-year variations in weather and hence employment and incomes neither of which follows any uniform pattern across states) — attempts to inquire into the relation between asset holdings and consumption on the basis of NSS data are somewhat risky. But considering its importance and the fact that this is a relatively neglected aspect, it seems worthwhile to explore the relation recognising of course that any inferences must be treated, at this stage, as being only indicative and rather tentative.

In rural India as a whole, the average per capita monthly consumer expenditure during 1983 is estimated at Rs. 112.4, with an average family size of 5.2, the average annual expenditure per household works out to Rs. 7,030. With the average holding of all assets per rural household in 1981 being Rs. 36,090, the asset to annual consumption ratio works out to 4:1 (Table 3), and the corresponding ratio for productive assets being 3.6:1. Since the price level in 1983 was higher than in 1981, the actual ratio is probably somewhat lower.

TABLE — 3

Average Asset Holdings and Consumption Expenditures of an Indian Rural Household

*Year**	*Mean Annual Consumer Expenditure (Rs.) Per Household*	*Asset Holdings Per Household (Rs.)*		*Consumer Expenditure (Rs.)*	
		Productive	*Total*	*Per rupee of productive assets*	*Total assets*
(1)	*(2)*	*(3)*	*(4)*	*(5)*	*(6)*
1961-62	1,335	3,824	5,267	0.349	0.253
1971-72	2,296	8,555	11,343	0.268	0.202
1981-82	7,030	25,588	36,090	0.274	0.195

* The years when the Debt and Investment Surveys were conducted. Except for 1961-62, the consumer expenditure data relate to different years from those of AIDIS. See text.

Across states, there is a strong positive correlation between average assets per household[6], and average consumption expenditure per household in the rural areas (Table 4). That states with higher endowment of assets relative to population also have higher consumption levels is not particularly surprising, though one must be careful to note that these correlations do not take into account the effect of regional variations in the prices of goods and services and in particular the prices of consumer goods relative to assets. Subject to this caveat, it is noteworthy that the level of consumer expenditure varies much less across states (CV=23 per cent) than asset per household (CV=67 per cent). Differences in assets per household are thus reflected in a less than proportionate difference in per household consumption. Thus, the average rural household in the Punjab, with five and a half times the assets of its counterpart in Orissa, has a consumption level which is barely double that of Orissa. In fact, the consumption to asset ratio itself bears strong inverse correlation to the average assets per household.

That the marginal consumption-asset ratio is lower than average could be due to one or more of the following factors: (i) the relative price of productive assets to consumption goods may bear a significant positive correlation with the assets per household across regions: (ii) marginal productivity of capital may be diminishing as capital-labour ratio rises; and (iii) savings propensities may be higher in regions with higher per capita income. How important each one is and whether they constitute an adequate explanation of the apparently small impact of differential asset endowment on consumption call for more information than is currently accessible. Overall, a rupee difference in asset per household in 1981-82 is associated with R=0.09 in consumption per household per year[7], which is about a third of the national average of 0.27.

The Gini coefficient for consumption in 1983 is estimated at 0.30, which is much below the coefficient for assets in 1981 (0.635). The coefficients are not strictly comparable inasmuch as the index for consumption relates to the distribution of population of households arranged according to per capita consumption while that for assets pertains to households arranged by size of household asset holdings. Since there is a strong negative relation between household size and per capita consumption, the inequality index for households arranged by household consumption would probably be higher than for population of households arranged by per capita consumption[8]. Quite apart from this, there are at least two strong grounds to expect that consumption distribution will be less unequal than the distribution of assets: (1) the income generated by the assets does not accrue wholly to asset holders and in proportion to their assets. A part of the income accrues to wage labour, a large proportion of whom have little or no productive assets. And, (2) given that higher incomes are associated with a higher propensity to save, the difference between the consumption of the poor and the rich is likely to be narrower than the differential in their incomes.

We do not have state level estimates of consumption inequality for 1983, but we do have the estimates from earlier years, and they suggest that consumption inequalities are consistently lower, and much lower, than asset inequalities. However, there is hardly any relation between asset inequalities and consumption inequalities[9], perhaps because some or all of the following factors, which affect their values, may be variable across state: (a) the relation between household size on the one hand and per capita consumption and total assets on the other; (b) the relative importance of asset-poor wage laboures in the population; (c) the income-consumption relationship; and (d) the relative prices of assets and consumption goods. Not enough is known on these aspects but much can be learnt by suitable retabulation of the data from the primary schedules of the NSSO.

Changes in Asset Holding and Inequality, 1961 to 1981

Taking the country as a whole, it is estimated that the average value of physical assets per rural household has risen from Rs. 5,267 in 1961-62 to Rs. 11,300 in 1971-72 and further to Rs. 36,100 in 1981-82. Buildings and durable household goods comprised about 27 per cent of the total assets in 1961-62; and their share in the total fell to 23.2 per cent in 1971-72 but by 1981-82 had recovered to a level (28 per cent) slightly higher than two decades earlier. The share of all productive assets taken together recorded a rise between 1961-62 and 1971-72, but fell in the subsequent decade to a level slightly lower than in 1961-62. The time pattern of change in the share of land (the most important productive asset) is similar. The share of other productive assets, comprising 9 to 10 per cent of the total, however, shows a progressive, if small, decline from 1961-62 to 1981-82. This decline is exclusively on account of livestock whose share fell from 7.5 to 5 per cent. There has been a significant rise in the share of machinery and equipment (Table 1).

The estimated increase in the value of assets per household no doubt reflects the combined effect of increase in real stock of assets and rise in their prices. The index of wholesale prices in 1970-71 was 80 per cent higher than in 1960-61 and in the subsequent decade it rose by another 156 per cent. The growth in the value of asset holdings is considerably more than in the general price level, thus suggesting a rise in asset holdings in real terms. But how much has been the real increase cannot be judged without more information than is currently available about the changes in the stock and quality of the various categories of assets as well as their prices.

At the all-India level, the extent of land and the number of livestock owned per household generally show a decline over the last two decades. However, the proportion of irrigated area (which raises the productivity and hence market value of land) has risen. So have the holdings of machinery and equipment. We do not have data on physical stock of building or durable household goods, but it is a reasonable presumption that the stock of these per household and possibly their 'quality' have increased. It should be possible to reconstruct price indices for different categories of assets and for all assets from the data collected by the AIDIS. But this has not been done; nor is it possible to do so on the basis of the tabulations which have become available to the public. This is clearly an important area for further research.

The rate and pattern of growth in asset holding again show large variations across states: During the sixties, Tamil Nadu and Andhra Pradesh recorded the smallest percentage increase in total assets while the Punjab recorded the highest. During the seventies, the regional pattern of growth is somewhat different, with Kerala recording the highest growth and Bihar least. Over the period as a whole, the average assets per household rose by 280 per cent in Tamil Nadu compared to a near 10-fold rise in the Punjab-Haryana and over a 15-fold rise in Kerala. The Southern states (with the significant exception of Kerala) have generally experienced a relatively slow growth in asset holdings, while Uttar Pradesh and the Punjab-Haryana recorded the highest growth.

While there is no systematic relation between the initial level of assets/households and their rate of growth, the ranking of states in terms of assets/households in not stable, particularly as between 1961 and 1971.[10] However, the data point to a widening in the interregional disparities in assets per household. The coefficient of variation in total assets per rural household has risen from 31 per cent in 1961-62 to 55 per cent in 1971-72 and further to 60 per cent in 1981-82. The regional variations in productive asset holdings has increased considerably faster. (Table 4).

Changes in the composition of assets also do not show any uniform pattern. In half the states, the share of productive assets in the total shows a rise between 1961 and 1971 and a

TABLE — 4

Inter-state Variability in Level of Asset Holdings Per Household and its Relation to Consumption, All-India

Year	Coefficient of Variation in Assets Per Rural Household		Coefficient of Variation in Consumer Expenditure Per Household	Correlation Coefficients between Total Assets Household and			
	Productive	Total		Gini coefficient of assets	Level of consumption expenditure	Gini coefficient of consumption	Consumption per unit asset
(1)	(2)	(3)	(4)	(5)	(6)	(7)	(8)
1961-62	0.315	0.313	0.22	0.238^{ns}	0.755*	0.485^{ns}	-0.580^{ns}
1971-72	0.610	0.549	0.266	0.111^{ns}	0.918*	0.295^{ns}	-0.743*
1981-82	0.669	0.599	0.232	-0.065^{ns}	0.924*	ns	-0.828*

* Statistically significant at 1 per cent level.

ns Statistically not significant.

fall in the subsequent decade. Some states (especially Andhra Pradesh, Bihar, Karnataka and Tamil Nadu) record a progressive decline in the ratio of productive total assets while in Uttar Pradesh, and the Punjab-Haryana the ratio shows a progressive rise. A similar diversity is noticeable in respect of changes in the relative importance of non-land productive assets in the total. In view of this, any generalisation[11] regarding the character of accumulation in the sixties and in the seventies will not be tenable; moreso because the published data relate to nominal value of different categories of assets at various points in time. Insofar as the prices of different categories of assets and of the same category of asset across space vary in a desperate fashion, the above comparisons may not give us a reliable picture of shifts in real terms.

At the national level, the Gini coefficient of concentration of total assets across classes seems to have changed little between 1961-62 and 1971-72 but perceptibly declined in the subsequent decade (1981-82), the GCC being estimated at 0.6524, 0.6551 and 0.6354 respectively. In seven out of the 14 states, for which estimates of total asset concentration is available for the entire period, there is a progressive reduction in the Gini coefficient. Only Orissa shows a progressively more unequal asset distribution. In the remaining states though there is no progressive fall, the concentration ratio, in 1981-82 is lower than in 1961-62 (Appendix Tables 1 to 3). In the Punjab and Haryana, the concentration of assets shows a decline between 1971-72 and 1981-82. (Separate estimates for these two states are not available for 1961-62). It would also seem that states with a relatively high level of inequalities have experienced a sharper fall in the GCC of total assets than in the low inequality states.

All this suggests that wealth is getting more equally distributed between the classes. But before such an inference is made, several caveats need to be stressed. In the first place, it is arguable that insofar as our concern is with the income earning opportunities from ownership of assets, we ought to focus more on the distribution of productive assets than on total assets. We estimated, for the country as a whole, the Gini coefficient for productive assets alone on the basis of the frequency distribution of households and of their holdings of productive assets by size class of total assets (Table 5). This suggests that while concentration ratio of land and livestock (at current values) has fallen between 1971-72 and 1981-82, that of other productive assets has risen.

TABLE — 5

Estimates of Gini Coefficient of Concentration in Total Assets, and Major Categories of Assets, Rural India, 1971-72 and 1981-82

Physical Assets	*1971-72*	*1981-82*
(1)	*(2)*	*(3)*
Total Assets	0.6551	0.6354
Total Productive Assets	0.6962	0.6742
Value of Land	0.7143	0.6874
Livestock	0.5089	0.4810
Machinery and Equipment	0.7070	0.7135

Computed from data on frequency distribution of households and assets by size class of total assets.

In the second place, all the estimates of asset concentration relate to households arranged by level of household assets. Given the variability of household size and its systematic relation to asset size, there is a strong case for using inequality indices derived from the distribution of population of households arranged by the level of per capita asset holding. As already mentioned, the estimate of the Gini coefficient is highly sensitive to the criteria by which households are ranked and whether or not it is calculated with reference to households or population. If the strength of the relation between asset holdings and household size is not stable over space and time, the concentration ratio computed on households arranged according to level of household assets could be quite a misleading basis to assess both spatial and temporal variation in inequality. And yet, for reasons which are far from clear, while the NSS tabulations of consumption distribution consistently relate to the population of households arranged according to per capita consumption, the RBI has followed a different practice in tabulating the asset data and gives only distribution of households by size of household assets. The RBI's practice, besides being questionable for reasons cited, also make it difficult to assess the relation between consumption distribution and asset distribution, and changes therein.

The above estimates of inequality relate to the distribution of assets valued at current prices. There are questions as to the basis on which the values of different categories of assets in different regions are computed. Is the market for assets sufficiently widespread, competitive and integrated to provide a reliable basis for assessing their 'value'? In any case, we need to take into account the fact that prices for the same kind of assets and their behaviour over time vary across regions. There are of course many difficult conceptual and practical problems of getting appropriate deflators. And yet without some effort at netting out the impact of differential price changes of different assets across regions, we cannot safely infer anything about the trends in inequality in real asset distribution on the basis of available estimates. Since the AIDIS has collected data on both the quantities of major assets and their values, such an exercise is in principle feasible with appropriate retabulations of the original data.

There are indications that : (a) the AIDIS tends to underestimate the total magnitude of land owned; (b) the degree of underestimation may be increasing; and (c) its incidence varies widely across states. The NSS estimate of area owned (120 million hectares each in both 1971 and 1981) is about 25 per cent below the total operated area as estimated by the Agricultural census (162 million hectares). The estimated total owned area in 1961-62 was substantially higher at 129 million hectares[12]. In 1971-72, the estimate of the area operated obtained from AIDIS was about 20 per cent below the figure from the All-India Agricultural Census; in 1981-82 the difference was around 24 per cent. The NSS estimate of operated area is lower than that of the Agricultural Census in all states. But the extent of difference varies from a mere 3 per cent in Uttar Pradesh to 45 per cent in Tamil Nadu during 1971-72 and from 4 per cent (Uttar Pradesh) to 36 per cent (Tamil Nadu) in 1981-82. Altogether the degree of underestimation by the NSS relative to the Agricultural census during 1981-82 was higher than in 1971-72 in respect of seven out of 14 major states. Since land accounts for the major portion of the value of all assets in rural India, and insofar as the incidence of underestimation is unevenly distributed across size class of holdings, caution is warranted in interpreting the trends in inequality from the NSS data.

Changes in Asset-Consumption Relation

The NSS data suggest that consumer expenditure per household has grown slower than assets per household; between 1961 and 1971, productive and total asset holdings of an average rural household more than doubled but consumer expenditure per household rose by only 75 per cent. While assets rose by 218 per cent during the subsequent decade, consumption rose by a somewhat lower proportion. As a result, there has been a substantial fall in the value of consumer expenditure per rupee of asset holding over the last two decades, the fall being more pronounced in the first half of the period. (Table 3).[13]

At the state level, the picture in respect of the consumption-asset ratio is again quite diverse. While between 1961 and 1971 most states show a decline in consumption-asset ratio, only three states recorded a decline in the subsequent decade. In some states the ratio showed a significant rise between 1971 and 1981. Taking the period as a whole, consumption per rupee of asset in 1981 is seen to be lower than in 1961 in only eight of the 14 states while in five they are higher. What is remarkable, however, is the strong negative relationship between the level of assets and the consumption-assets ratio in each of the three points of time (Table 3) and the progressive and sharp decline in the 'marginal' consumption to assets ratio computed across states. Thus a rupee difference in assets per household between states is associated with Re. 0.166 in the consumption per household, in 1961, Re. 0.102 in 1971 and Re. 0.09 in 1981. It also turns out that there is a strong inverse correlation between the rate of change in assets per household and in the consumption asset ratio both during 1961 to 1971 and 1971 to 1981. That is to say, states which experienced a relatively faster expansion of assets recorded lower rates of increase (or higher rates of decline) in the consumption-asset ratio.

The above relationship could arise from a number of factors: (1) Inasmuch as consumption expenditures are met out of the output and incomes generated by the assets of rural households, the above relations might reflect a progressive and steep deterioration in the productivity of assets (2) While assets of rural households may well be the most important source of real incomes, they are not the only source of rural incomes nor can it be assumed that all incomes generated by the assets of rural households accrue to rural areas. (3) Changes in the relative prices of assets and consumption goods in favour of the latter could make a significant difference to the pattern of variation in the consumption-asset ratio reckoned in real terms. (4) It is possible that incomes may have grown faster in states experiencing a faster accumulation of assets, but if this is accompanied by an increase in savings rates, the differences in the rate of growth in consumption may get muted. (5) There is the possibility that the NSS may not be equally efficient in capturing changes in asset holdings and changes in the consumption level.

The interpretation of the behaviour of consumption-asset ratio and its relation to the level and growth of assets, as well as its implications, depends on the relative importance of the above-mentioned factors. Clearly, if productivity of additional assets is declining rapidly, it is a matter of serious concern. If on the other hand savings proportions are so high as to dampen the increases in consumption relative to increase in productive assets, it could point to a worsening of income distribution in the rural areas. If the other three elements are important, the behaviour of asset-income ratio has to be located outside the rural economy. Unfortunately, we do not have sufficient data to enable us to hazard even an informed guess on this matter. There is however some reason to believe that defects in data may be a significant factor.

The extent of variation in the rate of change in assets per household is much larger than in consumption. The sharp rise in the coefficient of variation in assets per household is consistent with the progressive widening in the differences in crop output per capita across states. The coefficient of variation of consumption per household on the other hand has hardly changed. Moreover, in a majority of states the growth of nominal consumption expenditure taken together with state specific price indices (we have used Consumer Price Index for Agricultural Labourers as it is the one readily available) point to a stagnation or a reduction in real consumption levels per household (Table 6). Even in the remaining states, the highest increase in real consumption is only 28 per cent over 22 years or barely 1 per cent a year. That states like the Punjab, Haryana and Uttar Pradesh, which are known to have experienced relatively rapid growth of real income per capita, show according to the NSS a stagnancy or fall in real per capita consumption and that the widening dispersion of output per head is not reflected in the NSS estimates of per capita consumption raise doubts about the reliability of the NSS estimates of changes in consumption levels. There are also other independent grounds to reinforce this scepticism (Vaidyanathan, 1986).

TABLE — 6

Changes in Consumer Expenditure as Estimated by NSS Relative to Changes in Rural Price Index and Growth of Agricultural production by States

States	*Index of Nominal Consumption Per Household*		*Price Index**		*Average Annual Growth in Crop Output Per Head+*
	1961-62=100		*1961-62=100*		*1952-1978*
	1970-71	*1983*	*1970-71*	*1983*	
(1)	*(2)*	*(3)*	*(4)*	*(5)*	*(6)*
Andhra Pradesh	171	562	169	432	0.6
Assam	181	471	205	542	-1.2
Bihar	199	496	200	548	0.2
Gujarat	177	549	170	442	1.0
Karnataka	148	467	188	525	1.0
Kerala	183	657	202	552	0.7
Madhya Pradesh	168	512	192	511	-0.6
Maharashtra	193	544	196	519	-0.4
Orissa	172	587	208	589	0.9
Punjab-Haryana	171	512	187	494	3.5
Rajasthan	157	569	184	502	0.4
Tamil Nadu	139	515	174	528	1.4
Uttar Pradesh	161	472	447	525	0.9
West Bengal	168	518	196	500	0.1

* Consumer price index for agricultural labourers.

\+ Jose (1982).

This is not to suggest that data inadequacies are the whole or even the primary explanation. Given the strength and consistency of the patterns described above, a much closer investigation of the whole matter is necessary. It would help to narrow down the search if the NSSO could construct state-specific price indices for assets and consumption. This will enable us to focus on the relation between real assets and real consumption. It would also be useful to verify whether the consumption-asset relations across time and space as shown by the NSS data are corroborated by other independent surveys like those conducted by the NCAER.

Conclusion

This paper, as mentioned at the outset, is intended as "a small first step" to examining the trends in asset accumulation and their relation to consumption levels in rural India. Our collation of data, almost exclusively from the NSS, show fairly rapid rise in productive and total asset holdings over the period 1961 to 1981, accompanied by a much slower rise in per capita consumption. There is no pronounced or general tendency for inequality in assets distribution across classes to worsen, but there is clearly an aggravation of regional disparities in this regard. The consumption-asset ratio has declined in the country as a whole, the pattern being quite mixed when we look at state level data. However, there is a strong and persistent tendency for the asset-rich states to have a lower consumption-asset ratio, and for this tendency to aggravate over time. Finally states with relatively faster growth of assets tend to experience a markedly slower rise (or steeper decline) in the consumption-asset ratio.

Our attempts to explore the factors underlying these trends and relations are not particularly illuminating because of the numerous influences at work and the near impossibility, with presently accessible data, of sorting out their relative importance. A more detailed analysis, which should be possible by a proper retabulation of the basic data, is highly desirable for a better understanding of the dynamics of an important aspect of the rural economy.

Notes

1. The Gini coefficient of land-ownership for the country as a whole is estimated to have fallen from 0.73 in 1961-62 to 0.71 in 1901-72 and remained at that level in 1981-82 (Government of India, 1987, p.20). However over the same period the concentration of operational holdings has risen progressively from 0.58 in 1961-62 to 0.59 in 1971-72 and further to 0.63 in 1981-82 (Government of India, 1986, p. 19).
2. The first landholdings survey was conducted by the NSSO in the early fifties. This was extended to cover assets, debt and investment of rural households in 1961 and of rural and urban households since 1971-72.
3. Reports on the three All India Debt and Investment Surveys have been published by the Reserve Bank of India (1965, 1975, 1987). The NSSO by and large have concentrated on tabulations concerning characteristics of ownership and operational holdings (including land use, irrigation and livestock and asset holdings) by size class of holdings.
4. The basic data, state-wise, regarding the mean asset holdings (total and by major categories) of rural households, mean consumption expenditures, and the estimated Gini coefficients of concentration of total assets and consumption used in this paper are given in Appendix Tables I to III.
5. Our state-wise analysis is confined to the 15 major states (14 in 1961-62 when the Punjab and Haryana were combined). Jammu & Kashmir, Himachal Pradesh, the hill states of North-eastern India and Union Territories are excluded.
6. In this paper unless otherwise indicated 'assets' will refer to productive assets.
7. This is based on a linear regression of consumption per household per year on productive assets per household across selected states in 1981-82. The value of this coefficient was higher (at 0.102) in 1971-72 and even higher (0.166) in 1961-62.
8. That the ranking criterion makes a substantial difference to the value of the inequality index is now well recognised. But there has been hardly any attempt to empirically estimate the inequality coefficients on different criteria for ranking for sample households, and by taking distribution of population rather than of households arranged by per capita consumption, assets, etc.
9. The correlation coefficient between the two was barely 0.05 in 1961-62 and 1971-72.
10. The correlation coefficient between the level of assets per household in 1961-62 and the percentage increase over 1961 and 1981 is not statistically

significant even at 10 per cent level. The rank correlation coefficient of states arranged according to the level of assets in 1961 and 1971 is 0.71; while the correlation between ranking in 1971 and 1981 is 0.89.

11. Such as the sixties was a period of rapid accumulation of productive assets due to the green revolution, the subsequent decade saw a marked tendency to dissipate surplus in non-productive accumulation.

12. The figure of area operated as per Agricultural census is from Government of India (1986) and data area owned as estimated by NSS from Government of India (1987).

13. The fact is that the timing of the consumer surveys and that of the asset surveys are not always the same and the greater volatility of consumption, needs to be borne in mind in making these comparisons. Note especially that while asset data are for 1981, consumption relates to 1983.

References

Ahluwalia, M.S. (1978), "Rural Poverty and Agricultural Performance in India", *Journal of Development Studies*, 1978, Vol. 14, No.3.

Bardhan, P.K. and T.N. Srinivasan, (1974), *Poverty and Income Distribution in India*, Statistical Publishing House, Calcutta.

Bardhan, P.K. and T.N. Srinivasan (Eds.) (1988), *Rural Poverty in South Asia*, Oxford University Press, Delhi.

Mellor John W. and Gunvant M. Desai, (Eds.) (1986), *Agricultural Change and Rural Poverty: Variations on a Theme by Dharm Narain*, Oxford University Press, Delhi.

Divatia, V.V (1976), "Inequalities in Asset Distribution of Rural Households", *Reserve Bank Staff Occasional Papers*, Vol. 1, No. 1, June, 1976.

Frankel, F.R. (1971), *India's Green Revolution: Economic Gains and Political Costs*, Oxford University Press, Princeton, U.S.A.

Government of India (1974), *National Sample Survey: Seventeenth Round, September 1961-July 1962, No. 184, Tables with Notes on Consumer Expenditure*, NSSO, Department of Statistics, Ministry of Planning, New Delhi.

Government of India (1976), *National Sample Survey: Twentyfifth Round, July 1970-June 1971, No. 231, Tables with Notes on Consumer Expenditure*, NSSO, Department of Statistics, Ministry of Planning, New Delhi.

Government of India (1985), *National Sample Survey: Twentyeighth Round, January-December 1983, Report on the Third Quinquennial Survey of Consumer Expenditure*, NSSO, Department of Statistics Ministry of Planning, New Delhi (mimeo).

Government of India (1986), *National Sample Survey: Thirty-seventh Round, January-December 1982, No. 330, Report on Land Holdings-2: Some*

Aspects of Operational Holdings, NSSO, Department of Statistics, Ministry of Planning, New Delhi (mimeo.).

Government of India (1987), *National Sample Survey: Thirty-seventh Round, January-December 1982, No. 331, Report on Land Holdings-1: Some Aspects of Household on Ownership Holdings*, NSSO, Department of Statistics, Ministry of Planning, New Delhi (Mimeo.).

Jose, A.V. (1982), "Growth and Fluctuations in Indian Agriculture 1952-53 to 1978-79", Asian Employment Programme (ARTEP), International Labour Organisation, Bangkok (mimeo.).

Kurien, C.T. (1981), *Dynamics of Rural Transformation: A Case Study of Tamil Nadu 1950-1975*, Orient Longman, Delhi.

Reserve Bank of India (1965), "All India Rural Debt and Investment Survey", *Reserve Bank of India Bulletin*, Vol. 19, No. 6, June, 1965.

Reserve Bank of India (1975), All India Debt and Investment Survey 1971-72: *Assets and Liabilities of Rural Households as on 31st June 1971 (Statistical Tables*), Vol.1, Bombay.

Reserve Bank of India (1977), "Financial Assets of Rural Households As the end of June 1971)", *Reserve Bank Staff Occasional Papers*, Vol.2, No.1, June.

Reserve Bank of India (1987), All India Debt and Investment Survey 1981-82: *Asset and Liabilities of Households as on 30th June 1981*, Bombay.

Rao, C.H. Hanumantha (1975), *Technological Change and Distribution of Grains in Indian Agriculture*, Macmillan Company of India Ltd., Delhi.

Sundaram, K. And S.D. Tendulkar, (1988), "Towards an Explanation of Interregional Variations in Poverty and Unemployment", in P.K. Bardhan and T.N. Srinivasan (Eds.) (1988), *Rural Poverty in South Asia*, Oxford University Press, Delhi.

Vaidyanathan, A. (1986), "On the Validity of NSS Consumption Data", *Economic and Political Weekly*, Vol. 21, No.3, January 18.

APPENDIX TABLE — 1

Assets and Consumption of Rural Households in Major States, 1961-62

States	Assets (Rs.) Per Household		Gini Coefficient of		Consumption Expenditure (Rs.) Per Household	Consumption (Rs.) Per Rupee of	
	Productive	All	Consumption	Assets		Productive assets	Total assets
(1)	(2)	(3)	(4)	(5)	(6)	(7)	(8)
Andhra Pradesh	4,377	5,619	0.32	0.728	1,122	0.26	0.20
Assam	2,062	3,023	0.23	0.551	1,569	0.76	0.52
Bihar	4,354	5,491	0.28	0.694	1,202	0.28	0.22
Gujarat	4,508	6,496	0.27	0.618	1,470	0.33	0.23
Karnataka	5,272	6,864	0.37	0.667	1,655	0.31	0.24
Kerala	3,714	5,137	0.33	0.727	1,418	0.38	0.28
Madhya Pradesh	2,939	4,089	0.34	0.597	1,272	0.43	0.31
Maharashtra	4,093	5,072	0.28	0.658	1,242	0.30	0.24
Orissa	2,437	3,472	0.30	0.577	1,013	0.42	0.29
Punjab	7,059	10,113	0.35	0.633	2,314	0.33	0.23
Rajasthan	3,422	5,249	0.37	0.532	1,486	0.43	0.28
Tamil Nadu	3,901	5,033	0.31	0.719	1,141	0.29	0.22
Uttar Pradesh	3,357	5,182	0.32	0.604	1,425	0.42	0.27
West Bengal	2,807	3,898	0.28	0.656	1,298	0.46	0.33
Avg.		3,879.429	5,342.714		1,401.764		
Std.		1,223.411	1,674.399		308.078		
Cv.		31.536	31.340		21.978		

Source : Mean consumption: NSS (1974).
Gini coefficient of consumption : Ahluwalia (1978).
Assets : RBI (1965, p. 839).
Gini coefficient of assets : Divatia (1976).

APPENDIX TABLE — 2

Assets and Consumption of Rural Households in Major States, 1971-72

States	Assets (Rs.) Per Household		Gini Coefficient of		Consumption Expenditure (Rs.) Per Household	Consumption (Rs.) Per Rupee of	
	Productive	All	Consumption	Assets		Productive assets	Total assets
(1)	(2)	(3)	(4)	(5)	(6)	(7)	(8)
Andhra Pradesh	6,247	8,080	0.28	0.703	1,015	0.31	0.24
Assam	5,477	7,833	0.19	0.556	2,842	0.52	0.36
Bihar	9,972	12,828	0.27	0.671	2,386	0.24	0.19
Gujarat	9,237	12,874	0.28	0.634	2,608	0.28	0.20
Karnataka	8,026	10,762	0.29	0.655	2,453	0.31	0.23
Kerala	7,699	11,615	0.33	0.661	2,590	0.34	0.22
Madhya Pradesh	8,150	10,520	0.32	0.589	2,131	0.26	0.20
Maharashtra	9,122	11,682	0.26	0.649	2,392	0.26	0.20
Orissa	4,418	6,023	0.29	0.598	1,745	0.39	0.29
Punjab	25,837	31,833	0.30	0.683	4,139	0.16	0.13
Haryana	22,037	27,133	0.30	0.629	3,802	0.17	0.14
Rajasthan	9,158	12,750	0.33	0.559	2,341	0.26	0.18
Tamil Nadu	5,001	6,826	0.27	0.711	1,579	0.32	0.23
Uttar Pradesh	10,208	13,531	0.29	0.592	2,300	0.23	0.17
West Bengal	4,906	7,331	0.27	0.660	2,177	0.44	0.30
Avg.			9,699.697	12,775.13	2,493.20		
Std.			5,920.061	7,018.441	663.738		
Cv.			61.034	54.935	26.59		

Source : Consumption estimates relate to 1970-71, NSS (1976). Assets : RBI (1975).
Gini coefficient of consumption: Ahluwalia (1978). Gini coefficient of assets: Divatia (1976).

APPENDIX TABLE — 3

Assets and Consumption of Rural Households in Major States, 1981-82

States	Assets (Rs.) Per Household		Gini Coefficient of		Consumption Expenditure (Rs.) Per Household	Consumption (Rs.) Per Rupee of	
	Productive	All	Consumption	Assets		Productive assets	Total assets
(1)	(2)	(3)	(4)	(5)	(6)	(7)	(8)
Andhra Pradesh	18,577	26,047	—	0.661	6,301	0.34	0.24
Assam	12,814	20,503	—	0.545	7,390	0.58	0.36
Bihar	23,484	32,347	—	0.633	5,959	0.25	0.18
Gujarat	24,449	36,876	—	0.585	8,069	0.33	0.22
Karnataka	21,285	33,052	—	0.623	7,737	0.36	0.23
Kerala	53,612	76,476	—	0.605	9,322	0.17	0.12
Madhya Pradesh	21,461	29,725	—	0.590	6,512	0.30	0.22
Maharashtra	26,308	35,077	—	0.632	6,756	0.26	0.19
Orissa	12,641	17,630	—	0.605	5,946	0.47	0.34
Punjab	79,004	96,631	—	0.653	11,764	0.15	0.12
Haryana	67,218	90,590	—	0.559	11,094	0.17	0.12
Rajasthan	27,068	40,888	—	0.526	8,458	0.31	0.21
Tamil Nadu	11,419	19,520	—	0.666	5,870	0.51	0.30
Uttar Pradesh	32,646	44,660	—	0.575	6,721	0.21	0.15
West Bengal	13,710	20,710	—	0.608	6,728	0.49	0.32
Avg.	29,711.73	41,382.13			7,642		
Std.	19,887.13	24,770.89			1,770.88		
Cv.	66.934	59.360			23.164		

Source : Consumption estimates relate to 1983, NSS (1985).
Assets and Gini coefficient of assets: RBI (1987).

* Not available

17

Poverty and Economy

The Regional Dimension

THE existence of wide regional variations in levels of development is well documented (see e.g. GOI, Planning Commission, 1983; Mishra (ed.), 1985). Selected major development indicators for the year 1980-81 are summarized in Table 1 for ready reference. Large inter-state disparities are evident in the level of development, structure and productivity of practically all major sectors including social amenities and infrastructure. Per capita state domestic product (SDP) in the most well-to-do states is estimated to the nearly three times the level in the poorest.

The National Sample Survey also shows significant regional variation in the level of per capita private consumption expenditure as well as in the extent of inequality in its distribution. Their combined effect is reflected in the varying incidence of poverty. The overall poverty of the Indian rural population is of course highlighted by the fact that at least 43 per cent live below the Planning Commission's poverty line. What is more important in the context of this discussion is that the proportion varies from 13 per cent (in Punjab) to 68 per cent (in Orissa). Similar variations also exist in urban areas. However, the focus of this paper is mainly on rural poverty.

While there are serious and unresolved data problems, some

broad regional configurations can be seen: per capita SDP in the east Indian states is in general below the national average, while those of Haryana and the Punjab are clearly well above it. Much the same is true of agricultural output per caput of rural population and of per caput real consumption. The incidence of rural poverty (Table 1) is again well above average in Bihar, Orissa, West Bengal, Madhya Pradesh and Maharashtra, and considerably below it in Punjab, Haryana, Gujarat and Rajasthan. The majority of the rural poor (57 per cent in 1977-78) are in east and central India.

These disparities are in part a legacy of history. Even at the time of Independence, there were wide differences between regions in the availability of agricultural resources (land and irrigation) relative to population, in the nature and magnitude of manufacturing activity, in the productivity of resources, and in the development of socio-economic infrastructure. The British were not particularly concerned with the problem. At any rate it was not seen as meriting government action. But the situation changed after Independence. Given the country's linguistic and ethnic diversity, planners had necessarily to be concerned — or seen to be concerned — with preventing disparate development across states. With the rapid growth of public spending on developmental activities, the competition between states for resources became progressively more intense. 'Backwardness' was one of the widely used arguments in support of claims for larger plans, larger devolution of central resources and for preferential treatment in respect of central projects. With time, these considerations have also permeated discussion on resource allocation within states.

Reducing Regional Disparities: The Approaches of Planners

Balanced regional development has been a persistent preoccupation of planners from the First Five Year Plan. What

TABLE – 1

Interstate Disparities in Development, Selected Indicators, 1980-81

State	Incidence of rural poverty 1977-78	Per capita SDP (Rs)	Agricultural sector: Irrigation ratio	Agricultural sector: Fertilizer use (kg/ha) (1984-85)	Agricultural sector: Value per ha (Rs)	Agricultural sector: Value added per capita rural (Rs) (1979-81)	% work in non-agricultural activities 1981	Factory industry value added per capita (Rs)	Index of infrastructure devt.	Power consumption per capita (kwh)	Road length per 1000 km^2 (km)	Doctors per lakh population	IMR	Literacy rate 5+years
A.P.	45.4	1360	36.2	79.0	2785	836	28	111	98	102	457	45	86	30
Assam	n.a.	1135	21.2	4.1	3455	656	n.a.	60	93	34	757	38	n.a.	n.a.
Bihar	57.8	958	38.2	34.8	2500	450	20	73	97	74	480	29	n.a.	26
Gujarat	43.1	2150	22.3	48.0	1866	858	38	342	125	239	296	45	116	44
Haryana	23.2	2447	61.4	63.9	2710	1463	38	274	154	210	522	n.a.	101	36
J&K	n.a.	1549	42.9	17.5	3814	801	n.a.	31	73	75	52	48	72	27
Karnataka	53.1	1559	14.2	54.3	2093	837	31	167	101	146	572	59	69	38
Kerala	47.4	1540	11.1	48.6	4510	631	49	156	137	112	2673	49	37	70
M.P.	61.6	1237	12.8	18.3	1186	605	22	118	62	100	236	10	142	28
Maharashtra	60.4	2329	10.5	29.5	1844	922	36	486	118	245	381	50	79	47
Orissa	67.9	1286	19.8	15.3	1799	684	23	77	82	114	765	31	135	34
Punjab	13.1	2842	81.0	157.3	3135	1756	41	235	215	304	918	131	81	41
Rajasthan	33.5	1220	18.6	12.4	1205	771	28	100	77	99	187	27	108	24
Tamil Nadu	56.3	1413	47.2	104.7	2609	522	37	258	153	186	953	68	91	47
U.P.	49.8	1212	55.2	67.3	2401	648	25	69	107	83	513	22	150	27
W. Bengal	58.3	1586	26.8	53.5	3612	686	42	257	132	117	639	62	n.a.	41
INDIA	51.2	1564	30.0	48.3	2153	710	31	178	100	132	457	40	110	36

Source: Compiled from Centre for Monitoring Indian Economy (1985).

exactly constitutes 'balanced' regional development and how best to achieve it are questions to which planners have been groping for answers. While there is still no clarity on either point, one can discern some pattern in the evolution of thinking on the subject. Thus the Second Plan, where the regional aspect was first explicitly discussed, emphasized that due attention should be given to the 'special needs of less developed areas' and to the regulation of patterns of investment in order to lead to 'balanced regional development' without, however, defining 'balance', other than broadly in terms of wider diffusion of industry. A little later, the potential conflict between regional balance and the necessity for rapid overall growth came to be stressed. And at least in some formulations, faster overall growth was seen to be the most effective long-term solution for regional imbalances, as for mass poverty and unemployment. However, in practice the plans had to respond to pressures from different regions for special treatment.

The Third Plan therefore conceived of 'programmes with a direct bearing on the welfare of the people in different parts' and special programmes in particular areas suffering setbacks or chronic, basic deficiencies (*Third Five Year Plan*, p. 144). The former idea eventually led to the concept of the basic needs programme (formulated in the early 1970s) seeking to ensure a specified minimum standard of education, health facilities, drinking water supply and roads in all districts. This was reflected in a proliferation of special area programmes focused on scarcity tracts; drought prone areas; backward districts; tribal areas; and hill area development. The generalized anti-poverty programmes (IRDP, RLEGP, etc.) which have gained in prominence more recently, do not however pay any specific attention to regional priorities.

At a more general level, 'backwardness' came to be recognized as a criterion to be given special weight in determining the allocation of central assistance for state plans; in deciding the location of central projects; and in lending by financial institutions. Special incentives to attract private investors to industrially backward districts and discourage future growth in the metropolitan areas also belong in this category.

Acceptance of 'backwardness' as one of the criteria in deciding resource allocations, concessions and programmes for different categories of backward areas, naturally brought under close scrutiny the basis for identifying backward areas, especially when the unit of area planning came to be viewed increasingly in terms of districts rather than states or even regions. Several official committees of the Planning Commission[1] and at least one expert committee appointed by a state government (Maharashtra) have gone into the question of backwardness. Their reports highlight considerable divergence of opinion on the appropriate indicators of development, and on the feasibility or meaningfulness of trying to get composite indices of backwardness.[2] The balance of opinion seems to be against composite indices and in favour of indices capturing the degree of backwardness in respect of particular productive sectors (especially agriculture and industry) and of socio-economic infrastructure. However the matter remains unresolved. The National Committee on Development of backward areas — the latest to address the problem — came out against any index-based approach and argued instead for a 'problem-areas' approach. The Committee appointed by Maharashtra on the other hand adopted a sector-wise assessment of backwardness, based on quantitative indices.

The search for a composite index seems futile partly because reliable data for per capita income accruals or per capita real consumption levels, which could serve as a meaningful overall index, are simply not available at the district level. More importantly, such an index does not have much operational value unless the underlying causes of backwardness are identified and a coherent strategy derives from such analysis. Different regions are backward in different respects, in different degrees and for different reasons.

The Fourth Plan rightly calls for location-specific strategies. To that end it argues for a distinction between those backward regions which are marked by unfavourable physio-geographic conditions, terrain and climate, and those with adverse land-man ratios, lack of infrastructure or inadequate development of resource potential. But this is still far too aggregated. Detailed work on strategies appropriate to local conditions necessary for planning the development of backward areas has not been done. The plan stresses the need for strengthening district and local planning capabilities — the accent being more on technical expertise than on effective political decentralization.

Later plans have focused on the persistent and in many respects widening regional disparities. There has also been a significant expansion in the scale of anti-poverty programmes (including programmes aimed specifically at backward regions). There is, however, no attempt to confront questions about the effectiveness of the anti-poverty programmes generally and about the efficacy of the current approach to regional development in raising employment and incomes in the areas where poverty is high.

Major elements in the current strategy for reducing regional disparities thus include :

1. allowing a special weight to problem areas and backward areas in the allocations of central assistance;
2. preference for backward regions in the location of central government projects;

3. special programmes for the development of areas with relatively low incomes and/or underprivileged people;
4. providing basic minimum needs; and
5. incentives for location of industries in less developed areas.

Among the reasons justifying the relatively high degree of centralization of powers to mobilize and allocate financial resources in the hands of the federal government is that it gives greater freedom to make more resources available for the development of backward regions. The system to date has failed to accomplish this, however. This is because the formula governing the allocation of central assistance across states has given much greater weight to the size of population than to backwardness. Thus under the revised Gadgil formula, 60 per cent of central plan assistance is distributed pro-rata to population. A substantial amount is allocated to special problem states or regions but these are not always areas with a high concentration of poor people. About 10 per cent of assistance is allocated on the basis of the tax effort of the states. At present the relative backwardness of a state influences the allocation of only 20 per cent of the total central plan assistance but it is significant that the weight given to this criterion has doubled over the last decade. (Table 2 gives Fifth Plan figures.)

Plan assistance has accounted, over the last three decades, for less than two-fifths of budgetary resource transfers from the centre to the states. Roughly an equal proportion consists of transfers recommended by the Finance Commission, the balance being made up of other discretionary loans and grants by central ministries (Thimmiah, 1985). (The last category at one stage accounted for nearly one-third of the total.) However, none of these transfers, individually or in the aggregate, have been effective instruments for altering the allocation of resources decisively in favour of backward states.

TABLE – 2

Incidence of Poverty and Level of Expenditure on Anti-poverty Programmes and Total State Plan Outlays

	Incidence of Rural Poverty 1977-78	per capita expenditure under		
		Anti-poverty programmes (1980-81)	Total Fifth Plan outlay	
			State Plan	Central investments*
	(1)	(2)	(3)	(4)
Andhra Pradesh	45.4	11.56	210	46
Assam	n.a.	n.a.	159	45
Bihar	57.8	6.60	140	28
Gujarat	43.1	10.40	329	61
Haryana	23.2	17.37	420	91
Jammu & Kashmir	n.a.	n.a.	522	209
Karnataka	53.1	9.07	242	42
Kerala	47.4	10.09	203	29
Madhya Pradesh	61.6	8.44	224	41
Maharashtra	60.4	6.74	330	41
Orissa	67.9	8.01	186	86
Punjab	13.1	31.20	473	105
Rajasthan	33.5	11.39	203	82
Tamil Nadu	56.3	12.13	184	28
Uttar Pradesh	49.8	9.01	209	32
West Bengal	58.3	4.95	178	27
INDIA	51.2	8.83	232	43

Source: Columns (1) and (2): Hanumantha Rao (1985), pp. 7.9.
Columns (3) and (4): S.P. Gupta et.al. (1983), pp. 392, 457.
* Comprises central plan schemes and centrally sponsored schemes.

The correlation between per capita resource transfers on these accounts and per capita SDP across states turns out to be not significant. Indeed while the per capita resource transfers from the Centre to the states via the Finance Commission seem to be moderately redistributive (in the sense of poorer states getting more devolution per capita), the plan transfers are far less so (Guhan, 1988). The flow of institutional funds (during the seventies) also seems to favour the better-off states, there being a significant positive correlation between per capita SDP and the quantum of such funds per capita. And since the states with relatively high per capita output in general have better access to tax and non-tax revenues of their own, the per capita state plan outlays are also higher in the better-off states (Thimmiah, 1985 and George, 1985). It is also apparent (see Table 3) that states which have been growing relatively fast (in terms of SDP) have had a higher level of central assistance, institutional finance and plan outlays than have the slow growing states.

TABLE – 3

Selected Characteristics of States Classified by Rates of Growth of SDP

	Growth rate in SDP		
	3.75% to 5.50%	*2.75% to 3.75%*	*Less than 2.75%*
Annual growth rate 1960-63 to 1978-81	4.17	3.21	2.37
Per capita SDP 1960-63 (Rs)	369	292	217
Composite index of development mid-1970s	21.8	15.8	14.1
Per capita plan outlay 1956 81 (Rs)	1568	1344	1124
Per capita central assistance for plans 1956-81 (Rs)	482	426	373
Per capita flow of institutional funds 1973-81 (Rs)	718	405	276

Source: Ajit Kumar Singh (1985), pp. 2, 65.

Thus these financial resource-sharing mechanisms have not helped the backward states to get access to significantly larger financial resources per capita through the public sector than the relatively better-off states. However it is erroneous to suppose that the amount of public spending per capita has any direct or predictable bearing on the rate at which income and employment grow in a particular region. This impact depends a great deal on the purpose for which the funds are spent, the efficiency with which they are used, and the extent to which private sector activity is stimulated. It is legitimate to ask whether the programmes aimed specifically at backward areas and at providing minimum social amenities to all districts have had a significant impact on the condition of backward regions.

There is no convincing evidence that various special area programmes — the outlays on which have greatly expanded during the last two decades — have succeeded in accelerating the pace of economic activity in relatively backward tracts. The impact of the Basic Minimum Needs Programmes — which is now accepted as a distinct component of the Plans — in terms of raising the levels of education, health, water supply and other facilities at the district and block levels (and especially in the backward districts and blocks) remains to be properly assessed. Even in the case of anti-poverty programmes like IRDP and RLEGP, the amount of outlay at the state level bears no relation to the incidence of poverty across states. Indeed if anything, states where poverty incidence is high seem to spend less on anti-poverty programmes per head of population (see Table 2).

In view of the great variations in conditions of development within states, the state is obviously not quite the appropriate unit for a meaningful assessment of the impact of anti-poverty programmes. However, there is no way of knowing, with the available information, whether the backward districts within states get any special consideration in the allocation of plan resources, how much of the development programmes is located in the backward districts/blocks or what impact they have made in these areas. A detailed review of regional allocation in one state (Maharashtra) showed that an explicit commitment to allocate more resources per capita to its backward regions was not fulfilled.

In the allocation of central investments (central plan schemes and centrally sponsored projects) again, the better-off states seem to have got rather more per head than the poor states, the exceptions being the special category states in the north-eastern region and Jammu & Kashmir. Cumulative investment in central public enterprises in the early 1970s distinctly favoured the special category states and the poorer states, but by 1981 the difference between the groups had substantially narrowed, the better-off states gaining more than the middle-income and low-income states (Table 4).

TABLE – 4

Per Capita Central Investments and Gross Block of Central Public Enterprises During the Fourth and Fifth Plans

	Central Investments per capita		*Gross block per capita*	
	1969-74	*1974-79*	*1972*	*1981*
Special category states[1]	109	115	87	363
Richer states[2]	47	60	36	355
Middle income states[3]	38	39	72	268
Poor income states[4]	27	40	80	366
Total	34	43	67	333
Total state plan outlay per capita	141	232		

Sources : M.M. Ansari (1983), pp. 457, 458.

1. Includes Assam, Himachal Pradesh, Jammu & Kashmir, Manipur, Meghalaya, Nagaland, Sikkim and Tripura.
2. Punjab, Haryana, Maharashtra and Gujarat.
3. W. Bengal, Karnataka, Tamil Nadu, Kerala and Rajasthan.
4. Andhra Pradesh, Madhya Pradesh, Uttar Pradesh, Orissa and Bihar.

Overall, the available evidence (see Table 5) suggests that while interstate disparities have narrowed in a few respects – notably degree of urbanization, level of development of factory industry, electricity consumption and literacy, they have significantly widened in several important respects, notably in respect of productivity of land, foodgrain production per head and other indicators of agricultural development, as well as in respect of some infrastructural facilities (e.g. roads and hospital bed-to-population ratios). Interstate disparities in overall per capita SDP have also widened. A recent compilation of the relevant data — and one must always bear in mind their limitations especially in judging real income levels and changes therein — shows that poorer states have grown at a slower pace than the better-off ones. (Ajit Kumar Singh, 1985, p. 62; see also Table 19, Mohan and Thottan, this volume.) There are also indications that the interstate disparities in SDP per capita, after showing a fall in the fifties have been rising progressively since the early 1960s.[3] At a more disaggregated level also, judging from the coefficient of variation in per capita crop production across districts, the regional disparities in rural economy have been widening (Mahendra Dev, 1985).

This aggravation of regional disparities is a matter for concern and has been recognized as such. Of course faster overall growth would help mitigate the problem in as much as it gives greater opportunities for people from poorer regions to migrate to fast-growing regions. However, quite apart from the fact that the prospects of significant acceleration are rather doubtful, faster growth alone is not adequate. Ethnic and linguistic diversity and distances after all do limit the scope for migration. Also the ability of people in poor regions to take advantage of growing opportunities elsewhere is limited by their knowledge, skills and adaptability, which in turn is a reflection of the lack of education, training and health facilities as well as, in several cases, difficulties of access arising from physical isolation. Under these conditions, any strategy for regional balance must pay attention to achieving more diffused growth of incomes and employment and of amenities.

TABLE – 5

Changes in Interstate Disparities in Respect of Selected Indicators, 1960-61 to 1978-79

	Coefficient of variation during	
	1960-61	*1978-79*
1. Per capita state domestic product at current prices	19.6	27.6
2. Share of secondary sector in SDP	27.5	25.8
3. Urban population as % of total population	39.8	33.2
4. Irrigation coverage	60.5	65.2
5. Cropping intensity	11.6	13.3
6. Fertilizer consumption per hectare	67.4	71.9
7. Crop output value per hectare	36.5[1]	43.3[2]
8. Foodgrain output per capita	31.2[3]	59.1[4]
9. Factory employment per thousand population	74.8	65.2
10. Per capita consumption of electricity	61.3	48.1
11. % villages electrified	57.7	43.5
12. Road length per hundred sq.km.	54.0	75.2
13. Literacy rate	32.0	28.1
14. Hospital beds per lakh of population	41.3	42.7

Source: Tiwari (1985); Mishra (1985).

1. 1962-63
2. 1980-81
3. 1961-62 to 1963-64
4. 1975-76 to 1978-79

Regional development strategy must necessarily be multi-faceted, covering both agriculture and industry, rural as well as urban areas, infrastructure and productive investments. However, regions which are part of a national economy within which there is a great deal of scope for trade and mobility of resources (including labour), face a wider range of options than the country as a whole even as they are less able to determine on their own which option to follow. This makes the kind of intersectoral balancing characteristic of national plans rather inappropriate, at any rate difficult to implement for regional planning authorities (even assuming that they exist and are technically competent). It seems altogether more sensible to focus regional planning on (a) creating conditions for the more effective exploitation of the locally available land, water and other natural resources; and (b) ensuring investment in the infrastructure necessary to support developments in particular sectors and to improve the quality of human resources (education, health, water supply). In the case of industry, apart from providing infrastructure and lobbying with investors (government and private), they can do little to control how much and what industry will come to the region. Differential access to financial resources to support development of backward regions is clearly important; but how much and on what terms is a larger question which has to be decided at state and central levels, balancing the claims of backward areas with the interests of efficient expansion of the economy as a whole.

We do not propose to address these questions in their full range but will confine our remarks to the regional aspects of rural development. The vast majority of Indian people live in rural areas and depend on agriculture for their livelihood; and at present rates of population growth and income growth this will continue to be the case for the foreseeable future. And these features are likely, if anything, to be more pronounced in the poorer regions. Measures to accelerate growth of agricultural output and rural employment and to improve the quality of human resources in the poorer regions must therefore figure prominently in any strategy for reducing regional imbalances.

Regional Strategy for Agriculture

As regards agriculture, it so useful to distinguish between two types of regions deserving special attention: Those areas which have relatively low mean per capita output to begin with and those about or slightly above average but experiencing a decline in per capita output which, if unchecked, would push them into the ranks of the poor regions. The former category includes the greater part of east India (much of Bihar, east U.P., parts of Orissa, Bengal and Madhya Pradesh), coastal Kerala and Karnataka, most of Maharashtra and parts of Rajasthan. In these regions the incidence of poverty is generally higher than average and most of them have recorded a decline in per capita agricultural production. The second category is spread more widely and covers parts of Gujarat, interior Karnataka, parts of Tamil Nadu and Andhra Pradesh, and parts of Madhya Pradesh, Orissa and Bengal.[4] Poor regions by the above criterion can be further divided into four broad categories in terms of potentials and problems:

First is the western coastal belt, comprising Kerala, coastal Karnataka and coastal Maharashtra. This is characterized by high rainfall concentrated in 3-4 months of the southwest monsoon; a terrain which does not permit of surface irrigation. Paddy is an important crop. Since it is grown mostly in the monsoon season when water control is also difficult, there are serious problems in raising yields. Scope for dry season irrigation seems limited. Tree crops are important especially in Kerala and Karnataka, with Kerala facing serious problems of pest and disease in respect of coconuts. This region has traditionally been marked by net emigration. While their economic structure is more commercialized and diversified, unemployment rates are high.

Next is the relatively dry belt comprising the lower Deccan plateau, east Gujarat and southern Rajasthan. These have relatively low rainfall, comparatively low levels of irrigation, and agriculture is exposed to greater instability. But the density of population is relatively low. There is considerable unexploited irrigation potential, current utilization in Karnataka, Maharashtra, Gujarat and Rajasthan being less than half the estimated 'ultimate' potential. The impact of irrigation on productivity is also high. But even if all the potential were harnessed, barely a third of the area could be irrigated. Improvements in dry farming are therefore crucial to this tract.

The third region is in the east. Among the most densely populated parts of the country, it is also among the poorest. It has relatively high rainfall and also an abundance of exploitable water resources both surface and subsurface, which, if harnessed, could greatly increase cropping intensity and yields. But the productivity of existing irrigation systems — largely surface water based — is low; and the pace of private irrigation development has been slow despite the favourable position in terms of ground water endowment. The problems of this region are complex: In part they are technical in as much as effective water control is impeded by floods and waterlogging during the kharif season which carries over into the rabi season; in part they are institutional arising from the relatively small and highly fragmented land holdings (which reduce returns to irrigation), and from a land tenure system which has been characterized as 'semi-feudal'. Effective tenancy reforms and land consolidation seem essential to ease the institutional constraints and stimulate faster development.

The fourth category comprises parts of Tamil Nadu which has well developed irrigation and a high level of productivity, but is experiencing continued rapid growth in population along with a relative stagnation in output. The scope for extending irrigation is strictly limited; even existing supplies are under stress due to over-exploitation of ground water and increased use of water in upper riparian states. The problem here is partly one of increasing the efficiency of water use (calling for more sophisticated control devices and management) and partly one of identifying the factors constraining the improvement in productivity of irrigated lands. Improvements in rainfed agriculture — which will account for two-fifths of the cultivated area even after all the water potential is harnessed — are also important, though not to the same degree as in west India. In as much as the average rainfall and its distribution in this tract differs from that of western India, the nature of the technological improvements needed to raise yields in these tracts will also differ.

Clearly the problem of agricultural development in the poor regions, and the ingredients of their solution, vary greatly. Disaggregated studies of the type recently done for the eastern region under the auspices of the Planning Commission and the Reserve Bank of India are a good beginning. The reports (GOI, PC, 1985b, and RBI, 1984) do make a convincing case for augmenting the flow of resources to this region to enable it to harness its potentials and achieve speedier growth in output. While a larger flow of resources may be necessary to accelerate agricultural development in poorer regions, important institutional changes are also needed. In all cases it is important to see that agricultural programmes in the poor regions are oriented to their particular potentials and needs, which as we have emphasized are quite diverse. Whether in fact the institutional mechanisms for research, planning and policy formulation of the states and local institutions are geared to this task is therefore a matter of considerable importance.

The Problem of Wage Labour in Poor Regions

Accelerated growth of agricultural output is necessary but may not always suffice to make an effective dent on poverty in poor regions. A sizeable part of the rural population has no or only modest land or other productive resources. Their incomes are directly a function of the rate at which wage employment opportunities increase and the behaviour of wage-rates. In many of the 'poor regions' the incidence of wage-labour is high and wage-rates low. In fact, across regions, there seems to be a close connection between incidence of poverty on the one hand and the incidence of wage-employment and unemployment on the other. These in turn reflect the volume of productive resources per head, how evenly they are distributed and how productive the resources are (Sundaram and Tendulkar, 1983).

As a result of growing population against a near constant land base, and in the absence of any significant redistribution of land, the proportion of population depending on wage labour is bound to rise. (Changes in land distribution leading to greater concentration of operational holdings would also increase incidence of wage-labour but this seems to be — at least so far — in general far less important in the Indian context than demographic pressure). The growth of wage employment opportunities in agriculture however may not keep pace with the growth of agricultural production for several reasons: (1) even in 'normal' circumstances the total labour requirements of farming per hectare increase at a slower rate than production per unit of land; (2) the reduction in average size of holding per cultivator — a direct consequence of rise in population — increases the supply of family labour per unit area which is bound to dampen the growth in the demand for *wage labour*; and (3) there could be labour-displacing technical change.

The faster the rate of growth in agriculture, the better the opportunity for wage-employment both directly in agricultural operations and indirectly in commerce and transport, and resulting from increased demand for non-agricultural goods and services from the more prosperous cultivator classes. But this by itself may not suffice to absorb the growing work-force at rising real wage-rates unless growth reaches the levels recorded by Punjab-Haryana! In most regions, other sources of additional wage-employment need to be explored; without it the wage-labour class may have to contend, at current rates of growth of economic activity, with rising unemployment or lower wage-rates or both. For this reason regions which have a high incidence of wage-labour deserve special attention. While these are in general also marked by a high incidence of poverty, some regions (especially in Andhra Pradesh and Tamil Nadu), which seem to be about average in terms of poverty incidence, have a relatively high proportion of wage-labour (Table 6).

There are two possible sources of such additional wage employment: One consists of commuting to work outside the villages in nearby urban centres. The scope for this is directly a function of the level and growth of urban economic activity, its regional spread, and the costs of commuting relative to migration to the towns. The second is direct and indirect wage-employment generated by public expenditure of all kinds. Some recent data suggest that both of these may be becoming more important sources of increases in wage-employment opportunities for rural labourers. Their precise magnitude or mechanisms however are as yet unclear.[5]

Barring a dramatic increase in the rate of growth in non-agricultural activities, larger public expenditures must play an important role in generating more employment. Their impact on poverty will depend to a significant extent on the ability to ensure that areas where wage-labour incidence is relatively high, and the poor are concentrated, get substantially larger (and rising) outlays and/or the effectiveness of spending is greatly increased.

TABLE – 6

Selected Indicators of Rural Poverty, NSS Regions, 1972-73

Sl. No.	Region	Crop output per capita 1970-73 (Rs)	Incidence of rural poverty %	% farm wage labour	% in non-agriculture	Growth rate of crop output	PDUR %
1.	Kerala south	73	47.8	25.7	13.1	0.71	21.9
2.	Kerala north	121	55.7	24.0	17.4	1.60	25.0
3.	Bihar south	153	64.3	16.9	7.1	-0.90	8.2
4.	Bihar north	154	54.4	37.0	3.2	0.20	9.4
5.	Maharashtra inland central	159	54.6	24.7	4.6	-7.18	7.1
6.	Maharashtra coastal	160	59.3	18.7	27.8	-2.32	6.0
7.	Rajasthan west	174	28.3	3.0	5.6	2.79	5.0
8.	Maharashtra inland north	185	53.8	26.9	8.2	-5.39	14.5
9.	Bihar central	187	52.0	29.6	5.8	0.87	13.5
10.	J & K outer hills	190	44.4	0.5	2.5	5.67	1.0
11.	Karnataka coastal ghat	191	40.4	23.2	17.1	-0.66	5.2
12.	U.P. east	195	46.6	15.7	6.3	1.54	4.6
13.	J & K mountaineous	206	17.7	5.6	7.6	5.67	1.0
14.	A.P. inland north	207	46.8	29.4	10.4	-1.70	10.4
15.	W. Bengal central plains	217	45.3	34.8	22.9	1.82	9.6
16.	Assam plains	219	28.9	14.6	4.4	2.01	2.0
17.	Rajasthan south	226	78.9	6.0	5.0	2.10	1.3
18.	Orissa coastal	229	53.7	27.6	5.6	-0.16	17.1
19.	M.P. inland east	231	67.6	22.4	7.0	2.43	3.2
20.	Maharashtra east	234	60.4	31.9	12.3	-0.48	14.7
21.	Maharashtra inland east	247	61.6	38.6	7.2	-2.52	11.5
22.	J & K Jhelum valley	261	11.5	2.0	8.7	5.44	16.8
23.	U.P. central	268	48.8	11.2	7.3	2.06	2.3
24.	Karnataka inland south	278	34.6	23.8	11.5	2.55	8.1

(Contd...)

25.	W. Bengal western plains	280	58.0	30.8	5.7	2.49	14.2
26.	Gujarat east	282	60.5	20.6	9.6	-0.06	n.a.
27.	W. Bengal Himalaya	282	44.2	32.2	4.3	2.58	7.8
28.	Orissa south	284	83.9	34.6	3.7	-0.09	5.3
29.	Gujarat plains	299	26.8	26.4	10.7	-0.49	n.a.
30.	Orissa north	301	80.0	29.8	11.4	-0.44	10.7
31.	Tamil Nadu inland	313	41.1	28.9	13.5	1.18	9.5
32.	M.P. inland west	314	53.3	24.9	8.4	1.30	4.0
33.	M.P. north	317	40.2	10.1	5.7	1.95	2.0
34.	M.P. east	322	68.8	26.0	5.2	1.37	2.4
35.	A.P. inland south	334	37.7	29.2	7.4	0.01	11.5
36.	M.P. west	340	48.8	17.8	8.0	0.41	6.3
37.	W.B. eastern plains	340	59.5	33.0	7.2	3.02	11.4
38.	Assam hills	345	27.5	2.3	1.1	5.81	1.0
39.	U.P. Himalayas	347	47.7	5.1	3.7	2.15	1.2
40.	Karnataka inland east	350	36.8	32.4	6.3	2.29	5.6
41.	A.P. coastal	350	43.6	34.3	8.5	0.35	12.8
42.	Tamil Nadu coastal south	361	38.5	32.1	13.2	2.74	14.5
43.	U.P. South	362	49.6	12.6	5.0	2.46	3.3
44.	Rajasthan north-east	369	28.7	4.5	7.6	4.97	3.2
45.	Karnataka inland north	372	47.6	29.1	8.8	1.92	11.0
46.	Rajasthan south-east	377	47.2	7.7	7.0	4.35	1.3
47.	U.P. western	379	45.3	13.0	8.2	3.40	2.8
48.	Gujarat plains north	397	28.7	24.6	16.1	2.89	n.a.
49.	Gujarat dry areas	397	37.9	21.9	9.4	3.28	n.a.
50.	T.N. coastal north	423	48.7	33.9	13.4	3.24	14.6
51.	Maharashtra inland west	492	48.8	12.1	11.5	-4.25	8.8
52.	Haryana east	587	14.4	10.4	11.6	6.00	2.7
53.	Gujarat Saurashtra	641	20.0	14.6	11.0	2.28	n.a.
54.	Punjab north	644	11.8	19.7	14.3	8.02	6.2
55.	Haryana west	648	9.7	15.7	7.0	4.95	3.0
56.	Punjab south	1039	14.1	22.6	7.4	7.39	2.0

Source: Compiled from Bardhan (1982); Draft Fifth FYP 1978-83.

Implications for Programmes and Policy

Clearly the additional employment generated and the likely impact of future growth of the poorer regions depends on the totality of public spending in these regions. For it is not only the Food for work, IRDP and other special anti-poverty programmes, but also the normal rural development programmes and indeed public expenditure in general, which generate demand for labour and therefore affect the overall employment situation in a region.[6] The magnitude of this impact, the nature of jobs created and to what extent it is temporary or continuing depends a great deal on the activities and the efficiency with which the money is spent. Given that there are considerable leakages in public spending, one way of increasing the employment potential of public spending is to reduce leakages.

There are thus two problems — one is to find ways by which the flow of resources for development of backward regions with high incidence of poverty can be sustained at the necessary level; and the second is to ensure that the funds are used to maximum effect in terms of employment.

As for the first, under the present arrangements, the level and content of public outlays in backward regions is largely determined by the way the expenditures for various sectoral and target group/target area programmes are allocated by the concerned departments of the central and state governments. Instead it would be desirable to work towards an arrangement which provides explicitly for allocating a sufficiently large volume of total funds to make significant impacts in the backward/poor districts. This could be conceived in two parts: one part linked to an explicit commitment to ensure a specified standard of education, health, water supply and communication facilities; and the second to financing properly formulated productive investments in the districts identified as deserving urgent attention.

This calls for earmarking a substantial volume of plan funds and perhaps preferential treatment in loans, through financial institutions specifically, to correct the existing gaps in the poor districts. It also means the unit of allocation of these funds should be the district, and not the state, with the most backward districts being given the highest priority. This could be done either by the National Development Council earmarking, as a national commitment, a specified outlay for development of, say, the 100 most backward districts in terms of level of infrastructure and incidence of poverty; or by earmarking funds under the plan of each state for development of the backward districts/blocks in its territory. Exercises of the latter type have been attempted in Maharashtra.

With regard to the second problem, a serious review of the anti-poverty programmes with a view to rationalizing their scope and content seems in order. These programmes have proliferated under various heads considerable overlapping in a functional sense still persists, and the large subsidy/dole component in assistance oriented to individual beneficiaries is widely recognized to be a serious weakness. Once the poor districts deserving special attention are identified and an integrated plan is adopted, there is no need for keeping the numerous anti-poverty programme categories. This does not preclude maintaining programmes of special assistance to particular classes (e.g., scheduled castes and tribes) especially outside the selected priority backward areas.

Institutional Requirements

Such integration by itself should facilitate more effective use of funds — less duplication, less scope for leakages, — but only partly. It is equally important, especially in respect of programmes for the productive sectors, that the scale and content of schemes be tailored to the specific requirements and possibilities of local situations, and that schemes are properly prepared and implemented efficiently. The lack of local institutions to manage these tasks is obviously a serious lacuna. Better local planning calls for mechanisms for assembling the necessary basic information about local resources, potentials and problems; the machinery with the necessary expertise to formulate, appraise and execute projects; and institutional arrangements backed by adequate budget and personnel, for proper maintenance and management of facilities created on a continuing basis.

All this cannot be accomplished with the present system of centralized, bureaucracy-dependent and patronage-oriented planning. It calls for a drastic shift towards a more decentralized participatory system of local planning — which affords people opportunity to shape programmes in the light of local conditions, monitor and evaluate the use of resources, bring weaknesses in implementation (including misuse of resources) to the surface and generate pressures for corrective action. That the vested interests against such reform are strong is evident from the chequered history of democratic decentralization. But the fact that several states have thought fit to legislate such reforms — and some of these legislations are quite radical — and that some (like Bengal and Karnataka) are trying seriously to implement them are hopeful signs. These initiatives face heavy odds, and their progress needs watching closely. But there is no doubt that in this way there lies hope.

Notes

1. The following are the principal committees which examined the problem: Working Group on Identification of Backward Areas, 1968 (commonly referred to as the Pande Committee); the Chakravarthy Committee on Backward Areas; and the national Committee on the Development of Backward Areas, 1981.
2. For a brief summary and evaluation of the various reports see Govt. of Maharashtra (1984).

3. The coefficient of variation in SDP per capita is estimated to have risen from 19.5 per cent in 1960-61 to over 22 per cent in 1970-71. On the basis of a revised series the CV in 1970-71 is placed at 25.7 per cent rising to 36 per cent in 1979-80 (Ajit Kumar Singh, 1985:63). Also K.R.G. Nair (1985).

4. The use of per capita crop output as a basis for identifying poor regions is of course open to question in as much as the estimate does not cover all crops and crop production is but a part, though an important part, of total rural economic activity. However, it so happens that regions which classify as 'poor' by this procedure have a large overlap with those estimated to have a relatively high incidence of poverty on the basis of data on consumption expenditure (especially if one allows for the fact that the NSS estimates relate to individual years whose outcome would be strongly influenced by seasonal conditions). By either criteria east India, the west coast, and parts of Gujarat and Rajasthan fall in the category of poor regions. Much of Maharashtra in 1972-73 would also rank poor according to NSS, but 1972-73 was a drought year.

5. One of the striking features of the rural employment trends in the seventies is the sharp and nearly universal rise in the share of non-agricultural activities in total rural employment. The possible reasons for this structural change in the context of relatively slow growth of agriculture are discussed, if speculatively, in Vaidyanathan (1986).

6. There is some evidence that importance of direct employment in public services in rural areas though still small in relation to the total rural work-force (around 4 per cent in 1981) is increasing rapidly. Twenty years earlier, the proportion was only 2.4 per cent (Vaidyanathan, 1986).

References

Ajit Kumar Singh, 1985, 'Interstate Differences in Levels and Rates of Income, Growth of Income in India 1951-1981', in Mishra (ed.), 1985.

Ansari M.M., 1983, 'Flow of Financial Resources and Interstate Disparities', in GOI, PC, 1983, pp. 448-68.

Bardhan, P.K., 1984, Land, *Labour and Rural Poverty, Essays in Development Economics*, Oxford University Press, New Delhi.

Centre for Monitoring Indian Economy, 1985, *Basic Statistics relating to Indian Economy*, Vol. 2.

George, K.K., 1985, 'Interstate Disparities in Plan Outlays', in Mishra and Joshi (eds.), 1985.

Govt. of India Planning Commission, 1961, *Third Five Year Plan*, New Delhi.

———, 1981, National Committee on the Development of backward Areas, *Report on General Issues Relating to Backward Area Development*, New Delhi.

———, 1983, *Regional Dimensions of Indian Economic Development*, Govt. Press, Allahabad.

———, 1985a, *Seventh Five Year Plan 1985-90*, New Delhi.

———, 1985b, *Report of study group on Agricultural Strategies for Eastern Region of India*, New Delhi.

Govt. of Maharashtra, 1984, *Report of the Fact Finding Committee on Regional Imbalances*, Maharashtra.

Guhan, S., 1988, 'Issues before the Ninth Finance Commission', *Economic and Political Weekly*, 6 February.

Gupta, S.P. et.al., 1983, 'State Plan Outlay and Central Assistance', in GOI, PC, 1983, pp. 383-448.

Hanumantha Rao, C.H., 1985, 'Changes in Rural Poverty in India: Implications for Agricultural Growth', Rajendra Prasad Memorial Lecture, Indian Society of Agricultural Statistics.

Mahendra Dev, S., 1985, 'Directions of Change in Performance of All Crops in Indian Agriculture in the late 1970s', *Economic and Political Weekly*, 21-8 December.

Mishra, G.P. (ed.), 1985, *Regional Structure of Development and Growth in India*, Vol.I, Ashish Publishing House, New Delhi.

Nair, K.R.G., 1985, 'Interstate Income Differentials in India 1970-71 to 1979-80', in Mishra (ed.), 1985.

Reserve Bank of India, 1984, *Report of the Committee on Agricultural Productivity in Eastern India*, Bombay.

Sundaram K. and S.P. Tendulkar, 1983, 'Towards An Explanation of Inter-regional Variations in Poverty and Unemployment in Rural India' (Delhi School of Economics).

Thimmiah, G., 1985, 'Interstate Disparities in Financial Allocations', in Mishra and Joshi (eds.), 1985.

Tiwari, R.T., 1985, 'Interstate Disparities in levels of Development', in Mishra and Joshi (eds.), 1985.

Vaidyanathan, A., 1986, 'Labour Use in Rural India: A Study of Spatial and Temporal Variations', *Economic and Political Weekly*, 27 December.

18

Assessment of Nutritional and Health Status

THE purpose of this paper is threefold : (1) highlight certain measures of nutritional and health status currently in use and suggest some modifications; (2) review the adequacy of the data currently available for assessing nutrition-health status and the factors underlying its spatial and temporal variations and (3) outline an agenda for more effective use of available data and for improving their coverage and quality.

Nutrition and Health Status : Concepts and Measurement

Per capita food consumption or, in its more refined version, the proportion of population with food intake below "requirements", is widely used as a summary overall index of "nutritional status" along with life expectancy at birth and infant mortality rate, as indices of the health status of a population. The adequacy, and even the appropriateness, of these indices is however open to question. It is not possible to determine single norms of dietary needs for the healthy functioning of individuals. Mortality does not reflect the effect of morbidity on health status. We also need to take into account the interactions between morbidity and nutrition in assessing health status.

Conceptual Problems

Food Intake Requirement norms

Norms of food requirements for healthy functioning of individuals have conventionally been defined with reference to specified age, sex and activity status categories keeping in view climatic conditions and body mass. Given the composition of a population by age, sex and activity status, a norm of dietary requirements can be worked out for the population as a whole. The usual practice is to use the norm of per capita requirement for the "average" household as the basis for judging the adequacy of per capita mean intake and for assessing the proportion of households, and population, whose intake falls short of the overall norm (see for example GOI, 1994).

A single norm with reference to the 'average household' is inappropriate. Where, as in India, climatic conditions and stature of people vary widely from one part of the country to another, the requirement norms have to be region-specific. Moreover, there are large differences between households in respect of age and sex composition, activity status and size of people even within a region. And often these characteristics vary systematically across socio-economic groups: Thus poor households tend to be larger in size, have a relatively high dependency ratio and have a high concentration of female-headed households (Visaria). The body mass and activity characteristics of the poor may also differ from those of the better-off households (ICMR 1972). In principle, such differences can be taken into account by taking care to collect sufficiently detailed information on the characteristics (including size) of all members of each sample household in estimating "requirements". But even when such information is available, region-or group-specific norms are seldom worked out.

At a more fundamental level, the notion that there is a unique level of nutrient requirement for healthy life of any given individual has been under challenge.[1] It is argued that there are ways in which individuals can, and do, adjust to both temporary and sustained variations in food intake over a fairly wide range without impairing the level of their health and functional performance. Sukhatme (1989:16), one of the leading proponents of this view, points out that there would be "a direct and deterministic link between food intake and economic productivity" only "if energy used in metabolic maintenance, continuous secretion of immune response processes and free time activity was equal and all poor people were uniform in size." In point of fact, however, the size of humans, energy used for metabolic maintenance and the proportion of energy used for productive work are all highly variable. These considerations limit the significance of calorie intake per capita as a measure of nutrition status. The limitation is more severe in so far as there is truth in the claim that "whenever energy constraints are faced by man, powerful mechanisms are activated by the body to establish equilibrium between the internal and the external environment" which "enable an individual to increase metabolic efficiency and effect changes in discretionary work output". (ibid)

The scope for such intra-individual adjustment to persistent variations in intake is of course not limitless. The argument is rather that if this possibility is not recognised, measures of deficiency with reference to the unique norm of requirements for the population as a whole are likely to overstate the proportion of the population suffering from nutrition deficiency.

For this reason, Sukhatme suggested that it would be more appropriate to consider persons with intakes below the norm minus 2 standard deviations as being truly undernourished. An alternative would be to specify the requirement norm in terms of an optimum, a minimum and a maximum level of calories per kg of body mass (Sukhatme; 1989:21). This implies a range of intake within which there would be no serious health consequences. It is however not clear whether this procedure avoids the measurement problems associated with age-sex activity-group specific norms and those arising from the complex ways in which the human body adapts to nutritional stress.

Adjustments to variations in food intake take place in one or more of several dimensions including body mass and its rate of growth, the nature and intensity of activity and adjustments in the BMR itself. This means that sustained low intakes by an individual may be reflected in one or more of several dimensions: (1) relatively small size of the body; (2) longer time to reach the maximum size; (3) fewer working hours; and (4) lesser intensity of effort leading to lower productivity[2]. These adjustments however are not likely to be uniform across age and sex groups.

Under prevailing institutional arrangements the acquisition of food and its distribution to individuals are mediated through the family. Variations in the availability of food for a particular family — which depends on the size and composition of the family and its total income — affect the distribution of what is available among its members. Thus, when the availability is low (declining) it seems reasonable to suppose that the requirements of those who work and earn the family income will be given priority over those of non-working dependents, who are further differentiated by age, sex and intra-household responsibilities. Socio-cultural factors are believed to have a significant role in determining the allocation of food between adults and children, and between sexes, both among adults and children. Insofar as intra-family distribution is related systematically to its average per capita intake, one should expect intra-family differences in terms of size, activity and productivity also to vary systematically with the level of intake[3].

Relevance of morbidity

Nutrition status is not determined solely by the level and quality of food intake[4]. It is affected by, and also affects health status. Nutritionists have long recognised that the presence of infection has adverse affects on both appetite and absorption of food by the body (see e.g. Scrimshaw; 1968 and Sukhatme; 1989). In Sukhatme's words: "The majority of illnesses tend to synergise malnutrition both by demanding higher energy intake to meet the rise in BMR accompanying fever and by requiring higher intake of protein and other nutrients to form antibodies to fight illness and to replace damaged tissues. Most illnesses also tend to be accompanied by anorexia and loss of appetite" (Sukhatme, 1989;3).

The extreme case of severe and persistent shortage of food leads to famine and starvation death. But more commonly, low food intake reduces immuno-competence and thereby increases the risk of infection. A significant proportion of nutrition-deficiency diseases occurring in poor nations have communicable diseases as their underlying cause. For these reasons both food intake and morbidity ought to figure in any assessment of nutrition status especially in low income situations.

In any case morbidity has to be taken into account in assessing the health status of a population. Mortality rate alone does not give a complete picture. It is important to recognise that, especially in poor countries, public health measures (including the provision of primary health care) may reduce fatality without reducing morbidity. There is, in fact, a great deal of evidence that low (declining) mortality often goes with high (rising) morbidity. The interpretation of this phenomenon remains a matter of controversy. The controversy centres essentially around the possibility of getting objective measures of morbidity which are comparable across different countries, regions, classes and over time. This aspect is discussed later in the paper.

The foregoing discussion also suggests that in order to get a proper assessment of the nutrition and health status of a population, it is not enough to know levels and quality of food intake and morbidity per se. It would be more meaningful to focus on the effects of sustained differences (or changes) in intake on weight, weight for height, age at which maximum height or weight is reached and other measures of size; on the allocation of time between work and leisure; the nature and productivity of work; the extent of difference in these respects between social groups and between different age-sex categories; and the incidence of infectious disease (especially diarrhoea, respiratory infections and fever). Such an approach has the merit of avoiding several of the difficulties associated with the food intake measure and of focusing on the consequences of differences (sustained changes) in food intake and their multi-dimensional character. Several, though not all, consequences (especially size, time spent on various activities and nature of activity) can be defined with reasonable precision and the relevant information/measurements obtained more accurately than actual food intake.

The construction of a composite nutrition-health status index from these indicators does present problems. But insofar as there is an improvement (deterioration) in one or more of the dimensions mentioned above while others remain unchanged, one may unambiguously conclude that overall nutrition-health status has improved (deteriorated).

Measurement Problems

Available sources

The practicability of either the conventional or the modified measures of nutrition and health status depends critically, of course, on the availability of the relevant empirical data or at least on the feasibility of collecting such data at reasonable cost. The rest of the paper is addressed to this problem. The discussion is based on the Indian experience about which I have some first hand knowledge. Hopefully the points made will be of more general relevance.

Several systematic surveys of mortality, morbidity, food consumption and nutrition — some of them repeated at periodic intervals since at least the 'sixties — are available.

- The sample registration survey conducted by the Registrar General provides estimates of fertility and mortality at the state level annually and at the district level for the period 1971 — 1981.
- The National Sample Survey (NSS) conducted a pilot morbidity enquiry in the 'fifties followed by a national survey in 1973-1974. The latter is designed to give estimates, statewise, of incidence and prevalence rates for rural and urban areas and by age-sex categories (Sarvekshana 1980).
- The NSS started conducting periodic surveys (beginning the early 1980's) of education, health and other elements of social consumption. These surveys have generated data on morbidity, utilisation of different sources of health services and expenditures incurred (Sarvekshana 1992).
- A similar national survey was done by the National Council of Applied Economic Research (NCAER) in

1990 whose preliminary results have recently been published (NCAER 1992).

- We also have results of a comprehensive survey of morbidity and health care in the state of Kerala (Kannan, et al. 1991).
- The NSS consumption surveys give details of food consumption (by state and levels of total per capita consumer expenditure for rural and urban areas) and, for a few rounds, also the distribution of rural and urban households and the population of these households by level of per capita calorie intake. The National Nutritional Monitoring Bureau (NNMB) of the ICMR has been conducting since 1970 regular annual surveys of food intake and anthropometric measurements in ten states for a limited sample.
- A few indepth surveys of demographic behaviour, health and related aspects, have been done in particular areas, (including, in one or two cases, repeat surveys of the same regions), using both structured questionnaires and anthropological methods of inquiry.

For the most part, the data are obtained from large scale sample surveys. The NSS covered some 200,000 households in the morbidity survey of 1973-74, and 12,914 villages in the social consumption survey of 1986-87. The NCAER survey sampled 20,000 households all over India and the KSSP survey 10,000 households in Kerala. The NNMB surveys are relatively small in comparison, with a sample size of about 400 households a year in each selected state.

These surveys typically seek to elicit information from members of selected households with the help of structured questionnaires administered by full-time, paid and mostly male, field investigators. Only the NNMB surveys are conducted by investigators with specialized training and under expert supervision. The Kerala survey is notable for having used activists of the Kerala Shastra Sahitya Parishad (KSSP) and a sizeable number of female investigators after intensive training by professional doctors who were in charge of the survey.

These data have been used extensively in poverty measurement (Bardhan and Srinivasan eds 1974 and 1988 GOI; 1993) and addressing such substantive questions as the factors underlying the regional (and sometimes temporal) variations in the level of per capita calorie intake, sources and distribution of calorie intake by socioeconomic class (Panikar, 1980); the relationship between food intake on the one hand and the size of people, morbidity, and intra-family distribution, on the other (Vaidyanathan, 1985); the level and pattern of morbidity (Panikar and Soman, 1982; Vaidyanathan, 1985; Kumar and Vaidyanathan, 1988 and Kumar, 1990); and the sources and costs of health care.

Food Intake: Questions concerning the reliability and comparability of estimates derived from these surveys are prominent in the literature. Take, for instance, food intake estimates[5]. The NSS gives estimates of mean per capita intake of various food stuffs and of their calorie and protein content by State and by income class. The NNMB surveys also provide estimates of per capita calorie and protein intake, but these estimates differ substantially and erratically from those of the NSS: even the ranking of states according to intake levels from the two surveys are very dissimilar. Such differences reflect differences in concept, design and survey procedures adopted by the two agencies.

Thus the NSS seeks to ascertain the quantum of various foodstuffs consumed by each of a large sample of households during the 30 days prior to the date of the interview. Despite the care and thought which has gone into designing the schedules, several conceptual ambiguities remain. Moreover, the information provided depends largely on how well-informed the respondents were and how accurately he or she could recall consumption of each item during the reference period. Given the large number of items involved, the fact that respondents were usually males not well placed to know what goes on in the family kitchen, and further that there were unavoidable ambiguities (for example the distinction between consumption out of homegrown stocks and purchases; between food processed in the home and processed items, including purchased meals, got from outside) and difficulties of estimating food eaten in the household by persons who were not members of the household and food eaten outside the household by members of the household, the scope for non-sampling errors is considerable. What is more, some of these non-sampling errors could have varied systematically across socio-economic groups.

It is possible, therefore that richer peasant households reported some or all of the food they gave to their farm servants or workers rendering various services, as part of their household consumption. This means that the reported food intake of this class of households overstates their true intake. On the other hand, if the labourers do not fully report the meals they have taken in the employers' households, the reported intake of the poorer segments would tend to be understated.

The alternative of measuring actual intake, which in principle is the better way, presents other difficulties. It calls for specialised skills, careful supervision and cooperation from the sample households. (Even so, getting information on food taken outside the home will remain a problem). This technique is both more demanding and considerably more expensive than household interviews and therefore has necessarily to be on a relatively small scale. It is also difficult to make these measurements for long enough periods to get at the level of sustained intake. In fact, in India such surveys, conducted by the National Nutrition Monitoring Bureau, are limited to some 400 households in each major State with intake measurements done only for a single day. Intake on a single day being a hardly reliable indicator of sustained intake, it is not surprising that no correlation was observed between the per capita calorie intake as estimated from the NNMB survey and that obtained from the NSS.

Morbidity data: A review of the morbidity data from different sources shows a widely disparate picture both of the extent of morbidity and of the pattern of its variation by sex, between rural and urban areas and between income groups. (Table 1). Thus the NSS 1973-74 survey estimated the overall prevalence rate of morbidity in rural India at around 5 per cent per month. This compares with an estimated rate of 6.4 per cent on the basis of NSS social consumption survey of 1986-87 and 17 per cent on the basis of the NCAER survey of 1990.[6]

In the case of urban areas, while the NCAER estimate is much higher than the two NSS estimates, the NSS estimate for 1973-74 is higher than for 1986-87.

The KSSP estimates the two-week morbidity rate in Kerala at 21 per cent (equivalent to 43-44 per cent for 30 day period) which is 2.7 times the estimate given by the NCAER!

The 1973-74 NSS inquiry showed urban morbidity rate to be somewhat higher than the rural rate. Both the NSS 1986-87 inquiry and the NCAER show the opposite, the former showing the rural rate to be more than double that of urban rate. The difference according to NCAER is a modest 20 per cent.

TABLE — 1

Estimated morbidity rates according to different surveys, India

Morbidity rate per 100 persons over a period of 30 days		*National sample survey 1973-74*[1]	*National sample survey 1986-87*[2]	*NCAER 1990*[3]
Overall	Rural	4.8	6.4	17.1
	Urban	4.9	3.1	14.6
Rural	Rich	na	7.1	12.4
	Poor		6.0	16.5
Urban	Rich	na	2.6	10.1
	Poor		2.8	18.6
Ratio of female and male morbidity				
	Rural	.85	.98	.57
	Urban	.94	1.1	.53

1. Sarvekshana 1980
2. Sarvekshana 1992
3. NCAER 1992Again while the NSS inquiry of 1986-87 shows not much of a difference between the morbidity rates of males and females, the other two inquiries show male morbidity to be higher. According to NCAER the female morbidity rate in urban India is less than 60 per cent of the rate for males. A similar pattern is noticed in Kerala, but the KSSP survey shows no significant sex difference in morbidity.

According to the NSS, in 1986-87 the poor had a somewhat lower morbidity rate than the rich in rural India while the NCAER shows the opposite. In urban areas both surveys show higher morbidity among the poor than among the rich, the difference being much larger in the NCAER estimates than in the NSS estimates.

Finally, estimate of state wise morbidity — available only for 1973-74 and 1990 — show very different patterns of spatial variation. The rank correlation between the two sets of estimates is statistically non-significant.

Here again differences in concept, design and survey procedure present major problems in comparing the estimates and assessing their reliability. The 1973-74 survey of the NSS spread over a period of nine months broken into 3 subrounds. Information was sought on incidence and prevalence of temporary ailments during the 2 weeks prior to the date of interview and of chronic ailments at the time of the survey.

The NSS morbidity estimates for 1986-87 are derived from a survey spread over a whole year with a reference period 30 days. Unlike the earlier survey, this round focused on a number of items of social consumption (eg. education, health, access to the public distribution system). No distinction was made between incidence and prevalences, but hospitalised cases were treated separately from those not requiring hospitalisation.

The NCAER survey covered a three month period (May to July) in 1990, with a reference period of 2 weeks. Insofar as there is a seasonal peaking of infections in the monsoon, one would expect the NCAER estimate to be higher than those obtained from a year round survey.

This bias also affects the KSSP survey which was conducted during a two week period in July, at the peak of the monsoon. On the other hand, the fact that one-third of the field investigators in this survey were females who are better placed to get first-hand information on the illnesses of females and children, might be expected to give the picture of female and child morbidity reported by it, much greater reliability.

Apart from these differences, the utility of the surveys is further limited because they tend to focus on particular aspects of health and nutrition. Rarely are the surveys informed by a perspective wide enough to capture all facets of nutrition and health and the interconnections between them. Thus, the morbidity surveys do not canvass any information on food intake or size; the consumption surveys give only information on food intake; the NNMB surveys report food intake of the household on the date of the survey along with anthropometric measurements and clinical evidence of malnutrition for members of the sample household but nothing about health or activity status. Differences in design, timing and even concepts make it difficult to pool the data from the different sources for analysis in a wider framework.

Under the circumstances, a question arises about the utility of the available data for analysing variations in morbidity and the factors underlying it. Some attempts have gone into examining the relations between food intake, body mass and morbidity on the basis of data on inter-state variations in these characteristics. It is argued that such a study of variations is possible even if the absolute value of the relevant characteristics is not accurate, so long as the data give a reasonably reliable measure of the relative variations among regions and social groups as well as of distances between them. However combining estimates of various characteristics from imperfect data based on diverse surveys of doubtful comparability makes the results of these exercises far from robust. For this reason reported associations (or lack thereof) between calorie intake on the one hand and size and sex differentials in morbidity on the other, or the association between morbidity, illiteracy and access to health services, however suggestive, have been rightly viewed with scepticism.

There is of course scope for more disaggregated analyses by region and socio-economic categories. But there are severe limits to the extent to which such analyses could be taken for unravelling this complex phenomenon on the basis of available data. Better-designed surveys, informed by a wider theoretical framework comprehending the multi-dimensional and inter-related nature of nutrition-health status and their determinants, are obviously needed. In the process we have also to address the problem of ensuring reliability and comparability of data.

The question of bias

A major issue concerning the validity of nutrition and health data is the nature and extent of bias in the information provided by the households or, for that matter, observed/measured directly by outsiders. Information obtained through either means is subject to random errors of different kinds (including sampling errors and non-sampling errors arising from 'instrument' errors, differences among investigators in interpreting questions or carrying out instructions as well as among respondent households in their understanding of the questions or recall of relevant information). These errors affect the degree of confidence with which the estimated mean value of the characteristic under study may be taken as an accurate measure of its true value.

Insofar as the errors on this account are large, inferences which depend critically on the accuracy of the estimated values, are vitiated. But they need not necessarily affect the rankings of (and distances among) households/groups by the value of the characteristic. Therefore, even if the estimated values of a characteristic are subject to a relatively large margin of error, they could still be used for studying the pattern of variation within the selected population and factors underlying it. This possibility remains open even if there is a systematic, but constant degree of over-, or under-statement across all classes of informants. The real difficulty arises when the degree of over-, or under-statement varies systematically as between different segments of observers/informants.

We have already noted the sources of non-sampling errors, including systematically varying bias in the case of food intake.

These arise not so much from any inherent vagueness or ambiguity in the definition of food intake as in getting the relevant information accurately from the households. Much the same is true of mortality. But in the case of morbidity, fuzziness of concept compounds difficulties of getting accurate information; for this reason some scholars doubt whether it is at all possible to meaningfully compare, much less explain, variations in reported incidence of disease across different countries/regions and over time. (see for instance Sen, 1990; and the debate in the Health Transition Review 1991 and 1992).

Sen (1990) commenting on the fact that Kerala has the lowest mortality and the highest reported morbidity among Indian states, suggests that the Keralite being more literate and having better access to health facilities, perceives illnesses and seek remedies in a way very different from that of people less literate and poorly served by health facilities. It is for this reason that illnesses are reported more fully in some regions than in others and data of reported illness reflect not so much the differences in real illness but differences in perception.

The interpretation of the historically observed tendency for morbidity rates to increase even as mortality rates fall has also given rise to a similar viewpoint. Johanson (1991:43-44) argues: "...the difference between sickness and health has never been completely clear; this intrinsic fuzziness has always generated the need for interpretation, which can be either left to the imagination of each individual or can be culturally standardised. When the individual's interpretation of his or her own health has social and economic implications for other members of a household, family, lineage or community, society is unlikely to leave the individual decision makers to their own imaginative devices. Instead cultural pressures designed to standardise perception and behaviour will be brought to bear on private decision making with respect to health-related preferences." Perception of sickness and decision to seek professional assistance are thus influenced by "culturally constructed values and norms associated with health and disease"; health professionals have also been "... trained to interpret symptoms along culturally standardised lines."

This argument has been amplified in a subsequent paper (Johansson, 1992:81) thus: "...when an historian talks about sickness as if it were a biologically obvious state (like being dead) and proceeds to assume that some form of morbidity data can be used to measure biological sickness (as if measuring the biological extent of sickness over time were just like measuring height) and then attributes an observed trend to biological factors, he or she cannot be doing health history in a meaningful social science sense. Since all the available quantitative data on sickness are defective in some way and come in a number of inconsistent or incomplete forms that chronically confuse the biology of disease with the sociology of illness, the facts, even quantitative ones, can be made to say anything the historian wants them to say once he or she falls in the habit of treating morbidity as a simple, unidimensional, concept (like mortality and height) and the associated data as a direct reflection of the biology of disease".

The notion that morbidity data are essentially subjective and that the variable nature and extent of this subjectivity vitiates meaningful analysis of health and sickness across space, class and time, seems to be quite widely shared. If indeed morbidity data were so subjective, and nothing could be done to narrow down, identify and control for the sources of subjectivity, there is little more to be said or done. Such an extreme view is however unwarranted. It seems possible and worthwhile to concentrate on "...understanding the reporting system that provides morbidity data and how it reflects the way people and doctors are trained to perceive, detect and report sickness and differential incentive systems (social and economic) that shape reporting behaviour over time at the individual and institutional level."(ibid)

Determinants of Morbidity

Objective factors

Ideally we need a theory of morbidity which comprehends both biological and cultural dimensions. Though such a theory is not yet available, enough is known to permit us to identify some of the more important determinants of disease as well as some sources of bias in morbidity statistics. This fact, in turn, could facilitate better understanding of the sources of variation in reported morbidity rates even with available imperfect data and, more so, help improve the quality of morbidity inquiries in the future.

The literature (see Frenk et a., 1991; Johansson, 1991, 1992; Murray, 1992) in fact identifies several specific factors — both 'objective' and those affecting peoples' perception of health and their health-seeking behaviour which have a bearing on reported morbidity. The 'objective' factors include, for example, the economic costs of illness, the environmental conditions, the age composition of the population and the 'case fatality rates'. The 'subjective' factors, i.e., those affecting perceptions, include the way morbidity is defined, the characteristics of the respondents as well as the culturally mediated norms of diseases and their treatment.

Sickness leads to disruption of the activities of the affected person, and to claims on the resources of the household or community for assistance to meet the cost of treatment and/or to loss of income. The lower the income of a person relative to the cost of treatment, the higher is likely to be the threshold of pain and suffering which he or she is likely to put up with and hence the lower the probability of the person seeking treatment. This implies that reported morbidity is likely to be higher at higher levels of per capita real incomes; when the availability of services is more diffused; and when the services are subsidised directly (eg. by the state providing free medical care) or indirectly (eg. through publicly funded insurance schemes).

The relevance of environmental conditions — in particular, of the quality of water supply and sanitation — to health status needs hardly any elaboration. The lack of safe drinking water and poor sanitation are among the major sources of infectious and parasitic diseases. Immunisation, the spread of curative medical services and advances in medical technology reduce case fatality for a wide variety of diseases (both infectious disease and diseases like diabetes and cardio-vascular disorders) but do not eliminate them. Indeed, by improving the chances of survival of 'weaker' individuals, who are more frail and prone to infection, it is apt to increase both the incidence and prevalence of disease. (Murray, 1992).

Differences in age composition is another important source of variation in both the overall level and pattern of morbidity. Older people tend to have higher incidence of disease, especially chronic and degenerative diseases, than do persons in young age groups. And insofar as the propensity to infection also varies in some systematic fashion with age, differences in age composition have a direct bearing on the overall morbidity rate. However, given the age structure and the age specific morbidity rate, it is a relatively simple matter to estimate overall morbidity rates corrected for age structure differences. (see e.g. Murray, 1992)

Perception Bias

The determinants and consequences of 'perception' bias are more complex. Estimates of morbidity are usually based either on information relating to illness obtained from sample surveys of households or from statistics compiled by doctors and hospitals. In the former case, morbidity is generally defined as any illness during a specified reference period which was treated with external assistance or self-medication. Individuals may not be aware of all their illnesses: some types of disease (e.g. hypertension, cancer) can only be discovered by proper clinical examination and testing. The informants may not all follow a uniform criterion in reporting self-medication or home treatment.

More importantly, the above definition leaves out a whole lot of conditions in which an individual may feel unwell but does not resort, for one reason or the other, to any treatment. Differences in the distance between the point of feeling unwell and getting treatment for that condition — which is a useful distinction proposed by Johansson — could be an important source of variations in self-reported morbidity across space, classes and time.

Another factor is the extent to which interviewers are able to get accurate information on the illnesses of individual members of each sample household. There is reason to believe that adult males, who are generally the principal informants, are unlikely to be as well-informed about the health of all family members (and especially that of women and children) as women are. One may therefore expect female morbidity, and hence overall morbidity, to be understated in the usual surveys. If this is true, canvassing of schedules from female members of the households with the help of female investigators should make a substantial difference to the estimates and probably give a closer approximation to the real state of affairs.

We have already noted the importance of economic factors (especially the potential income loss from allowing sickness to disrupt productive work and the cost of treatment relative to income) in determining the point at which persons feeling unwell take recourse to treatment. When incomes are high and medical services are not expensive, people are likely to seek treatment earlier than when incomes are low and medical services are expensive. People's attitudes to illness are also influenced by education and exposure to modern medical practice. Better education, in so far as it raises health consciousness and improves preventive care, may well lead to lower incidence of at least certain types of disease.

On the other hand, the medical profession itself has an influential role in shaping people's perceptions of, and attitudes to, disease. "The more diseases there are, that is, the more diseases for which patients and professionals have names, the more likely are individuals to think of themselves as sick or to be diagnosed by a professional to be sick. In this sense the incidence rate is a function of the culturally recognised stock of diseases" (Johansson, 1991:44).

Other examples of 'cultural' influence on perceptions regarding morbidity are sex discrimination and the notions regarding 'normal health' prevailing in a society. It is widely believed that there is sex differentiation in matters concerning health as is the case in several other spheres. It could be that women are more reluctant to disrupt their home care, child rearing and other functions; and that they have a higher threshold of pain tolerance than men. In this event, women might ignore feelings of being unwell for longer than men would and also delay the point at which they seek treatment.

People are also conditioned to adjust their norms of health depending on the level of discomfort and pain most people bear in the normal course in a given community. For instance it has been noticed that in parts of Africa where a majority of people are affected by a parasitic disease involving the passage of blood in the urine, the discomfort is not considered serious enough to disrupt work or seek medical assistance. Runny noses or parasitic infections or frequent diarrhoea are not thought of as symptoms of sickness justifying treatment when most children have these symptoms (Johansson, 1991:50-51).

The effect of socio-economic influences cited does not manifest in the same manner in all categories of disease. Sex differentiation seems likely to be pronounced in respect of diseases which are both perceived and observed or discovered only by clinical tests. It could take either of two forms: Women having palpable symptoms of illness may not resort to any form of treatment; and/or they may not have medical check-up as often as men have. Johanssen cites the following example to illustrate the point: A survey in two Indian villages showed 92 per cent of women to have one or more gynaecological and sexual disease; 98 per cent were anaemic; 12 per cent had filariasis; and 10 per cent had leprosy. "Almost all women had more than one serious disease even though none was hospitalised at that time and none had disrupted their daily routine to any great extent. In a cultural sense these women were healthy although many had symptoms they regarded as painful or unpleasant" (ibid 52).

Given these and other sources of perception bias in self-reported morbidity, the possibility of cross-checking their validity with clinical data assumes some importance. Prima facie such cross-checking would seem difficult. There are few surveys which give a representative picture of illness in the society as a whole on the basis of clinical assessments. Most clinical morbidity data relate to patients who get treated by doctors and in hospitals. This group of patients is unlikely to be representative of the general population.

More importantly the criteria used by clinicians to assess illness are very different from those used by individuals. In the case of self-reporting it is the individual's sense of pain and suffering which is the decisive criterion. Clinical assessments, on the other hand, are based on professional examination and diagnostic tests. The criteria used by the clinicians are not standardized nor are they invariant with reference to place, time and the extent of specialization of the professional. Advances in medical science are constantly adding to the stock of identifiable diseases even as improvements in diagnostic techniques enhance the capacity to identify them.

An individual's sense of pain and suffering must, of course, be the principal basis for judging his health status. Johansson rightly points out thus; "No amount of research or clinical advance will allow us to measure the pain and suffering of an individual except through self-reporting. Clinicians are well aware that pain is the exclusive province of history-taking rather than diagnostic tests. Unfortunately for those who are uncomfortable with our capacity to independently validate pain and suffering, it is precisely this dimension of pain and suffering which gives import to all morbidity".

And yet it seems possible to use clinical data, properly collected, for cross-checking self-reported morbidity, to some extent. Diseases have been classified into three broad categories in terms of perception:

(i) diseases perceivable by individuals - and this category includes the most infectious and parasitic diseases - and also observable by clinical examination;

(ii) diseases which may not be perceived by individuals

(like hypertension and cancer) but can be identified by clinical examination; and

(iii) pain and suffering perceived by individuals which may not meet clinical criteria of disease. (Murray and Chen, 1990).

Diseases in category 3 can never be independently validated. For category 2 clinical tests are in fact better than self-reporting which would almost certainly understate their incidence. In respect of diseases of the first category it is, in principle, possible to cross-check self-reporting with clinical assessment provided both are based on a representative (if not identical) sample of households and self-reporting surveys define morbidity broadly to capture the existence of symptoms associated with such illness rather than only the conditions which are treated.

Directions of further work

The main thrust of the foregoing argument is that there is no warrant for assuming that perceptions of illness are so subjective as to preclude any confident inferences about even the relative incidence of morbidity, not to speak of analysing the factors underlying such variations. We have seen that the literature is replete with implicit and explicit hypotheses regarding the influence of identifiable 'positional characteristics' of individuals and households (such as the characteristics of the member of the household providing the information, accessibility and costs of medical care, sex and educational status of individuals) on reported morbidity. The list is by no means exhaustive and the influences may be inter-related in complex ways which need to be unravelled in order to sharpen and refine the 'bias' hypotheses.

Not all the hypotheses can be tested with available data, partly because of defects in the scope, design and conduct of the surveys and more importantly because they relate only to treated morbidity. Nevertheless, it is worthwhile to explore the extent to which it is possible to proceed with the help of disaggregated, household level data from existing surveys. Specifically it should be possible to test whether there is any systematic relation between reported morbidity on the one hand and income, social class, education and sex, and availability of medical care facilities, on the other; also to filter out such biases wherever found significant; and to get more comparable and closer-to-objective estimates of relative morbidity.

Over the longer run, we need to improve the design of surveys to permit more rigorous and complete analysis of differences in the real burden of disease, adjusted for at least the more important sources of bias, and the factors contributing to these differences. The following are some of the more obvious lines of improvement which should be taken into account in the design of surveys:

In surveys of self-reported morbidity a clear distinction should be made between 'feeling unwell' and 'getting treatment' and information should be obtained on both the aspects.

Some thought needs to be given to developing a standardised classification of symptoms whose presence or absence can be ascertained with reasonable accuracy from informants. It is also necessary to devise ways in which the confounding of symptoms and specific diseases can be minimised, and a post-stratification by type of morbidity (as proposed e.g. by Murray and Chen) facilitated. This will help in better mapping of the 'break points' in the health continuum, sorting out cases of morbidity with no specific, identifiable clinical cause from those which have, and permitting more rigorous comparisons of what differences the individuals' and the physicians' perception make to the assessment of morbidity.

The relation between the level and pattern of self-reported morbidity and the characteristics of the household member from whom the schedule is canvassed needs to be looked into. A methodological inquiry to compare responses from different types of informants (the male head or senior males only; from wife or senior females only; both together; and each member of the family individually) and responses to male and female investigators would be useful.

It is necessary to conduct carefully designed small scale inquiries to explore the possibility of correlating morbidity data obtained from household surveys with those obtained from clinical assessment, preferably for the same set of sample households taking care to capture seasonal variations in morbidity.

Surveys on incomes, food intake, anthropometry, activity characteristics and morbidity need to be integrated so that their inter-relations could be better analysed.

Given the high level and diversity of skills needed, and the cost involved, ways of designing surveys of different aspects of nutrition and health in such a way so to ensure that they relate to comparable socio-economic and environmental conditions need special attention. One should perhaps start with detailed and carefully supervised surveys in a relatively few selected locations representing different 'typical' situations and incorporate the insights gained in designing larger scale, representative surveys.

Notes

[This paper was originally written at the Harvard Center for Population and Development Studies, Mas, where the author spent 6 weeks in late 1992. The visit was sponsored by the Research Project on Strategies and Financing for Human Development financed by the UNDP. The present version incorporates revisions in the light of comments from Lincoln Chen, Peter Berman, TN Krishnan, Sudhir Anand and Amartya Sen and participants in a seminar at the Centre for Population and Development

Studies. The author gratefully acknowledges his debt to all of them.]

1. An extensive literature exists on this aspect in the context of measuring under-nourishment and malnutrition as well as on the use of food intake as a central element in measuring poverty. For an excellent overview of the issues involved and of the various view points on the subject see Srinivasan 1986; Osmani (ed.) 1988; Dreze and Sen (ed.) 1990.

2. Sukhatme (1989) questions the assumption that poor nutrition affects amount of time devoted to work or the nature of work and its productivity.

3. Sex discrimination in intra-family food allocation has been widely discussed (see especially Sen, 1988). But the relation between level of intake and the extent of such discrimination has not received much attention.

4. This is now well recognised in the literature on poverty. For example Anand and Harris (1990) point out that consumption of goods and services "...does not really make, an adequate allowance for illness which does affect an individuals well being. Inadequate consumption of food, prevention of drugs and fuel increases the risk of illness...." The utility reduction associated with illness will be greater than utility reduction due merely to lower consumption.

5. For discussion of various aspects of reliability of NSS consumption data in general and data on food intake in particular see eg. Bhattacharya and Chatterjee, 1975; Vaidyanathan, 1985; Minhas 1988.

6. The 30 day rate for 1973-74 and 1990 are estimated by a pro-rata adjustment of the two week rates given respectively by NSS and NCAER.

References

Frenk, et al. (1991), Elements for a Theory of the Health Transition, *Health Transition Review*.

Indian Council of Medical Research (1972), *Studies on Growth and Physical Development of Indian Infants and Children*, Hyderabad.

National Institute of Nutrition (1991), National Nutrition Monitory Bureau: *Report of Repeat Surveys 1988 90*, Hyderabad.

Johansson S.R. (1991), The Health Transition: The Cultural Implication of Morbidity during decline in Mortality, *Health Transition Review*.

Kannan K.P., Thankappan K.R., Ramankutty V., and Aravindan K.P. (1991), *Health and Development in Rural Kerala: A Study of the Linkages between Socio Economic Status and Health Status*, Kerala Sastra Sahitya Parishad, Trivandrum.

Kumar B.G. and A.Vaidyanathan (1988), *Morbidity in India Some problems of Measurement Interpretations and Analysis*, Paper presented to Annual Conference of the Indian Society of Medical Statistics, mimeo.

Kumar B.G. (1990), *Quality of Life and morbidity: A Recommendation of some Paradoxes for Kerala India*, Centre for Development Studies, Trivandrum, mimeo.

Minhas B.S. (1988), Validation of large scale sample survey data care of NSS household consumption Expenditure" Sankhya (Series B 50:3)

Murray Christopher and Chen K. (1991), *A Conceptual approach to Morbidity in Health Transition*, in Chen et al.

NCAER (1992), *Household Survey of Medical Care* (New Delhi).

Osmani S.R. (1988) (ed.) *Nutrition and Poverty*, Oxford University Press, India.

Panikar P.G.K. (1980), *Inter Regional Variation in Calorie Intake*, WP No. 111, Centre for Development Studies, Trivandrum.

Panikar P.G.K. and C.R. Soman (1982), *Health Status of Kerala Trade*, Centre ofr Development Studies, Trivandrum.

Sen A.K. (1988), *Family and Food: Sex Bias in Poverty* in Srinivasan and Bardhan (eds.)

Sen A.K. (1990), *Objectivity and Position: Tolerance of Health and Well Being* (CPDS, Harvard University).

Srinivasan T.N. (1986), *Nutrition in Developing Countries: The State of Knowledge of some extent of its Prevalence, its Causes and its Consequences*, Yale University, New Haven, mimeo.

Srinivasan T.N. and P.K. Bhardhan (1988) (ed.), *Rural Poverty in India*, Oxford University Press.

Scrimshaw N.S., Taylor C.I., and Gordon J.E. (1968), *Interaction of Nutrition and Infection*, Geneva, WHO.

Sukhatme P.V. (1989), *Food, Physical Growth and Work Output*, Nehru Memorial Lecture, IASR, New Delhi.

Sarvekshana

Vaidyanathan A. (1985), *Food Consumption and Some of People*, EPW, June 27.

——— (1986) *On the Validity of NSS Consumption Data*, EPW.

Visaria Pravin (1977), Living Standards Employment and Education in Western India, 1972-73, *DFCE World Bank*, Washington.

This paper grew out of collaborative work on the assessment of nutritional status with the late Gopalakrishna Kumar (Gopu to his friends) of the Centre for Development Studies, Trivandrum beginning 1988. I would like to dedicate this paper to the memory of Gopu who met an untimely death in Jan 1993.